Pentimento

Diary of a Walk-In

bj King

Pentimento: Diary of a Walk-In

bj King

Copyright © 2025 by bj King

Published by 1st World Publishing
P.O. Box 2211, Fairfield, Iowa 52556
tel: 641-209-5000 • fax: 866-440-5234
web: www.1stworldpublishing.com

First Edition

ISBN Softcover: 978-1-4218-3577-8

LCCN: Library of Congress Cataloging-in-Publication Data

All rights reserved. No part of this book may be reproduced or utilized in any form or by any means, electronic or mechanical, including photocopying or recording, or by any information storage and retrieval system, without permission in writing from the author.

This material has been written and published for educational purposes to enhance one's well-being. In regard to health issues, the information is not intended as a substitute for appropriate care and advice from health professionals, nor does it equate to the assumption of medical or any other form of liability on the part of the publisher or author. The publisher and author shall have neither liability nor responsibility to any person or entity with respect to loss, damages, or injury claimed to be caused directly or indirectly by any information in this book.

I would like to thank Ede Durfey and her husband, who have read years of my newsletters and compiled the information for me, and added global historical facts. And the many people who edited and appreciated my story.

Thank you.

Author's Note to Readers

The word "Pentimento," in the title of this book, usually refers to pictures painted in oils and means that the artist painted over the original image. The obliterated images, forms or strokes on canvas begin showing through the newer painting, because the over painting is becoming transparent. When pentimento happens, in some pictures the lines of the original painting may show through the new painting. For example, a tree (in the old painting) may show through a woman's dress (in the new painting); a child may make way for a dog; a boat may no longer be on an open sea. "Pentimento" can also result because the painter repented – changed h/her mind and chose not to stay with the first painting.

The first time I heard the word pentimento, I instantly got goose bumps. I understood its meaning and resonated with it even though I wasn't an artist at the time. Being a walk-in, I often find the "original lines" of the previous entity's life bleeding through into my own experiences, reactions, feelings and plans. I am sometimes blind-sided by an emotion that does not seem to fit with the current conversation or event, but the reaction is coming from the cellular body.

"Walking in" is a rather unusual process of incarnating into a physical body on the Earth plane. It can happen when a soul, who originally inhabits a physical body, agrees or decides to vacate that body. In so doing, the vacated physical body, left by the departing soul, becomes available to another aspect of the same Oversoul.

The outgoing soul leaves physical embodiment in a manner similar to that usually experienced by Human beings at the time of death. The soul may depart during a near-death experience, through a serious illness, an accident or even during sleep. The agreement to have a walk-in is sometimes made before the first entity incarnates, and sometimes it happens as a need to rescue a soul aspect that has become despondent, depressed and unwilling to complete their contract. The incoming soul, the "walk-in," inherits the memory of the departing soul aspect and assumes all of the remaining karma and responsibilities of that outgoing soul aspect. They must complete the host's karmic contract before they are free to begin to accomplish their planetary contract.

An incoming soul is simply a different "soul projection" or "soul aspect" of the same Oversoul as the outgoing soul. (Oversoul refers to a group, or family of souls, similar to a family tree, descended directly from the Source of all things, or God. Each Human being is a member of a family of souls, or an Oversoul.)

Because of the Universal Laws of Non-Intervention and Free Will, one species is not allowed to intervene or meddle with another civilization's evolution. One way to overcome this obstacle is for members of a more advanced civilization to agree to be birthed into the less advanced society, to raise the vibration and consciousness of that species, and to provide permission for assistance to be given. The other option for overcoming the obstacle is for an extraterrestrial member of an Oversoul to "walk in" to the body of another member of the same Oversoul for rescue at the Human level. My soul aspect came from another galactic system; as an extraterrestrial inhabiting a Human form, my purpose is to participate fully as a Human being. Because I am fully Human and conscious, I can give permission to other extraterrestrial forces to assist the Earth and Humanity in their evolution.

The consciousness that moves through this vehicle causes activation of memory cells in other individuals. When this happens, they become consciously aware of themselves as spiritual beings inhabiting physical bodies, rather than Humans trying to become spiritual. The memory cell activation usually reduces the feelings of separateness from the Source (felt by many walk-ins) and causes conscious multidimensional awareness to take place.

Pentimento, Diary of a Walk-In is the story of my experiences as a walk-in from another dimension in space. It is an account of my merging with, and then inhabiting, the body of a member of my Oversoul who had become very depressed in her life on Earth and wanted to commit suicide.

As you participate in my life's experiences – as you read my life's record – be aware that the name of the entity that originally inhabited this body (was born through the birth canal) was Betty Jean. The representative, who came from the same Oversoul as Betty Jean to merge with this body, and to eventually take full charge of the body, was known galactically as Jovanna.

In Spirit's communication with me, which began September 30, 1982 – long after I had first joined this physical body – Spirit always referred to me as "bj," in written correspondence. And "bj" was always expressed in lowercase letters with no periods, more like a symbol or calligraphic character.

The personality/soul now occupying this body uses the name "bj King" to express itself and to acknowledge the vibrational change. In other words, I use the name "bj King" to express myself here on the Earth plane since the departure of Betty Jean.

In this book I use the pronoun "I" throughout for several reasons. One is that doing so makes it easier for readers to follow; another is that when a walk-in completely merges with the personality/body of the person already living in that body on Earth, that merger includes becoming a part of that personality/body's happenings even before the "walk in" occurred. For example, the walk-in inherits the cellular memory in the body and is able to be conscious of the life happenings of all the years before the actual merger, going back perhaps to even before the body was born.

Another reason I use the pronoun "I" throughout the book is to express the corporate energy of both Betty Jean and me as one individual. A further reason is that "I" also expresses me, bj King, as the lone inhabitant, now in this body, since Betty Jean's departure. However, whenever there is a reference to something that pertains to, or happened to, Betty Jean before I "walked in," I try to make that distinction clearly.

Pentimento: Diary of a Walk-In is my story, which I have chosen with some trepidation to share with you. Living through it at times was very confusing. I hope that in the way it is written it will be less confusing for you. It will be important for the reader to pay close attention to the dates before each chapter so you will be able to be aware of who is in the body and the time frame referred to by the participants.

I choose to finally write this story now, because more and more walk-ins are coming to Earth to assist in this stage of evolution of Earth and the Human species. It is a methodology and circumstance I feel needs to now be exposed and understood.

Foreword

As I began writing my story, I vividly recalled the first faint whisperings that prompted me to begin the undertaking in earnest. It was a few years ago, in June . . .

Seated on a chaise lounge on the wooden deck, the surfaces still wet from last night's rain, I, bj King, listened to the birds, heard bees buzzing on the dogwood and feasted my eyes on the beauty of Mount Shasta and the beautiful redwoods of Northern California. I watched the squirrels and jays vie for peanuts and birdseed left for them by my partner.

As I did so, I asked myself, "Where do I begin this very complex, oftentimes bewildering tale, so that readers and seekers of truth and wisdom might believe, hopefully understand and be encouraged?"

I closed my eyes and took a few deep breaths, hoping to clear my mind and to solve the confusion. I breathed deeply, held the breath, focused at the center of my brain, counted three, three, three . . . and exhaled; breathed deeply, held the breath, focused at the center of my brain, counted two, two, two . . . and exhaled; breathed deeply, held the breath, focused at the center of my brain, counted one, one, one . . . and exhaled.

I breathed normally and began to count ten, nine, eight, seven, six, five, four, three, two, one – as if descending a stairway inside myself. I waited to feel the now-familiar subtle shift within my head from my left brain to my right brain consciousness. Then I waited, listening expectantly . . .

"Begin where you are, right now, sitting on this lounge. Begin now. Feel Peace."

Since no further words came from Spirit, I began to count in reverse of my previous counting – one, two, three, four, five – and allowed awareness to return to my physical body. Once again I became conscious of the warm breeze caressing my skin.

As I opened my eyes and looked down at the grass, I was startled, yet pleasantly surprised, to see another blue feather lying there. As I moved to pick up the feather I remembered the cover of Illusions, a book by Richard Bach, subtitled, *The Adventures of a Reluctant Messiah*. The front cover displayed a blue feather against a night sky. The back cover recounted this quotation from the book: "Here is a test to find whether your mission on Earth is finished. If you're alive, it isn't."

This book had continually touched my life since November 4, 1979. The feathers had appeared since September 30, 1982, at various times of doubt. Whenever I had become too discouraged to continue, or questioned my direction, a blue feather has appeared on the ground. Could the blue feather in the grass be confirmation of the message that I should "begin now" to get my story down on paper? Several times I had started writing about my life. I had even double-spaced the first memories so that additional ones could be added.

At that time, as I had begun my inner search, much of my childhood memories was blank. However, I had recorded whatever memories did surface.

Later, a Priest read my original writing and added marginal notes. He wanted to collaborate with me on a novel about my life. He felt that the story of my withdrawal from fifteen years of Valium addiction could be an encouragement to many persons who get hooked on prescription medication – perhaps help them to KNOW and BELIEVE that there really IS hope that they CAN quit taking drugs; hope to begin again.

At the time the Priest had suggested that we write together, I had just finished reading Ruth Gordon's book, *I'm Dancing as Fast as I Can*. I had felt that Ruth said more than I could ever say about the subject of Valium addiction and withdrawal. Also at that time I was more interested in healing myself, attempting to remember my childhood and trying to find MY identity (as separate from the roles I played for other people) than I was about writing. Too, I felt that I had not experienced anything, up to that point, which would help anyone else. Since then, many events have occurred in my life to change my opinion. I now realize that part of my confusion stemmed from my being a walk-in, which I did not know at that time.

1
Lady Venus

Aboard a Venusian Mother Ship - Earth time -1968

"*Jovanna!*" The name rang clearly and authoritatively inside my head. I recognized the energy vibration of Lady Master Venus.

"Yes?" I asked telepathically.

"*Please leave your station with another and come to the conference room.*" The voice was her usual loving vibration, yet it seemed to contain a sense of urgency.

I was a Novan aboard the *Venusia*, a Venusian Mother Ship, monitoring planet Earth along with several other team members. We sat in plush, high-backed chairs containing headsets. Computer-like keyboards were built into the armrests. Viewing screens lined the circular room.

When Lady Venus called, I had been monitoring the events of my assigned sector of Earth on several screens in front of me. The screens allowed me to see the actual weather, medical, political, economic, and spiritual conditions of the planet. They also provided overall readings of the Earthlings' thought patterns. Through the headset in the chair, I heard certain information produced by digital computers and satellites. The satellites monitored the planet's surfaces. The dolphins and whales produced a sonar recording of the inner Earth magma so it could be received aboard the ship. Through the armrests, I controlled the energy Rays suggested by thought projection into my mind.

The other team members in this circular room and I were part of a larger crew from other parts of the galaxy. Those in the room did the same type of monitoring and energy adjusting that I did (and had been doing prior to the call). Our job was to adjust energy vibration to continue the evolution of all species on the Earth and to continually raise the vibration of Earth itself.

The Divine Plan of the Creator of All Universes is stepped down through the various dimensions, through thought projections, into the minds of the Spiritual Hierarchy and the Angelic Communion. This information is acted upon and disseminated through "group minds." Assignments are given to various groups within the 47 civilization-members of the Intergalactic Federation. Venus is one of the members of the Federation. I had been assigned from Nova, which is beyond this Omniverse (a collective of twelve Universes), to spend an apprenticeship on the planet Venus

In order to fulfill Lady Venus' request that I come to the conference room, I thought-projected a request to Adrianna, a standby member of the team, to relieve me of my duties. Relinquishing my place, I quickly made my way to the conference room where a holographic image of Lady Venus waited to speak privately with me.

I was, as usual, overwhelmed by her energy of beauty, peace, grace and love. Her light and energy totally filled the room, and my body and mind melded with hers.

"Welcome, Jovanna. The Council has a request to make of you. You have served with us faithfully since Sanat Kumara and I agreed to help Terra and her people through these difficult times. It has not been necessary for you to lower your vibration into an Earth body for a very long time.

"We understand the seriousness of that which we are asking of you. You understand the gravity of conditions on Earth because you have been working with the energy team monitoring and dispersing energies to the planet. You are also aware of current conditions there, but have been shielded from remembering its history.

"It is now time for you to know more of the history of creation, the reason for creating Earth and the situations contributing to the conditions there. It is also time for you to know the Creator's original plan for this planet. These you must understand before you can make an educated decision concerning that which the Council asks of you."

Lady Venus gestured for me to be seated.

"I shall refer to this Omniverse as twelve Universes within this sector of the physical and spiritual creation of the Creator. In the beginning of this Omniverse, the Creator projected two great Rays of energy: The Gold Ray and the Silver Ray. From these Rays, the creation of physical matter and life began in this sector. The Rays created the first Universe within this Omniverse around an energy axis. This axis is a highly concentrated

vertically intensified energy field from which the rest of this Universe radiates out horizontally as it is created.

"After creating the first Universe, the Rays realized that to continue their creations they would need to create assistants. These assistants would monitor and record what these Rays had created. They would also hold the energy patterns in place so the created life forms could continue. This would also maintain order and continuance in the Rays' Universes. So they created the twenty-four Elohim to assist them.

"If we consider God the Creator as Level 24, and Level 23 as a protective energy field around that Source, Level 22 contains the energies of the Elohim.

"My energy pattern resonates at Level ten, with the other Ascended Masters. Your Ship resonates at Level six. To accomplish the mission the Council is suggesting, you would be asked to lower your vibration to Level three, the density of Earth."

Her words brought fear to my heart.

"After birthing the 24 Elohim, the Silver Ray, apart from the Gold Ray, created 11 sub-Rays. The first created was called Silver Ray 'minor' and was very powerful. This Ray later rebelled against the Creator God and became the Dark Ray, or that which we refer to as the Dark Force.

"Only seven of these Rays are visible to the density of Earth and then only occasionally, when certain physical conditions create what is known there as a rainbow. You, however, are very familiar with the use of all 12 of these Rays in your work here on the Venusia Mother Ship. If you accept this assignment, eventually you will be expected to assist us in anchoring additional Rays of energy on the Earth to assist Earth and Humanity in their evolution.

"To lower your vibration to the density of Earth, to take on physical embodiment again, you would need to suspend temporarily – seemingly forget – the knowledge you now possess about creation, the Rays and their usage. I realize how frightening and foreign that would feel to you. In many ways you would feel as if you had amnesia and had been sent back to kindergarten.

"You would have to relearn from written material, as well as from that which we will channel to you. Once you had complete control of the physical vehicle (body), you would join and open it to hear our vibrations.

"Many walk-ins, while going through this period of forgetfulness before their remembering process begins, become so depressed they themselves try to destroy the physical bodies they've taken. They try to return to something they only vaguely remember, or they simply want out of the physical and emotional pain of the vehicles they've taken on. There are many challenges involved in that which we ask of you. However, if we did not feel you capable of the challenge, we would not ask." Lady Venus spoke reassuringly.

"Let me continue with an explanation of what led up to the grave conditions on the Earth at this time.

"By the time the Gold and Silver Rays had created eleven Universes, their experience was great. They created the twelfth Universe around the Sun, which is held in place by two great energy force fields we know as Helios and Vesta. This Solar System includes the Milky Way Galaxy. The planets of this Solar System were to be 12 in their creation.

"When the two Great Rays conceived of this Solar System, they chose the family design concept and caused each planet to have a relationship to all the others. This required them to work out a system of orbits, of circles and near-circles, and gravitational pull within each planet and then its gravitational relationship with the other planets.

"Of the planets, Mars was created first, then Jupiter and then Earth, Mercury, Maldek, Uranus, Neptune, and Saturn.

"When it was time to create the next planet, Sanat Kumara and I were called to bring our energies from the Nova system, outside of this Omniverse, to hold the focus for the creation of this next planet, Venus. Many Novans came near to Earth at that time to assist us in founding Venus.

"The next planet which was created is not yet visible to Earth because of its lack of density. Pluto, which your scientists value as a planet (but is not), was created after that, and the final one that was created is also not visible from Earth because of its vibration.

"Our Solar System was created over four and a half billion years ago and revolves around the Great Central Sun at the center of the Milky Way. Each orbit takes 206 million years as Earth calculates time. In the Will of Divine Mind, or the Creator, this completes the time cycle in which our entire Solar System is to remain in its present state of evolution.

"In the next stage of evolution, Earth, which has been the laggard planet vibrationally, is scheduled to raise its vibration through the Fourth Dimension and shift vibrationally to exist as a Fifth Dimensional Love Star.

"However, when Maldek exploded because of her occupants' misuse of atomic power, the souls from there were allowed to inhabit bodies on Earth, rather than being sent to one of the dust planets in another galaxy where they would have started over in their evolution. This decision by the Council has caused the evolution of Earth and Humanity to be behind schedule.

"The Council is asking for additional volunteers to come into Earth vehicles from the higher vibrational planets to raise the vibration of Humanity. The condition of Earth (remaining in her present orbit and the evolution of Humanity) affects the entire Solar System.

"We of this Universe are all related. Therefore, we are taking this request very seriously and are recruiting a team of individuals such as yourself to incorporate themselves into the populace of Earth Humanity."

For the first time during this conference, the Lady's voice contained sadness.

"When Maldek exploded, the debris created an asteroid belt and threw solid rock mass out into space, affecting some faraway stars as well as neighboring galactic planets. Much of the debris was drawn toward the planet of Saturn because of its gravitational field and its close proximity.

"Saturn was allowed and assisted, at that time, to protect itself by creating a reversed gravitational force field to stop the debris from smashing into the planet. This choice also kept the debris from affecting several other planets.

"You see, one of the properties of hydrogen is that it can continue to perform in a chain reaction going through a space meridian and harming all it contacts within that specified area.

"As a consequence, following the destruction of Maldek, a cosmic agreement was made to prohibit such an event from ever happening again. However, the beings of Maldek retained most of their knowledge and later destroyed much of the landmass of Earth when they annihilated Atlantis, Lemuria and Mu.

"At that point, it was decided to erase much of the memory of the Earth Humans. By disconnecting ten of the twelve strands of the helix of their DNA, it was felt this move would limit their destructive powers.

"Through the knowledge we brought from the Nova system, and with the assistance of representatives from the Pleiades, the constellation of Orion and the star system of Sirius and a few systems from outside this galaxy, Earth was reseeded.

"At this time, the Council also decided to create a 'ring-pass-not' around Earth. This ring is a vibrational barrier to contain Humanity's negative thoughts to keep them from polluting the rest of the Universe.

"The Sirians sent beings to inhabit the forms of whales, dolphins, porpoises and the giant squids to monitor and pass back to us the sonar readings of what is happening to the interior magma of Earth. They are able to monitor the activity of Earth's geological plates and ascertain information about potential Earth movement.

"These volunteers, who came at that time, made an agreement that they would remain on Earth until their work was finished. They became a part of the planet's population and there was to be no interference from their former home planets.

"So far as the individuals of the donating planets and stars were concerned, these emigrants were gone for an indefinite period of time. They would not return until their mission on Earth was completed. Their mission is to assist in raising the vibration of Earth and Humanity and preparing them for evolution into the Fifth Dimension.

"It was at this time that Sanat Kumara and I dedicated ourselves and our energies, not only to maintaining our beautiful and peaceful planet of Venus, but to assisting Earth to overcome her retardation and to join her in preparing for her evolution. This includes assisting as many of Humanity as will hear the call to raise their vibrations in order to move with Earth into the Fifth Dimension.

"Many Venusians lowered themselves into the Fourth Dimension to prepare Shambala not only as a way station for Sanat Kumara's energies, but as a home base for those who would periodically visit Earth from higher realms, for many would come to assist in the task of preparation. When the station was complete, Sanat Kumara enjoined his energies with Earth as well as Venus."

Again there was sadness in the Lady's voice at the thought of his commitment on such a mission.

"It is very difficult for those entering the Earth's system to retain memory of their purpose for entering. When they lower their vibrations from higher densities into the density of Earth, they get caught in the mass consciousness of Earth. The sensations and emotions of the physical bodies of Earthlings, the work of maintaining these bodies and the density of the thought-forms surrounding the planet itself, make it very difficult for even high-minded beings to retain their focus and intentions. Often such beings lose sight of their objectives once they inhabit the Third Dimensional flesh bodies."

Her words again struck fear in my heart at the possibility of subjecting myself to such a situation.

"Earth Humans did not always have physical bodies. The original caretakers of Earth were Light Beings approximately seven feet in height, from a high-density level of eight, as are most Venusians and Novans. Of this you are well aware. The great director of the Blue Ray, Archangel Michael, recruited these Light Beings.

"Because the planet was so unique and beautiful in its extensive varieties of plant, mineral and animal kingdom creations; and because the volunteers would have such a rare opportunity to assist in the development of additional botanical and biological forms, many souls wished to go to Earth. Earth – and Free Will – were the most novel experiments in the Twelfth Universe.

"Although Archangel Michael was the coordinator, he was frequently absent after the initial stage of the work had been accomplished. None of the souls who came together to be the original caretakers of Earth as Free-Will beings had ever lived in anything but a high spiritual vibration of cooperation and caring. Therefore, it was easy for them to live harmoniously with little supervision while attending to the details of the planet's needs. It was also easy for them to develop further variations of botanical and biological life forms.

"This state of evolution lasted for approximately 800,000 Earth years. Another ten million souls volunteered to join these forces approximately 200,000 years after the original immigration. These beings were all aware of the Creator and the Source of the energy used for creation.

"These Earth souls had never experienced fear or evil up to the time when the Dark Force, or Jehovah, sought to win their reverence and to take the planet from his position on Maldek as a base for his own power. Consequently, since these souls were not expecting an enemy, they did not call their home forces of Light for assistance. At first the Dark Force, or Jehovah, used intelligence and created many rules and laws. Later, sound frequencies were added to distort the reverence the Earth Humans had for their Creator. The persuasion of the Dark Force and the sound frequencies influenced and confused many of the Earth souls. The outside influence caused them to lose their memories and distorted their perceptions. Many could not remember how to access the inflowing energies of their creator. Therefore, their lights diminished and they lost contact with their Source." The Lady's voice was a bit agitated as she recalled these events.

"Michael became aware of the situation when the planet began to lose its glow. He came to the defense of the caretakers of Earth. It is with great sadness that we report that a great cosmic war took place between Jehovah and the Archangel Michael.

"Michael lost this war, and Earth came under the influence of Jehovah. The souls of the caretakers were affected, but because cosmic agreements must always be honored, it was still necessary for the diminishing souls to complete their planetary caretaking functions and achieve the mastery that went with that promise. The souls had to be retained on Earth to finish their chosen task.

"The only hope of bringing these souls back to their original vibrations is to encase them in protective containers. The Silver Ray created physical body containers that can hold fading and dimming soul Rays until they are raised back to a higher dimension. The original bodies were of a much higher frequency than the Earth bodies of today, and not totally physical. An invisible guardian was assigned to help and care for each soul; what some Humans think of as their Guardian Angel.

"After this disastrous event, the Gold Ray intervened. It once again projected its Ray throughout the Twelfth Universe and embraced Earth with its energies.

"It was decided to draw a veil over the traumatic experience and memory of the planet so that these souls would wish to continue. This is what the Earth scriptures refer to as 'the fall' or 'the separation,' because after this experience the souls who remained suffered deep depression and felt pain, sorrow and unidentified guilt. In this recent, all-out effort to heal the Earth and Humanity, this separation has been healed. Full access to higher knowledge and energies has been returned to Earth inhabitants.

"New cellular release methods of healing are being given to Earth for use by her inhabitants for healing these obscured memories. If you accept this assignment, one of your tasks will be to assist this healing. You will be expected to channel methods of healing that require higher energy, DNA cellular memory release and reconnection of the twelve strand helix of the DNA.

"Many of the Earth's scientists and anthropologists try to trace the history of Human evolution from the ape, a species brought much later from another galaxy. They try to create this explanation without understanding that there was a species prior to caveman, Cro-Magnon man and Neanderthal man. These beings did not start out as physical. However, through the fall and their separation, or turning away from the Source toward Jehovah, they continually reduced their vibration to evolve into these species. They evolved into Homo sapiens only through the efforts of extraterrestrial assistance, through genetic engineering. Now again, through the assistance of these same influences, Homo sapiens are being engineered to evolve into the Homo universalis species. This species could energetically live through Earth's shift into a Fifth Dimensional Love Star. These beings are in a process of remembering their Source and how to draw energy from that Source through the Rays. They are remembering the knowledge and use of the Universal Laws that govern and control this universe.

"Veils are being dissolved within the brains of Homo sapiens to allow for this expansion and the memory of the truth about their existence, creation and the Source. They, once again, will not be physical, in the Third Dimensional sense, as they evolve into the Homo universalis species. They will merge with more and more of their Oversoul energies and become less dense. This merging will be referred to as overlighting or soul braiding and is different from a being becoming a walk-in, as no aspect of the entity will walk out.

"You are already aware of much of the history I have relayed to you, at least in a vague sense. It was advised, however, that I refresh your memory of what has gone before in the evolution of Earth and the Human species before I explain to you the full spectrum of what you are asked to do. Put another way, it was felt I should refresh your memory concerning the potential difficulties you might encounter, if you accept this assignment. Now I will acquaint you with the individual situation.

"One of the other members of our soul family who is incarnate on Earth at this time has herself in a situation that she feels is more than she can psychically and emotionally handle. She is considering terminating her physical body before finishing her karmic contract. We need a volunteer from the Oversoul family willing to overlight her energy, merge with it, take her place on Earth and finish the karmic responsibilities she accepted prior to incarnation. That in itself would be a big assignment, but there is more to be considered here. I wish to make you aware of the entire plan before I officially put the request to you."

Lady Venus spoke with compassion and deliberation as she continued. "As you have been observing from your station, Earth is in serious danger of destruction by the Humans who are now incarnate there. These Humans have discovered and are experimenting with various atomic and hydrogen devices that could destroy the plant, animal and Human populations, as well as Earth herself, as happened with Maldek. Since the veils were created to obscure memories of Maldek, these Humans are repeating the pattern of self-interest. They do not seem to understand that Earth itself is a living organism, and they are using her resources as if they were endless. They also pollute her waters without thought of the future." The Lady spoke precisely and without hesitation.

"We need volunteers to incarnate at this time to speak for peace, spiritual awareness and the Oneness of all life. We need individuals who <u>will not be afraid to speak and be public examples of spiritual beliefs</u>. The graveness *of the situation on Earth does not leave time for all of the individuals who are needed to be born into the bodies of infants. A plan has been devised through which you can merge your energies with those of an individual who wishes to leave life on Earth. You would co-habit this body until you feel comfortable with the environment, family situation, language and the body itself. The preceding entity would then be allowed to leave the planet to rest before reincarnating."* Lady Venus made it sound like a simple procedure.

"You will be expected to finish the karmic contract of the body you take, which in this case includes physically creating two bodies, or vehicles, for other entities to inhabit. You will create these children with the husband that entity has already chosen. You may then be allowed to choose your own partner and begin the actual work that we are sending you to do.

"You are being sent to express spiritual ideals of Oneness and the existence of other life in the universe; to understand and to teach the Universal Laws; to assist the Spiritual Hierarchy to anchor additional Rays of energy into Earth; and to usher in the beginning of a new species on Earth, the Homo universalis." She continued to speak with clarity, concern and controlled emotion.

"I must warn you, however, that the entity whom we are monitoring as a possibility has continually abused the body she inhabits by taking a tranquilizer and several other substances. She also suffers from poor nutrition, which has severely weakened some of the major organs. We feel, however, that you will be able to take over the body, discontinue the drugs and rebuild the body's stamina to hold a much larger focus of the soul's energies." She made her statements with confidence.

"Before you consider what I am saying any further, I would like to show you an image of the woman I've been speaking of and allow you to mind-meld with her to get an impression of her condition."

The Lady stopped her discourse. Before me was a holographic image of a man and a woman involved in an emotional discussion. The woman appeared to be about 28 Earth-years old. She was attractive, by Earth standards, with auburn hair, blue eyes and very light skin. She weighed approximately 125 pounds and was about 5'7" tall. The man had curly dark hair, blue eyes and darker skin. He weighed about 175 pounds and was approximately 6 feet tall.

As I merged with the woman's mind and the discussion, I was overwhelmed with a sense of sadness, aloneness, desperation and depression. I realized the two were discussing events of the past seven years. These events included their previous marriages to other individuals, marriage to each other, the construction of a custom-built home in another city, and the abrupt move to the present town. The events also included the woman's unhappiness at having to sell her home, leave her family and move to a strange town where she felt like an outsider. She hated the house they now lived in and the neighborhood.

The woman was experiencing nausea as she was speaking. As she ran to the bathroom, I broke the mind-meld with relief.

"There is another energy in the room with them. Is the woman aware she is already pregnant with one of the children she is to have?" I inquired of Lady Venus.

"No, she is not. Even though she will be overjoyed with the news of the baby, we feel that because of her already complete sense of defeat and depression it will add to her feelings of inadequacy to care for a child. She has no knowledge of children or their care. We are planning to monitor her carefully to see how she adjusts during the pregnancy. The doctor will obviously take her off all medication. Her mental and emotional conditions, however, may improve without the drugs. She may be willing and able to stay off them once the child has arrived. If so, we will be pleased to leave her to finish the life. If she is not strong enough to maintain herself without the drugs and continues the depression after the birth, for the sake of the child and the soul, we will have to recommend letting her leave, to rest. We will have you or another member of the soul family fulfill the contract as well as accomplish the additional work I have mentioned. We would like you to consider this as a possible assignment, Jovanna, and to periodically mind-meld with this individual. We will check with you at a later time to discuss your feelings and observations. You are aware that you have free will to refuse this request. However, we of the Council see that major work could be accomplished through this body if it does become available through default. Do you have any questions?"

I was so overcome with information and emotion I could only shake my head in a negative response. No words could have expressed the overwhelming feelings running through my body or my thoughts.

Lady Venus shocked me with much more information than I was able to summarize here. As I left the conference room I thought to myself, "I will think more about this later, but for now, back to work." When we are in other dimensions and working aboard the ships, our identity, thoughts, goal and intentions are always to accomplish "the work."

2

Assignment

My steps were heavy as I, Jovanna, left my workstation at the end of my shift, and my thoughts returned to the Lady's message and my mind-meld with the Earth entity. I proceeded down the corridor to my cubical living quarters. The door to my private area opened as I approached, activated by preprogrammed soul vibrations. Any other person's vibrations would not trigger the sliding door to respond without a coded phrase entered in a small terminal to the right of the doorway.

The room was dimly lit as I entered, but brightened as the walls reflected my own energy light. A raised padded platform, my resting place, and a recliner facing a viewing screen were the only visible objects in the room. The space would have appeared austere to an Earthling.

I lowered myself into the chair and sat for some moments, thinking about what Lady Venus had asked of me. "Return to Earth . . . be densely physical again . . . agree to co-create other physical bodies . . ."

These thoughts tumbled about in my mind. I normally had total control of my thoughts and contact with the Oversoul. I asked myself, "Why does this come as such a shock? Why did I not feel this request coming from the Oversoul? Have my precognitive powers become defective?"

"NO. You have merely been concentrating on the larger vision of what is happening on Earth to the extent that you have not recently monitored your other soul aspects."

The answer came to me telepathically from Matthew, my Eighth Dimensional soul self.

"If we had challenged you with a question concerning the overall status of Earth, your precognitive projections would have been accurate."

I was a little agitated. Matthew paused in his speech when I interrupted with, "What do you know about this new assignment I am being offered and what do you recommend?"

"*I am aware of the subject's history and soul performance record,*" he responded.

"Please share with me what you know, Matthew," I implored.

"*The soul aspect which energizes the personality calling itself Betty Jean was aspected onto the Earth by the Fifth Dimensional level of our Oversoul on September 28, 1941, at 10:30 a.m. Earth time, to very young parents in a small West Texas town. Already another soul (a son) had been assigned to the care of these parents years before Betty Jean's arrival.*"

"*Betty Jean stated in her Earth re-entry contract that she would become a spiritual communicator, remember the Universal Laws, honor the Source, and write and speak of these memories during this life. She also agreed to co-create two physical bodies for other entities to come to Earth. She further agreed to expose these souls and all members of her biological family to universal spiritual principles during their life together.*" Matthew spoke as if literally reading from a written document.

I broke in with, "Why is she so depressed and considering leaving? By Earth standards she seems to have what would be necessary for happiness. She has her health, a husband and parents who love her, a nice home, a car and a job." My tone made my confusion obvious.

"*She chose to be born into a family with no spiritual focus or particular desire for self-achievement. She felt she would be able to overcome the environmental limitations and genetics because the mental capabilities would be highly activated in the body being created for her by these particular parents.*"

"*She managed quite well as a child and as an adolescent by being a loner and an introvert. She spent most of her time studying or absorbing herself in the lives of others through books and movies. She always sought religious education and has consistently tried to remember about God. This education has been limited and erroneous, however, because the only institution and examples available to her as a child were the nearby Baptist churches. Such churches are prolific in the area of Texas where she chose to be born,*" Matthew offered.

"Matthew, what is a Baptist Church? I have witnessed spiritual energies from the overall views we have of the various countries of Earth from my terminal in the viewing room," I declared. "But I have no specific knowledge of churches or any types of individual religions, which seems to be what you are speaking of, if I am following you correctly."

Matthew explained, "On Earth (as Lady Venus had begun to tell you) Humans have evolved genetically and in consciousness through several stages. During their evolution these Humans have forgotten they are part of a Oneness, which is all – both the Creator and the created. In their amnesia, they have further divided themselves into small groups headed by individual leaders. Thus, they have mostly given over their true identities and abilities to communicate directly with God the Creator.

"They have created various myths or stories of creation, which they profess to believe. Many of the people also believe that these leaders, or ministers, priests or Rabbis, as they call those who head these groups, are the only ones who can communicate, interpret and know the Will of God. One of these groups is the Baptist Church.

"These Humans seem to profess a belief in the book known as the Bible, which is divided into two major sections. One of the sections is called the Old Testament and the other is called the New Testament. The Old Testament is basically a historical record handed down from memory for several generations before it was recorded. This is the history of the reign of the Lord Jehovah over the Earth and most of her people.

"The New Testament is a similar historical record of the reign of Yahweh over the Earth and of the Christ Consciousness energy returning to Earth through Jesus and the being known in the Bible as John the Baptist. Actually, John the Baptist was a twin Soul to Jesus and agreed to come in with him to channel the energies of the Christ Consciousness, or Holy Spirit. The energies flowed in when he submerged Jesus in the water and called forth the Holy Spirit to bring these energies. Therefore, baptism became an important ritual to the Christians and particularly to the Baptists. They believe a person cannot enter the Kingdom of Heaven unless they have undergone this ritual." Amusement was evident in Matthew's voice.

"They even have a book in their Bible which they attribute to me during my incarnation with Jesus when I assisted with anchoring the Christ Consciousness energies. Some of it is even quoted correctly." Matthew's comment seemed full of smiles.

"Those who grew greedy have mostly deliberately destroyed the true historical records of Earth and Humanity's evolution. These avaricious ones wished to control the masses by promoting fear and the belief that not everyone can hear God.

"Some of the true historical records are now being recovered and translated. The original Sumerian and Aramaic histories describe reincarnation, the Oversoul and the truth that several extraterrestrial civilizations have seeded colonies of life on Earth."

"How much of the truth does this being whose body I am being asked to use understand?" I inquired.

"Not much, as I have stated. Her viewpoint is narrow because she has been limited to a strictly Christian version of history. She has never been exposed to other versions of spiritual truth.

"Betty Jean has always questioned and been confused by the Christian belief that the references in the Old and New Testaments refer to the same God. Her confusion comes from the blatant differences in the actions and attitudes of these two gods. The traditional ministers have always hushed her when she has made these observations. They can't seem to explain these contradictions and try to embarrass her for questioning them. She knows nothing of the Oversoul, reincarnation, meditation, telepathy or any form of soul communication. The Christian Churches thus far only teach prayer, a form of entreating God, a Being who they feel is outside of, and no part of, themselves."

"Is she aware of the various Rays of energies coming from the Creators who keep the universes balanced and the Universal Laws by which all things operate?"

"Not at all. These concepts have been taught thus far to only a limited few on Earth through something they call Mystery Schools. In the past it has been necessary to limit the exposure of Earthlings to the information because of the combative and competitive natures of Humans.

"One of your assignments, if you agree to walk into Betty Jean's body, will be to remember these Laws and to share them with many souls. These souls will be ready to be reminded of these principles between the Earth years of 1990 and the year 2012."

"That is a long time from now, as time is measured on Earth, Matthew. It is now only 1968 on Earth."

"Yes," Matthew agreed. "For Betty Jean's body, it is December 1968. What you don't seem to realize, Jovanna, is that if you choose the challenge of this form of incarnating, it will take many years of adjustment to her body, emotions and environment before you will begin to remember that you are a walk-in and start recalling our conversations and what you now know and understand.

"As Lady Venus has explained to you, it will be necessary to temporarily veil your consciousness of these memories in order to make your adjustment into Earth's density less traumatic. This is one reason you are being given a while to consider your decision.

"You see, Jovanna, it is a very different process to merge with another's consciousness and learn to use a mature body than to join an embryo and enter through the birth canal. When you join an embryo, you have only your own agenda with no one's previous concepts, possible addictions and habits to overcome, nor must you assume a lifestyle that is already in progress.

"Infants sleep a lot. They have much time for thought and integration of the consciousness with the body. Walk-ins, more or less, must hit the ground running in bodies that are fully formed. In many instances, they walk into bodies that have been abused by drugs, alcohol or food. In this case, Betty Jean's body has been given poor nutrition and tranquilizers."

"Why has she used the drugs?" I inquired. "Doesn't she realize this slows down her vibrations?"

"She doesn't know about vibrations," Matthew responded. Then, after a few moments, "Jovanna, let me tell you a little more about her history so you can try to better understand.

"In the culture in which Betty Jean grew up, females are raised to become wives and mothers. They are more or less owned by their fathers and then by their husbands. She had an early awareness of her desire to be a writer. During her period of education, she worked on what is known there as the high school newspaper and was on the yearbook staff. These are a group of people who write papers and books about school life. Her desire was to go to the university to become a journalist, a person who writes for a newspaper. A newspaper is a daily written report of the events of the World and of a particular part of the country".

"Why didn't she accomplish this if it was her desire?" I demanded, still confused.

"Because of fear. You see, on Earth, people are basically afraid. She was afraid of her parents and wanted to please them more than she wanted to please herself. She was afraid she was not intelligent enough, nor strong enough, to go to school and work at the same time since she had never worked.

"Her mother had always told her that she was weak and warned her not to overstress her nerves. Her mother is a very fearful person who uses many chemicals in her own body. This is another reason Betty Jean feels justified in taking the tranquilizers."

I was still confused. "If her family did not have the money to send her to school for higher education, why did she not go to work first and go to school when she had earned the money?" Many of the Earth systems were unclear to me. Money and the lack of freedom were two of the most confusing.

"As I tried to explain," Matthew repeated, "*she was afraid. In her culture it is more important for the males to become educated and more important for the women to be wives and mothers. She married only months after her graduation from high school. She went to work as a bank teller to help finance an education for the male she married.*"

I thought for a moment. "Then she at least understands this Earth concept of money, which I have so much trouble comprehending energetically on my Earth monitor." I smiled, and for the first time I felt hopeful.

"*Yes, she understands it, but she doesn't have much money of her own. She is used to handling massive amounts that belong to other people.*"

"Then these other Earthlings must trust her a great deal. They seem to be very possessive and concerned about this energy substitute they call money."

"*Yes, she has high integrity and is well thought of by the people around her. She works very hard, both to keep up appearances and to be a good friend and is loving and trustworthy. In some ways her lifestyle will be difficult for you because of how hard she tries to please everyone.*"

"If she married so young, why has she waited so long to conceive this child?" I questioned. "Don't most Earthlings have children at a younger age than twenty-eight?"

"*Yes, it is a little unusual. But her first marriage right out of high school, which I referred to earlier, lasted only 4-1/2 years, so this is her second marriage. She was young and inexperienced sexually when she married the first time, as was her husband. Most of his sexual encounters had been with males, so he was very confused about himself. Therefore, his rejection of her after the marriage caused her to become even more mixed-up about herself and about sexuality as the marriage progressed. This was the original reason she was given the tranquilizers by her doctor.*"

"How long has she been married to the dark-haired man I saw her with this morning when I did the mind-meld?"

"*The soul sent him to meet her the night she moved out from the home of her first husband to get her divorce. He was dating her best friend from high school. He had graduated from the same high school as Betty Jean but they had never met because he had moved to the school as a junior from another town when his parents had both died suddenly. This man's mother, who was a nurse, committed suicide because she believed she had cancer. His father died six months later in an accident when a fork lift filled with canned goods fell on him in a warehouse. The souls of these parents have been waiting around him to reincarnate with him to continue their relationships. He and his mother were very close, since he was the youngest of five children, but he was never close to his father.*

"*If you agree to create bodies these two can use to return to be with him, you will not be required to stay with him to raise them. The karma they have to work out between them does not involve you. You will be finished with the primary segment of Betty Jean's soul contract for this life when the children are six and ten years of age. I must return to my duties now,*" Matthew then told me. "*We will speak of this matter again before you make your decision. You have the Oversoul's permission to begin monitoring the entity Betty Jean and observing her habits, thought patterns and progress during the pregnancy.*"

Matthew withdrew his energies from the room. I felt very much alone and more than a little overwhelmed by his explanation of the circumstances surrounding what might be my next life's adventure. For example, he had said it would take many years of adjusting to the body, emotions and environment before I would remember that I was a walk-in. He said that it was easier for a soul entering the Earth Plane through the birth canal because babies sleep a lot. That allows them plenty of time for thought and the integration of consciousness with the body.

Matthew's words were scary to me. The idea that it would be necessary to temporarily veil my memories to make my adjustment to Earth's density less traumatic was frightening.

At the time he gave me this advice I thought it would be impossible for me to forget what either Matthew or my beloved Cosmic Mother Lady Master Venus had told me once I went to Earth.

3
Further Instructions

Two days after my discussion with Matthew, Lady Venus' voice broke gently, but authoritatively, into my train of thought. *"Jovanna, it is time for me to give you more information concerning your possible mission to Earth."*

As I took my place before the Lady, she began: *"You have been observing the entity Betty Jean during her pregnancy and periodically experiencing what it feels like to share her body while she is sleeping. This is good preparation. It makes you understand the limitations of the physical bodies of Humans. You will not remember these experiences when you first arrive in her body, if you decide to take this opportunity.*

"There is a need on Earth for a new pattern to form. This new pattern will change both the helix of their DNA and the psychological makeup of the way men and women of the Human species relate to each other. During this period of linear time on Earth, men and women are living under what is basically a male dominated society called a patriarchal society. This form of society is not serving the planet as a whole. The reason is that industries created by this patriarchal influence are destroying the environment. These influences are also using the resources of Earth disproportionately to Her ability to replenish and detoxify Herself.

"Within the next one hundred years of Earth time, it is mandatory for the Human species to evolve – not only through DNA changes, but psychologically – in order for the species and Earth to survive. It will not be useful for them to become a matriarchal society. They must become an androgenarcal society. They must learn to use all of their male and female qualities simultaneously.

"One of your missions, if you decide to serve Earth in this capacity, will

be this: You will live through a series of events that will create a matrix for changing the consciousness of how men and woman relate to each other physically, psychologically, and spiritually.

"Within their psyches and within their DNA, Human beings carry the seeds for both the destruction and the salvation of Earth. We wish to encourage them to survive both as a species, and to reclaim loving dominion over the plants and animals of the Earth instead of destructive dominion.

"The energies which will be assisting you in creating this new matrix will be the energies of the Goddess Psyche, and myself. Psyche is known selectively upon Earth as a figure of mythology.

"Most of the population on Earth at this time is unhappy. The things they believe will bring them happiness are failing them. Human beings have been seeking to control their planetary environment, as well as each other's behavior. They have forgotten the Universal Laws and are searching for solutions outside themselves.

"A team of entities, not unlike yourself, is being organized to take Human form on Earth. Team members will live out another reality in order to create a matrix that will serve as an example of drawing from within for solutions. They will also create forms of integration from which the mass consciousness can draw, within the perimeter of Earth.

"At this time, we are very limited in ways to assist the beings of Earth. This is because of the Universal Law of Free Will, under which Humans live. We can only intervene in the lives of individuals when we are asked directly.

"But if we have more beings on Earth who know they must ask directly for assistance, and who are willing to be used as terminals, we can channel energies to change the mass consciousness. We can also channel energies to change the Human, plant and animal DNA and to adjust the frequencies and pressures building within the Earth's physical and energetic body. nsitional phases which will, of necessity, take place on Earth during the next twenty to forty years.

"The changes must take place first within the females of the species. This is because the males only develop their masculinity fully through encouragement from the females.

"There are four tasks that women must accomplish in order to end their unhappiness and thereby lead the males to end theirs.

"The majority of women on Earth are living their lives in a very limited fashion. They are not allowing themselves to fully express their spirituality, sexuality, creativeness or passion. This is because of the injunctions, which have been placed upon them by their society as it has developed.

"This must change, if it is to be possible for the species to remember why it was created in two distinct sexual forms yet carry within themselves the genetics of both sexes. It will take courage for women to learn to live freely, sexually, passionately and creatively within the framework of society as it is now.

"In order to create this new matrix, you will be required to disobey what Betty Jean has been taught was right and good and true. You and she will experience panic and bear the wrath of the culture in which she lives. You will be condemned for your actions.

"The first and primary task will require that you and she learn how to differentiate between who she *is*, and what she needs and wants, from what everyone else tells her she is and what she needs and wants. The Myth of Psyche calls this 'the sorting of the seeds.'

"Relative to your experience of joining with Betty Jean's body and consciousness, a preliminary plan has been laid out. Of course, variations will occur depending upon the daily choices you and she make during the first few years of the merger.

"You will join with her body and begin to experience the periodic and limited use of that body in December of 1969. The changes, which will take place in the body itself, will be slow and gradual. This is to permit you both a reasonable amount of comfort within the body, while not being too noticeable to outsiders.

"The second child is scheduled to be born in 1973 and will be a male. When this male is three years old, Betty Jean's body will undergo the removal of certain female organs. This will help in the transference of genetic information and establish a freer vehicle for the further events of life."

Lady Venus continued giving me information, most of which would mean more to me in later years. For now – once again – she had given me much more than I was able to assimilate.

Later, when alone, I tried to summarize a little of the information I'd been given so far: If I agreed to do this Earth assignment: (a) I would have to accept and complete the woman's karma, including accepting the husband she now had (for a while); (b) The woman (whose name was Betty Jean) and I would create two other physical vehicles (for one male and one female child); (c) Betty Jean and I would need to live together in the body in order to create the new matrix for the species; we would also need to confront Betty Jean's fear of males; (d) We both would need to examine and understand all the "roles" she had played for other people; (e) Betty Jean would eventually leave her body and I would take it over completely;

(f) I would not recall any of this conversation until about 1991, after I had been given primary custody of the body.
 Could I do this? Did I want to do this?

4

Betty Jean

In December 1969, I, Jovanna/bj King, merged with the body of Betty Jean King on Planet Earth.

At the time of my merger, Richard Nixon had begun a second term as President of the United States, the war was still raging in Vietnam and the United States was preparing to place a man on the moon.

Betty Jean, 28, and her husband were living in Amarillo, Texas. Her body was pregnant with a female. They had agreed to name the baby Marjorie Elizabeth after his mother, not knowing that the soul coming in was indeed the reincarnation of his mother. Shortly before the birth, Betty Jean felt strongly that the child should be named Kelley Kay.

Betty Jean was not consciously aware of my entrance, or that I would now be a part of her, sharing energies – everything – or that we would become one. Neither was anyone else.

Although a decade would pass before I, Jovanna/bj King, would <u>begin</u> to recall details of Betty Jean's early life, it seems appropriate here to recount some of the background of the woman whose life I was to share.

Betty Jean was born September 28, 1941, to a very young couple living in a small community in west Texas. She was their second child, following a boy who was then three years old. (More details of her early life appear in other Chapters.)

In July 1960, two months after graduating from high school, Betty Jean married a young man she hardly knew. She worked very hard at creating a home and being a "good" wife. The man went to college and worked part-time. The couple had very little social life, except with their families. A sexual relationship between the two never developed.

During the years of this first marriage, Betty Jean was confused about herself, her husband, and what she had read of love and sex in romantic novels. She had no experience, nor firsthand knowledge of sexual relationships. Before marriage she had always been fearful of getting pregnant. Her parents told her that her virginity was her most important asset and that no one would want to marry her if she was not a virgin. Now that she was married, she was confused. She was still a virgin and her husband showed no sexual interest in her.

After four years of marriage, Betty Jean developed ulcers and sought medical advice. When she tried to talk to the doctor about her frustration, he suggested among other things that her husband might be homosexual. He prescribed a tranquilizer. (Later, information surfaced through Betty Jean's mother that this same doctor had delivered Betty Jean just twenty-three years before!)

Betty Jean did not know what a homosexual was, but she went to the library for information. As she read explanations and descriptions, she blushed profusely. With the new knowledge, she began to observe her husband's behavior. Six more months passed before Betty Jean decided to leave her husband.

She was terrified by the thought of living alone. Returning to her parents' home was not an option. Her parents' attitude was, "You made your bed, now lie in it." They insinuated that if the marriage was not working, it must be Betty Jean's fault. Also, divorce was seemingly as unacceptable to them as pregnancy out of wedlock. She had married as a virgin, because they had taught her that to have sex before marriage would ruin her reputation and keep anyone from wanting to marry her. They insinuated they would rather see her dead than pregnant out of wedlock.

Betty Jean asked her father and brother to meet with her and her husband to try to convince him to agree to a divorce. The four met at her father's home. When her father and brother learned that her husband opposed the divorce, they fled, leaving the couple alone in her parents' house. Later, when Betty Jean confronted her father about his abandoning her, he said he thought if the two of them were left alone they would have intercourse, make up and her dilemma would be ended.

Betty Jean was incensed that he believed one sexual occasion could melt away all of her marital problems! She could not believe her father's ignorance or insensitivity.

Betty Jean could never bring herself to tell her father that she suspected her husband of being homosexual. However, being abandoned by her father and her brother – the two male role models in her life – affected her for many years. She allowed it to cause her to mistrust all males and to feel that no man would ever be there for her emotionally.

At this time, one of Betty Jean's few girlfriends from high school returned to Texas from California where she had lived for 4-1/2 years. Susan had been married to a sailor and had worked as a telephone operator. Susan told Betty Jean that one night she, Susan, had come home early from work and found her six-foot-tall husband clad in her baby doll pajamas, playing with their four-year old son. He admitted that he was a transvestite.

Susan returned to Lubbock to live out the required year of residency with her parents, before being allowed by Texas law to file for a divorce.

Betty Jean confided in Susan that she, too, suspected her husband of being a homosexual and that she wanted to move. With Susan's help, Betty Jean moved out of her home and into a duplex. She chose to move while her husband was away at school, since he did not want the divorce. He saw nothing wrong with the marriage. All his needs were being met.

The day of the move was quite strenuous. That evening the two women stopped by Betty Jean's boss' apartment for a drink and to relax. Her boss, an older man, was separated from his alcoholic wife at the time.

Susan got their permission to invite her boyfriend over to share the evening. She made Betty Jean promise that she, Betty Jean, would "not make advances" toward Susan's boyfriend now that she was "available." Betty Jean was shocked by Susan's suggestion and declared emphatically, "The last thing I need in my life is another man! You have nothing to worry about from me!"

When Susan's friend, John, arrived, Betty Jean was sitting at the counter in the kitchen, visiting with her boss who was standing. When Susan introduced John, Betty Jean turned only her head, nodded a greeting, and simply said, "Hi." She and her boss continued visiting while Susan and John sat down on the couch.

Later, Susan came into the kitchen and announced she was leaving with her friend. Betty Jean understood, thanked her for her help, gave her a hug and turned back to continue visiting with her boss. Shortly thereafter, Betty Jean fell asleep on her boss' couch, unwilling to face the new home, until the next morning.

The following day was Sunday. Betty Jean went to her apartment, the first home she would occupy alone, to set up housekeeping. She deliberately had not given her phone number or address to anyone except Susan and her boss. Because of her family's attitude, she had not given her address to any of them.

After a long day of emptying boxes, weeping and feeling very much alone, Betty Jean bathed, shampooed her hair, set it in pink foam curlers, donned an ancient, stained, terry-cloth robe and creamed her face. Looking at her exhausted reflection in the mirror she thought, "I look worse than I ever have in my whole life. What is to become of me?"

She sat on the floor, checkbook in hand, in the center of her living room, surrounded by her bills. The television was on, just for the company of the sound. The eleven o'clock evening news was ending. Just when she thought she could not possibly contain any further tears, they began again. Fear and frustration gripped her. How would she survive alone? She heard a knock on her door. Terrified, she approached the door and managed a, "Who is it?"

"It's John," a male voice replied.

"You have the wrong place." Betty Jean tried to sound certain and authoritative.

"No, I don't. I want to talk to you. Let me in," the male voice persisted.

"No. You have the wrong place. I've just moved here. You must want the person who lived here before me. No one knows I'm here. I don't know anybody named John. Go away!" Her voice was getting louder and louder, and she could feel her heart pounding inside her chest and head.

"You know me. We met last night," he responded to her growing hysteria.

"I didn't meet anybody last night!" Betty Jean said emphatically, believing her own statement.

"You did too. I'm Susan's friend. We met at your boss' house."

"My God, no!" Betty Jean yelled. "You get away from here! How did you find me? Never mind, just go away. I promised her I would not even talk to you. You must be crazy. It's so late." By this time Betty Jean was shouting through the solid door at the stranger.

The door to the other side of the duplex opened and another man's loud and angry voice yelled, "Lady, let him in or send him packing. Give us all a break; we gotta get some sleep here."

Embarrassed and more confused than ever, Betty Jean began whispering loudly through the door, still determined not to let this stranger into her space. She didn't want anyone to see the way she looked, not even this strange man. She was equally determined not to revoke the vow she had made to Susan. She had emphatically agreed not to have anything to do with Susan's boyfriend, but here he was at her door.

"What do you want?" Betty Jean whispered loudly, enunciating carefully.

"I just want to come in and sit and talk to you. I need someone to talk to," the man responded in a loud whisper.

"Why don't you talk to Susan? She's your girlfriend."

"She's not exactly my girlfriend. We've only had two dates," he persisted. "She's just someone I knew in high school. She was a friend of my wife's. What I need to talk about is my wife." He was becoming emotional.

Betty Jean interrupted him in mid sentence. "You mean you're married? My God. As if this wasn't complicated enough! You've got to leave! Now! I mean it!" She was shouting again.

"I'm getting a divorce. I'm not really still married. My wife left me for someone else. Please. Let me come in. I promise to just talk. I'll sit across the room from you. Just let me come in. I won't stay long. I promise," the man pleaded.

"OK, but you have to promise you'll leave if I tell you to," Betty Jean responded warningly. She felt she couldn't possibly be in any sexual danger, since she looked so awful and this man was Susan's friend.

"I can't believe I'm letting you in," she complained as she opened the door. "I promised Susan I would do nothing to take your attention away from her. She plans to marry you when her divorce is final."

John grinned at the sight of her with pink foam curlers covering her head. She said sarcastically, "Don't laugh at the way I look! You didn't exactly make an appointment to be here, you know! So what do you have to say that's so urgent?" She frowned as she spat the words at him.

"What is someone like you doing with that old man?" he asked bluntly.

"What old man? What are you talking about?" Betty Jean was confused by his question. "Your boss, the one you were with last night."

"None of your business!" she snapped. "What right do you have, barging into my house, questioning who I spend my time with. You're a nut! Susan must be crazy to be in love with someone like you!" She spewed anger out with every word. She was bitter with ALL males, felt betrayed by ALL males, and this male was going to be the recipient of ALL the feelings she'd had bottled up for years!

The two talked, argued and drank coffee for hours. John told Betty Jean his life story and she responded with hers. Finally, at 3:30 a.m., she pleaded, "You've really got to go. I've got to get some sleep. I've got to be able to count money in the morning."

"Will you promise to have lunch with me tomorrow?" the man asked as he rose to leave.

"No! Absolutely not! Haven't you heard a word I've been saying? I'm

Susan's friend. She wants to marry you. I promised I would have nothing to do with you. I'm getting a divorce. I don't want to ever have another thing to do with men! You're not listening to me!" Her voice rose again and grew shrill.

"OK, calm down, what do I have to do to get you to change your mind?" he asked in a matter-of-fact manner.

"You can't. Not even getting a written permission slip from Susan would be enough!" Betty Jean had to laugh at the absurdity of the thought.

"Then I'll explain it to her and have her call you and give you verbal permission to see me. I want to see you again. I have no intention of marrying Susan. She needs to understand that." His voice was emphatic.

Betty Jean pushed him playfully out the door. Confused by the events of the week and especially by her attraction to this man, she fell into bed totally exhausted.

The following morning at work, Betty Jean received a phone call from Susan. "I know it's not your fault he wants to date you. I saw you did nothing to encourage him the first night you met. He begged me for your address. It's my fault. I told him how to find you, but if he doesn't love me, keeping him from you will not change that. It's better for him to be with you. He's really a wonderful person. You both are. I hope it works out for you. Keep in touch." Betty Jean could hear the disappointment growing in Susan's voice, as she offered her friend a verbal permission slip to date the man she had wanted for herself!

John and Betty Jean were married four months later. (The two were still husband and wife when Jovanna merged with Betty Jean in 1969.)

5
Earth Life

Early 1979

By this date Earth time, a decade had gone by since I, bj King, had first begun sharing the body and consciousness of Betty Jean. Although she was still in the body, we had truly merged energies and become one complete entity.

Because I had no recollection of what I was or where I had been before, or of any other life or time, this was my life for all intents and purposes.

At that time, 1979, I would describe my life as normal (although now, I chuckle at that description and wonder, "what is normal?"). In 1979, "normal" was middle class suburbia. I was thirty-seven years old, Caucasian, married with two children, a daughter, nine and a son, five. I had a husband who loved me, a mother, father, brother, grandmother, and aunts and uncles living in the same town as I. My parents loved John and felt I was lucky to have such a wonderful husband. I had never again trusted my father or my brother, but I appeared to have a friendly relationship with them. I was respected as a pillar of the community, an example of morality, a God-respecting Episcopalian, a favored daughter of the Church. I knew my place as President of the Women of the Church and Secretary of the Women of the Diocese. I had even been allowed to become a Lay Reader in the Sunday services, the highest position women were then allowed in the Episcopal Church. I was a Camp Fire leader, homeroom mother for both my children and a paid PTA member. I spent my days shopping, planning socials, playing bridge, carpooling and staying attractive. I "numbed out" to any feelings or thoughts that would contradict this perfect life, by taking four prescribed Valium tablets every day.

My husband, John, was a firefighter and, in addition, had his own automotive garage. He worked at least 100 hours a week. He demanded very little of me, personally, other than to keep up a positive community image and to care for our children and our home.

Our relationship took very little of my time or energy. I was sexually frigid. I filled my hours reading novels, playing bridge with three other mothers whose children were similar in age, volunteering for everything at church, attending my son's soccer games, sewing, reading to and caring for my children, caring for 200 houseplants in my garden room, fixing meals and baking thousands of cookies.

As president of the Women of the Church and Secretary of the Women of the Diocese, I attended Women's Bible study groups and planned events connected with the church.

As "normal" as my life seemed, I had strange feelings at times, feeling as if I were living in a cocoon, waiting to emerge as something else. I often experienced confusion and restlessness. I spoke to no one of these feelings.

One morning in February 1979, my depression was intense; my first thoughts upon awakening were, "Oh, God, why do I have to wake up?"

I moaned and rolled over in the empty king-sized bed. The alarm could no longer be ignored. The persistent thought, "I can't live this way any longer," would not leave my brain. Each morning lately I had awakened with the same panic and feelings of aloneness, helplessness and utter frustration. I continued to have a very strong urge to end my life. I did not understand this urge to die when I seemingly had so much to live for.

As I drifted in and out of sleep, I thought, "This is like 'deja vu'. When? Why?" My brain fought to remain conscious and tried to remember something that seemed to be at the edge of my consciousness.

The thoughts would not come clear. In my half-asleep, half-awake state that February morning, the thought of "children" began to surface and crowd out the possibility of remembering, what? I burrowed deeper under the satin comforter. I heard myself groan again, "Oh, God, why do I have to get up?"

Sleep became impossible as I became aware of the familiar sounds of my nine-year-old daughter, Kelley. Alone in the kitchen she banged the cupboard doors and noisily slammed kettles as she went about preparing and eating her breakfast and packing her lunch.

I felt guilty about not getting up to help her. But several months before, we had agreed that I should remain in bed to avoid our early morning confrontations. They had become unbearable for both of us. My staying out of the kitchen had cut down on the unnecessary yelling that seemed to always happen when the two of us were together. I preferred the mess that Kelley always left for me to the scenes we had acted out for months before our agreement.

Kelley entered my darkened bedroom hesitantly. "Mom?"

"What is it, Kelley?"

"Have you seen my tennis shoes?" she inquired.

"No, Kelley, I have not. I do not wear your tennis shoes; therefore, I do not remember where you left them."

Sarcasm and disgust were obvious in my voice. This was one situation we had not been able to correct by my remaining in bed. Kelley still found excuses to come into my room to ask questions, which seemed totally unnecessary and unanswerable to me.

As Kelley left my beautifully decorated pale yellow bedroom, she slammed the door. She opened it again, stuck her pretty, auburn head back in and shouted, "Sorry, Mom!" Then she closed the door, slowly this time.

My head felt as if it was in a metal vise and someone was slowly tightening the crank. I felt that Kelley's slamming the door was a personal insult aimed at increasing my pain. I believed that many people did things to deliberately cause me pain. My head had ached all my waking hours for more years than I could remember.

"I must get up and take something for this pain," I told myself. I slipped my bare feet onto the plush, celery-colored carpet as I perched my slim body on the edge of the bed. I glimpsed well-manicured nails as I began running my fingers through my thick auburn hair. I looked down at my feet as I wiggled brightly lacquered toes to help the circulation.

I stood up to my full height of 5'7" inches and began slowly approaching the marble-topped vanity. I tried to get a clear image of myself in the large gold-framed mirror. Without my glasses I could not see clearly. I could have been staring at any well-kept female in her mid-thirties.

I turned slowly and reached for my thick horn-rimmed glasses. Slipping them on, the image came into focus. I immediately became more critical of my appearance. "Maybe I should bleach my hair. John likes blonde hair. He bought me that blonde wig immediately after we got married."

Removing my glasses I began to insert my faithful contacts. My hand trembled noticeably as it moved the small blue circle of plastic closer to my eye. I hated the shaking. I hated the pain.

With only one lens in, I ran a glass of water and began fumbling with the caps of the six medicine vials I kept in my makeup drawer. The pills had become as much a habit as putting on my makeup or brushing my teeth.

I dispensed a Valium, a Darvon for my headache, a sinus pill, a hormone supplement and two vitamins. I did it routinely, yet that day I stopped to look at the red, blue, yellow, gray and pink-and-white pills in my hand. I asked myself, "Does everyone start the day this way?"

Some part of my being responded immediately, "*YOU NO LONGER NEED THESE.*" The thought seemed to be prompted, but I immediately argued, "Yeah, right. How do I do this without them?" No response was immediately there.

"Surely there has to be a better way to live," I thought as I swallowed the last pill and methodically cleaned and inserted the other contact lenses. The world focused, and I turned to survey the closet.

Three large racks of fashionable, color-coordinated garments faced me. I stood and stared with eyes fixed on nothing. I was unable to make the simple decision of what to put on.

I wrapped my arms tightly around my shaking middle. I rocked back and forth, back and forth, tears streaming down my cheeks. I was unable to finish my daily routine of camouflaging myself in the role of successful wife, mother, daughter, bookkeeper, Camp Fire leader, churchwoman . . . I crumpled to the floor.

As I lay huddled in the closet, a kind of "dawning" seemed to take place in my consciousness: Although some 17 years had gone by (including 12 years of this, my second marriage) and I'd had two children, I was still being plagued with awful headaches, shaking insides, feelings of inadequacy and the nagging question of whether life was really worth living.

"Maybe all of these pills for all of these years are only treating the symptoms, not the disease." I began questioning myself. "Maybe I'm not really sick. Maybe I'm only afraid. Yes! Afraid! But afraid of what?"

A small warm hand touched my arm as Cory, my son, knelt beside me. He seemed not to notice my distraught condition.

"Mommy, do I have to go to school today?" he breathed sleepily.

I smiled through my tears. At five, he was the joy of my life – fair skinned, blond haired, with big mischievous blue eyes and a pug nose sprinkled with freckles. "Angel kisses" we fondly called them.

"Come here, Love."

Cory snuggled up against my breast and slipped his arms around my neck. His fine blond hair still smelled of baby shampoo from the night before. The fragrance aroused memories of his babyhood and all the hours I had rocked him through the night when he could not breathe lying down because of asthma.

"Don't you want to go to school today and play with your friends and learn to draw?" I was bringing up the positive aspects of going to school, trying to change his mind.

"Aw, I guess so," he answered a bit disgustedly. "I just thought maybe it was cartoon day, and I wished we could stay home together."

"So do I," I thought. His remark made me realize that we were almost always on the run and in and out of the car.

"Why do I feel the need to go so much?" I wondered, almost out loud. "We have this lovely house with a new sun room just added for my plants, yet I always feel the need to be out, away from here – playing bridge, shopping, volunteering, my part-time job at the bank – seemingly anything to keep from staying at home; anything to avoid being alone. I can't stand to be alone."

This last thought still nagged at me as I helped Cory dress for school. Cory insisted on wearing a well-worn shirt with a motorcycle on the front. I had wanted him to wear a new shirt because I wanted his teacher, who was also a personal friend, to think, "What a good mother she is. . ."

I did not know, on that February morning while half asleep, that I had been tapping into Betty Jean's and my combined Oversoul, that the soul was prompting me to begin to remember who we really were. I did not realize then either that Kelley and Cory were children of the <u>one</u> entity that Betty Jean and I had become. All I knew was confusion and depression.

I would also later come to know that the wonderings and whispers of that morning were but the faint stirrings of my "remembering." The tangled threads of my life were beginning to unravel.

6

Life Changes - 1979

February faded into history and the days moved into March. I still, somehow, managed to live my "normal" busy life in middle class suburbia. (Betty Jean was still in the body.)

At that time I had no clues, other than depression and a growing sense of restlessness, that my life was about to take a drastic change. Since my return to Lubbock from Amarillo, one of my familial responsibilities included fixing my (and Betty Jean's) mother's hair twice a week. On this particular Monday, after a morning of bridge with three of my closest friends, and lunch at McDonald's with our small children, I went to my mother's home to perform the familiar service of doing her hair.

At first sight of her I was aware she was ill. She explained she had been experiencing arm pain and nausea. Her face was ashen. When I saw her, I now vividly remember thinking, "Mother is going to die from this." (This realization is my first remembered precognitive awareness.)

I reacted in my usually efficient manner. I was frantic inside but calm on the outside. I arranged for her to get to the hospital. She had already driven herself to the doctor's office once that very morning and had had an EKG. My father and brother were at work and had been unavailable to take her, and I was playing bridge. She had (by choice) no friends she could call on for help. The doctor had sent her home to rest. She had just driven herself back to her house when I arrived.

Mother's week in the hospital passed in a blur. I spent many hours sitting beside her bed, just holding her hand. She slept most of the time. I left her only long enough to attend to my other essential duties. On Saturday, I began to feel ill myself and went home to take a shower and change clothes. While I was in the shower, a final heart attack claimed her life. It was as if she waited until she was alone to leave her body.

Before Mother's transition, while she had still been able to recall life's incidents, and to talk, she cleared up a gap in my (bj King/Betty Jean's) memory that had puzzled me for a long time. I had decided to ask her about it because I was concerned she might take the memories with her and I would never know.

Mother had told me she remembered that once, when I was nine, for the first time in my life I had seemed really happy. I had just been elected Queen of the third grade. I had a boyfriend and my own pet, a little beige, short-haired dog I had named Peanut. We were living in the first home we'd owned, which had been built by my grandfather; prior to that time we had always lived in rental property and moved every two years within the city.

She related that about that time she began to suspect that my father was having an affair with her best friend, who was also the wife of his business partner. She said she felt the only way to save her marriage would be to move away in order to keep the two apart.

My folks gave my little dog away, and we moved overnight to Ft. Worth, Texas, without explanation at that time, or ever. They claimed Peanut could not be taken with us because we didn't know what our circumstances might be in the new town.

Betty Jean must have gone into shock at that time, due to the loss of her school, friends, security, home, and pet. She must have stayed in shock for the nine months they were in Ft. Worth, because there were almost no available memories of that time period in her body.

After nine months, we moved back to Lubbock. Mother revealed she had extracted a promise from my dad that if we returned to Lubbock, he and his business partner's wife would never see each other again. By the time of our return, the partner and his wife had divorced and she had moved to another city. Mother never allowed herself another close friend.

At my mother's funeral a woman came up to me, very hesitantly, and said, "You won't remember me, but I used to be your mother's best friend. I want to extend my sympathy to you. I have missed her . . ." and she burst into tears before she could finish. The only response coming from me was, "I know. She missed you, too, and she forgives you, and so do I." We embraced and a warmth of energy passed between us.

That same week, one of my bridge partners made up with her mother from whom she had been estranged for several years. My mother's death and my loss made my friend realize that she wanted a mother more than she wanted to have her anger, and more than she wanted to be "right."

The night of Mother's funeral, my husband John asked me to join him and his visiting family from Abilene at a local restaurant. As we all left the restaurant, he handed me the car keys and asked me to drive his sisters-in-laws to our house while he took his brothers to his shop to show them some new equipment he had just acquired. I was shocked by his insensitivity. I was angered by his expectation after the strain of the week and the funeral. Did he not realize I had put my mother's body in the ground only hours before?

I took the keys and dutifully drove the women to our home. I was in a daze as I prepared and offered them coffee. I was unable and unwilling to join in their small talk while we awaited the men's return.

That night I decided I no longer wanted to be John's wife. I was no longer willing to pretend that everything was "fine." I was no longer willing to live emotionally abandoned.

7
Edward - 1979

My husband, John, and I were members of St. Christopher's Episcopal Church. In addition to being President of the Women of the Church and Secretary of the Diocese, I had also volunteered to be the librarian and bookkeeper.

During the week Mother was in the hospital, Ed, the priest of our parish, turned in his resignation and announced he was leaving the priesthood. He and his family planned to move to Oklahoma City where he planned to return to geology, his profession before seminary.

In the three years they had lived in Lubbock, Ed and his wife, Mary, had become two of my closest friends. He and I had worked together on church projects, and she and I belonged to the same Bible study and prayer groups.

I was shocked by Ed's announced resignation, yet I totally understood his frustration with the rules handed down by the national church. The national organization was demanding that individual churches be run as corporate businesses, and that ministry become secondary on the priest's list of duties. Ed now felt that being a parish priest was interfering with his own spiritual life and his ability to minister to the needs of the people he served. The vestry of St. Christopher's was uncomfortable with his focusing on people perusing their individual relationship with Jesus and God. He was veering away from Episcopal theology. The "old guard" rose up and asked for his resignation.

It had been the evening of the day Ed and Mary left Lubbock for Oklahoma City that Mother had her final heart attack and permanently left her body. I called him the following morning. They were staying temporarily at the home of the Bishop of Oklahoma. They offered to return to

Lubbock to be with me for the funeral. Since I am a very practical person, I refused their offer. I could not imagine expecting them to make such a sacrifice, when they were in the midst of relocating.

Humans have a built-in psychological protection system they use in times of emotional disturbance or trauma. It is called shock. Humans have also created rituals at such times, which require them to make decisions and perform various duties. The enactment of these duties and rituals enables them to get through the first few days of a loved one's death. The shock of my mother's passing kept a blanket of fog between me and the world. I was as if I was able to wrap my feelings in a wet blanket and put them in a trunk to be exhumed at a later time when not so much was being expected of me. I (Betty Jean was still in the body) operated as my usual efficient self during the funeral planning, the service, and the clearing and distribution of my mother's personal belongings. I broke down, emotionally, when I uncovered a single long-stemmed red rose in the bottom of her lingerie drawer.

The rose, a vase, my card and a note had been ritualistically wrapped in an abundance of aluminum foil. Mother's note read, "This rose fulfills a lifetime fantasy, that someone would care enough to send me one red rose." Tears flooded my shaking body as I recalled that when Mother was alive, she had been severely allergic to flowers, perfumes and all fabrics except cotton. This required that she sew her own clothes from 100-percent cotton fabric. As for the rose, when I was 28 years old, I (Betty Jean) had decided to send her a single, long-stemmed red rose on my birthday, thanking her for my life.

In sending the rose, I had concluded that she could keep it in another room, if she had to. But it had been important for me to send it to her, because the rose was symbolic of my love and gratitude. After birthing my first child, I had a new appreciation and gratitude for what she had gone through to give me life.

The week following my mother's death, I received a long letter from Ed. The letter was consoling and included descriptions of his feelings at the time of his own parents' deaths and Bible quotations. He said he thought all of this might be a comfort and might assist me somehow in my grief. He also included a suggestion that I might wish to quit taking the tranquilizers, to quit masking my feelings.

Ed was the first person who had ever suggested to me that taking four prescribed Valium tablets a day might not be a normal way to live. In the 1970's, it was seemingly a status symbol to be living a life so stressful that one required such medication!

I was touched and moved by Ed's concern for me. He offered to be emotionally and spiritually available to me by mail and by phone, at any hour, to assist me to get off – and stay off – the drug. I found his offer overwhelmingly generous. It brought a new torrent of tears. I had never had a male make himself available to me, emotionally. I did not believe I could trust him. I did not understand how to regard such an offer, since I was cut off from my own feelings by the effects of Valium. After all, I seldom thought, "How do I feel about this?" I only thought in terms of, "What does this situation require in order for me to look normal and competent. What is needed?" And I certainly never thought, "What do I want." I followed his suggestion because I wanted to please him. I also wanted to test him, to see if he could be trusted to be there for me.

The first few weeks after my mother's passing were difficult, both because my routine was altered and because I was going off the Valium. I slept almost not at all. The anxiety attacks were horrendous! My skin crawled and my insides shook. I was alternately freezing and burning up. My thoughts and feelings were rampant and chaotic. I found it difficult to concentrate. I had memory lapses. Twice I forgot to pick my child up from day care. I cried with almost no provocation. I felt raw, as if a layer of my skin had been torn away and I was totally exposed. My head ached as if someone were inside with a jackhammer tearing out the walls. I had flashes of myself in scenes I didn't recognize. I had no way of knowing if they were real or imagined. I now realize some were scenes of Betty Jean's past, which she had kept from herself through the Valium use, and some were precognitive scenes of my future. I felt as if I were losing touch with reality.

The most difficult thing was grocery shopping. I would enter the store with resolve; by the time my basket was half-filled, and I had reached the back of the store, the anxiety would be so intense, the shaking so severe that I would flee the store without purchasing what my family needed. I had no idea I was empathic, that I was picking up all the emotions that previous shoppers had psychically left in the aisles. I only knew I couldn't manage to shop for a full list of groceries. I learned to shop in five-minute increments. I would enter the store with a list, concentrate on finding and purchasing the first six items and rush from the store before the anxiety forced me to run to my car.

A constant stream of encouraging, helpful and inspiring books and letters from Ed filled my mailbox. Devouring his writings, the books and following his suggestion to write out the story of my life made continuing possible.

After the first week, Ed began calling daily. He took time from his busy schedule at his new job to check on my progress and condition. He encouraged me to call him if I needed to talk. He suggested I write, just for myself, or to him if I felt I could trust him enough. But he said it was important to <u>write my feelings as they surfaced</u>. He suggested that I write my life story from my earliest possible childhood memories to the present. He said if the memories are blocked, you may need to write your story backward. Start with today and write what you remember of yesterday, but don't worry about the chronological order, write the memories as they occur to you. He jokingly said he knew this would be difficult for me, writing not in order, since order was so vitally important to me. Inside I questioned, "How does he know that would bother me? He must know me better than I realized. He must have been paying attention to me all these years we have worked together." The thought was a little frightening. "What else had he noticed that I thought I was successfully hiding from everyone?"

I had huge gaps in the memories of my childhood! (I would like to say here that many other walk-ins I have since met experience this same situation. The original entity, which in this case was Betty Jean, stored difficult or traumatic memories in a special section of the brain. This section can be veiled from the conscious mind. Retrieving such memories takes special concentration and a *willingness* to *experience* them, although they may be upsetting and difficult. I was ripe for, but suspicious of, the emotional support offered by Ed's calls and letters. I was drowning in a sea of emotion which had been held back successfully for years. The emotions were increased by removal of the dam the Valium had held in place. (I came to know, years later, that Betty Jean was preparing to leave the body during this time. It was time for her to return to the Oversoul. The potential of her departure, although not known to me at a conscious level, was affecting my emotional body. The potential of being left to cope with life alone added to my feelings of fear, confusion, grief, guilt, and conflict.)

Withdrawal from the drug, confrontation with death and the unblocking of childhood memories were increasing the tension in my marriage. John withdrew even more because of my increased sensitivity, unexpected angry outbursts, and my need to talk about death. Ed's letters and calls continued to come daily. He invited and encouraged me to talk and to share my innermost fears, desires, questions, memories and frustrations. He was offering me what I so desperately needed and wasn't getting from my husband.

I felt one door closing and another one opening, moving me from my fear, my deep commitment to John, family, my children and the church toward the unknown – and to Ed.

I was torn apart. I still loved John. I loved my home, my children, my security and my positions in the community. I loved the respect all of my dedication had earned me, yet I began to be increasingly aware that I wanted and needed something more. (Years later, I recalled having tried to explain to ten-year-old Kelley that I needed to go away "to find out who I am." She could not understand and kept emphatically telling me, "But I know who you are. I can tell you who you are. You are my Mommy. Now, you don't need to go anywhere.")

I wanted to experience more of the feelings I had when I talked to Ed, the excitement of ideas, philosophy and spiritual awareness. Strong emotions filled my body. A passion I had always previously been able to control welled up from my depths.

I wrote, read and talked to Ed. I read and reread his compassion-filled letters and felt his growing love for me.

During these months he threw himself into his new position in the oil business. He filed for a divorce and registered to work on his master's degree at an Oklahoma university. I was amazed and appalled by how swiftly my life and his were changing.

I was constantly torn between what was "right" and what I felt I needed and wanted. I hated myself for betraying his wife, who had been my friend, my husband and my own values. I also had the fear of discovering or not discovering, and/or possibly losing, my "real" self, even though I had no real understanding of what those words meant.

I withdrew more and more from John, my friends and my children as I tried to "find myself" through the writing. Ed's letters encouraged me "not to be afraid to know the truth," but I had no concept of what that meant. I fought to hold onto my sanity, to function, to fix meals, to dress myself and to care for the needs of the children. I tried to behave as normally as possible when other people were around. At the same time, I was feeling that all things inside and outside of me were moving faster and faster, seemingly taking on a life of their own, without my consent.

One morning, Ed called after he knew that John would have left for work. "Love, I just heard a message from God as I was waking up this morning. The message is:

Blame no one.
Assume nothing.
Hope everything.

Be still, be patient,
Wait in love...

"I truly feel God is with us in this," he said. "You won't believe what else has happened. In the divorce agreement, Mary asked for a ridiculous amount of alimony. I received another job offer yesterday. It includes a raise amounting to exactly the amount she is asking for child support and alimony.

"I wish you, and, of course, the children, would consider moving to Oklahoma. If you don't want to marry me, I will understand; but I want to commit to taking care of you and the children financially so you can go to college and get a degree. I know you want that and you deserve it. You have a beautiful mind. You will be a wonderful counselor and I just know you have artistic talent you haven't explored.

"We can buy a small wooded place here in Edmond, close to the university." His words tumbled out, one on top the other. "The kids can have some animals, and we can be close to nature and you can walk to school. If things work out, eventually we can move to south central Texas and start the retreat center so that when other people are going through these sorts of life changes, they will have a place to come to sort things out and explore their creativity."

He was speaking very rapidly now. "We can call it 'Genesis, a Place for New Beginnings.' Don't answer me now, just think about it. I'll call you back later this afternoon." All of his ideas were tumbling over each other in my mind, and obviously in his.

"I don't want to put more pressure on you. I know you are barely handling the pressure there in your house already, but I love you so much, and I want to take care of you and be with you. I want to spend the rest of my life with you. Just think about it."

I was racked with grief and passion. I had an unquenchable desire to be held and comforted. My mind was so full of thoughts, possibilities, and fear of change that I could only sob my reply.

"I'll think about it. I love you. Goodbye."

Ed's life changes were opening him to his own creativity. He began to paint, exercise, write poetry, and to play the piano again. He even began writing a novel about my withdrawal from Valium and our relationship. I was absolutely astonished that he was able to do all of these things, write to me several times a day, deal with his divorce and handle his new job.

Ed's love and support gave me freedom from the fear of remembering, the fear of truly knowing myself. I was able to go deeper and deeper inside myself. I became even more emotionally overwhelmed as old memories began to surface. I dealt with each of them by writing to Ed and then talking them through with him each day when he called. Uncovering the memory of incest with my great-grandfather staggered us most of all.

The same week I uncovered that memory, my father called to tell me he had met someone new, fallen in love and was getting married. I was appalled! I could not imagine him with another woman, or another woman in my mother's home. He explained his loneliness and that this woman was full of life and fun. He added that she had had her children by caesarean section as I had and therefore making love to her was similar to what he imagined making love to me would be like. I gasped. I could not believe what he was saying to me.

"She loves to dance and has her own band," he told me excitedly.

I was appalled by the idea of his even thinking of making love to me and by the idea that he was remarrying so soon, but I wanted my father to be happy. I wanted him to be happy for me, too, but I could not share my thoughts, feelings, struggles, or awakening memories with him. Instead, I lied. I overlooked what he had just said and told him I was happy for him. I hung up the phone and crumpled to the floor, once more collapsing in tears.

The phone rang again almost immediately. It was Ed. "I'm coming to Lubbock to take care of some business. Can you get a sitter and spend the afternoon with me?"

"I don't know," I whispered through my tears. "What would we do?" I was confused and afraid.

"We can do anything you want, or nothing," he replied. "Or we can just talk. I just want to see you, to be able to hold you, even if it's just your hand. Whatever you can be comfortable with, please?" He sounded almost desperate.

"OK, when?" I groaned.

"Day after tomorrow at 10 A.M. I'll be at the airport. Can you get a sitter that early on Wednesday? You don't play bridge on Wednesday," he added with amusement in his voice. He knew my schedule almost as well as I did, and better than my husband. He was aware I had a grandmother-type sitter who was available on call, so long as I took my son to her home.

"Yes, I'll be there if I can arrange it. I'll let you know before your flight takes off."

"How are you doing?" he inquired. "You sound tired and stressed, even more so than when we spoke earlier this morning. I don't want to add more stress to your life, but I want you to really understand how much I love you and how much I want you to be here with me. I want you to know how much I want to make a life with you, a reflected life, a life with meaning and purpose, a life with fun and joy in it. I know it's possible. We just have to make it through these changes. I know we are meant to be together." He spoke with great conviction.

"You seem so sure," I stammered, "and I'm not sure of anything at this point. There is so much to think about, so much feeling happening in my body that I'm not used to. What do I do with all these feelings?" My voice had become almost inaudible, yet was shrill with panic.

"Has anything new happened? Have you remembered anything new since yesterday?" Concern and love filled his voice. "You are so brave to keep going with your process, in the midst of everything. You have no idea how brave you are to quit the drugs."

"Brave? No. Stupid? Yes. To try to deal with all this without tranquilizers is crazy. The doctor offered me a new prescription just this week, and when I couldn't sleep last night, John said, "Just take something and come to bed and quit pushing yourself so hard."

I went on shakily, "Today my father called to announce he's getting married again already. I can't believe it! Yes, I guess I can. I mean if I can fall in love with you and yet still love John, of course I can believe he can fall in love with someone else and still love my mother. But at least mother is dead. John and Mary are not dead and they are going to both be devastated if we make a choice to be together." I hated the whine in my voice.

"Bless your dad's heart. It's really difficult to lose someone you've spent your whole life with. You said in your writing that they were married at sixteen and seventeen. My God, they were only kids. They were together 41 years." His voice was filled with empathy.

I was silent as I thought about Ed's caring, his recall of details I had written and things I had told him about. I marveled at his coming up with 41 years from other facts and figures I'd mentioned. It was not a thought I had as yet put together, even for myself. I was amazed that he, being a man, paid so much attention to what I thought and felt.

"At least he will have someone to be with and I won't have to worry about him. I guess it is a good thing. I was just shocked by the suddenness of it. I'll be OK with it once I'm used to the idea, if I can get used to the idea of someone else in my mother's home." The doorbell was ringing so I ended the conversation and hung up abruptly.

A day later, I met Ed at the airport. This first meeting since his departure, was tense at first. Neither of us knew exactly what to do or say. I drove him to his business appointments and we talked between stops. Each time our eyes met or our hands touched, so much energy passed between us we were both physically shaking.

"That's the last stop," he breathed a sigh of relief as he reentered the car. "How about we get some sandwiches and go on a picnic?"

I started to laugh. Tears filled my eyes.

"What is it? What did I say?" He turned to me anxiously.

"The basket and cooler are in the trunk." My words spilled out through tears and laughter. "I never cease to be amazed at how similarly our minds operate. I decided last night that going out to eat would be foolish. We would probably run into people we know and to try to explain what we are doing together would be impossible. So I planned to drive outside the city, about an hour, to a state park, if that's OK with you." As I pulled out of the parking lot I turned back to see a grin spread across his face.

"You're a wonder and a delight," he chuckled. "I am always astounded by how organized you are and how much you accomplish and still always look so cool. I think I shall call you 'Ice Princess.'"

I felt anything but icy as my body flushed from his compliments and the intimacy in his voice.

We laughed, cried, ate, walked, swung, hugged, and kissed our way through the afternoon. It was an idyllic time. I felt a sense of freedom, joy and openness I had never experienced with another *Human* being.

After we'd finished eating, Ed gave me a cashier's check for $1,000 made payable to me. He said he hoped having it would make me feel less trapped. He added that if I needed to delay coming to Oklahoma to be with him, at least he could provide a way for me to start school in Lubbock in the fall. Not only was he offering me emotional and financial support, he was offering me freedom.

We both cried as we parted at the airport. I felt even more torn apart as I returned to my life of children, home, and my husband's birthday dinner.

Daily, I became more and more uncommunicative with anyone except Ed and my writing. John began to notice my detachment.

During his family reunion I wrote my first poem, entitled, "Stillness." I mailed it to Ed. At the end of the week, John and I returned home from the reunion. I entered the house through the garage; John went to the front door to retrieve the mail and newspapers. A telegram was attached to the front door. Thinking that a telegram meant bad news, John tore it open, although it was addressed to me.

"Bravo, My Love

'Stillness' is wonderful.
I applaud your breakthrough to the source of your poetry. I wrote a poem by the same name on the same day.

All my love
Edward"

John entered the house. I could feel his anger. I thought it must be because of the five letters addressed to me in the mailbox, all from Ed. He laid the telegram on the table in front of me. I read it without picking it up. I felt my decision to leave was being taken from my hands; was somehow being forced and speeded up by God.

"What does this mean?" John demanded angrily. "Why does he refer to you as 'My Love' and sign this, 'All My Love'? Doesn't the man know, care, or recognize that you ARE MY WIFE?!!" He was more angry and hurt than I had ever known him to be. I had never seen him express so much emotion. I was amazed and terrified.

I felt totally defenseless, afraid and inept to even try to explain the feelings I had for both him and Ed. I knew I was guilty. I knew I deserved to be punished. But I could not imagine what the correct punishment should be, for someone who loved both her husband dispassionately, and her friend's priest husband, passionately and with her whole being.

The following hours are a blur. John left for the fire station. I fed and put the children to bed. As I read their bedtime stories I noticed that one part of my brain was reading the story with animation, which pleased the children, while another part of my brain was busy planning how I would leave my home, my husband, my friends, my family, my positions, and all that I knew and was familiar to me. I wondered at being able to read a story and have another separate train of thought at the same time. I questioned, "Have I become schizophrenic?"

By morning I had made my decision. I would leave John, take the children and go to Ed, regardless of the cost to all other parties and my fears.

After taking the children to school, I called Ed at his office. He was elated by my decision, but distressed that his telegram had caused such a furor. We made a tentative plan: I would file for divorce and move to Oklahoma City the first of December. The day I made the call was July 6, 1979.

8

Getting To Oklahoma City

By the time John returned home from his shift at the firehouse, he had come to a decision about us: We would go for counseling and he would take a two-week vacation. He had made this decision and arrangements without calling me. He planned a ten-day "honeymoon" in New Orleans, so that I could have his undivided attention. He also arranged for a sitter for the children. He told me I was to cease communicating with Ed for one month to give him time to prove his love for me and to prove, also, that he could be open and communicative.

I was, once again, thrown into a state of total confusion. How could I possibly leave this man whom I loved, had lived with for 14 years, and who had fathered my two children? Didn't I have to give him at least a second chance?

In my duress, I agreed to his terms. The next morning I called Ed. I explained that I had changed my mind; that I simply <u>had</u> to try to make this marriage work. I asked him to please not try to contact me. We were both miserable with my decision, but he agreed to honor it.

The "second honeymoon" in New Orleans was a disaster. I found my body even more unresponsive than usual to John's touch. My mind was completely filled with thoughts of things I wanted to tell Ed – experiences I was having that I wanted to share. I felt I was in the right city, but with the wrong man.

We returned to Lubbock and entered what I thought was to be marriage counseling. We went to three different psychologists for counseling. I thought we were attempting to find one with whom we could both feel comfortable. The third psychologist asked me two questions, which still stand out in my mind. The first one was, "What is the worst thing that can happen if you choose to leave your husband and go to live with this other man you hardly know?"

To this I answered that I would leave everything I knew to be with Ed and if he abandoned me, I would be there alone, with no one.

The second question was, "Could you live through what you just told me if it were to happen?"

I replied, "Yes. I don't want to think about it, but I know I would survive." My voice had a surety about it that I did not feel. The counselor turned to John and stated, "She's one of the sanest people I have ever had in my office. She knows what she wants and she is willing to risk everything to have it. You would do well to let her go."

He spoke to John as if I were not even in the room. I became aware that I had just passed a sanity investigation and had not been involved in a marriage counseling session at all! John had every intention of keeping me as his wife, even if it included having me temporarily committed to a hospital for reasons of being emotionally out of control. I later learned, from the divorce lawyer, that by Texas law a husband has the authority over his wife to have her committed if he can find three attending physicians who agree to her instability.

The shock of his attempt to once again control me cleared my mind and strengthened my resolve to leave. I remember my next thought clearly: "I <u>have</u> to leave. This person does not have my highest good in mind, only his own. He is even willing to have me committed rather than face, and admit to, the real problems!"

The following morning I called Ed. He was in a meeting and had to return my call.

The anxiety of that hour's wait is indescribable. My feelings of relief and happiness when I finally heard his voice are not possible to express in words.

He was relieved and elated by my call. We talked and cried and laughed for two hours. We jointly made the decision that he would send me a check that would enable the children and me to move out of the house and live, while we arranged my final move and the divorce. We also admitted to each other that while the letters had gone unmailed, we both had continued to write daily during the past weeks. It was amazing how we had continued to communicate with each other mentally and spiritually. I did not know at this time that we are from the same Oversoul.

I arranged to fly to Oklahoma the following weekend to look for a house. When John came home from work that evening, we talked honestly for the very first time in our lives together. We both spoke without anger. He admitted that he realized he had lost me. He said that if I could just agree to remain in the house with him and the children until the divorce was final, he would try not to interfere further in my decisions, nor impose any physical demands on me. I agreed to try. I was able to stay because I knew that I had the freedom to leave any time I desired. Ed's offer of financial assistance made that possible.

The next few months were very stressful, but the two of us fell into a new pattern of honestly communicating, which we had never had before. And we talked for hours.

Now that I was leaving, John gave himself permission to be vulnerable. It made my commitment to a divorce even more difficult. I had to remind myself constantly that I was not "running away" from anything; I was "making a choice to move toward something," another way of life. During the extra months of waiting, it became increasingly apparent to me that I was making the right choice.

I made two trips to Oklahoma City. The first trip Ed and I both experienced sexual healings. He had been impotent with his wife for several years; I had been frigid for 38. Together we were completely free to express ourselves and found we were sexually compatible.

The second trip, the children went with me. We had a wonderful weekend together. They were excited about the possibilities of our new life. We made a down payment on an old farmhouse, with acreage, four blocks from the University in a suburb of Oklahoma City. We planned to move in December.

Toward the end of October, Ed and I both became anxious about waiting, he more than I. His divorce was now final and he was free to rent a townhouse for us while the contract on the farmhouse was being completed and it was being renovated.

At his insistence, we arranged for a moving van to arrive in Lubbock November 9, 1979. John was understanding and helpful and worked hard to control his emotions. Ed flew to Lubbock to drive the van, the children, and me to our new life in Oklahoma City.

The day before we departed, I purchased a book to read aloud to Ed while he was driving us in the van. The book was *Illusions* by Richard Bach. *The Manual for Reluctant Messiahs* fascinated us both. I was still unaware of metaphysics and what it meant to be psychic.

The townhouse was light, airy and adequate. It overlooked a golf course filled with trees, squirrels and birds. The four of us laughed our way through the adjustments and awkwardness of moving in. The first night, Ed prepared to leave for his apartment (for propriety's sake and the children's adjustment). Cory, nearly six at that time, adamantly opposed his leaving.

"You didn't move my mother and my sister and me here so you could live by yourself," he accosted. "You're staying here with us. He can sleep with you, Mom. He's going to be your husband," he stated, grabbing Ed's hand and dragging him toward the stairway and bed.

From the beginning, I had never experienced a period of my life that felt more "right." The fourth morning as we awakened and snuggled, Ed confirmed my feelings. "I have never felt happier or more content in my life. How about a picnic today? I'll take a long lunch hour and drive back out to get you and Cory about noon. We can eat in the park and then go to the bank to open our joint account so you will have money to run the house."

He kissed my forehead once more before he lunged from the bed to take a shower.

Cory, awakened by Ed's riotous singing in the shower, knocked at the bedroom door and then scurried in to grab Ed's "still warm spot" in the bed beside me.

"You sure picked a 'funny' man to love, Mommy," he said as he snuggled up next to me to listen to Ed sing "I had a dream . . ." When Ed came out of the bath, a towel wrapped around his waist, he began to tickle Cory through the blankets, giving his now famous imitation Dracula laugh. The three of us were roaring hysterically when Kelley entered, rubbing her eyes and yawning.

"You guys are nuts," she exclaimed.

Ed surfaced from under the covers, raised his arms menacingly over his head and deepened his Dracula laugh. As he did so, he moved around the bed toward Kelley. She ran screaming down the hall and flew down the stairs yelling, "Stop that! You know I hate it when you do that!" But she was laughing all the time and loving the attention. When Ed left for work, the four of us laughed and hugged and kissed. As he started to leave the porch, he said gratefully, "I've never been happier or more content in my life. Thank you for coming to be with me."

This brought tears of joy to our eyes as we watched him drive away. We rushed to dress and to get the children to their new schools on time for their first day.

I returned alone to the townhouse and to the stacks of moving cartons to be emptied. I poured myself a cup of coffee and set to work. As the knife cut through the tape on the first book box, the phone rang. I answered with a smile on my face and in my voice, as I knew it would be Ed.

"Hello," I said with happiness in my voice.

"Hi, there. I just wanted to let you know I arrived safely at the office. I thought of you all the way to work and wanted to tell you again how much I appreciate your moving your schedule forward to come to me before your divorce is final. I know how difficult it is for you to be living with me before you are legally free. But, Love, I know that God means for us to be together and these are all man-made laws. Your friends – our friends, the ones who are REALLY our friends – will understand that later and get over being angry. Maybe even John and Mary will eventually understand."

The smile left my face and tears welled up in my eyes. A lump filled my throat as the conflict of both the happy and sad emotions met once again in my body.

"I know," I managed to whisper almost inaudibly into the receiver. "I know. I pray they will, but it is so painful that no one but you and I understand."

"I didn't call to make you sad." Ed sounded almost apologetic. "I called to tell you how happy I am and how much I love you and your wonderful children. I talked to my crazy friend Tim this morning. He's arranging to have a limo pick everybody up and take us all to Molly Murphy's for Cory's sixth birthday party." He sounded so happy and excited that my mood returned to one of elation.

"What's a Molly Murphy's?"

"It's a house of ill repute," he answered, chuckling.

"A what? Don't you think he's a bit young?" I started to laugh.

"He'll love it! It's a restaurant that's decorated really crazy. The salad bar is in a red 1970 Jaguar. The waiters and waitresses are dressed as characters from movies, TV and the comics. It's really a zany place and they have a dance floor. I'll finally get to dance with you. There are so many things we haven't done together yet. I want to make every first time we do things special."

"Speaking of special," I smiled happily, "what would you like to do for your birthday? You don't turn 52 every day and take on a new family."

"Can you make cheesecake?" he asked softly.

"I don't know. I've never tried to, but if that's what you want, I'll try it," I offered.

"That's what I want, cheesecake, and you and the children and dinner at home together. I don't care what else we have. You're such a great cook anything you fix will please me."

"How do you know I'm such a great cook? I've never cooked for you," I challenged.

"Ah, but you have, at a hundred church potluck dinners, remember? And you put your recipes in the cookbook you gals published last year for the church. We've known each other for three years. That's a lot of meals, but now it's different because we're really finally together, thank God."

"Yes, thank God is right. There's no other way I could have done all this so quickly unless it was an act of God." I laughed, but I was serious.

"Speaking of acts of God, it's going to take several to get all these boxes emptied, make a picnic, pick Cory up at school and meet you at noon. Don't you have work to do, or do they pay you to talk on the phone," I teased happily.

"Don't worry about the lunch. I'll stop at a deli on my way home and bring the lunch. Oh yeah, I almost forgot the other reason I called. Could you hold off on unloading the books until we can do it together? Books are so special to both of us I think it would be fun to do that part together and talk about them as we put them away," he requested. "Also, I'd like to have you show me your scrapbooks tonight. I want to know everything about you."

"Sure, I can wait. I'd love that. I loved all the books you put on the shelves of my office when you left the church. I often thought you left them just for me and not just for the church library," I confided.

"I did," he replied, "once I found you were going to be the church librarian, as well as everything else you did at the church. I left the ones I thought you would enjoy the most."

"I thought so, but you did that before you left – before we fell in love as a result of all that letter writing," I commented joyfully. "Yeah, some part of me must be very smart, or maybe I'm a little bit psychic," he joked. "I've got to go now. The meeting is about to start. I'll meet you in the park by the library at noon. I love you. Thanks for being crazy enough to love me," he added.

"I DO LOVE YOU very, very much. See you at noon. Bye." I hung up the receiver, a happy smile once again covering my face.

I worked at unpacking the kitchen boxes until time to pick up Cory from kindergarten. I noticed I was singing to myself and couldn't remember ever feeling so happy. As the little fellow got into the car, a big mischievous grin spread across his freckled cherub-like face.

"What's up?" I asked.

"Nothing. I'm just glad to see you. Where's Father Ed?" he inquired.
"He's meeting us at the park," I answered.
"Good. I was afraid he had changed his mind."
"No, he's bringing the lunch, so we'd better get going. Buckle up."

As we pulled away from the curb, I once again said a prayer, thanking God for the happiness I was feeling. The day was warm, clear and sunny for November.

Cory's eyes began searching for Ed as we approached the park.

"There he is! There he is, Mom! There's Father Ed and look! He's got a kite for me!" As he spoke he began bouncing up and down on the seat, as much as the belt would allow. He was out of the car and running across the grass the second I got it unfastened. He grabbed Ed around the waist from behind.

"Let me try! Can I try to fly it, please? Can I?" He jumped up and down in his excitement.

"Sure! It's yours, Sport. I was just holding it 'til you got here," Ed teased as he handed the controls over to Cory, grabbing me around the waist at the same time.

"God I missed you! I missed you more now that you're here in town than I did when you were in Lubbock. Then, I knew you were inaccessible. Now, I know I can talk to you, hold you, see you, and that's all I want to do." He cupped my face in his hands and looked deep into my eyes. "Now, nothing can separate us," he declared as he kissed me firmly and passionately.

We had a delightful picnic lunch, and made it to the bank, all in the two hours Ed had allotted himself. We even drove by the house we had under contract. As we said goodbye for the second time that day, it seemed even more difficult to part than it had been that morning. Once again he said, "I am happier and more content than I have ever been in my life."

Cory and I returned to the townhouse and to the chore of unpacking. He quickly tired of helping and fell asleep watching a cartoon. The afternoon flew by as I emptied carton after carton, broke them down and shoved them under the beds for the move to our own home. Kelley arrived on the school bus, flushed by excitement and the unusual warmth of the November day.

"Mom, do you think we could get me the new Carpenter's album sometime soon?" she asked.

"Well, probably. What's it called? And how was your first day at school?"

"OK, I guess, OK, it's different. It's called, 'Close to You,' and I REALLY want it." She stressed the _really_, as she returned to the subject of the album.

"We'll see. I'm sure we can find it. Father Ed will know where the record store is. He's been living here for a while and is really into music," I offered.

"Are you always going to call him 'Father Ed' even after you marry him, Mom?" Kelley asked, wrinkling her forehead.

"No. I don't call him that when I talk to him. I only call him that to you and Cory because that's what you call him. I call him Edward. Once we began writing each other it was like we were two new people with each other. So in our writing, I called him Edward and he called me 'bj,' so now we use those names," I explained.

"I like that," Kelley said. "A new name for a new life. Do we have any Dr. Pepper?" She ran it all together as if it made perfect sense to her ten-year-old mind.

Ed called later in the afternoon, just to "check in" and to ask the children about their first day at school. I mentioned the tape request and asked about the location of the record store.

"No, problem. Do you think she'll mind if I just stop and get it on my way home, or is she invested in shopping for it herself?" he inquired.

"No, I think she's more invested in having it than in going to get it," I said, continually amazed at this man's sensitivity, generosity and caring.

"Cassette or eight track?" he asked.

"Cassette," I answered, "and thanks. You're a love."

"It's nice to be appreciated. I like that," he responded. "I'll see you soon. Maybe you should sit down and put your feet up for a while or go sit in a hot tub, sounds as if you've been really busy. I think I'll get a bottle of wine on my way home, too. We can probably both enjoy a little relaxation. Any preferences?"

"No. No preferences, really. I do like Asti Spumante. Do you like that?"

"Perfect. Asti it is. See you soon."

Dinner in the oven, I took a quick shower and ran a comb through my hair. I was coming down the stairs when the doorbell rang. Both children shouted simultaneously, "I'll get it," and ran for the door. As they flung it open, Ed nearly fell through, flowers and wine in one hand and briefcase in the other. He must have rung the bell with his elbow or his nose.

"Hi, hi, hi! How's everybody?" he questioned, grinning from ear to ear. He kissed me on the forehead and handed me the bouquet and wine.

"I've got something in here that I think will interest you guys," he said rather mysteriously. He clicked the latches on his briefcase and looking at the children, he wiggled his bushy eyebrows like Groucho Marx. He extracted the Carpenter tape for Kelley and a tape-book set of *Peter and the Wolf* for Cory.

"Wow, how did you know I wanted this?" Kelley exclaimed, shocked at how rapidly her request had been granted, as if by magic.

"You've heard of fairy Godmothers?" Ed asked with a twinkle. When she answered, "Yes," a little reservedly, he went on, "Well, you have a Godfather who's not a fairy," and he ruffled her bangs. She threw her arms around him. "Thank you, Father Ed, thanks a lot," she exclaimed with feeling.

"You're welcome, Princess. You deserve it. Both you kids have been great about this whole ordeal. We've put you through a lot, without asking your permission," he declared, emotion creeping into his voice as he drew all of us into a family hug.

"When's dinner, Mom?" Cory inquired excitedly. "Do we have time to listen to our tapes first?"

"I think we'd better eat now. Maybe we could listen to Kelley's as dinner music while we eat and then you can listen to yours as a bedtime story," I suggested. I tried to encourage a planned evening progression to allow Ed and me time alone to go through the scrapbooks as he had suggested.

After a talk-and-laugher-filled dinner, Ed helped Cory bathe while Kelley and I cleared the dishes. We tucked them both in bed with lots of hugs and kisses. I started Cory's tape before retreating downstairs to our wine and quiet. As I put on a tape of love songs, Ed popped the cork.

We spent three hours pouring over scrapbooks and school annuals of my history, stopping periodically to exchange stories and to just feel the pleasure of being together.

As we showered together, we tried to be quiet, but could not help giggling and tittering happily from our joy and the wine. In bed, Ed read to me from a book of poetry, <u>My Beloved</u>, which he'd also had in his briefcase. We made love – from our hearts, our bodies and our souls. Later, I propped myself up in the middle of the bed, faced him and read to him from *Some Men are More Perfect than Others* by Merle Shain.

At one point, he stopped me and went downstairs "to check the lock on the front door." The next day I found evidence that he had taken an Alka-seltzer. When Ed returned, I detected he was getting sleepy and suggested we turn off the lights. As I righted myself in the bed to pull up the blankets, I saw him fall across the foot of the bed, clutching at his chest. He gasped for breath and was unable to speak. I was horrified and confused. I was torn between trying to help him breathe and trying to get to the phone to call an ambulance. The phone was downstairs.

I called 911 and flew back upstairs. Ed was turning gray and gasping.

I began mouth-to-mouth resuscitation. An eternity passed in the next fifteen minutes. He was breathing but was still unable to speak. I heard the ambulance miss the turn into the townhouse complex. I heard the sound of the siren retreat as the ambulance passed us and drove up the hill. Frantic for help and knowing Ed was suffering, I raced, barefoot and robeless in a black see-through negligee, screaming for help into the cold blackness of the night. Porch lights came on; people stepped outside. One man jumped into his car and sped after the ambulance. Someone draped a blanket around my scantily clad body.

The children were awakened by my screams. Fortunately they followed the sound of my voice and came downstairs without looking into our bedroom. The paramedics worked with Ed giving him injections and oxygen. Neighbors from Afghanistan, who I did not know, stayed with the children; other neighbors I did not know put clothes on my body and whisked me to the hospital three blocks away.

By the time the ambulance arrived at the hospital, Ed was dead. The unbelievable had happened – the thing I had described to the psychologist had happened. Ed had abandoned me.

9

The Abyss

Ed being gone forever was utterly inconceivable to me. How could this possibly be happening, after all the changes we had gone through, and the effort we had made to have a life together? He and I had abruptly changed the lives of at least 18 people so we could be together, and now this was forever denied us! I would be alone! How could I tell Mary he was dead? It was bad enough for her to have given him up to me. Now, we BOTH had to give him up – to death.

Most of the memories of the few days following my beloved's death are very sketchy and blurred; a few are vivid. Kelley took the responsibility of phoning Mary and explaining that Ed had a heart attack and was at the hospital.

The next day I received three calls; one was from John. He offered sympathy. He offered to come get the three of us. He offered to drive us back home to Lubbock "where we belonged." He suggested he and I just start over – "just forget what has happened" – learn from it. "None of us know how long we have," he suggested. I agreed that he should come to help with the children. I admitted that I simply could not think. The pain was too much – too much death, too much grief. My mother's death, my father's betrayal and now this.

It had been only eight months since Mother's death, followed by my father's remarriage. It was to me as if they both had died at the same time. My father now had a new wife, a new family – we hardly saw or heard from him.

Most of my friends had turned against me. The divorce, leaving Lubbock, my new home – the grief seemed larger than my body. I simply did not know what to do.

The second call was from a priest friend of Mary's. "The family insists that you not attend the funeral. You have already caused everyone too much pain. They can't bear to see you, not at the funeral. If you must, go to the mortuary and view the body prior to the service, but do not attend or you will be asked to leave. That would be painful and embarrassing for everyone," he admonished.

I was shocked by his lack of concern for my loss and the children's. Then I realized he was right; I had caused enough pain, even to myself. I agreed to stay away. I realized Ed's spirit was still with me and not with his body, but this awareness did not lessen my intense pain. I so desperately wanted him to be physical, to be with me.

The third call was from the Bishop of Oklahoma informing me that I was no longer welcome to take communion in the Episcopal Church because of what I had done.

"What have I done that results in this?" I demanded.

"You've broken the commandments. The sacraments are holy. You need to reevaluate how you are living your life before we can reconsider having you partake of communion. Think about your actions. I'm sorry for your loss. I'm sorry for all of us that this has happened as it has," the Bishop said as he hung up the phone.

I was both devastated and furious. How dare he judge me as unfit! How dare he presume to know why I had made the decision I had! Within a few days I received a letter from the Bishop of Northwest Texas recommending that I return to my husband "where I belonged." (I wondered how they, the Church officials, would have treated Ed, had I been the one who had died!) But I hadn't died. I was still physically alive, although a huge part of me felt as if it were dead.

Through the mercy of shock, the first few days following Ed's passing are foggy. I remember that John arrived and stayed with the children. He was consoling and loving.

He encouraged the three of us to return to Lubbock with him. But I felt incapable of making any further decisions. I felt I had created chaos in all of our lives through my decisions. I felt I had been selfish in not considering how my choices would affect everyone. I felt that, through Ed's death, we were somehow all now being punished for my choices and actions. My thoughts and emotions were at war again, the truce having lasted only four days – like a temporary holiday respite during wartime.

The battle of thoughts and emotions continued day and night. Should I return to John, agree I had been "bad," repent my sin of adultery, take my continued punishment from the Church, family and friends? Was Ed's death punishment from God for allowing me to finally feel my femininity, explore and express my sexuality – for allowing myself happiness? I had always had trouble believing in a God of retribution. I had difficulty with "God" as he was described in the Bible. I could not understand the radical differences between the stories of God in the Old and the New Testament.

I made a temporary decision to remain in Oklahoma City, but to allow the children to return to Texas with John. I needed to think, to try to determine what this all meant. I needed to know how there could be so much difference in what Ed and I thought God wanted of us and how the events had worked out.

Ed and I thought that being together to create a reflective, spiritual, creative life, as well as Genesis, a retreat center where others could come to begin again, was what God wanted of us. How could all that love, all that emotion and feeling, and all that passion, not have been the will of God?

John took the children and their furniture and belongings back with him to Lubbock. I remained in an empty environment, foreign to me, to think and to pray.

Days passed in which I did not even get out of bed. Some days I bathed and put on a bathrobe. Some days I ate; some days I did not. Dressing to go out for groceries was a fear-filled ordeal. When in the grocery store emotions overwhelmed me, guilt overwhelmed me, too. Sadness that I was not with my family, shopping, cooking, caring for them, washed over me. The anxiety continued. I would often have to leave the store, before I had completed the impossible chore of deciding how to shop for just one person instead of four. The entire thought of food was repulsive, but I knew it was necessary. I had to stay well. Knowing my insurance would be canceled with my divorce filled me with alarm. I had no one I could talk to or depend upon. The sadness of realizing Ed was no longer alive and that my mother also was not there to judge me, or to comfort me, overcame me as well. Logic, fear, emotions and grief fought for control of my body and over my sanity.

Years later, I realized that the major contributing factors in my conflict were between Betty Jean and Jovanna. I now have greater appreciation for the decisions and resolutions that were trying to work themselves out from the level of the soul. But at the time, I felt as if I had "descended into the aloneness of hell." I vacillated between doubt that a God existed, belief that I was being punished by God, and very brief periods of feeling absolute peace. I usually experienced the peace when I was first awakening in the mornings or on days when I stayed in bed and drifted in and out of consciousness. I must have drifted in and out at night, too, because I was hardly aware of time passing. I now know that I experienced the periods of peace when I, Jovanna, was in the body alone.

Periodically, during this time, John would call and beg me to return to him, the children and my former life. I would try to talk to him and the children. I cried and felt very inadequate, unable to express myself or to make any decisions. I knew I was not stable enough to try to be out in public. I knew I could not return to work. I could see a black void, an abyss, on either side of the rocking chair in which I sat. I knew, or felt, that if I made a move too quickly, or made the wrong decision, I would fall into the blackness and lose my sanity forever. I intuitively knew that I must rest and not expose myself to pressures or demands.

At the conclusion of one particularly emotional conversation with John, on Thanksgiving Day, I agreed to plan to return to Lubbock for Christmas. I regretted the decision immediately after I had hung up the phone. I realized I could not possibly return to John, the children, or to responsibility. I could not even keep a train of thought long enough to carry on a conversation. I could not remember from my chair to the refrigerator door why I was making my way to the kitchen.

I tried to write, to clear my mind, to make my mind have sequential thoughts. I tried to examine "Who am I?" on paper and in my heart. If I was no longer my mother's daughter because she was dead, who was I? If my father did not want or need to relate to me, because he had a new family, then, who was I? If my friends were angry with me, I had no job, no position in the community or church, who was I? If I was not John's wife, because I chose to leave, and I was not there to mother my children, then, who was I? If I was not Ed's lover, because he was dead, who was I? Was I anyone other than the roles I played for other people? Was this black void the answer to not playing roles? I sat in a rocking chair with a pencil and paper on my lap and wrote: "I AM...? I AM....? I AM...? I AM...? I AM...? I AM . . .?" I was unable to come up with a description of what was left when all the roles were removed. I did not at all understand the message of what I was saying to myself on the paper, nor the enormity of the message coming from my soul: "When all else is stripped away, the I AM, which equals God Presence, remains. Before and after all else, we are God playing roles as Humans."

At this point within my aloneness, in which I had no roles to play for anyone, I spent my time thinking and asking such questions as: "Why am I here? How did I get here? What should I do next? Who should I work for? What kind of work should I do? Do I want to live?"

An answer to the last question came back, "Not particularly," which gave me very little enthusiasm for answering the others!

You will note in my questioning that not once did I ask, "What do I WANT to do?" Only the "shoulds" were there. In getting the divorce and moving to live with my new love, I had done what I WANTED to do, and the price and consequences were overwhelming. My family and friends were angry with me and convinced that I had lost my mind. The church officials also added their disapproval. I felt I was near insanity, a nervous breakdown or suicide.

10

An Awakening

May 1981

Within a year or so following Ed's passing, I began to feel strong and alert enough to return to the working world. I was still living in Oklahoma City. (Betty Jean and Jovanna were still sharing the body, although I still did not know this.)

I chose to go back to work in the only field I really knew: banking. Eighteen months of applying everything I had read in the most recent self-help books brought me a new lover, a promotion to management, a teaching position with a state university giving bank seminars, and an eventual offer to consult for a savings and loan association. Just when I seemed to be getting "control" of my life again, my lover married someone half my age and the savings and loan association terminated its entire consulting staff – all in the same week!

The same day I was let go from the savings and loan association, I received a call from Peter, a man who periodically came through Oklahoma City on business. He was a very wealthy older man who lived in California. He had asked me several times to visit him in California and I had always told him I couldn't because I had to work. Well, now I was unemployed and had no excuse. Having been raised to believe men should take care of women, I chose to pursue marriage. I took Peter up on his offer to fly me to California for a ten-day sailing trip on his 35-foot Trimerand. He assured me he could sail the boat by himself and that very little would be required of me. Having never been sailing, I imagined lying on the deck reading books while he sailed the boat. I wasn't naive enough to believe there would not be some sex involved, but I was willing. I planned to get

Peter to marry me so I would not have to figure out what to do with my life.

I should have been suspicious when the air conditioning in the plane failed on the way to California. It was August. I was wearing a while polyester dress, nylon underwear and nylon stockings. When I arrived in California, I was exhausted and soaking wet from sweat. All I wanted was a shower and a nap. Peter seemed excited to see me and our first stop was at a dive shop to get me fitted with a wet suit, because we would be scuba diving off the boat. The wet suit the shop owner offered was still damp from its last user; he offered no talcum powder to make it easier to pull it on. My body was damp and sticky and the suit was damp. I struggled. Cursing under my breath, "This suit was built for a 14-year-old boy with no ass, unlike me." I waddled out to the show room with the suit hanging down twelve inches in the crotch thinking they could obviously see they needed to get me a larger size. The oriental shop owner made an OK sign with his thumb and forefinger and said, "Perfect." I headed back to the dressing room muttering, "There is no way in hell this is perfect; you must be blind." By the time I got the thing off I was even more exhausted and my arms were aching from the effort.

When we arrived at Peter's townhouse he did not even give me time to take a shower, much less a nap, before he had me across the bed. I stared at the digital clock as he raped me. The man had an erection recovery time of six minutes. I didn't even know this was Humanly possible. I wondered if his sexual appetite and endurance were somehow connected to his surviving Auschwitz. When I was finally released to take a shower, I cried and wondered what I had gotten myself into.

The next morning before we set sail Peter took me to The Bodhi Tree, a large bookstore in Los Angeles. He insisted on buying me three books. One on numerology, one on the I Ching and a novel called *A Hundred Years Of Solitude* by Gabriel Garcia Marquez. His buying me books on subjects I had no desire to pursue made me think him even more strange than I had the night before, but I was determined to see this vacation through to the end and to attempt to get to know him better.

The ten days on the boat were misery. I was seasick. Peter was constantly yelling at me to move, to get out of the way, to hold this or that. When he wasn't yelling he was attacking my body or cooking Hungarian goulash. I knew quickly I had taken myself to hell, but in the middle of the Pacific I saw no way out. On the tenth day I had had enough. I put on the full scuba diving gear, without putting the air in my mouth, and jumped into the Pacific to kill myself. During the night a huge yacht had anchored next to us. The men on the yacht recognized that the right kind of bubbles weren't coming up where I had entered the water and one jumped in to rescue me. Peter expressed his disappointment in me, and we headed back into the harbor. My plane ticket was not good for four more days.

On the sail back I tried to come up with a plan. Peter was unwilling to pay to change the return date on the ticket, and I had no money to change it myself. During the year after Ed's death and after the children had gone back to live with John in Texas, I rented out the extra bedroom to a college student who was from Afghanistan. She had been the daughter of the president of Afghanistan. When she left school and my home she had moved to Los Angeles, and we had not kept in touch. When Alia lived with me I always drove, because even though her family had furnished her a car she was afraid of driving on freeways. I called the operator to see if I could locate Alia and see if she would come get me. The operator asked what suburb of Los Angeles she should look in, and I told her I had no idea, but that finding her was an emergency, I was desperate, and to please just look in all of them until she found her. Fortunately, Alia has an unusual last name and the operator quickly found she was living in Hollywood. I called Alia and through my tears explained my situation and asked her to come get me. I really couldn't imagine her driving on the Los Angeles freeways, but she got to Brentwood in less than an hour and took me and my luggage to her apartment.

When Alia lived in Afghanistan, she had three servants and a chauffeur-driven Mercedes. She had never learned how to care for clothing or herself. Around the perimeter of her rooms, clothing was thrown into piles. She did not understand laundries or dry cleaners. Everything had always been done for her. I spent two days doing laundry and taking her dry cleanable clothes to the cleaners. The bottom half of her refrigerator was the freezer and would not close because so much ice had accumulated. It took two days of it being unplugged and my chipping away to defrost it. I colored her hair and gave her a perm. After two days, I was even more exhausted than when I'd left the boat. I felt like a servant. Not that I wasn't grateful for her rescuing me, but I knew I needed to get back to Oklahoma City and return to work; the idea of getting married to save myself no longer seemed like the answer.

That night, when Alia came home from her job at the immigration office, I asked her to take me to the airport the next morning, not realizing how far away the airport was. She said she couldn't take me until the weekend when she would be off work. I asked her to just take me to a bus stop and I would catch a bus to the airport. The next morning I was standing on the corner of Hollywood and Vine (no longer a nice neighborhood) waiting to catch a bus that I wasn't sure would stop at the corner to take me to the airport to use a ticket that still wasn't good for two more days.

Standing there with all of my luggage, which was too heavy for me to lift, I felt totally alone in the world and even more abandoned. The bus pulled up to the curb and the sign on the top of the bus scrolled to read airport. The driver got out and rolled up the side panel of the bus and stood there looking at me, waiting for me to put the luggage in the open space. I uttered a silent prayer, "God help me." Walking toward me was a six-foot-plus black man in a straw cowboy hat. He tipped his hat to me and said in the most wonderful southern accent I had heard in a very long time, "Can I help you, miss?" I mutely pointed at the bags.

He lifted them as if they weighed nothing and placed them in the luggage opening of the bus. The driver closed the compartment. The southern gentleman said, "Have a nice day, ma'am," and once again tipped his hat as he walked away. I entered the bus and breathed a sigh of relief. I knew I could stay at the airport for another day if the agent would not change my ticket without charging me.

Miraculously, after hearing part of my dilemma, the female agent put me on the next plane headed out of Los Angeles for Oklahoma City.

Once I returned to Oklahoma City, I realized insanity, an emotional breakdown or suicide were no longer options; I became determined to learn why I was still alive and what I was here to do.

September 30, 1982

Two days after trying to drown myself, I noticed a quotation on the back cover of the book *Illusions*. I had bought the book to read to Ed in the moving van the day I left Texas, not knowing it was a metaphysical book. I had kept the book on my coffee table. The front cover is black with a suspended blue feather, which would later be significant to me. At that time, the message on the back cover pushed me over the edge. "Here is a test to find whether your mission on Earth is finished. If you're alive, it isn't." The quotation didn't give me an answer, it merely highlighted the problem: I was alive, but with no purpose. Reading the quotation did, however, make me angry enough to cry out to God, "What do YOU want of me? What do YOU want me to do? I'll do anything, I'll go anywhere, I'll say anything YOU want, just tell me what it is YOU WANT!"

After saying these words aloud, my hand literally flew up to my mouth: I realized I had just turned MY will and MY life over to God!

I had never before fully turned MY will over to the Creator, although I had attended many church services in which the minister had pleaded from the pulpit, "Not my will, Lord, but thy will be done." My observation had been that most people who had totally turned their wills over to God became missionaries in Africa, or monks or nuns. I had never had any desire to be any of these; therefore, I had held on to MY self-will until I was so miserable and desperate that I was willing to say, "Even Africa."

For a long while I sat still, mentally "digesting" what had just happened to me. (As I would realize later, this was my most significant breakthrough.)

After a while, since no big booming Charlton Heston voice responded to my commitment with, "I hear you," or "go to Africa," or anything else, I decided to go to a bookstore and look in the "Self Help" section for anything written on how to find your life's purpose.

I entered a neighborhood B. Dalton bookstore. I walked past the Occult Sciences section. Normally, because of my inherited and well-ingrained beliefs, I would have avoided anything occult or psychic to the extent that I would have walked <u>around</u> that section of the store. After all, psychic and occult practices were declared by Christianity to be of the devil. However, this day my depression was so great, I forgot my precautions and prejudices and walked right by the Occult Science section.

As I passed through the section, a book entitled, *Psychic Energy: How to Change Desires into Realities*, by Joseph Weed, suddenly fell off the shelf onto the floor directly in front of me. Being aware that I had in no way touched or jarred the shelf, I was greatly puzzled by this event. I picked up the book and examined the cover.

The book didn't impress me. It was a red, white and purple paperback, and the print was crooked. In fact, everything about the book offended my librarian sense of beauty and order. I turned it over and read the back: "*Psychic Energy: How to Change Desires into Realities*, by Joseph Weed."

"This is a valuable book, a precious book which you will want to keep near you and read again and again. It lifts the veil of mystery and superstition that have for too long shrouded the puzzling phenomena so often seen today.

"In truth, there are no deviations from natural law. Everything that happens, no matter how exotic it may seem, can be explained and understood. Many of these so-called 'wild talents' are described herein and their functions analyzed in simple, non-technical language.

"Habitually, we all think in terms of the visible, the material. Yet man is not an animal and he cannot live like one and be happy. On the other hand, neither is he a god and any attempt to deify his higher nature at the expense of his Human heritage is equally doomed to fail. A balance is necessary, and the suggestions given herein will guide you to the attainment of proper harmonies.

"In this book you will find information that will surprise and often amaze you. For example . . ."

I placed the book back on the shelf and proceeded to the Self Help, Psychology, Philosophy and Religion section, where I felt I should find help. There I read cover after cover, but found nothing that spoke directly to the issue of finding one's life's purpose.

Disappointed, and even more depressed, I prepared to leave the store. As I once again passed the Occult Science section, I glanced toward the shelf where I had replaced the copy of *Psychic Energy*. To my utter amazement, the book was now lit up! A white glowing light was emanating from and encircling the book!

Many thoughts went through my mind: "I am now having a nervous breakdown. I've earned it, I deserve it and it is now happening to me. This light is proof. Books don't just fall off shelves and objects don't just light up."

I am very pragmatic. Curiosity overcame logic; I purchased the book and took it home. Though still very skeptical, I thought, "I'll do what we used to do with the *Bible*. I'll close my eyes, ask a question, open the book and put my finger on that page with my eyes shut. If, when I open my eyes, the message on that page makes sense, I'll read that page. If it doesn't, I'll take the book to the dumpster. I seated myself on my couch with the book between my hands and said a prayer before I opened it: "If this book is of God, I will open it to one page and there will be a message from God."

I opened the book to a page in the center and read: "Instructions for Inspired or Automatic Writing." It said meditating in this particular way would make it possible to get answers from God or one's higher self. After all, that is what I was asking for.

If you would like to experiment with automatic writing, follow these instructions.

1. Always take a bath before any automatic writing session. This is not only to cleanse yourself physically of impurities that may be clinging to you, but it is also symbolical of a spiritual cleansing, which should take place before exposing yourself to any foreign influence.

2. Sit at a desk or table where you will not be disturbed, take the phone off the hook and compose yourself.

3. When you are completely relaxed physically, emotionally, and clear mentally, take three deep breaths, letting each one out quite slowly.

4. Then take pen or pencil in your hand, place it on the top line of the blank pad before you, see that your arm is comfortable and relax.

You may get a response the first time, but more likely not. So try again and repeat the preparation here outlined each time. After a serious attempt, on five different occasions, if you get no result, set the idea aside temporarily and try it again in a year when you and conditions about you will have changed.

If your hand starts to write, it may turn out serious material or it may write nonsense. If the latter, stop immediately and try again another time, making sure you prepare yourself most carefully. Foolish, childish or confused writing is evidence of a poor connection (so to speak) or contact with a low-grade personality. If this occurs, try the next time to raise the level of your consciousness by clearing your mind of low-grade thoughts and impulses. Usually you can establish a satisfactory mood by prayer, or by reading a passage from the Bible *or another inspirational work.*

When you get a serious response, do not hesitate to ask aloud, "Who is this?" You will, as a rule, get a completely candid answer to this and to any other legitimate question that may occur to you. Once you have learned how to relax your hand and arm and have caught on to the proper 'don't care' attitude, interesting results should ensue.

Automatic writing is not something new, or strange, or so very different. Many people practice it and there are literally thousands of books, documents and reports written this way that are available for examination.

I finished reading the two pages, laid the book aside and made a conscious decision to try this foreign-to-me form of communication. I took a shower, dressed in a robe, took the phone off the hook, gathered pencil and legal pad, lit a white candle, sat on the couch with my back straight, bare feet on the floor and recited the Lord's Prayer. I began to breathe deeply, becoming aware of my breath as I exhaled slowly.

My conscious mind – or as I later learned, my left brain, my ego – pointed out, "This is really dumb. This is the dumbest thing you've ever done. This is not going to work. You should be out looking for a job, not sitting here doing such a weird thing. Go get a job. At least put the phone back on the hook so it can ring," and on . . . and on . . . and on . . . I tried to ignore my doubts and continued to breathe deeply and waited, wishing my hand would begin to move.

After what seemed about ten minutes, I had another set of words in my mind separate from the objections, which continued; still in my own voice, the other message was simultaneously there: *"Through this pen will come . . . through this pen will come . . . through this pen will come . . . through this pen will come . . ."* Since I was expecting the writing to be automatic, I just kept listening. After the fourth repetition I asked mentally, "Will come what?"

"The words you need."

At this reply, I began to realize that I was to write down the words that were coming into my mind, instead of expecting my hand to automatically write the words. It was a little like taking dictation: I was writing down inspired words, instead of my hand automatically moving as it wrote down words.

The words continued:

"Through this pen will come the words you need to express the feelings of the world and how you feel about them. I want you to now relax, accept, identify and examine your motives for this experiment. This day has been given for your use. It is a free gift. You may however, be placing a price that I have not required. Try accepting MY gift without reservation or reluctance. Test this program for thirty days. I will make manifest to you my Will for your life and can guarantee you will be amazed at how closely it will parallel your own true desires.

"Forgetting all else that troubles you, CHOOSE to accept each new assignment as it appears before you in whatever form it takes, whether a person to be entertained, a task to be accomplished, a chore to be done or a piece of creativity for which you will be given the strength, knowledge, ability and insight to reach a level of awareness you never dreamed imaginable.

"Take this opportunity to reflect . . . What do you really want to do? Where do you really want to be?

"Try this method of putting yourself in contact with the answers to these questions by listening to a pattern of speech coming from your unconscious awareness. If the phone rings, answer with the attitude that you are willing to comfort, be with, or respond to the person on the other end. Create an atmosphere of acceptance for yourself, your faults and your imagined shortcomings. With MY power you have the ability to create, activate and accomplish many marvelous things.

"I choose you as MY instrument of peace to be used by ME in a World

that truly needs peace. I will activate in you an energy supply unequaled by any other. My energy I give to you this day as a free gift to be accepted or rejected as you choose. I am willing to see you as an equal to ME, ready to respond at a moment's notice to the needs of others, and in so doing be aware that you are not only accomplishing MY goals, but your own. Now, take your pen and express the feelings I give you in MY words and I will reward you with MY grace. Try as you will with MY love and you will succeed beyond your dreams.

"*I have a plan for Our life in you. Give it a chance to materialize, and I will reward your efforts by being near you to comfort, guide and direct these efforts in the way for which I have created you to flow.*

"*This is not a test of endurance, but a test of faith. You cannot fail; you can only stop to begin again. When you feel yourself take control of your life – STOP – examine your results. Do they agree with what you truly want to do with your life? If not, pause, listen and redirect your thinking to ME and to MY words as I give them to you. You are MY child and I care what happens to you in this life. I expect you to care what happens, too. This is your life, freely given by ME. I need your life to accomplish MY plan. I am willing to assist in any situation where you desire MY help. Because you are willing, I can use you for MY projection into the World at the Human level. Take MY hand as I lead you today and don't fear the outcome. Just trust the process that takes us there. We can accomplish things together, which cannot be accomplished in any other way.*

"*Support for your efforts will be made available through an unexpected source and should not be a concern for you at this time. Redo your work when you feel you have not pleased yourself because you are aware of the need for quality in OUR approach.*

"*Accept the things I send as gifts, not questioning why they should be yours. I will create the material needs you have to be fulfilled. Right at this moment there is a need that I will make you aware of shortly, to be accomplished as quickly as possible. Now, replace the telephone receiver and wait.*"

After seven pages, I heard no more words and stopped writing. Then I read what had been written.

"Amazing!" I thought. "I must be making this up, but I can't be; my mind was thinking something else all the time. But a person is not supposed to have two voices in their head at one time, isn't that what schizophrenia is?"

I went back over the words. "*Examine my motives?*" I felt my only motive was my desperation to have answers about my purpose for being. "*Test this method for thirty days.*" That seemed fair. I apparently could reserve judgment. I knew I would never set myself up to do anything for thirty days. This made me even more sure I wasn't the creator of the message.

"I will make manifest to you my Will for your life and can guarantee you will be amazed at how closely it will parallel your own desires." This gave me hope that I would not be sent to Africa as a missionary.

"Choose to accept each new assignment as it appears before you in whatever form it takes, whether a person to be entertained, a task to be accomplished, a chore to be done or a piece of creativity for which you will be given the strength, knowledge, ability and insight to reach a level of awareness you never dreamed imaginable." Somehow, put in those terms it didn't feel as if I would be asked to do anything weird or something that I could not do with the help, which was seemingly being offered.

I replaced the telephone receiver. It rang immediately, startling me. The call was from an elderly neighbor who needed a ride to her doctor's office. *"If the phone rings, answer with the attitude that you are willing to comfort, be with or respond to the person on the other end."*

I agreed to chauffeur my neighbor. As you can imagine, I was in a state of awe and disbelief from my writing experience!

When I returned from my chauffeuring, I grabbed my writing and continued where I had left off. *"What do you really want to do? Where do you really want to be?"*

This was more difficult for me to define. Since I had experienced little of the World, how could I know what I wanted? I felt like shouting, "If I'd known what I wanted, I wouldn't be asking you!" However, more questions didn't seem like a good answer to my original one. I thought deeply and seriously. Then I began to put a list together:

I want to do something creative.

I want to do something that helps people to communicate.

I want to work at home in case my children want to come back and live with me.

I want to do something I can't be fired from.

I want to teach adults something they really want to learn.

I want to help people to self-actualize. (I wasn't sure exactly how, but I did know I wanted to learn to become all I could be and do what I had come to Earth to experience, and to share that with others. I now admit I was trying to impress God – if this was indeed God – that I knew a big word like "self-actualize.")

I laid the brief list beside my bed and slept soundly for eleven hours.

11

Messages From Spirit

The morning following my experience with the book, *Psychic Energy*, I was still confused and disbelieving that God had actually spoken to me and that I had received this message through inspired writing. Since the message had suggested I try the method for thirty days, I decided to try again. I took a shower and then repeated the same meditation as the night before. The writing began almost immediately:

October 1, 1982

"*Time is of the essence now that you have laid the groundwork for what you are to accomplish at this point in your life.*
 "*Retreat from all confusion.*
 "*Explain your actions to no one.*
 "*Walk into the path I have placed before you.*
 "*Take time to examine the principles behind the plan you have established. Does it fit your needs?*
 "*Reach out to a person whose needs are similar to your own.*
 "*Correspond with the party; try to bring peace without allowing your feelings to interfere.*
 "*Explain your needs, wants and desires.*
 "*Explain what is happening in your life.*
 "*Talk as freely as possible without emotion.*
 "*Explain where you have been, where you are going, and how you intend to get there.*
 "*Retract nothing you have said in the past, for it was all truth as you*

saw it at that time.

"My purpose will become clearer to you as we progress.

"Do not become afraid.

"I AM WITH YOU.

"Be at peace.

"Explain nothing to anyone for any other reason than because you want to. Do not be forced.

"Rescue your feelings when necessary.

"Calm yourself and others.

'Refine your thinking to include concepts that are foreign to you at this time.

"Propose an alternate route for the life you were expecting to happen and feel good when you believe this is MY will for US.

"Think about trying a new method of writing that involves putting aside what you have done up to this point and starting over from a totally new perspective. You will eventually become an example and a key to understanding for your biological family, the group of people involved in this transition. (I pointed out to God later that I thought He had forgotten who the members of my biological family were and that His suggestion that I was somehow going to help them to understand spiritual subjects was ludicrous.)

"Through this method of writing you can reach the mass of Humanity WE desire to touch by your story. Take time now to reread what you have written. Close your mind to confusion. Accept all things as MY will. Create a new beginning, both for yourself and for the book.

"Treat the material as you would a work of art, trying to experience the time lapse and expressing your emotions to those you encounter as if you were feeling them again. This will be painful, but you are not alone and I care that you are willing to re-experience today all of the feelings of yesterday for the sake of speaking to the mass of Humans who are missing MY message and are therefore in constant pain.

"Tape your thoughts as you go and attempt to recreate an image of yourself as you were then, explaining in detail what brought you to this point in time.

"Take up your task and prepare to accomplish more than you intended, simply because I AM WITH YOU THIS TIME. You will succeed."

Although many of the messages I received during this time did not make a lot of sense, they have made perfect sense to me since. For example, at the time of these messages, I had been in the process of writing a book about my life, including my withdrawal from Valium.

I was having difficulty deciding just how to start my story. While the messages did not help me that much then, years later, when I was emotionally ready to begin writing, the directions made a great deal of sense.

October 2, 1982

"Think in terms of trying to succeed and you will fail. Think in terms of doing MY WILL and you will succeed.

"Think about today's assignment as closely as possible. Be at peace with your surroundings, trying to see at all times that effort is not necessary for the result; WILLINGNESS IS NECESSARY. Take time to promote good will. Accept the outcome of whatever you are able to achieve with the arrangements that are made for you."

At this point, I began to believe that I might have become schizophrenic. I wondered if the Voice I heard was an alternate personality, an alter ego of myself that had split off because of all the trauma I had experienced. I knew no one else who had this experience. I'd never heard of channeling. I didn't even know what it was to be psychic. I wondered if I was being led down what seemed to me to be a very unproven path?

I asked the source of the writing this question: "If you really are God and we really are going to do these things together, could you give me some kind of concrete sign, like maybe a burning bush, to prove to me that I am not crazy?"

The message came:

"Look for a type of huge triangle atop a configuration of granite. This is where you will begin to experience your walking into another realm of today's time, a time of which you are not now aware. You will learn to transcend time and space."

I didn't want to transcend time and space. I only wanted to be sure I wasn't crazy.

At this time, I was asked to return to my hometown and to visit certain individuals whose names I was given. I was told that when I visited these individuals, I would be given messages for them, which I would deliver during conversations.

This assignment was very uncomfortable for me since the people whose names I was given had been close friends before I moved from Texas. They were also the very people who had been so angry and disappointed with me, because I had chosen to leave my husband and that community.

Nevertheless, I began to trust. As a result, much healing was accomplished, because I became WILLING to again encounter those individuals. Messages for the people I encountered were always given to me at the time of the visit and never before.

The personal messages continued as I meditated:

"*Observe your thoughts without judgment. Be aware that thoughts are things. Your thoughts become your reality. Everything that exists in your life started as an idea, a thought. All that you have, all that you are, all that surrounds you is a result of your thoughts, ideas, rules, concepts, wishes, desires, fears and beliefs. Your life is also a result of what you have avoided. You have the ability to change your thoughts and your beliefs and thereby change your reality – and thereby the reality of the World. Observe your thoughts, without judgment, and then shift them to thoughts that align with what you want.*"

During this period, I was also asked to create a line of hand-painted greeting cards. I was given the name of the company (bj Originals, Inc.) the price of the cards, the messages and the type of paper and envelopes to buy.

I felt that Source (the Voice) had misunderstood my request to "do something creative." I quickly explained that by "creative" I had not meant that I knew how to paint. By "creative," I had meant "not boring."

The Voice assured me that I could paint, that all I needed do was buy watercolors, brushes and a book, *Drawing on the Right Side of the Brain*, by Betty Edwards. I was asked to do the exercises in the book and was told (in a meditative state) that I would be able to "allow" the painting to "happen through me."

The greeting card idea did fit most of the desires I had listed when Spirit had asked me what I really wanted to do and where I really wanted to be, namely: Making cards would be creative; I could work at home; cards could help people communicate; I could not be fired from my own company; creating cards might be a way of becoming all I could be, doing what I came to Earth to experience; and certainly would be shared with others.

I knew nothing about marketing or painting. I had taken six calligraphy lessons just before leaving Texas. Besides that, I had only $105 and was on unemployment compensation, since being terminated from the savings and loan association. Still the messages (in meditation) were emphatic:

"*Take $100 of the $105 and open a business account in the name of "bj Originals, Inc." Notify the state that you can no longer accept unemployment compensation, for you are now self-employed.*"

You might imagine how well I took that suggestion!

The advice did not compute to my left-brain logic. First, I explained to the Voice that it obviously did not understand much about banking. I explained that a person does not open two checking accounts when one has such a small amount of money because the bank service charges would eat up what was there. I further explained that I wasn't making any money as yet, being self-employed. I agreed, though, that when I <u>was</u> making money, I would quit accepting the unemployment. I began to doubt, even more, that this voice was God. Surely God would be smarter than this.

Every day for the next six days, I received the same identical message from the Voice.

I now understand that the majority of lessons I have to learn in this life have been in the area of money and relationships, particularly male/female relationships. Therefore, this has been where my tests of faith – or of necessity, my leaps of faith – have been. After the sixth identical message, I somehow came to the conclusion that I must either quit trusting and working with the Voice and the messages, or go with the advice.

I gave up the unemployment and opened the bank account. I bought the parchment paper, watercolors, calligraphy pens, ink, envelopes, and *Drawing on the Right Side of the Brain*. I felt encouraged when I went to the bookstore and such a book actually existed. I began to do the exercises in the book and found, to my surprise, that I WAS able to sketch and do an oriental form of brushwork. A flower with a butterfly suspended over the flower would come out of the end of the brush each time I sat down to paint.

I began doing what the Voice suggested. I painted greeting cards. Money started coming in: I received a check for $50 from my father for my birthday. It was not in my father's nature to remember or acknowledge my birthday. An insurance refund check came in the mail; the IRS sent a refund from my return two years prior. I began selling my cards to friends.

I received a call from an ex-lover who had moved to Houston. "Let me send you a plane ticket," he said. "Come down and visit for a couple weeks and take time to think about what you want to do. Rest a while. I would love to see you, spend time with you, talk to you, hold you."

I knew I could continue painting the cards even if I was in Houston, because David would be at work during the day. I did need time to think and rest, and I needed to be held. Even more than that, I needed to talk to someone about what was happening to me. I felt I couldn't talk to David. He was an ex-police chief. I didn't think he could possibly believe that I was talking to God and that God was talking back. Nevertheless, I agreed to go. I was to leave on Saturday afternoon.

Friday evening my phone rang. A male friend I had made when I recently visited a Methodist church was on the line.

"There is a psychic fair at the college tomorrow. Would you like to go with me?" Al inquired.

"No, thank you. I don't like to be around fortune-tellers. They're really weird people with gray hair, long dangly earrings, shawls and crystal balls. Anyway, incense gives me a headache." I really wasn't interested in going.

"You don't know much about being psychic, do you? There's a lot more to a psychic fair than fortune-tellers. Come on, go with me; you might learn something. Make up your mind after you get there and if you don't like it you can leave. How about it?" Al was talking me into it.

"Well, OK. I'm catching a plane at 3 p.m. for Houston, so I'll take my car and go on to the airport from the college. What time shall I meet you there?"

"I'll meet you in the parking lot at 10 a.m.," he replied, and hung up the phone.

I slept better than I had for weeks. The next morning I awoke refreshed, loaded my bags in the car and headed for the campus, never imagining what a turning point I had reached.

12

Test Of Faith

November 1982

In the parking lot, Al greeted me with a smile and a hug. Together we walked to the auditorium housing the psychic fair and entered through the back door.

The first lecture was about Kirlian photography, a way of photographing the energy field or aura of a person or object. It was a very scientific, very left-brained film. I was impressed, but as we walked down the hallway filled with psychic reader booths, the smell of incense filled my head. I headed for the door and air. Al followed.

As we strolled side by side around the quadrangle enjoying the fresh air, I suddenly noticed the huge sculpture in the center of the patio. It was an immense bronze triangle, suspended by three enormous granite spires. I gasped in disbelief. The sculpture was my "burning bush!"

I almost passed out and I wet my pants. Then I began laughing. After all, I HAD asked the Voice for some kind of a "concrete" sign, like maybe a burning bush, as proof that I wasn't crazy. And IT had given me granite!

"At least this Source has a sense of humor," I thought. Maybe the "not boring" part of my plan WOULD BE more exciting than what I had imagined!

In my excitement and amazement I tried to explain to Al what the sculpture and symbol meant to me. I'm not sure he ever understood exactly, or grasped the significance of the Voice and its messages. We trekked back into the auditorium. Inside, the first booth we passed was on The Silva Method. I picked up a brochure. I was also handed brochures on "Touch for Health" and "The Course in Miracles." By then I was in "overwhelm."

What did all this mean? What was I going to be asked to do? Had I really turned my will over to God? Was this really God? I thanked Al for inviting me to the fair, excused myself and left for the airport.

Arriving a little early for the plane, I went into the gift shop to get a present to mail to my children in Lubbock. I browsed through the paperback bookrack and was intrigued to find a copy of *The Silva Method of Mind Control*. I purchased the book and boarded the plane, feeling excited, yet a little frightened, too, by the possible meaning of all these recent occurrences.

Arriving in Houston, David's greeting was a blessing; loving and sincere. I was bursting to share what was happening with me, but felt our relationship could not withstand the truth of what was taking place in my life.

While David was at work each day, I read, painted cards, meditated and wrote. The fourth day of my vacation the message came through from the Voice: "*Return to Oklahoma City immediately to take The Silva Method of Mind Control course.*" I explained to David that I felt I needed to get on with getting a job, that I was becoming increasingly uncomfortable being unemployed. He understood and, although disappointed, consented to pay to change my ticket and to take me to the airport.

Upon returning to Oklahoma City, I called the phone number listed on the brochure for Silva Mind Control. The woman who answered was pleasant enough, but when I asked how soon I could take the course she answered, "I'm sorry. You will not be able to take it until next month because we are right in the middle of a course. We taught the first half last weekend and will be teaching the next half this weekend."

I didn't speak for a moment as I realized that today was Wednesday; there were two days between now and the weekend.

"Is there any way I could learn what the others learned last weekend between now and Saturday and still get into this group?" I inquired excitedly.

The woman sounded offended by my question. "We do not give private instruction." "Please, just take my number and think about it. This is very important to me, to do this while I am unemployed, and do you accept credit cards?"

"Let me think about it, and I will call you back shortly."

In approximately 20 minutes the phone rang. When I picked it up the woman explained, "After I hung up the phone I meditated on your question and received the answer that I am to allow you to do as you requested."

I was ecstatic, but concerned as to how I would pay for the course.

"Do you accept credit cards?" I asked. I had two credit cards and they were both almost maxed out.

"Yes, we do," she replied.

"Where do I need to come to take the course tomorrow?" I inquired.

"We are being told to bring the information to you, if that is agreeable to you." Surprised, I exclaimed, "Sure! Great! What time should I expect you?"

"Is nine o'clock too early?"

"No, that will be fine." I gave her directions to my apartment, and replaced the receiver.

For a few moments I just sat by the phone in utter disbelief. The woman was going to teach me the first half of the course right here in my apartment. Then it dawned on me that the tuition of $395 would max out my Visa card. I had been able to function for daily necessities by charging groceries and gas to my Visa. My MasterCard was getting close to its maximum.

Fear began to rise in me again, but I breathed deeply and challenged myself to BELIEVE that I would not have made it this far if what was happening was not truth.

When Human beings finally relinquish control and EXPECT the assistance of the Universe, something organic happens. People find themselves assisting us. For example, I again encountered this instructor seven years later and she confided that she had never before or since given a private class like she gave me back then. She was still amazed she had made such an exception.

The Silva Method was fascinating to me. It is an experiential method of learning to be either in your right or your left-brain at will. The method is simple and easy to accomplish and I was a ready and willing pupil. This is a channeled message I received several years later:

February 2, 1988

"The Silva Mind Control course is currently the most concise and available method to teach individuals to control levels of awareness.

"The methods offered in the Silva course are a composite of many modalities and expressions of truth – the truth of inner communication with aspects of self in various levels of one's Oversoul, as well as intergalactic communication. The exercises have been created to hypnotically suggest

trust in self-awareness and healing of the body, mind and spirit. The purpose of the repetitive wording of the exercises is to remove blocks in consciousness, which have kept the individual in a state of fear and/or doubt about their abilities.

"The inner programming that occurs is subjective and causes the consciousness to allow a breakthrough to inner awareness of the power to bi-locate one's energy, to take excursions out of body and into matter, as well as 'mind merging' with others and the Infinite.

"The sense of self, which has been developed through the lifetime up to the point of exposure to the method, is expanded to include the Oneness of self with all energy of others, as well as Oneness with all life and matter.

"This method is highly recommended for breaking the bonds of limited consciousness."

After I completed the course work, I was able to hear the inner Voice without having to enter meditation.

The next morning I awakened and began painting before getting dressed. The Voice suggested I go to Albertson's, a large chain of drug and grocery stores in my neighborhood.

"But it's raining outside," I argued. "I was just there yesterday; I don't have any money to buy anything; I'm not dressed, my hair's not done; I haven't showered; I need to paint."

The Voice continued suggesting, "Go to Albertson's."

Finally, still not understanding, I threw my coat over my sweat suit and, with no makeup on, I drove to the nearest Albertson's store. I grabbed a shopping cart and began pushing it through the aisles.

I wondered to myself, "Just how weird is this going to get? Are the cans of peas now going to light up and start talking to me?"

As I passed the bread rack, a man's voice surprised me with, "What are you doing? I haven't seen you in the longest time."

Startled by the voice, I turned to see the Rainbow Bread man stocking the rack and recognized him as having been a customer at the bank where I had worked when I first returned to banking in Oklahoma City.

I hesitated to tell the Rainbow Bread man, "God has designed a line of greeting cards through me and is looking for a place to market them." Instead, I simply said, "I'm not at the bank anymore."

"I know that," he said. "The question is what are you doing now?"

"Designing greeting cards," I blurted out.

"Where do you market them?" he continued.

"Well, I don't have a place to market them yet. I'm trying to find one."

"Why don't you market them here?" he questioned, beginning to give me a sales pitch on the number of customers that came into the store daily and reminding me the store was open 24-hours a day and that there were eight stores in the metroplex area.

"I don't know anything about marketing. I wouldn't know who to talk to. Besides, they wouldn't market a handmade product, made by one person, in a national chain store like this," I argued for my limitations.

"How do you know if you don't ask them?" he confronted me. "The regional drug manager will be in town tomorrow from Tulsa and he is the person you will need to talk to. Tell me your phone number and I'll make you an appointment to see him. Give me a call in the morning about 9:30 at the North May Avenue store and I can let you know the time of your appointment."

When I began rummaging through my purse for paper, he stopped me, and said, "Just tell it to me. I'll remember."

I told him the number, thanked him, and stumbled away in an absolute daze.

I returned home and painted for the rest of the day with renewed enthusiasm.

The following morning I woke up to ten inches of snow on the ground. I called the store the bread man had indicated. The person who answered said he had not yet arrived and offered to take a message.

I waited – less than patiently – until 11 a.m. when the phone rang.

"This is the manager of the North May Avenue Albertson's store. You left a number earlier for Sidney Shelton?"

"Yes, I did."

"Well, he still hasn't shown up. What do you want me to do with the message?" Confused, I blurted out, "He was going to get me an appointment with the district drug manager."

"The district manager called and will not be in town this week because of the snow, so you won't need to wait around for him." He thanked me for my call and hung up.

I felt absolutely devastated. What had happened? This didn't seem possible after the way the connection had been made the day before. I was furious! I yelled and ranted and raved at God, telling him that I did not want to do this. "If the information isn't going to be accurate, I don't want to do this!"

"Be patient. I'm taking care of it. Keep painting," was the reply to my ranting.

"Easy for you to say. You're not down here with all these bills and you don't have to eat either. You don't have people wondering if you're crazy, because you're not out looking for a job," I stormed.

"Be patient. I'm taking care of it. Keep painting."

I didn't find it easy to be creative under such pressure. However, I continued to paint while waiting as patiently as I could.

Ten days later at 10 a.m. the phone rang. It was Sidney. He had remembered my phone number and his promise.

"The district manager is in town today. You have an appointment at 1 p.m. at the North May Avenue store. The guy's name is Randall. Good luck." He didn't wait for a reply.

I dressed as I would for a job interview, created a small wicker rack of sample cards. I arrived at the store and the manager's office at 12:55 p.m. The district drug manager was a nice man, very businesslike.

"Yes, I like these," he said, as he read through the cards. "We will start them in the store closest to where you live, so you can easily monitor them. After we see how they are selling, we will decide whether or not to put them in all the stores in the Oklahoma City area. Take four hundred cards, with this purchase order and your rack, to the Bethany store. Thanks for coming by and good luck."

I left the store and went immediately home to meditate on where to get a rack. "Look in the Yellow Pages." Sure enough, there was a wholesale greeting card company listed.

I drove to the location. The sales clerk showed me a variety of styles that would fit my cards. The least expensive was white cardboard and I could paint a logo across the top. The cost was $12. I bought the rack, took it home and created a logo. The next morning I took the cards, rack, and purchase order to the store.

The shipping agent seemed a little surprised to see me standing on the dock, but honored the purchase order by counting the cards, signing the document, and handing me a copy.

"It will be about six weeks before you can expect to receive a check," he told me. "Checks are generated from our home office in Salt Lake City. Since you are a new account, that's how long it will take for them to get you on the computers. After that, you can expect a two-week turn around."

"Six weeks! How could I possibly survive another six weeks," I asked myself fearfully.

13

The Benefactor

January 1983

After I completed the Silva class I joined a Silva cottage group made up of graduates who met once a week to meditate and use techniques learned in the course. Group members were very enthusiastic about my greeting cards and the method through which they were created. All six members were unemployed and mentally programming for new, perfect jobs. I was relieved to be with a group of people who were attempting to receive messages from their souls, attempting to do what was already happening to me.

One member of the group was a man named Joseph who had been involved in Silva and metaphysics for fifteen years. I was surprised to see him in the group. I had met him at the Silva area Christmas party six days after my graduation from the course. (I eventually learned that Spirit's primary reason for returning me early from my trip to Houston, to take Silva at that particular time, was to meet Joseph.) Two weeks had passed since I had begun marketing my greeting cards. I had started borrowing small amounts of money from friends to buy parchment paper and envelopes. I was confident I could return the cash now that I knew how I would be making my living.

A week after I joined the meditation group, I was pleasantly surprised to receive a call from the district drug manager at Albertson's inviting me to market my cards in all of the Albertson's stores in the Oklahoma City metropolitan area. My first reaction was elation. Then the manager told me I would have to furnish permanent metal racks, inventory the cards myself and keep the racks full at all times.

Hesitantly, I agreed to do all of this, wondering to myself how much the racks would cost and how I would manifest the money for their purchase. I hung up the phone and immediately called the wholesale greeting card company to inquire about the availability and cost of racks.

"What size are your cards, Lady?" the dealer inquired.

As I described the cards he began chuckling. "Are you in luck. I've got a ton of those racks hanging from the ceiling in my warehouse. I ordered them for a guy in 1977 and his company went under before he even picked up the racks. Hope you have better luck. Tell you what I'll do. Hang on a minute and let me pull the invoice and I'll give them to you for what the price was in 1977." He put me on hold as country and western music blared in my ear.

While I waited I asked God, "How will I pay for these racks?"

The reply was immediate. "Write a check. You will have the money before the check gets to the bank."

I was stunned! I had been teaching bank teller security for two years for the University of Oklahoma, showing how to recognize people who were passing insufficient or forged checks. I could not imagine deliberately writing an insufficient check. I knew if I wrote the check and God did not come up with the money in time I could be prosecuted or at least never be bondable as a banker again. It would mean the end of the only career I knew.

"That will be $800 for eight racks." The man's voice startled me out of my stupor. "I'm going out of town today, but if you want, I can meet you at the warehouse on Sunday afternoon at 1 o'clock and let you pick them up."

"Eight hundred dollars!" I fairly yelled into the mouthpiece.

"That's the best deal you're going to get anywhere, Lady, I can promise you that! What do you say?"

"OK, fine. I'll meet you at 1 p.m. Sunday, and thank you," I answered, a bit dazed.

When I hung up the phone, I heard Spirit suggest I take another Silva class, this one on healing. It would be held on the weekend, including the Sunday I'd promised to pick up the racks. I pondered this, realizing the class cost $285, which would max out my only remaining credit card. I had maxed out my Visa to take the first course. I knew I couldn't pay the $800 on my card. My only asset, my car, was already mortgaged beyond its value. I could not imagine how God could create money on Saturday or Sunday when the banks weren't open and the mail wasn't delivered. Therefore, I saw no obvious ways for miracles to happen through computer errors or mishandling of mail.

My mind continued to calculate, conjure up possibilities and worry how I was going to handle my dilemma.

Saturday morning arrived and I attended the first lecture of the Silva healing course. As I sat listening to the speaker, I felt someone staring at me. I looked across the room and caught the eye of a tall, white-haired, tan-skinned gentleman. As he smiled at me, I felt a sense of recognition, although I could not remember where I had met him. At the first break I walked closer to get a better look at him and to read his nametag. I didn't recognize his name.

We both smiled. "I apologize for staring, but I thought I knew you," I was now standing in front of him.

"Yes, I know," he replied. "I've been staring at you all morning."

Realizing the man might think I was trying to pick him up with the oldest line in the World, I blushed furiously, blundering, "Must have been in another lifetime." (I didn't even believe in past lives at this point, so I felt even more foolish for making such a remark.) I very quickly walked away and took my seat across the room.

At the lunch break, I found the man standing in front of me. "Can I take you to lunch so we can try to find out how we know each other," he invited.

As I looked into his smiling brown eyes, I realized I didn't have enough money in my purse to buy my own lunch, so I agreed.

Over lunch, we discovered we were both from the panhandle of Texas, but we could not find any obvious places where our paths could have crossed.

The man also explained that he had recently sold his business and retired to pursue his spiritual growth. "I want more than anything to hear the voice of my Higher Self," he confided.

As a result of his confidence, I told him the story of my inner Voice. I also showed him some of the messages I had received and some samples of my greeting cards. He was fascinated and envious of my obvious clear connection to what he called my Higher Self.

At the end of the day's lectures the two of us had dinner, after which I trusted him with my meditation journal to read overnight, although it was the only copy I had.

I slept restlessly that night, separated from my journal and still unsure how I would pay for the racks I had promised to purchase the following day.

"This is fascinating reading," the man told me the next morning as he handed me my journal. "Can I take you to lunch again today?"

"I can't" I replied. "I have to run an errand during the lunch break; I have to pick up the racks for my greeting cards. Thank you anyway."

"When you come back, come and sit with me. I'll save you a seat," he offered.

"Fine, I may be late though."

"I'll see you then." He squeezed my arm as we parted.

At lunchtime I left the seminar, met the man with the racks and wrote the check – on blind faith. More tense than I ever remember being, I returned to the class and took the empty seat my new acquaintance had saved for me.

As I sat down he turned to me, grinned, and patted my leg under the table, leaving his hand casually on my thigh. Leaning toward me conspiratorially, he whispered loudly, "Did you get your racks?"

I was appalled at the volume of his whisper. I suddenly realized that because of his hearing aids, he did not realize how loudly he was whispering. It sounded to me as if he had just spoken through a megaphone!

I nodded my head numbly, unable – and unwilling – to speak.

"How much did they cost?" he again whispered loudly.

My body stiffened. How could I get this man to stop asking me questions? I was also indignant that his inquiries were so personal. I wanted to say, "The price is my business – God's business – not yours! I don't even know you and get your hand off my leg!" but I could not speak a word.

I quickly wrote $800 on a scrap of paper and shoved it toward him. I was trying to get him to shut up – to stop telling the whole room I had just written an $800 hot check, for which I could be prosecuted and sent to prison, never to be bondable again; never to be employable by a bank again!

The man looked at the note and appeared to turn his attention back to the speaker. I tried to do the same. I was unable to focus on the speaker's message.

Moments later I felt him slip paper into my hand under the table. I brought my hand out from under the table so I could read his note. Instead of paper, the man had filled my hand with hundred dollar bills!

My body began to shake. Every admonition my mother had ever given me about not taking money from men began passing through my mind in red neon letters.

"I can't do this," I thought. "I can't go to bed with this man for money.

God wouldn't expect me to do that. I really need this money, but I don't want to get it that way . . . I really need this money . . ."

As the speaker finished I turned to the man, speech still nearly impossible. I stuttered, "Wh-wh-what is th-this? Wh-wh-wh-why are you p-p-putting this money in my h-h-hand? Wh-wh-what do you want?"

"I want to help you. It seems to me you need it. You need help to do what you're being asked to do."

"Yes, I need the m-m-money," I confessed shakily, "but I can't take it from you. I don't even know you. I can't borrow it; I have no collateral. I don't know if I would ever be able to pay it back – if I will ever make enough to give it back to you."

"Who asked you to? I don't want it back. If you send it back to me, karmically it won't do me any good. When you do get it, sometime in the future, give it to someone who needs it as badly as you do now. Then it will do some good for all of us." His statements were emphatic.

I did not know what karmically meant. I could not believe my ears. He was actually willing to give me – trust me – with the money! My eyes spilled over with tears. As he put his arms around me and kissed the top of my head, my body stiffened again with mistrust.

"I've got to go now, but I would like to have your phone number. It's a long drive back to Texas. Good luck," he said as he pulled away and smiled. I handed him my number.

I went out to the lobby and fell into a chair. I had to get my bearings. What was happening? Then I recognized one of the seminar participants, an older woman, sitting near me. "I didn't get to meet you during the weekend. My name is Valerian Smith," she said.

I came out of the fog long enough to introduce myself.

"What do you do?" she asked.

"I design and market greeting cards at Albertson's," I replied.

"My daughter designs and manufactures greeting cards also," she replied, smiling.

"No kidding! Where does she live?"

"She lives in Hurst, Texas, down between Fort Worth and Dallas."

"What kind of cards does she make? What do they look like?" My interest was mounting.

"Well, they are long and thin, done on parchment paper. The messages for her cards come to her in her meditations," the woman confided.

By this time my curiosity was really piqued.

The stranger asked to see my card samples and was amazed by the similarities between my cards and those of her daughter. The paper and size of the cards were identical. Even the company names were similar, hers being "dr Originals, Inc.," mine being "bj Originals, Inc." Both of our initials for our names were even done in lower case letters, with no periods. Further, the messages on our cards were nearly identical, as were the prices.

When the two of us discussed the possibility of my meeting her daughter, the woman confided that her daughter was facing heart surgery and therefore would not be traveling to Oklahoma City any time soon. She was very encouraging that her daughter would love to meet me.

We exchanged numbers. I explained that my car was in no condition to be driven to Texas; therefore, I would not be planning to go anytime soon. We hugged and parted.

14

The Benefactor Returns

Two weeks after the Silva class, I was awakened one morning by the phone. "Hullo," I groaned groggily into the mouthpiece.

"Hi. How's it going?" a cheerful male voice inquired. I lay very still for a few seconds trying to place the voice. "I'm going to be in Oklahoma City tomorrow and I'd really like to see you," he said.

"I'm going to be very busy tomorrow delivering cards to the stores." I began making excuses when I realized to whom I was speaking. My first thought was that my benefactor (the man who had given me the eight one-hundred dollar bills at the Silva class) was returning to Oklahoma to collect on his investment by wanting to spend time with me.

"How are the cards selling?" he asked brightly.

"Very well," I answered, "but I've created a monster. There is no way one person can create and deliver this many cards. I'm painting twenty hours a day and not getting any sleep. Not getting any sleep is killing me!"

"Haven't you got your photocopy machine yet?" he questioned.

"What, are you kidding?" I screeched. "How in the hell do you think I would buy something that costs that much money when I can't even afford peanut butter and crackers?" (I called him a few names I later regretted. Sleep deprivation truly makes one crazy.) "You have obviously never been broke. You have no idea what it is like to be in my position. A photocopy machine costs a lot of money. I haven't even been paid for any of the cards I've delivered yet. It takes six weeks for a new vendor to get a check back from the home office of this company. Not only do I not have enough money to buy a photocopy machine, I still haven't paid my rent, my utilities or my car payment. I could be evicted from my apartment any day now!"

"Calm down. Everything is going to be alright. I want to buy you a photocopy machine tomorrow. You need to be able to make a master of the calligraphy on white paper and reproduce it onto the parchment. Then you will be able to paint twice as many cards," he stated excitedly.

"Go out and find one large enough to do what you need to do and tomorrow I'll go with you and pay for it." I realized immediately I was not only feeling a lot of resistance to a man telling me what to do, but certainly had mixed emotions about what he was going to expect of me in return for the copier. I felt totally exhausted from lack of sleep.

Because of my exhaustion and fear, I made my decision. I would accept his offer. We would either get the price of my body up to where I could comfortably negotiate it later, or this man and his generosity were really gifts from God. Either way, I felt too tired to argue.

"What time will you arrive?" I managed wearily.

"I'll leave early and be there around noon. Wait to eat and I'll take you to lunch."

"Fine, I'll be waiting." As the words flowed from my mouth I asked myself, "What am I getting myself into?"

By the time he arrived the following day, I had worked myself into a state of agitation. At this point in my metaphysical education, I did not know the importance of ending my list of affirmations with the closure, "I accept this or something better through the grace of God and to the highest good of all concerned." Because I did not realize this subtlety of manifestation, whenever I had claimed money from the Universe, my car was the vehicle that was used to get it. Money paid by the insurance company to repair my car had been used to live on. Therefore, my car never received repairs. I asked the Universe for $1,000. It happened that my car was damaged in a hailstorm. The insurance company sent me a check for $1,012, which I had used to survive. When my insurance premium of $286 came due, a client accidentally backed into the door of my car. Her insurance paid me $289, which went to pay my premium.

By now, though, my car's engine was using almost equal amounts of gas and oil. It would barely make the weekly rounds of the eight stores in the Oklahoma City area. In addition, I had had to use my credit cards to the maximum in order to follow Spirit's directions. Despite working 20 hours a day, I was broke. I was desperate. I had concluded no one person was capable of painting, lettering, channeling, inventorying and delivering as many cards as the market now demanded.

As I opened the door to let the man in, he enfolded me in a long embrace. Holding me by the shoulders in front of him, he grinned as if he held a major secret.

"I've missed you! I'm starving. Let's get this show on the road," he roared with great enthusiasm in his deep husky voice.

While we ate lunch, I bolstered my courage to ask, "Why are you doing this for me?"

"Because you are doing something God obviously wants done and I can't do what you are doing. I didn't tell you before, but before I left Texas to come to the seminar I felt compelled to go to my safety deposit box and to take out the eight $100 bills. I never carry cash with me when I travel. I always use credit cards. That's why I was so sure when I heard your story that you were the person I was to give the money to."

"Do you have a picture with you of your priest friend who died?"

"Yes, I do," I said pulling Edward's photo from my wallet. "Why do you want to see it?" He took the photo and looked deeply into Edward's eyes. "I had a very strange experience the week before I met you. Have you seen the movie, *The Thorn Birds*? he asked.

"No, but I read the book."

"It was on television the week before we met," he related. "I never watch television, except for the news. I seemed to have a compulsion to see that program. I was drawn emotionally to the priest. For four nights I sat on the floor, right in front of the TV, mesmerized by that story."

"Every time my wife talked to me, I felt intruded upon by her presence," he confided. "I even tried to get her to leave the house so she wouldn't disturb me. Now that I have met you, I realize I saw you in my dreams for several weeks before we met. I wonder if it was your priest friend trying to communicate with you through me? I think he was trying to get me to feel his pain in leaving you, trying to get me to come to help you," he ended wistfully.

I was speechless. As he talked, chills of confirmation covered my whole body. When I finally found my voice, I croaked, "I guess it's possible. I don't want you to do anything for me that you might regret later, or that you feel coerced in any way to do for me."

"No, I really want to help you. I really believe in you and what you have told me. I know you are telling me the truth. I just wanted to tell you about the feelings I had during the movie, because I didn't understand them at the time. It really makes more sense to me, now that I've met you and heard your story, than it did at the time it was happening. I felt a little crazy. It is so unlike me to watch hours of TV, especially anything other than the news – very unlike me."

After lunch, we purchased the copier we felt would best serve my needs. It was delivered and set up in my apartment by mid-afternoon. The man paid for it with hundred dollar bills. I wondered how many he had in his safety deposit box and how he had acquired them, but certainly wasn't prepared to ask him. I also assumed he had to handle the situation with cash so his wife would not know what he was doing.

As we both stood looking at the machine, the man said, "You must really be in debt by now. How bad is it? You've been on unemployment, off unemployment, trying to start this business. I know you also wish you could help your children in Texas. And even when you did work, we know banks never pay women much anyway."

"Well, all my credit cards are maxed out, my rent's two months past due, my utilities are all past due and my car payment is due. I have no food in the house and no cash." My eyes filled with tears as I admitted my situation.

"Let me have your credit cards," he instructed.

I fumbled in my purse for the cards and a tissue, thinking to myself, "I can't use the cards anyway."

As he took them from me I thought he did so in order to remove the temptation to try to overcharge on them, which would worsen my financial situation.

We said goodbye with a long hug. I thought he was departing for his doctor's office and then returning to Texas.

When he returned a few hours later I was absolutely shocked to see him. I had been totally absorbed in running off volumes of card verses on the new machine. I was even more shocked when he handed me my credit cards along with receipts that showed he had gone to the bank and spent nearly $4,000 to pay off the balances!

"Apparently you will also need this," he said, handing me a miniature tape recorder he had obviously just purchased.

"What would I need this for?" I managed, tears of relief streaming down my face.

"Spirit says you will be writing books and you will need to keep notes by talking into the tape recorder," he responded. He grinned at me as he took a white handkerchief from his pocket and wiped away my tears.

"Would you like some coffee?" I stammered, "I'd like to show you the results of my afternoon's work."

"I'd love that, thanks." He moved to the kitchen table sitting with his hands folded in front of him patiently waiting for me to share the copier's results.

"I was told about four days ago in meditation that I would be expected to write books, but it's a surprise to hear it coming from you too," I confessed as I busied myself with coffee preparations.

"Well, I was surprised when I heard the Voice tell me to stop and buy you the recorder. I don't usually hear messages in that way or that clearly," he responded.

"I told Spirit," I confided, "that I don't feel I'm capable of writing books. I don't know how to write. I only have a twelfth-grade education. I don't think of myself as smart enough to write a whole book. When I told Spirit I would if they sent me some help, the reply came back, 'Bach will help you.' The only Bach I've ever heard of is Richard Bach who wrote, *Illusions* and *Jonathan Livingston Seagull*, and, of course, Bach the composer, but he's dead, which would probably make it easier for me to talk to him than it would Richard."

I surprised myself by laughing out loud. It had been a long time since I had anything to laugh about. "Spirits are easier to locate and communicate with than embodied people, and much less suspicious." I laughed again, feeling my own spirit lifted by the day's events, even though I still felt suspicious of his motives.

As we drank our coffee, I shared another message with the man that I had received while he had gone to the doctor and bank. "Spirit is insistent about my going to a place between Dallas and Ft. Worth to meet Donna, another woman who's making greeting cards. I met her mother at the Silva class. Donna is facing heart surgery and they want me to meet her and do a healing treatment on her heart before she enters the hospital for the surgery. It seems ridiculous to me. My car won't make the trip and I don't feel that I know enough about healing to offer myself as any kind of help. All I know is what we learned in the Silva class, and I was so panicked with buying the racks and writing that check that I missed most of what the speaker was saying."

The man regarded me thoughtfully. "I'm leaving for Dallas in the morning to visit my cousin who lives there, on my way back to the Panhandle and home. Why don't you call the woman you met and ask if her daughter would be receptive to meeting you? If she's receptive and it's a convenient time for her to meet you, you can ride down with me in the morning. I'd love to have your company on the trip and I'll buy you a one-way ticket and you can fly back here when you finish." I thought to myself what's another plane ticket compared to what he's already invested in me.

I made the call immediately. Valerian called her daughter and called me back quickly to say Donna was thrilled that I was coming. We agreed to leave the next morning.

After dinner and a walk through the park, the man left me at my apartment and spent the night at a nearby motel.

The next day we were joyful. The October weather was sunny and clear. The foliage was beautiful. The trees and wild sumac were a riot of gold, red and orange. I felt as if a huge weight had been lifted off my shoulders – and my soul as well – with the ending of my debts and the freedom of having credit again. The creative possibilities of the copier would make it possible for me to continue the cards and support myself without working twenty hours a day, too! The two of us laughed all the way to Dallas. I read the man more of the channeled messages I had received and told him the story of my life in Texas. He was easily entertained and also seemed to enjoy my silent presence when my voice tired.

As the Dallas skyline came into view, he inquired, "Would you be willing to go to dinner with my cousin and me? He's a commercial artist. He might have some helpful ideas about your cards. He also used to be on the National Board of the Church of Religious Science, so he's used to people who channel and meditate and all aspects of metaphysics."

"Yes, thanks, I would. I'm getting hungry and he sounds like someone I would enjoy meeting," I responded.

His cousin was charming and similar to the man in age and appearance. He was quietly amused and moved emotionally as I relayed the stories about how I began channeling and the events that had followed.

At the end of our four-hour dinner, the cousin spoke casually. "I have a cousin I feel would really enjoy meeting you."

"Really? Where does he live," I inquired.

"California."

"Well, I'm certainly not planning to go to California, my car wouldn't even make it to Dallas, but maybe you should give me his name in case I ever do get out there so I can contact him," I replied.

"His name is Marcus Bach," he said, writing as he spoke.

I felt my mouth drop open as I heard "Bach," the name Spirit had mentioned as a possible source of assistance with my writing.

"What does he do for a living?" I asked.

"He writes metaphysical books. He's written and published about 25 metaphysical books."

"Do you think he has any connection with Richard Bach, the man who wrote *Illusions* and *Jonathan Livingston Seagull*?" I asked.

"Yes, as a matter of fact, he is Richard's uncle," he answered.

As he spoke, goose bumps engulfed my body. (I had come to recognize this response as psychic confirmation. It's a physical response in the body to a spiritually delivered message or event.)

"In that case, I'll definitely need his address and number," I responded, as I explained Spirit's message when I had argued about my inability to write books.

"This could really get to be fun and interesting," the cousin grinned as he handed me the name and address. "You're a very brave lady and I've really enjoyed meeting you. I'm very glad to hear your story. It encourages me to start meditating again. I've been really lax lately on my listening." He smiled broadly and held out his arms for a hug as he rose to leave.

The man and I made our way to Donna's, where he left me. As we parted, he slipped more money for plane fare into my hand. I had the strange sense I would never see him again. He seemed sad to leave. Donna sensed my exhaustion and insisted I go to bed immediately. She assured me we could spend all of the next day visiting, which we did. In fact, we spent two talk-filled days together and I admitted I was apprehensive about my healing skill.

"You have to remember, bj, the healing is up to me. You only have to be WILLING to channel the energy. I have to ALLOW it to work," she encouraged.

"Willing," I thought. That's what my guidance had said when I questioned why I had been chosen to channel, to receive messages. I felt so unworthy of this kind of work.

But Spirit had admonished, *"It's not worthiness that's important, Dear One, but WILLINGNESS that's necessary. You were not chosen, YOU VOLUNTEERED."*

My faith started to build and my trust increased more and more. I recalled Spirit saying, *"Faith and trust are like muscles. If you exercise them they will grow and serve you well. If you don't use them. they atrophy and you will feel fear again."*

15

Joseph

One week after I returned to Oklahoma City from my visit with Donna, I attended a service at a Church of Religious Science. This was the first time I'd ever gone to the church and I was hopeful that I might meet other people like Ken, the man who had bought the copier for me, and his cousin . . . the type of people with whom I could communicate. I was hungry for someone to talk with about all the seemingly mysterious things going on in my life.

"Hi, my name is Joseph. I think I met you at the Silva Christmas party, didn't I?" The man's face opened in a broad, engaging smile. "I'm not sure. I met a lot of people that night and I've not mastered the Silva method of remembering names. You do look familiar, though," I responded.

"I remember you because the instructor mentioned you were interested in being a part of a Silva weekly meditation group. I've been involved in Silva for 15 years, since my wife's death, so I've had a lot of group experience. Here's my card and if you're interested, give me a call. By the way, have you read this book?" The man offered me a copy of *The World of Serendipity*, by Marcus Bach. Waves of goose bumps swept over me as I looked at the title.

"No, I haven't, but I guess I'd better buy a copy," I commented.

"Here, borrow this one. I don't have time to read it right now. We will be starting the meditation group the first Wednesday in January at 7:00. You can bring it with you then when you finish," he stated as he walked away, not waiting for an answer.

I spent the afternoon and evening devouring the book. I was fascinated with the concept of "serendipity" (the gift of discovering unsought-for desirable things by "accident").

Toward the end of the book, the author advocated a National holiday called "Serendipity Day." You could spend the day honoring all of the people you had met by "chance," or by serendipity, during the year. The idea intrigued me in view of my stream of recent serendipitous encounters.

"What a perfect opening," I uncharacteristically spoke aloud to myself. "I'll make a dozen cards that have the author's recommended message:

Thanks to chance

You came my way

Three cheers for

Serendipity

"I'll send them to Marcus Bach with a letter of introduction saying, 'quite serendipitously, I met your cousin in Dallas last week.'" (I won't mention the book.)

I began to attend the Silva meditation meetings, which were held in the home of a woman named Susan who had taken the Silva class at the same time I did. I seldom spoke to Joseph beyond the initial greeting as we entered the meeting. I was genuinely puzzled by my reaction to this man. He was not the physical type I was normally attracted to, since he was overweight, blond and fair skinned.

When Spirit began mentioning him in my meditations, I was even more puzzled. The man behaved almost as if I didn't exist personally, although he seemed infatuated by my greeting cards. He even asked if he could take some on consignment to offer his friends.

As time went on, Spirit repeatedly encouraged me to elicit a relationship with Joseph.

One evening after a session, group members went out for ice cream. Afterward, Joseph walked me to my car and hugged me platonically and wished me a good week.

I found sleeping difficult that night. What Spirit was indicating seemed so inappropriate in view of Joseph's seeming lack of interest in me as a woman.

Each week, I felt more and more love for this man who seemed so distant and almost secretive. The only thing I knew about him was his original offering – that his wife had died fifteen years before, that he was raising his 15-year-old son alone, and that his 19-year-old daughter had moved into her own apartment. I knew he was a computer programmer and that he was from Kansas. I didn't know if he was romantically involved with someone else, if he had ever married since his wife's death or how he felt about me.

Coming from a Christian background, I had no belief in past lives and actually had never thought of such a concept. In my meditations Spirit encouraged me to explore a past life regression with a certain psychologist who did hypnosis (actually giving me the counselor's name in meditation). Spirit kept mentioning that it would be appropriate for Joseph and me to marry. Spirit intimated that the regression could help me alleviate some fears of marrying again by understanding my past karmic relationship with him. I was encouraged to do the regression before beginning a romantic relationship with him.

It all seemed so preposterous. To begin with, I was not accustomed to pursuing men, especially men who seemed to show no interest in me as a woman. To follow Spirit's suggestion to confront Joseph and express the growing intensity of my feelings for him made me very uncomfortable.

The more I wrestled with my fears of rejection, the more I considered doing the regression to gain insight before making what seemed like a potentially threatening declaration of love to a virtual stranger.

Spirit confirmed: *"We would not have brought you back from Houston early to take Silva Mind Control had it not been important for your growth to meet Joseph at the Christmas party and lead him into this relationship. He will be willing, although stunned by your declaration. He is very shy and finds it difficult to approach you because he feels you have many other men in your life. He does not date because of taking care of his son. Do not be afraid. Trust the process and have the regression."*

The following day I called the psychologist whose name Spirit had given me in meditation to discuss the possibility of a past life regression. I asked the price of the session.

"Seventy-Five dollars," he replied.

"Do you take credit cards?" I asked.

"No, but if paying is a problem I do sometimes barter. What do you do?"

"I paint and do calligraphy."

"Well, I can't use those services, but I have been interested in trying a new technique I have thought of with an artist to prove we can improve a person's creative abilities through hypnosis. If you would be willing to come for four sessions of hypnosis for creativity and write up the results, I'll trade that for doing a regression for you," he offered. I could hardly believe my ears! It sounded as if I were the one gaining all the benefits. I agreed, made my regression appointment and thanked him profusely.

I arrived at his office later in the week, very nervous and unsure of myself. But Dr. Ben is a huge, soft-spoken gentleman and he gained my confidence immediately. He explained what might happen during the regression and that I would at all times be in control of the situation and my body. I lay on a couch. He sat beside me and asked me to close my eyes and to deliberately begin to relax.

After I had taken a few deep breaths he began to speak, "Four, three, two, one . . . You have now entered a state of deep relaxation. Your body feels heavy . . . You will begin to see colors, images . . ."

The psychologist's voice was smooth, relaxed, reassuring. Immediately I felt my body temperature drop, but a flood of warm light enveloped me. I was floating as if all gravitational restraints had been removed.

I floated through a purple cloud, then a yellow mist and settled into a female form, more petite and fragile than the one my soul normally inhabited in this lifetime. A tightness in my chest let me know I was anxious, afraid. I was exhausted from the trip, afraid, and my breathing was constricted by the stays in my corset. My hand smoothed the horsehair cushion of the train seat.

I was aware this was my first train trip. I felt a long way from Baltimore. I knew I was leaving a family of ten, headed only by my mother - no father image. I felt cast out, rejected, sold to the highest bidder.

The brakes of the train screeched and the steam hissed as the train ground to a halt. Chills ran up and down my spine as I braced myself against the seat. I was apprehensive about meeting this man I had been sold to by my mother. I was a mail-order bride.

My feet felt like lead as I made my way down the corridor with my one bag – my total life's belongings. My eyes searched the platform. I feared the man was not there to pick me up. I also feared that he was.

Since I had learned of my plight a month before, my dreams had been filled with rape scenes, abuse at the hands of some faceless man whose hands violated my body. I stiffened as I saw a tall, broad-shouldered, round-faced, bearded stranger approach the train exit. His eyes were happy and twinkling.

"Rebecca?" The stranger's masculine voice was tentative, but melodious. I could only muster a nod. My voice escaped me. I searched frantically for words to express my relief.

"I'm Joseph," he said. "Thanks for coming."

The man took my bag and my hand, gently guiding me to a wooden wagon hitched to a beautiful bay horse. His huge, reddened hands encircled my waist and hoisted me into the wagon as if I were a feather and fragile as an egg. He took equal care with my bag.

Gently he placed me respectively in a position of equal importance on the seat. He climbed up beside me and took the reins masterfully and with authority. Though terribly frightened, I observed that he did not slap the horse with the reigns, but made a gentle clucking sound with his tongue against the roof of his mouth.

As the animal moved forward, understanding its task, the giant man turned his full attention to me, observing my face, my hands, my hair. He said very little, but he communicated a warmth with his eyes that I had never before experienced. He seemed to hold some hidden message that I would understand very soon.

For two hours we traveled through beautiful green rolling hills. Then, upon rounding a bend in the road, I observed a small log cabin nestled in some trees. As I sat in the stillness of the wagon, I heard the sound of a brook nearby.

Joseph lifted me effortlessly to the ground and took my hand, leading me to the stream. He motioned for me to sit on a rock protruding over the water. He removed his boots and stepped into the water. As he did so, he gently unlaced my high-topped black boots and put my stocking-clad feet into the water. His actions seemed to say that asking _me_ to remove my stockings would be premature, too familiar.

His massive hands gently massaged my tiny aching feet that had been encased in my boots for three days.

I was filled with awe, confused by my expectation, which was so opposite of what I was experiencing. However, a part of me was still not trusting. I felt as if I were dreaming, having been transported from my struggling, nightmare existence to this fairyland in the woods, my faceless monster turning out to be a tender, gentle giant.

The next four days included the man's washing and combing my hair, showing me his land, massaging my back. Nights were spent on a bearskin rug in front of the fireplace as he vividly expressed his dreams, his plans for our future. After all else and an established feeling of trust, his lovemaking was as gentle as any lover I had ever created in my girlish fantasies.

I awakened from my past life regression knowing it would be safe to marry Joseph.

I could not get my mind off Joseph for the rest of the week. I was haunted by the regression and the intense feelings of love and passion, which continued to grow in my mind, heart, soul and body. However, whenever I thought of exposing my feelings to this seemingly uninterested man, my face flushed, and I trembled with fear of rejection.

Spirit continued to reassure me daily of the appropriateness of the relationship and its importance, and thus convinced me I would not be rejected. Joseph was Spirit's choice of a mate for me. I rationalized that with his background in metaphysics, he would be able to accept my growing psychic and channeling abilities. He seemed to trust the information that came through me for him on other subjects, so I became encouraged to share with him my feelings, fears, my regression and, if necessary, Spirit's messages. I hoped he would accept me because of my feelings, and I would not need to encourage him with Spirit's recommendations. I did not want him to feel manipulated. Still, since I had no desire to marry again, the entire situation seemed really ridiculous to me.

After the next group meeting, I approached Joseph with, "I realize you need to get home to your son, but I wondered if I could stop by on my way home and visit for a little while. I need to share something with you."

He looked at me quizzically and then said, "Sure. Give me about 45 minutes to get home, get Eric to bed, pick up the house, and then I'll be free to visit."

"Fine, I'll be there in 45 minutes." As I spoke, my body was already beginning to shake so hard my teeth chattered. I felt an intense desire to take two Valium and go home to bed rather than face the challenge of learning the truth about Joseph's feelings and his romantic status with other women.

I parked my car down the street from his home and began taking deep breaths to calm my shakes. This went on for thirty minutes while I waited for him to get his son to bed.

As I approached the open door, I heard the television in the background and then his voice over the sound of the news, inviting me to come in. I made my way through the unfamiliar kitchen and moved in the direction his voice suggested.

"Your tea's on the counter, if you want it," I heard him say. "Come on in."

"Have a seat," he invited as he nodded toward a place on an adjoining couch near where he sat, his stocking feet propped up on the coffee table. He looked at me over the top of his reading glasses and suspended newspaper as if it were perfectly natural for me to be there.

I took a drink of tea. I thought he would surely turn off the TV and quit reading his paper to pay attention to me, and what I had come to say.

"You remember the stocks you channeled last week?" he inquired behind his paper. "They have gone up in price this week."

"Really? Well, I didn't come to tell you – to talk about stocks; I came to tell you I've fallen in love with you, and I need to know if that's going to cause you a problem or if that's OK or awkward for you, or are you involved with someone else already?" I ran it all together without taking a breath in hopes I wouldn't cry from fear. My heart pounded so loudly I was afraid he hadn't heard what I said over the newscaster's report.

"You what?" He lowered the paper in line with the bottom of his glasses. So I couldn't see his full facial expression to judge his response. Asking me to repeat myself when it was so difficult to even say it once didn't help either.

"I said I'm falling in love with you as a result of sitting across the room from you in meditation every week and listening to you speak, and I feel really insecure and a lot crazy allowing this to happen not knowing if you already have a girlfriend or a fiancé or someone special in your life. So I need to know how you feel about me, if you've ever even considered the possibility or anything," I stammered and gulped, my heart pounding.

"The possibility?" he questioned as he finally laid his paper in his lap and took off his glasses. He looked at me for what seemed like the first time, possibly even just now recognizing me as a member of the female species.

"I'm not sure what you mean, the 'possibility,'" he acknowledged. "Usually, when I feel this confused or confronted by something, I say something funny to keep from dealing with it. But I can see from the look on your face you are really serious about what you are saying and that kind of response would hurt your feelings."

He sat staring at me for what seemed forever, then he rose to turn off the TV. He was either going to give me his full attention, or buy himself time to think of a response, I wasn't sure which.

"Your mate is your mirror, reflecting back to you parts of yourself you may like to pretend do not exist," wrote Martha Baldwin in *Self Sabotage, How to Stop It and Soar to Success*.

16

More Joseph

After turning off the TV, Joseph began talking to me, a conversation that lasted for several hours. He talked about himself, his dead wife, his son, his daughter, his work. He said he was not involved with anyone else, nor had he been for several years, not since his move to Oklahoma City.

At 3 a.m., he finally patted the couch beside him and said, "I think if we are going to discuss such a serious subject, we should at least be on the same couch."

As I rose to sit beside him, he took my hand and asked me to sit on his lap. He simply held me for a very long time, my head resting on his broad shoulder. He kissed the top of my head and ran his fingers through my hair. The image of the regression and the experience of his washing and brushing my hair welled up inside me as tears of relief flowed profusely, soaking his shirt.

"It's OK. It's OK. It's OK," he gasped. "I was just shocked . . . I had no idea you felt this way. I can't believe I was so blind to you as a woman until you walked into this room. God, it feels so good to hold you, to smell your hair. I desperately want to share love with you. Will you spend the rest of the night with me . . . sleep with me? Can you do that?" He took my face between his hands and kissed my lips gently.

As he accepted the passion of my returned kiss, he took me in his arms and lifted me off the couch. He carried me to his bed and placed me upon it. As gently as I had remembered from the regression, he removed my clothes and, as gently, caressed and kissed every part of my body. Our passion seemed inexhaustible.

Sleep finally captured us in its velvet grasp, and we remained entwined until awakened by his son Eric taking a shower before leaving for school.

Concerned by what the child might think if he found an unexpected woman in the house or in his father's bed, I asked Joseph if I should leave before the boy finished his shower or if I should remain in the bedroom until he had left for school.

"No, I'll not hide you from my son. You need to meet him. I have a strong feeling we will all be spending a lot of time together," Joseph predicted happily.

Shortly after the relationship with Joseph began, I started to feel the need for a house. My income had still not caught up with my expenses, so the idea seemed impossible.

The following week at the group meditation, one of the members mentioned that her father was retiring to his lake house and wanted to rent his family home. He did not want to rent to strangers. The woman suggested that I might want to look at the place and meet her mom and dad.

Although I did not know how I would afford the rent, I went to see the property.

I loved the house. It was immaculately cared for, inside and out, and had large rooms.

"When can you move in?" my friend's father asked after we had finished viewing the place.

"I don't know, Mr. Jones. I don't think I can afford your house even though I would love to live here so my children could come back to live with me," I expressed my doubts and my desires.

"How many children? What ages?" he inquired.

"Two, a boy, eleven, and a girl, fifteen." As I answered, I figured he did not want to rent to anyone with children.

"This old house has been a good place for us to raise our family. The schools are good in this area and the place could benefit from the sound of children again," he mused. "I'm asking $650. How much do you think you can pay?"

"I can only pay $500," something said through me.

"Fine. I'll take it! What else do we need to do about a contract, or deposits, or whatever? You've rented before, and I've never rented, so I don't know these things," my new landlord confessed.

"Well, it's customary for a person to sign a lease, pay the first and last month's rent in advance and make a damage deposit. And I can't do any of that for you. Maybe you should find someone else," I said, trying to talk him out of it from my own fear that I could not produce that much money for rent.

"No, I don't want someone else," Mr. Jones said emphatically. "I want you to live here. You're a friend of Susan's and she trusts you. I trust you. Besides, you need a place for your kids to live. We'll just leave the rest up to God and waive the deposits if you can move in next week. We also need to leave some of my wife's antiques here with you, if they won't be in your way. We've got no room for them at the lake cottage. How much furniture do you have?"

"Not enough to fill up this house, so I would be more than glad to take good care of whatever you need to leave here," I assured him.

"Good. It's settled. We'll move out on Friday and you can move in over the weekend. It's important to me not to leave the place vacant." He smiled as he handed me a key and added, "We'll just leave our phones here and call the phone company and change the name on the number to yours, if that's OK with you. That way you can refer calls that might come in to us at the lake and save yourself an installation charge. Besides, if Mildred can't stand living with me at the lake and comes back to town, she will have her same number. That's also why I'm waiving the lease. If she hates lake living, or I kick the bucket, we may have to ask you to leave with very little notice."

"No problem. I understand," I responded in disbelief at his generosity and my good fortune.

I moved into the house alone in May. In June my son came to live with me.

On July 4, Joseph proposed that we live together, share expenses and allow our sons to become better acquainted. We would do so with the thought of marrying in September if we felt, after the summer, that we were at all compatible. I agreed, and he and his son moved in immediately. I now knew why my guidance had directed me to this house and how I was to cover the rental expense. I was still hesitant about the idea of a formal marriage. I felt that I was already as committed – as married – as any piece of paper or words could convey. With his strict Catholic background, however, Joseph felt a real need to formalize our living arrangement for the sake of his aging parents.

I went through the marriage ceremony for Joseph's sake. My son, Cory, came to stay for the school year, and Joseph started his own computer business in an office space Mr. Jones had created in the garage. I ran my card company from the living room.

We fell quickly into a routine. Joseph would rise early, prepare food for the boys and take them to school. I would stay in bed to write channeled information, or simply to rest. When he returned from chauffeuring the children, he would make breakfast for the two of us. Often, mealtime was the only opportunity we had to share. Joseph worked long hours to create his company, and I was most often asleep before he came to bed.

The relationship between Joseph and his son was confusing to me and seemed based equally on love and hate. I would periodically ask Joseph about his attitude toward his son, but he would deny my concerns. Eventually, the behavior became so obvious and Joseph seemed so oblivious to his attitude toward his son that I resorted to asking Spirit to explain the basis of the situation to me.

Spirit commented: *"His son is actually his brother."*

"That makes no sense to me, what do you mean?"

A vision formed in my mind of two children, one about twelve and one about six, inside what appeared to be a wooden, dirt-floored garage. The twelve-year-old pointed a rifle at the younger boy and pulled the trigger. The younger child fell to the dirt floor.

Was Spirit showing me that Joseph's son had been his brother in a past life? The vision haunted me for days before I mentioned it to Joseph.

One afternoon, while the boys were at school, I entered Joseph's office. "I think I've seen why you have this love/hate relationship with Sean," I offered.

"What do you mean?" he looked surprised that I was still trying to figure out something that he clearly didn't see as a problem.

"I asked Spirit for an answer to why you treat each other the way you do. You don't seem to realize how much tension it creates in our home."

"What did they tell you?"

"Spirit said Sean is your brother, but you don't have a brother."

"What else did Spirit tell you?"

"Nothing else. They just showed me a vision."

"What kind of vision?" His face began to lose its color.

"I would rather not say. Do you know what they would have shown me?"

His voice changed, and he became demanding. "Tell me exactly what you saw."

"I saw two young boys in a dirt-floored, wooden garage."

His face grew even paler. "What were they doing?"

"I'd rather you told me."

"No, you tell me right now what you saw," he demanded.

"The older boy shot the younger one with a rifle. It seemed to be an accident. He didn't seem to think the gun was loaded."

Joseph's face was now as white as his shirt, and he was shaking. "I shot my brother accidentally with my father's rifle when my brother was six years old. Sean must be the reincarnation of my brother and that's why I've had complete responsibility for him since my wife's death when he was nine months old." He had tears streaming down his face.

I moved to be near him behind his desk, but he rose abruptly and left the garage and entered the house and locked himself in the bathroom. I was shaken, confused and hurt. How could he marry someone and not tell her something so significant? How could he keep such a secret? What would he do now that I knew it?

Joseph, the boys and I were together for nine months.

One night I was suddenly awakened from a sound sleep. Joseph was sitting up in bed, eyes closed, shouting: "Get out of my head!"

The next week he asked me for a divorce. He said he felt he was not the right person for me; that he was intimidated by my psychic abilities.

I was devastated!

Shortly after the divorce, my daughter came to live with me for a school term. I worked hard, meditated regularly, enjoyed having my children, and tried to forget Joseph. I also tried to forgive Spirit for bringing him back into my life.

I can now look back and understand how we all benefited from our nine months together, but at the time, the pain of rejection was intense.

I had not yet learned "apocatastasis," the ability to see the seed of inherent good in every seeming disaster or crisis.

17

A Dawning

May 1984

I had believed, because Spirit had so obviously chosen Joseph and because he had been involved in Silva and metaphysics for years, that my abilities would not intimidate him. I had a lot to learn about the difference of studying and talking about spirituality and living a spiritual life.

After the divorce, and while my children and I were still living together in the rented house, I had an unusual experience during one of my early morning meditations. I felt my room fill with light and a presence so powerful that loving tears of joy streamed down my face, wetting the paper lying in my lap.

An image of the Master Jesus stood at the foot of my bed. The energy made my body feel totally weightless. I have never experienced so much joy or love.

Much was communicated telepathically as He stood there, including a dialogue about The Lord's Prayer and what He really meant in the Beatitudes. He extracted a promise from me that I would eventually write down His definitions of the words He used in the Beatitudes. I later learned that many of the Aramaic words He used could have as many as 12 different definitions.

He suggested I create Retreat Centers and call them, "Namaste, Inc."

Visions of 12 Centers were shown to me, Centers in various parts of the country where people came to experience their creativity, emotions and divinity during times of stress, transition or extreme phases of growth.

The word "Namaste" recalled my first exposure to the word and to yoga during the intense depression I suffered in 1969, after having just joined this physical body.

My consciousness had joined the original consciousness of the body in 1969 and was living in Amarillo, Texas. I was flipping through TV channels looking for *Sesame Street* so my three-month-old daughter could watch it while I made dinner. I stopped changing channels at a yoga program. The instructor greeted the viewers at the beginning and end of each program with "Namaste," and each of her hands joined in a prayerful position touched at her heart level as she bowed from the waist.

I had an instantaneous connection to the word and felt chills all over my body. At that time in my life, I had no idea the chills were psychic confirmation of how important the word would be later in my life.

Viewers were told that "Namaste" is a Sanskrit word meaning, "The Spirit within me acknowledges the Spirit within you."

As for creating Namaste Retreat Centers, I felt absolutely inadequate to such a task. At that time the only attitudinal healing centers I had heard about were the ones being created from a model started in Tiberon, California, by Gerald Jampolsky.

I thought, "Me, create retreat centers? How can this be possible? I have no money, no credentials for such an awesome task! How can I possibly do that?" I confronted my Spirit with these doubts.

"You will be the instrument, the catalyst, for the creation of the twelve attitudinal healing centers. Many will be sent to help. Many will participate. You are called to hold and ground the energy form in your mind and are asked to travel to the various places where we have already etherically located these temples of healing. You will join your energies with others who will be given similar visions, similar guidance.

"It is now time to release the past and move toward this next phase of your growth. The mission could best be served by your selling the greeting card company (the suggested price is $3,000,) returning your children to Texas for the summer to live with their father, buying a new car, giving up your house, putting your belongings in storage and traveling for three months to visit other healing centers, retreat centers and spiritual communities.

"If you agree to this, it will be important for you to meditate each morning in order to know the next city to travel to, and each evening to know the most beneficial place to spend the night."

I was instantly overwhelmed by the message, the thought of sending my children back to Texas, the thought of putting my belongings in storage and being a homeless person. I began to cry.

How, I questioned, could my Spirit expect me to leave my children again when we had just re-formed our family? How could It expect me to buy a new car when I still owed money on the car I was driving and it was falling apart? How could It expect me to sell the business for $3,000, pay off the debts of $1,500 and travel for three months on just that $1,500? How could It expect me to tour with only a day-to-day or hour-to-hour itinerary?

It all felt totally unreasonable to me, totally ridiculous, totally impossible.

I was very depressed. I seriously questioned how I could go on trusting this Source which had brought Joseph to me, encouraged me to marry him, and then not arranged for him to stay to join me in the work I felt we had been asked to do. I felt betrayed by my soul. I spent hours in self-argument, plying myself with questions.

Did I want to continue with the guidance? Did I believe it could be trusted? Had I seen enough evidence to keep me going after such a major disappointment? Could I face giving up everything again, including my children, to travel alone to unknown places to meet strange people I had never seen before? How could I expect these people I had never met to take me in and take care of me?

Then I remembered one of the main things that had drawn me to Edward. It was our shared dream of a retreat center in the hill country of Texas. He had named it "Genesis, a place to begin again." So I meditated daily, taking the memory of our dream and my questions into my meditations.

Then one day, tears of relief and joy filled my body as I realized Edward's dream had not died with him; I was indeed being prepared to hold the creative energy form for not one, but 12 such centers! I didn't understand it then, but I would be prepared through my travel and a series of consciousness-raising experiences!

I saw further why Edward had chosen to leave this planet, and why (as he explained through my guides) it had _not_ been in the interest of my highest good to live in his shadow, to expect him as a religious authority to contact God for me. And I understood that it was important that I not be his secretary, his helpmate, because my soul needed to develop its own potential.

For years I had experienced intense anger with Edward for abandoning me and our dream. I was also angry about my inability to communicate with him from the world of Spirit, and I thought my guides were blocking this communication to keep me from creating a dependence on his guidance. After all, I seemed to be able to connect with almost anyone else in the spirit world except Edward and my mother.

Now, I finally came to understand that it was the anger itself that had blocked me from communicating with Edward. I realized that because about that time, a dear friend channeled him and this was his message:

"Love, I have never left your side, could never leave you, for we are a part of the same Soul. I will never abandon you. You have only to ask for me; I am here. Only your anger with me for dragging you from your false security in Lubbock and leaving you physically alone in Oklahoma City has made it impossible for you to hear me, to forgive me, to give up the anger.

"Let's be friends again. Let's work together again. I want that so much. Your anger toward me blocks so much good, so much joy from you. It interferes in your relationships and makes it impossible for you to bond with someone else as a mate.

"Let it go, My Love. Be free at last to love again as we did, completely, abundantly, without restraint and reservation. Love can and must be shared for total joy to be present."

Tears of happiness and relief flood my being even now as I feel his presence here in the room with me as I write these words.

The blockage to hearing my mother's voice was also resolved a few years later. I had never sought to hear my mother, because I knew she would be in judgment about my leaving my husband, my children, the security of my home in Lubbock and my father.

I was traveling from Denver to Sedona, Arizona. When I arrived in Sedona, Spirit asked me to keep driving and to go on to Cottonwood – ten miles west – and to stop at the KOA campground. My agreement with Spirit in the traveling adventure did not involve camping out, so I did not know why I would be sent to a campground. When I arrived at the KOA, nothing being obvious, I parked and went into the clubhouse to get a Coke and see who was there.

I stopped just inside the door and looked around. Two women were seated at a corner table across the room. They saw me enter and began to wave for me to join them. I looked behind me to see if someone else, someone they must know, had entered with me. There was no one there. I went to their table.

"What took you so long to get here? We've been waiting for you all morning. We are both tea-logged from sitting here so long waiting," the woman who introduced herself as Jackie said.

"I think you must have me confused with someone else," I protested.

"No, my husband is a medium, and he said this morning that Spirit said we were to wait here in the clubhouse and that someone important would be arriving."

I was amazed that someone else was so clearly being told what to do and following through with the information. We visited for a while and I learned that one of the women was from Colorado and had been traveling around the country, recently driving from Alaska to Arizona. Her stories about her travels were inspiring. They asked me about myself and I told them my story. The other woman, Honey Lee, was and is a bookkeeper/accountant and has for years done the tax work for Namaste, Inc. Had I not gone to the KOA, Spirit would have had to arrange a whole other set of circumstances through which we would have met each other and become friends.

Jackie, whose husband was a medium, insisted that I have a session with her husband the next morning. I didn't see the point, as I could receive any information I thought I needed from my own soul. He would create picture of my guide in the process. I didn't want a delicate pastel picture of my guide to carry around in my car. My car was full enough with my clothes and what few belongings I kept. I didn't want to spend $40 for a session and a picture I didn't want. The message was clear from my soul that the session was necessary. I agreed to return the next morning.

Jackie and her husband traveled around the country in a fifth-wheel trailer. I had breakfast with Honey Lee and Jackie around their campfire before knocking on the door of Jackie's trailer for my appointment with her husband. The door was opened by a six-foot tall, thin to the point of looking emaciated, man with a toupee sideways on top of his head. His face reminded me of a caricature I had seen of Ichabod Crane. I controlled my first reaction, which would have been to laugh, had the odor coming out of the trailer not overpowered the urge. The smell was a combination of body odor, old cooking smells and mildew. I couldn't believe I had to enter. I couldn't believe my soul thought this was necessary.

I entered with great resistance and trepidation. Steve led me to the front of the trailer, to a chair next to a window, which was blessedly open enough for a little fresh air to enter. His easel was set up in a small cleared area. I pasted a smile on my face and became determined not to throw up.

He channeled the drawing of an Indian chief he claimed was my guide, White Cloud. I was convinced he was a fraud. I have no Indian guides. After a few minutes of drawing his eyes filled with tears. "What's wrong?" I inquired as I experienced a dramatic shift of energy in the room.

"There is the presence of a woman, a mother-energy who has just made contact with me," he explained. "She's expressing so much love for you that the beauty of it brings tears to my eyes. She wants to talk to you."

I was used to talking with Lady Master Venus, my cosmic Mother, but definitely didn't want to hear from my biological mother. "I really don't want to talk to her," I told him. "I know she's going to be in judgment about my leaving John and the children and Lubbock and my dad, and I don't want to hear any more of her judgments. There's no way she can understand why or how I've made these choices."

"I think you might be misjudging her at this point," the artist said. "She's learned a lot since she left her body. She's sitting in the midst of a field of multi-colored flowers. She says she was allergic to flowers, perfume, cigarette smoke and many foods when she was here. She says her clothes no longer have to be all cotton. She seems to be saying certain things to make sure you realize it is really her before she gives you her message; otherwise, she says you won't believe the message."

"She's asking you to remember the single red rose you sent her on your birthday to thank her for creating your body."

At this I began to sob, "OK, OK, tell me the message. I believe she is talking to you."

And then the words came.

"I'm still trying to get through to Dad and Jim to help you. What you are doing is more important than being a mother or a wife. Teaching people that they really don't die and removing the fear of death is the most important thing on Earth. I support you in your work from here and I will continue trying to get the rest of the family to hear you. But don't let their rejection or judgment stop you. Keep going, Baby. It's going to be worth it. I love you."

The day of my mother's funeral, my father insisted that my sister-in-law and I go through my mother's belongings and give them away to his sisters who had come to town for the funeral. When we reached the bottom of her lingerie drawer we found the single red rose I had the florist send her on my birthday. The rose, the vase, the card were wrapped in a whole roll of aluminum foil to preserve them. She had attached a note to the outside, which read, "Receiving this rose fulfilled a lifetime fantasy."

Even now, as I write these words, I remember the intense burden of guilt and fear that was lifted from me by that one message – the guilt that I had not lived up to her expectations of me as a daughter, a perfect mother and supportive wife; the fear of her judgment of me and my involvement in the spiritual, psychic and metaphysical.

I finally had to laugh out loud – through my tears of relief – that she, of all people, was able to support my decisions to give it all up to follow the Voice of my own Spirit at the expense of "everything." And that she would choose such a bizarre setting and medium through which to deliver her message.

Again I realized that, truly, there is no death.

18

A Change of Lifestyle . . . and Cars

It is appropriate to understand that at this stage of my working with Spirit I believed that since I had turned my will over to God everything I got in meditation was an order. I thought of myself more or less as a pawn who had to obey my guidance, <u>which I later found is not true</u>. For years I tried to accomplish everything that was suggested, without argument and at the expense of my credit cards. I later learned the soul will never take our will, even when we've given it. We always maintain our free will. The messages are just suggestions; we always have the right to accept or refuse, to make a list of conditions under which we feel more comfortable tackling the assignment. But at this point in my story, I was still following what I thought were "orders."

When Spirit encouraged me to sell the greeting card business, return my children to Texas, buy a new car and put my belongings in storage – not to mention traveling – I seriously questioned the wisdom of continuing to follow the guidance. However, Spirit continued to suggest I begin my "trusting" process with the purchase of a new car.

I knew I needed a more dependable vehicle just to return the children to Texas, whether or not I chose to meet the challenge of traveling. Therefore, I listened attentively to Spirit's suggestions:

1. *Blue cars are involved in collisions less often*
2. *28 miles per gallon*
3. *Five doors*

Armed with this information, I decided to visit some obvious car dealers. While I didn't feel as if I were being told the order in which I should approach each one, I intuitively chose the Chevrolet dealer first.

The salesman who greeted me was interested and courteous – until he saw the condition of my trade-in and my financial statement.

"Lady," he stated flatly, "you can't afford a new car." Then he took me to the used car lot and dropped me off with another salesman who was to fix me up with a secondhand car. He did not introduce me to this man.

I was angry and upset. "I don't need a used car! I already have a used car! That's the whole idea; I need a NEW car!" I clenched my fists and shook with anger at having to deal with the ignorance, logic and inflexibility of these sales people.

I left the lot frustrated and frightened. I understood THEIR logic, and I understood MY need. I was angry that there was not a man in my life to negotiate what to me was a seemingly male transaction. John had always dealt with car salesmen. When I had car trouble, I called and he sent someone from his automotive garage to rescue me and bring me another car. I had never had the responsibility of taking care of or purchasing a car.

After days of searching for a new car and dealing with rejection, I gave up, exhausted. Also, my son had developed chicken pox and needed my constant attention. In my frustration I yelled at God, "If you want me to have a new car you will have to have someone deliver it to my driveway. I'm too tired and discouraged to do this anymore!"

In the next day's mail I received a letter from the new owner of the Chevrolet dealership. The letter stated that because of my visit to the company and the appraisal of my trade-in, the dealer was aware that I had left without purchasing a vehicle. This new owner requested that I call him personally to tell him why I had not bought a car from his dealership. He wanted to know if his salesmen were rude, if his cars were overpriced, or if they had not had the model I desired.

It occurred to me that if I were ever going to be able to afford a new car – or negotiate a really good deal on one – I had to work with the owner who could make exceptions to rules of credit and trade-ins. I called the owner immediately. I explained to him that yes, the salesman had been rude, telling me I could not afford a new car, and had dropped me off at the used car lot without introducing me to the person with whom he was leaving me.

He was appalled and apologetic. "What kind of car do you wish to purchase, and what kind of payment do you feel you can afford?" he inquired politely over the phone.

I described the small blue car to him as Spirit had described it to me, and added, "$200 a month."

"I have that car in the show room right here in front of me," he said.

"You come back down here, and I'll fix you up personally."

"I can't do that for a few days because my son is home with the chicken pox," I explained. "I'll have to get back to you when he's better."

He thanked me for my time and hung up. Twenty minutes later the phone rang. It was the salesman who had taken me to the used car lot. "Mr. Smicklas told me to call you and to offer to bring this car and a contract out to your house, if you have time to drive the car this afternoon."

The salesman did indeed bring the car out, and it was perfect. We traded vehicles in my driveway, I signed his contract and he drove back to the dealership in my dilapidated car to pay off the debt on it at the bank and to sell it for salvage.

The power, method and humor of Spirit amazed me once again.

After buying a car, which was the first move Spirit had suggested I make to begin my trusting process, I sold the greeting card company. A woman I did not know called the day after Spirit had made the suggestion and asked if I had ever considered selling the greeting card company. She said she was an artist, and that she and her partner were looking for just such an outlet for her talent. I never even had to run an ad. They came by with a check the same afternoon.

Since the garage of the rented house was heated and air conditioned, when I met a woman who was getting a divorce and didn't have money or a place to move until her divorce was final, I let her move into the garage. There were nice cabinets out there because that's where Mr. Jones had spent a great deal of his time. All we needed was hot and cold running water and a small refrigerator. We wrote out a request to the Universe for both. The next day the Ozarka water salesman knocked on the door and asked me if I would consider renting, for ten dollars a month, a water dispenser that dispensed hot and cold water and had a small refrigerator in the bottom. God moves in mysterious ways, seemingly, sometimes fast and sometimes slow.

Since the children were eager to spend the summer in Lubbock with their father, I reluctantly gave up our home and put my belongings in storage. The woman who had been living in the garage wanted to go to Oregon, so I agreed to let her travel that far with me. We made it all the way to Amarillo before she decided she couldn't stand waiting around while I talked with people and did readings and wanted to go back to Oklahoma City and her husband. I spent two more days bringing her back and then set out alone.

After all that, I traveled for three months alone, guided daily by my

Spirit about where to go and with whom to speak. In my experience and opinion, calling someone you've never met on the phone and saying, "Spirit gave me your name in meditation this morning and your soul has a message for you. Could I come by and visit with you?" is the worst cold call a person can ever be expected to make.

The children decided they would spend the next school year in Texas, so at the request of my Spirit I continued traveling. I covered Texas, New Mexico, Arizona, California, Oregon, Washington, Idaho, Utah, Nevada, Colorado and Kansas. Finally, seven months later, I returned to Oklahoma City.

After my return to Oklahoma City, I went out to the storage unit one day to have a look. As I viewed my belongings, I was absolutely amazed at how heavy they felt to me. I realized that I no longer needed to own all of these items. During my travels, all my needs had been met. Most of my possessions now, somehow, felt like an unnecessary burden, especially if I was going to continue to travel.

I sold almost everything I owned, keeping only my clothes, books and a few personal items. Some things were very difficult to part with. For Mother's Day, my children had given me an acrylic box filled with real butterflies suspended on a real branch. I didn't want to part with it, so I put it on a shelf at the back of the garage and marked it an unrealistic garage sale price of $40. On the second day of the sale a woman stopped abruptly in front of the house, exited her car and went directly through the garage to the shelf. She picked up the acrylic box and brought it to the card table where I was seated. I was stunned. "Did you see the price?" I asked her.

"Yes, I want it, but I need to tell you why and what I'm going to do with it."

"No, actually you don't. I'm sorry, it's just that this has sentimental value to me, which is why I priced it so high."

"No, actually I do need to tell you. It's a birthday present for my daughter who is turning 30 this week. When she was nine she was sitting on the front porch while we adults were inside having a prayer meeting."

"Oh, boy," I thought. "She's a Christian. Hide the Tarot cards."

"After the meeting ended she came inside. A butterfly had landed and was still sitting on her hand. I told her it was probably her Spirit guide."

I breathed a sigh of relief and listened closer to her story.

"She wanted to keep the butterfly in her room, but I convinced her that it would die if she kept it inside so I watched her take it back outside and leave it on a bush. Two days later, while I was cleaning her room I found a dead butterfly like the one she had shown me under her bed. She assured me she had not brought it back inside. She is really going through a difficult time in her life right now and I want to send this as a reminder to her that her spiritual guidance is available to her."

Needless to say, I had tears in my eyes and realized that Spirit was releasing my possessions to those who needed them more than I did at that moment. I asked her to wait and I went inside and got my autographed copy of *I, MONTY* by Marcus Bach for her to send to her daughter with the box of butterflies.

Spirit continued to encourage me to travel. It was also suggested that I trade my little blue car for a blue mini-van.

This time when I approached the dealers to try to trade cars, the salesmen said, "You are upside down in your car, lady. We can't trade with you." I learned this meant that I had no equity in my car; that I owed more than what it was worth. Discouraged, I began repacking my car with what was left of my belongings. As I packed the items in my little blue car, the phone rang. It was a friend I had met when traveling through Amarillo, Texas.

"bj, I've been thinking that if you are going to continue to travel, what you really need is a mini-van."

At my friend's words, I began to laugh into the phone. "I know. That's what Spirit keeps suggesting. I wish you could convince a car dealer of that."

"Maybe I can. My daddy buys all of his cars from a dealer in Borger. I think if I took you there, Jim might make you a deal. Come on to Amarillo, and let's give it a try."

"Well, we've got nothing to lose, Sara, and Spirit keeps insisting it's possible. I will be there tomorrow afternoon."

The next day when Sara introduced me as her friend to the dealer and told him I needed a mini-van to travel in, he responded, "Well, young lady, which one do you like?"

With her help I was able to acquire a mini-van, as Spirit had suggested. It is important to realize there are other people who are also listening to their Spirit and are willing to follow what they are being asked to do. I continued to travel for five years, as my guidance directed, including trips to Peru, Mexico and Guatemala. My needs were all met. I experienced many miracles, much serendipity and generous, generous people.

I have learned that many times the goal, mission or purpose we seek changes in appearance several times as we journey toward it. Our Spirits reveal to us only "the next single thing" that we should do, or "the next single step" that we should take to accomplish our goals. If they were to show us the long-range picture of what we would be doing, most of us would be afraid to step out. For instance, when I was encouraged to travel, way back then, had I been shown what I would be doing, I probably would still be in bed with my head covered or even under the bed.

Today, I feel I know my life's purpose: To use my creativity, enthusiasm and humor to support and inspire others as we all freely express our talents in joyfulness, harmony and love. I am dedicated to making a positive difference in the quality of life on planet Earth and beyond.

19

Accounts of Synchronicity and Serendipity My First Extraterrestrial Encounter

About 1986

I had left Oklahoma in May 1985 to travel for what I thought was to be three months.

Early in my travels, about 1986, Spirit asked me to attend the Earth Stewards gathering at the Big Springs Ranch outside Wendover, Nevada.

Norman Paulsen, author of *Christ Consciousness*, was responsible for organizing the commune of individuals at Big Springs. He had been one of Paramahansa Yogananda's original disciples and had assisted in building Yogananda's first ashram in California.

I did not really know what to expect when I went to the place, as was often true (and still is) when I am asked to go to a certain event or location.

Many people were in attendance from all over the country, along with numerous speakers and presenters.

One of the speakers was a professor from Stanford University who offered a slide show of the pyramidal faces on Mars. He made his presentation outside on a large screen.

It was the first time this slide show had ever been presented. Although the pictures had been taken by government cameras, they had not been revealed to the public.

During the show, the extraterrestrial ships hovered unseen over the event. They were very obvious to me. Beings from them kept telepathically tapping into my consciousness, insisting that I allow them to speak to the professor <u>through me</u> after his presentation.

I was very resistant to the idea of approaching him with such a suggestion, but finally I reluctantly did so.

He was very abrupt, fearful and skeptical. He kept saying he did not believe in psychic anything, that he was a scientist and that he was NOT interested <u>in anything</u> that I might have to say.

I cried myself to sleep that night.

The next morning, I mentally prepared myself to get into my car and drive to the next location – even though I wasn't sure where that was. All I had been given as a destination in meditation that morning was "California."

For breakfast, I went to a restaurant on the highway that was run by the commune. While I was eating, I overheard two women sitting in the booth behind me discussing past lives. I heard them say they wished they knew someone they could trust who could regress them to find out about their past life connections.

Spirit asked me to interrupt their conversation and offer my services to regress them.

I did so and learned they were attending the gathering from Palo Alto, California, and were leaving to drive back there. One was a massage therapist on a cruise ship, and the other was the secretary for the professor of Stanford (whom I had been asked to approach the night before).

I agreed to drive to their home in California to do the regressions. I stayed there two days. On the second day the phone rang. They were both at work, but I could hear the woman's voice leaving a message and got goose bumps. The woman calling was named Ruth. She wanted to leave word that she was in town from Carmel and wanted to see one of the women before returning home the following day.

I knew instantly, energetically, that I was supposed to meet Ruth. When Linda came home I asked her about Ruth and explained that I needed to meet her. (Ruth had assisted in writing an early metaphysical book, *The Betty Book*.)

When Linda reached her, Ruth explained that she and her friend Betty were much too tired to see us that evening (both women were in their seventies.) However, with my urging, Linda assured Ruth we would just stop by long enough to make introductions, give them a hug and then leave.

When we arrived, Ruth did invite us to sit for a moment. She was a large woman with beautiful, white hair and penetrating eyes that seemed to stare right through me as she gazed down at me from her chair as I sat on the floor.

"Who are you, and what are you about?" she inquired of me.

I began telling my story. As I talked, the energy in the room seemed to get stronger and stronger. About an hour and a half later, both women were lively and laughing. They did not want Linda and me to leave!

The following day, at her insistence, I drove to Carmel to see Ruth. During our visit, Ruth told me about a friend of hers, her former employer, Kay Ortmans. Ruth and Kay had been pioneers in the metaphysical movement. Kay had developed a method of massage, which she did to classical music. The method released trauma from the body. Ruth knew Kay had just returned from a trip to Russia and that she was quite depressed.

Ruth's one-room apartment was too small for me to even sleep there with my sleeping bag. Later in the day, she called Kay to inform her that I was on my way to Ben Lomand to visit her.

At first Kay was even more resistant to me than Ruth and Betty had been the night before. She had explained to Ruth that she did not want to have company, especially someone she did not know. Besides, she was busy reproducing a musical score that had been partially destroyed by fire.

As Linda had done the night before, Ruth kept insisting to Kay that she must see me. "You will enjoy her; she is quite amusing," Ruth soothed. "She'll be arriving in Ben Lomond about seven. I would so appreciate it if you would feed her and give her a place to sleep for the night."

I could feel Kay was unimpressed, but Ruth was adamant that I should go.

I arrived at dusk at the top of the mountain in the redwoods where Kay and her secretary, Mary, lived. Mary answered the door and helped me with my bags. She warned me Kay was in a foul mood and didn't want company. I said I understood and that I would go to bed immediately and not bother her if that would be best, but Mary insisted that she had prepared a wonderful vegetarian meal for the three of us.

As I sat down at the table, Kay inquired sternly, "Exactly who are you, and what are you about? Why was Ruth so insistent that we should meet?" Kay was English, imposing, authoritative and had the energy presence of an army general.

I was exhausted, tense, hungry and intimidated, but I began to tell them my story.

The women began to soften, relax and to laugh. As I talked, the energy in the room grew very strong. Two hours later the two were energetically high and wanted to continue talking! I only wanted to go to bed. It was already midnight.

Kay made me promise to give her a reading the following morning, saying she would give me a massage afterward.

She got me up at six o'clock. (I'm not normally an early riser, especially when I've gone to bed at midnight.) I did the reading and her guidance really came through.

When I tuned in to Kay's soul, a man began to speak in very intimate terms to her. At that time I had never heard of Rudolph Steiner, so I was not as impressed as she when he spoke to her through me. He talked not only about her trip to Russia, but about her work and what she was doing with the staff of the Santa Cruz Waldorf School. She took me to her bedroom and showed me a picture of him she kept beside her bed.

After the reading, Kay was so impressed that she demanded I stay another night and do a group reading for the staff of the Waldorf School. Members were to assemble in her living room for a board meeting the next morning.

I had no idea there had been tremendous conflict among board members and teachers. Neither had I ever heard of the Waldorf Schools (which had been created as a result of Rudolf Steiner's teachings). I stayed, and the next morning he counseled the board members and teachers through me. Everyone was pleased and seemed quite impressed. I left for my next destination.

During our conversation the second night Kay mentioned that she had a benefactor who provided the beautiful home she lived in and that she had "life estate" to the property. I asked what the term meant. "It means I can stay here as long as I live or as long as I want to, without the possibility of having to move." Like the word "Namaste," I knew this word was significant to me. I knew I wanted a beautiful place to live and I wanted "life estate" to the property. It would be 18 years before this desire became a reality for me.

A few months later, Kay offered a massage workshop in Apache Canyon outside Santa Fe, New Mexico, and asked me to be her guest. She wanted me to be present in her sessions with the participants, and for me to reveal to them what I was seeing and hearing while she performed the massage. When I arrived at the workshop, I learned the food provisions for the week-long affair had not been arranged. Kay promptly put me and a woman from North Carolina in charge of shopping and planning meals for the week.

At the end of the week I accompanied Kay to Santa Fe to meet her benefactor, whose son had recently committed suicide. But Kay was now a friend and wanted to be able to bring some closure to her friend and benefactor, and I needed money to get to my next destination, even though I didn't as yet know where that was. Channeling the spirits of persons who had recently died was not something I routinely did or wanted to do. However, I successfully communicated with the only son of Kay's friend.

After the session the friend and her husband were in such an emotionally and energetically altered state, they did not think to pay me for my services. The husband, a UFO enthusiast, had contributed to printing a very thick book called, *UFO Contact the Pleiades*. He gave me an unopened copy as I walked out the door to get into my van and drive alone to my next destination.

I was tired, irritated, nearly broke and depressed. I did not know how I was going to have enough funds to get to my next assignment. I had no interest in extraterrestrials and UFOs, and no conscious belief that they really existed. If they DID exist, I was pretty damn sure they had nothing to do with me. I considered myself a channel only for my soul and the Spiritual Hierarchy. I did not read the book. I tossed it, still encased in its cellophane wrapper, into the back of the van.

I drove to Denver to rest and be with friends who I knew would take care of me. While there I met a young man named Rocky. He wanted to learn to channel. He and I were from the same Oversoul, and Spirit asked me to assist him to open to the soul. He and I began working together in meditation.

The first regression I did with him involved a lifetime he spent on ALDERON. He was the first person I had regressed who actually showed up on another planet. The information we received was very disconcerting for me <u>and my belief structure at that time</u>. I was relieved the next morning when Spirit informed me I was to leave Denver and drive to Sedona.

When I called Rocky to explain that we would need to discontinue our sessions, he asked to go with me. His request disturbed me.

"I never have any idea where I will go next, I can't be responsible for you, where you will sleep, how you will eat, and all that," I tried to explain to him. "But if you want to follow me in your own car and be responsible for yourself, you can go."

The two of us left the next morning.

When we arrived in Sedona, Rocky drove on to Phoenix to spend the night with his grandparents, and I spent the night with a woman I had met on a previous visit to Sedona.

The following morning I was having breakfast alone at the Coffee Pot Restaurant. A nice looking man walked up to my table and asked if he could sit down and have coffee with me. I said, "OK."

He began asking me questions, like what did I do, who was I, where was I from, what was I doing in Sedona . . .

I answered most of them, but I had to admit that I did not know why I had been asked to come back to Sedona. Then he said, "I have a video I would like to show you."

I sat quite still for a few moments thinking about his offer. Was this a new, "Wanna come to my place and see my etchings" routine?

"I've seen a lot of videos. What's the name of yours?" I inquired cautiously.

"*UFO Contact the Pleiades*," was his reply.

Chills went up my spine and the hair stood up on the back of my neck. I really hate it when that happens in context of something I think I don't want to know.

"I'm traveling with another person who I am sure would want to see your video. Is there a time we could arrange to see it?" I inquired.

"Meet me tonight at seven here in the restaurant parking lot, and we'll drive out together to a friend's house who has a video player," he instructed as he stood up to leave.

Just as we were shaking hands, Rocky walked into the restaurant. When we made him aware of the video and our arrangements, he became very excited.

We did tourist things during the day and were at the restaurant at seven.

Three cars filled with people were going to see the video, so we caravanned out Highway 89A, toward Red Rock Loop Road, as darkness fell.

When we arrived at the turnoff to Red Rock Loop Road, we were amazed to see seven disk-shaped objects hanging in the air above the rim of the canyon. The objects were obviously not stars in the distance, but saucer-shaped objects with green lights around their edges. They hung motionless and soundless, but the energy field caused every hair on my body to stand up. Having my pubic hair at attention and my heart pounding was decidedly not a familiar feeling, nor one I enjoyed.

We parked the cars quickly beside the road and got out to watch.

All the time it was happening I had a sense of dread. I wished I were alone so I could pretend this was not happening. Some part of me knew that the events of this evening would change my life forever. The ships disappeared. We got back into our cars and proceeded to the house to see the video.

The video was actual film footage of Pleiadian Beam ships taken by a man named Billy Meyer who lived in Switzerland. It was about an investigation into their authenticity. All the time we were watching the film, I was receiving the telepathic message, "We want to speak to Rocky, we want to speak to Rocky, we want to speak to Rocky."

I telepathed back to them, "So, speak to Rocky and leave me the hell alone. I don't want to talk to you. This has nothing to do with me!"

Rocky could not hear them, but he could sense they were still near and that they wanted to communicate. He got up off the floor and went outside to see if the ships were visible. I continued watching the footage with intense fascination and dread.

When Rocky came back into the room he whispered, "bj, bj, they want to talk to us! I know they want to talk to us."

"I know, Rocky, but I don't want to talk to them. I'm a 'spiritual channel.' I don't want to have anything to do with them. You listen to them. They are using your name. They want to speak with you." I was really irritated with him AND the voice within my head. "Just hush and let me finish watching this video, and then I'll decide what I'm willing to do," I told him and myself.

When the video was over we got back in our cars and headed back to town. Just as we arrived at the same place on the highway, a huge Mother ship appeared in the sky above us. This vehicle was so large it could have contained all of the previous ships, plus all of the people in Sedona and Oak Creek! It arrived and disappeared just as silently as the other ships had, leaving us all with a sense of wonder and lightheadedness.

I agreed with Rocky to go back to our lodging and meditate to try to find out from my soul what was going on and what was expected of me.

We lit a white candle, stretched out on the floor in front of the fireplace and began deep breathing and counting ourselves down into a meditative state.

Just as I had reached the alpha level, we heard BAM! BAM! BAM! on the front door! I just about wet myself. I thought the beings from the ships had come to take us away, and I was definitely NOT ready to go with them! I still didn't know who they were or whether their intentions were benevolent. I was still sure this could have nothing to do with me.

Rocky jumped up off the floor and threw open the door. Outside were all the people with whom we'd watched the video. They'd all gone back out to the canyon to watch for more ships. They'd come back to get me, since I was the only conscious channel in the group.

I finally gave in and agreed to go with them.

By the time we'd reached Boynton Canyon, the extraterrestrials had created a dense cloud cover, like fog. They had done this to conceal what they were doing from the eyes of those who were not supposed to see them that night.

As we had driven slowly to the Canyon, one of the extraterrestrials tapped into Rocky's body and wanted to speak. Since Rocky's body was not energetically ready, it caused him to have difficulty breathing.

At that time I felt as if I was being blackmailed into allowing the extraterrestrials to speak through me. At the same time I was fearful for Rocky's health. (And I did not want to have to explain to his little Baptist mother in Amarillo, Texas, that her son died when an extraterrestrial attached itself to him energetically in the front seat of my car!)

When we had arrived in Boynton Canyon, I got out of the car and listened. There were 29 extraterrestrial civilizations in ships circling the Earth that night to change the magnetic grid system of the planet. They explained to me that both Rocky and I were from other galaxies and had agreed to come to Earth to assist in the evolution of the Earth and the Human species.

I found what they were saying difficult to believe – until later in the evening remembering the truth about myself. I began to remember the conversation with Lady Master Venus; my responsibilities aboard the ship I had come from; when I walked into this body in 1969. The energetic connection with the ships removed the veil the soul had so carefully constructed between my personality and the truth of who I AM at the level of my soul and when I AM out of my body while I'm sleeping.

A few years later my son, Cory, and I were traveling in California. I received a telepathic message to once again stop in Ben Lomond to see Kay Ortmans.

Though Kay was recovering from two knee replacements and was packing to move from California to another state to live with her son and family, she was very gracious about having Cory and me stop for a visit.

During our stay, she told me about the woman and her husband who had purchased the natural amphitheater – the mountain top on which she (Kay) had been living.

Cory and I walked up the hill to meet Barbara and Jim Thomas, the new owners and stewards of the mountain and natural amphitheatre.

I did not know then how important these two would become in my life . . .

> **"I cannot gather enough material to make perfect decisions in my life.**
>
> **I must become still and let the creative flow of ideas influence my decisions."**

20

A Mysterious Reading

In February 1988, I went to Lubbock, Texas, to stay with my two children while their father and stepmother took a trip. While there, I received instructions from my Soul to call a woman living in a small town in the Texas panhandle and make an appointment for a psychic reading. Since it is not my pattern to ask people in the Third Dimension to read for me, I assumed my Soul meant that I was to give this person a reading so that her soul could speak to her through me. At this time, I was still very much a novice concerning spiritual methods. I had only been traveling for two-and-a-half years, in response to my daily spiritual messages, and then only in the United States.

I made the appointment, which happened to be on the day following the return of the children's family.

The morning of the appointment I awoke to a West Texas blowing snowstorm. I asked for guidance as to the possibility of canceling the appointment. The immediate reply was, "*No. This is important.*"

With more confidence in the reply than in my ability to drive a car in the snow, I prepared to depart.

By the time I reached Plainview, the highway was declared closed. The wind was howling at 60 mph, the snow was severe and visibility was nearly zero. Moreover, the ditches on either side of the road were filled with cars and pick-ups. I had stopped to put 500 pounds of bagged sand in the back of my van, yet it seemed very light and fishtailed constantly on the slick surface of the non-visible highway. I invoked Angels to hold the van on the road between lines I could no longer see. I continued to drive. I must have been invisible because the highway patrol did not try to stop me.

I arrived at the psychic's home feeling tense, exhausted and "put out" that this meeting was not planned with better attention to weather conditions.

The woman was amazed that I had not called to cancel. She had telephoned all of her other clients and canceled appointments, but had no way of reaching me. She offered me coffee and led me to a back bedroom that had been converted to an office where she did her readings. She was short, jolly, round faced and overweight.

She wore a loose, flowered muumuu, sat at a coffee-stained card table in a folding lawn chair opposite me. She was the physical epitome of why I didn't want to be thought of as a psychic. She joked a lot and her sincere amazement that I had come through a snowstorm to keep my appointment kept coming up in her conversation. "Well, honey," she said, "since you've gone to so much trouble to get here, I'm going to give you a really good reading. Let's start by doing a brief astrological reading of the major players in your life – your children, boyfriends, your ex-husband, etc. Give me their birth dates."

I gave her all the information she requested. She filled out some small forms in front of her for a few minutes and then began to talk about the characteristics of the people in my life. She used what I call "astrologicalese" and I attempted to look interested even though I understood little of what she was saying.

While she spoke, I carried on a running conversation with myself in my head about what a waste of time this was and how I wished she would hurry and get through so I could read for her and get the heck out of the place. She chain-smoked in a small room ventilated only by an oscillating fan. It only swirled the cigarette smoke around as there was no place for it to escape. My head began to ache.

After completing the astrological portion of the reading, the woman handed me a deck of tarot cards. She asked me to shuffle them while thinking about my life and what I wanted to know. The cards were unlike any I had ever seen before.

While I shuffled the cards I was thinking, "Why am I here in this room with this woman, and how quickly can I get out of here?" I gave her no information about myself except my name, birth date and the place I was born. I did not tell her I was psychic, a walk-in, a teacher of metaphysics, or why I assumed I had come to see her.

After I cut the cards, she laid them out on the table in front of her and chuckled. "Well, we can certainly see that this is not your first time at the rodeo!" I was not at all clear about what this statement meant.

"I see here there are five significant men in your life." She began.

I immediately denied this statement, assuring her that I had recently narrowed my involvements to one man.

"Well, let's see here," she responded, "maybe we have someone else's cards. Sometimes that happens if the client isn't concentrating on themselves when they shuffle. My feeling is that this man's name is Ed." She pointed to the first court card lying on the table. "I also feel he is not still in a body, and that his death and funeral were very difficult for you. Looks like you have experienced several funerals recently.

"This next man's name is John, and he seems to be connected with these other two cards, which represent young people, possibly your children. This card seems to represent a man named David. This other one is a man named Robert, who is probably the one you think you have narrowed this down to. This one is a man named Jack, but we don't have to think much about him. It looks like he has just left on a long-distance trip and is getting married and will no longer be a consideration. Does any of this relate to you, or do we have the wrong cards?"

I'm sure my mouth was hanging open and that I was as white as a ghost. Everything she had said was totally accurate. I had never met any psychic who could tell the names of individuals by looking at the images on tarot cards! I could not even do it myself! I was extremely impressed and began to feel I may have misjudged the woman.

I stammered, "Please continue. You are absolutely accurate. Thank you."

After the tarot reading, the woman proceeded to look into a crystal dove, setting on the edge of the table. She seemed to use it as another psychic might use a crystal ball. According to her, images would form in the dove that related to either my past, current or future life.

The first things she said formed in the crystal were white birds. They, to her, meant her client had some association with Atlantis.

I listened, but I couldn't see what this had to do with me.

Suddenly the reader straightened in her chair and gasped, "Something else is forming here. I see a small, very old, dark-skinned woman who is sitting on a dirt floor in a grass hut in the middle of the jungle. She wants to talk with you. She has some things she needs to tell you and some things she needs to give you before she leaves the planet." The reader glanced at me, seeming to look straight through or past me, at the wall behind me.

"Stand up and look at that country in South America on the left," she commanded. "I think it would be Peru and look at the long name of a town there that would be in the Amazon jungle."

I thought to myself, "What a joke. This woman may be the best I've ever seen at tarot reading, but she's not worth a damn on a crystal ball. No one in Peru wants to speak to me. And I certainly have no intention of traveling to Peru or to any jungle."

Dutifully, I stood up and faced the world map hanging on the wall behind where I had been sitting. I stumbled over the pronunciation of "Puerto Maldenado."

"Right," the reader exclaimed, "That's it. That's where she is, or at least she's near there. Well, I see things are getting ready to change dramatically in your life as a result of this trip to Peru." I heard little else of what she said after that. Fortunately, about an hour later, she handed me a tape of the entire reading. Following that, I read for her, about her career in music and other aspects of her life.

When I prepared to leave the woman's home for Denver, the storm had ceased and the sun was out. Changes in weather like this are not unusual in West Texas. My eyes watered from the cigarette smoke, and now from the sun shining brightly on the snow. Maybe there were a few tears too . . .

"What if she's right? How could she be so accurate on the tarot reading and so far off on the other stuff? My God, what if I AM going to have to go to the jungle!"

As I drove north, my mind raced. I moved from fear to laughter at the absurdity of such a trip and to the disbelief in the entire experience.

I stayed with my spiritual family in Denver for several weeks. Shortly after my arrival there, Matthew, my Eighth Dimensional higher self, began to awaken me regularly about 3 a.m. to give me messages. It isn't unusual for him to do this, because at that time, the early morning airways are less filled with Third Dimensional activity. However, during my conversation with him each time, the image and awareness of a little lady sitting in the middle of the jungle in a grass hut would come into my mind and I would telepathically hear her speak.

In a meditation (February, 1988) I received this message:

"You expected me to speak in short broken sentences and less than adequate English. You think all who are not of your own culture are stupid, ignorant. We will proceed to ignore and overcome your prejudices of those with darker skin than your own.

"The stones which you have been shown in your vision were brought by the Brothers of Light when they came in their ships from the stars, planets of the Eastern Lights, for not all ships came to us from the East. Many came from other areas.

"As you have read, many of us have been on your planet for hundreds of years, aging without our physical vehicles. We are well preserved for 710 years, are we not?

"The time has come for me to leave your dimension. The ships will come for me and return me to our home planet of Venus. From there I shall continue to communicate with you.

"The greenery that is perceived in your consciousness, and the hut and the cave are all of my location. It was decided that I could work more effortlessly in this setting than had I chosen a more public location as you yourself did. Since our missions have been very different, yet the same, locations and styles were necessarily different. I would be an oddity in your civilization and you would be an oddity in mine. Yet our missions are the same: to assist Mother Earth, and her beings to survive their ignorance and greed.

"Each galaxy has its own attunement to the Source of its creation through sound. The vibrations are centered within each planet and individual Soul that inhabits each galaxy. The sounds themselves can be heard and reproduced by each one to attune to their Source. The Universal sound of "Om" or "Aum" is the key. However, many other sounds are possible and necessary for the shaping, procuring and manifesting of physical objects as you know them.

"The stones, or crystals themselves, are attuned to the various star systems from whence they came. They can be used when properly aligned around the Earth in a harmonic fashion to produce a force field to withstand any invading frequency.

"Symbols, which you will begin to remember, can be combined with tones and colors to cause materialization, dematerialization, reconfiguration of molecular structure, and change in density of the affects of gravity."

The small, dark woman appeared almost nightly, speaking of when I would come to Peru to meet with her at The Temple of the Sun. She said her village was 15 miles southeast of Puerto Maldonado and that she would be waiting to gift me with the information and artifacts that her father had left with her.

I did not speak to anyone about what I was hearing because it seemed so bizarre. I had no idea how I could physically, emotionally or financially get to Peru.

After several sessions communicating with "Maitreya," I became "willing" to go. However, I had been traveling for several years on my credit cards when cash was unavailable. This enabled me to journey to the various places to which I was told to go in meditation. But I was unwilling to incur more plastic debt in order to follow my guidance. I explained my terms to Matthew. "If it is important to the Soul for me to go to Peru, I ask for three things (1) a round-trip ticket, paid for up front; (2) someone from Peru to travel with so I will not get into trouble with the language and customs of the people, and (3) someone fun to travel with. Then I will go."

Henry Ford is quoted as saying,

"Whether you think you can or whether you think you can't, you're right!"

21

Peru

Spring and early summer, 1988

After stating the "conditions" which I wanted met before I would even consider making a trip to Peru, I felt completely confident that I would not be expected to physically go to Peru, much less into the jungle. However, within two weeks I received a phone call from North Carolina. A woman I had originally met Third Dimensionally at a Marcel Vogel Crystal Seminar outside Reno, Nevada, three years before, was calling to determine if I could meet with her in Frisco, Colorado. She told me she had just purchased a condo there and needed to fly out to inspect it.

Since Margie and I had enjoyed each other's company in Nevada, I agreed to drive into the mountains to "catch up" on the past three years.

I drove through yet another snowstorm to reach our meeting spot. When I arrived, Margie and I talked non-stop for hours. However, it was about 3 a.m. in the morning, and we had consumed half a bottle of wine before I mentioned the little woman in the hut in Peru who was invading my meditations. I prefaced the information with, "You're probably going to think I'm nuts, but I'm having this strange experience, and I really need to share it with someone."

Margie listened without interruption as I described the psychic in Texas, my reading and the messages I had received in meditation. When I finished I asked hesitantly, "What do you think? Am I crazy?"

"I don't think you're crazy at all, in fact the trip is already planned," Margie explained. "My friend Cecila, who was born and raised in Peru, is the tour guide and my friend Ann, who is a specialist in Latin American studies, will be going. You would make the twelfth person in the group going from the United States and Mexico."

Margie went on, "We will be picking up a doctor once we get to Peru; he'll be the thirteenth. We will be doing planetary energy work while there. All of these people are meditaters and believe they are being called to go to Peru. The location there that you mention isn't on the itinerary, but that shouldn't pose a problem. I would think if you once get into the country, that the woman will come to meet you."

I was overwhelmed by Margie's complete acceptance of what I had told her. I was even more surprised that a trip was already planned, but I protested. "I'm willing to go with you, and you and Cecila fulfill two of my conditions about making the trip. But there is still the question of the paid round-trip ticket." I was still determined not to incur more plastic debt.

"We will pray about it and I am sure we'll wake up with the answer," Margie declared confidently. We finally went to bed.

About 6:30 a.m., Margie woke me up, very excited. "bj, bj, I've got it! I'll sponsor you to come to Charlotte, Winston-Salem and Wilmington to do readings and workshops about walk-ins. That way you can make the money to go to Peru."

Since working for the money was not included in my "conditions" to Matthew, my Eighth Dimensional self, I just sat there staring at Margie as I considered her words.

"Oh, yes, and I am to buy your tour ticket and plane ticket as my contribution." She said with even greater excitement.

I burst into tears. All my conditions had been met. I had to now follow through on my promise to be willing to go "if" . . .

At the end of May, I went to Charlotte, North Carolina. Margie and I traveled within the state for three weeks doing workshops and giving readings. This did indeed provide me with money to spend while out of the country.

On June 18, 1988, Margie and I arrived at the Miami Airport. We were filled with anticipation, anxiety and fear, yet we were extremely excited too, about finally being on our way. At 5:55 p.m. we began the 17-hour flight to Lima, Peru.

We had properly prepared ourselves for this trip, or so we thought. We had been eating strictly vegetarian food for three weeks and drinking lots of water. We had also been doing yoga daily, including some rather rigorous psio-physic exercises to build stamina for climbing and lung expansion to assist in adjusting to the high altitudes of the Andes.

However, about an hour into the flight I began to feel very nauseous.

My liver and gallbladder were on fire.

Our spiritual sources had warned us that we would need additional protection. Because of the nature of the Universal energy work we were going to be doing, we would be causing tremendous interference in the efforts of the negative forces in the area. The conflict began in my body. I actually thought I was going to die before I reached Peru.

Nearly everyone on our team was an experienced energy worker. One of the members was an indigenous healer from Mexico City. When Margie told Luis how I was suffering, he immediately began working on me with crystals and energy. We all began to meditate. We took turns sleeping and watching each other energetically to counteract the attacks being made on each of us, which began nearly as soon as we were airborne. It took 11 of the 17 hours of the flight for the disturbance in my body to calm.

We arrived in Lima at 11:25 p.m. June 19. Our tour guide's family, whose members reside in Lima, met us with bottled water, fruit and bread.

The airport was chilly, with cold marble floors. No seats were available. We pulled sweats and jackets from our luggage and huddled together on the floor like homeless people. We also took turns napping on our luggage.

At 6:30 a.m. June 20, we left for Cuzco, Peru, the sacred city of the Incas. We were an exhausted, irritable group. Our salvation lay in the fact we were on our way to hotels and real beds in Cuzco.

Cuzco is referred to as the "navel of the world," a major energy chakra (or energy center) in the Earth's cosmic grid. The elevation is 11,400 feet above sea level.

The altitude did not help the nausea and light-headedness of group members. Our hotel, just off Cusipata, the town plaza, was authentically Peruvian (not a Hilton or Holiday Inn). The rooms were cold and sparsely furnished with hard cots. It was considered winter in Peru, with temperatures from 30 to 60 degrees.

The group's local tour guide met us and gave us some facts and information about Peru and Cuzco. At that point, however, we couldn't have cared less and fell into our bunks, exhausted.

But we found sleep impossible because of the nausea. The compassionate hotel owner brought us tea to drink that was made from coca leaves and the rinds of a special citrus fruit we were supposed to inhale. However, the nausea and headaches continued.

I and some other members of the group were taken to various hospitals and clinics to receive oxygen. The hospitals were incredibly dirty. The uniforms of the doctors and nurses, and the sheets on the beds, were spattered with blood.

However, the staff was amazing. They simply could not have been more considerate or compassionate. They hooked each of us to an oxygen tank and then sat with us for an hour while we breathed. They were extremely curious about America and Americans and asked us dozens of questions. The two physicians who attended me, husband and wife, seemed too young to be physicians.

Since some of us had made friends with the doctors, we were charged only about $6 for the oxygen. Some of the other team members, who went to other facilities, were charged as much as $75, since fees are not preset. Some were charged more than that simply because they were Americans and could obviously afford more. All types of medication are available over the counter without prescription in Peru. We were told what to ask for at the "pharmacia."

As we returned to our hotel, we were finally able to sleep with the help of ear plugs. (Our rooms were adjacent to a local cantina that played VERY loud music until about 6 a.m.) Water for showers was available for just one hour a day, too, so if we wanted a hot shower, we had to take it at 6 a.m.

On June 21, after unpacking and showering, we wandered out into the plaza in search of breakfast. The restaurant we chose offered delicious coffee with steamed milk, as well as omelets and French fries. Because of this food, we stayed with this eatery the entire time we were in this part of Peru. Cuzco remained our home base, too. From there we traveled to other cities and regions.

An additional guide – who was a member of the Universal Great White Brotherhood, an International and multi-dimensional spiritual organization – joined us. Ohenyio (Eugene to us) took us to the Sacred Valley of the Incas. (The word "Inca" means king or emperor.) We traveled 62.5 miles in a small van from Cuzco to the Valley. The Urubamba River flows through the Valley. We visited a stone altar, built October 7, 1962, during the *LaCumba Maila* (a great spiritual celebration). The occasion, in their opinion, was the commemoration of the 27th year of the Age of Aquarius.

When we returned to Cuzco later that day, we went to a cathedral in the city, formerly a Temple of the Sun. Years before, the Spaniards destroyed the temples and built Catholic churches on the same sites to dissuade the people from worshiping their own gods and to encourage them to become Catholic. I was discouraged to learn that each site was referred to as "Temple of the Sun." How would I know at which Temple of the Sun Maitreya intended to meet me?

While at the Inca Temple, we psychically felt the vast catacombs beneath our feet. Legend has it that the Incas buried golden artifacts in the underground tunnels rumored to extend all the way to Lima. We anchored the energy of the Cosmic Christ Consciousness into each location we entered.

Our trip had been arranged to fall during the week of June 24 because during this week, each year, thousands of Peruvians and tourists gather in Sacsahuaman to witness the Festival of the Great Winter Solstice and a reconstruction of the ancient *Inti Raymi* festival.

That year was no different. People came from all of the surrounding villages. The city of Sacsahuaman was filled to absolute capacity and military troops were brought in to keep order. Guards with machine guns were on duty at the entrance to many stores and restaurants.

We were taken to the massive fortress of Sacsahuaman where we visited Coricancha, another Temple of the Sun. The Temple had originally been the size of four football fields.

As I toured the ancient site I was thinking of Maitreya. In our nightly meetings sometime earlier, she had told me she would meet me at the Temple of the Sun. At that time I had assumed there was just one Temple. Now, I was totally confused.

I began searching the face of every older female we encountered, seeking recognition. By the end of the fourth day I was very discouraged. I had believed that if I made it into the country, Maitreya would seek me out, and I would not have to go into the jungle to find her. I slept fitfully at night, as did the other members of the group. We were tormented by the nightly psychic attacks, as well as by the loud music of the villagers celebrating in the cantina next door to our rooms.

I did not feel up to attending the *Inti Raymi* celebration in Sacsay-huaman. Some members of the group took slides with my camera of the 10,000 people crammed into the area and the majestic Incan ceremony.

I never regretted not going. I was overcome with exhaustion from the altitude, the energy transfers, psychic attacks, lack of sleep and all the climbing.

On June 23, we visited the caves of Csicuchay (cave of the monkey) and Kenko. Most of the temples were located at elevations of 11,000 to 16,000 feet. The views were awesome and always worth the struggle we went through to get there. Later, we took some time off to shop and visit with the natives who lived in the Square in Cuzco.

As I awoke on June 23, my guidance told me that after breakfast I was to enter the Catholic Cathedral on the Square to anchor the energy of the Cosmic Christ Consciousness. Ann and Margie went with me. We took incense with us and lit it before entering the Cathedral.

When I entered the Cathedral's foyer, I was stopped in my tracks by a large poster of the Pope. The message on the poster was that the energies of the Christ, as they were at the time of the Apostles, would be offered to the people of the Catholic Church on June 23!

I had to smile. The Pope and I finally received the same message! This somehow made me feel better, even though I had never actually believed that the Pope was directed by the Christ that I knew.

The caretakers of the Cathedral were most curious about the three American women carrying incense all around the church, mumbling prayers. When they stopped us to ask what we were doing, we just replied, "praying." They maintained their distance, but were obviously greatly relieved when we left.

In the afternoon we were taken to Ollantaytambo and the Tambo Machay fountains. There we performed a group ceremony, working on the grid system of the Earth and sending the energies of World Peace in twelve directions out into the World. Later that day, we repacked for our early morning excursion to Machu Picchu.

On June 24, we were to take an early morning train to Machu Picchu. We had been warned that while we were in the station we should watch our belongings very closely.

The station was soon teeming with people. Many persons were not leaving on the train, but were there to press up against tourists to steal wallets, etc.

As the swarms became denser, people pressed against us on all sides. Falling down was impossible. The children had been trained to razor slit the bottoms of backpacks and purses. As the contents fell to the floor, the children scooped up every item they could while adults made paths for them to escape and held us captive with their bodies pressed against us.

I felt objects fall out of packs on either side of me. Instinctively, I dropped straight down into a squat, bending over being impossible. I quickly picked up every thing I could reach, whether it belonged to me or not.

As we boarded the train, I asked if what I had retrieved belonged to anyone around me. Many of our group's important belongings – address books, wallets, passports, plane tickets – were in my hands. My own passport, plane ticket and monies were in a security packet next to my body. However, the bottoms of our backpacks had been slit open by razors.

Margie's makeup was stolen. She felt this was a lesson from Soul suggesting she needed to come out from behind her mask. Later, she replaced the makeup, including the brand of eyeliner she used. Though the liner wasn't legally available in Peru, she bought it from a street vendor wearing a large raincoat. The entire inside of his coat was filled with eyeliner pencils, just like in movies we had seen of men having an array of stolen watches pined inside a raincoat! He was concerned that she would turn him in for not having a vendor license! He could not have imagined how relieved she was to find a source for the brand of eyeliner pencil that she could easily acquire in America, but was not supposed to be available in Peru.

Hers was the most amazing manifestation I had ever witnessed. I could not have been more surprised if she had made the liner appear in the palm of her hand. She REALLY wanted her makeup! I'm sure I would have felt the same way had it happened to me. After all, didn't I take a butane-powered curling iron with me, just in case the electrical outlets were incompatible?

Once we were aboard the train, we sat for hours in the cold before it finally began to move. As the sun came up, the views were so beautiful through the jungle and up the steep inclines. We stopped in a village halfway up and were inundated with natives selling their wares through the windows of the train.

We stayed at the base of the mountains at a tourist hotel with "aqua caliente," hot springs. The springs were wonderful for our stiff, cramped bodies, but the hotel was worse than the one in Cuzco. We had to sleep in bunk beds, dormitory fashion, and use coed bathrooms in the halls. People knocked on the doors of our room all night and the smell of urine was nauseating.

The following morning, we got up early and boarded a bus that took us up a very narrow winding road to Machu Picchu.

Our first glimpse of the city itself nearly took our breath away. (Seeing Shirley MacLaine in *Out on a Limb*, and the version in National Geographic are just not the same as seeing it in real life). The view and the energy brought tears of familiarity to our eyes and opened our hearts. We were all immediately in an altered state of consciousness.

While we climbed around the ruins, we were mentally contacted by the Pleiadians and given information about their base, their point of entry and their use of the location.

While in the ruins I spoke with a man who was an astronomer from Washington, D.C. He asked us questions about why we were there. I was instructed spiritually to tell the truth. He was skeptical and kept trying to explain to me that the Pleiades were too young a configuration to have been involved in the events I was describing. He did give me his card, however, and asked me to send him whatever I received from them.

We had several past-life flashbacks during the day. At the end of the day we planted crystals and did various meditations.

We walked the distance back along the railroad to the hotel at "aqua caliente." How welcome the baths were to our tired bodies. We stayed up late listening to everyone's experience and the memories brought up by the energy of this awesome location.

On June 26, as I awakened to the street noises and reentered my body, I heard Matthew's voice (in my head) say, "*The energies do not support going to Arequipa today. Tell the others.*"

We assembled for breakfast at the usual restaurant. At this time I was under the impression that I was with a group of persons who meditated regularly and whose members received information from their souls. Therefore, I was sure I was not the only one aware that we should not go to Arequipa that day.

When I asked if anyone else had received the same message I had, everyone looked blank and incredulous that I should even mention a change in plans! The tickets had been purchased for our trip by train to Arequipa, and so far as the group was concerned, we were GOING to Arequipa, regardless of what the energy was like!

When I mentioned Matthew's message to the group their immediate rejection made me feel confused, disappointed and personally rejected. I felt that fear had caused the group members to begin operating Third Dimensionally.

I knew I should not go to Arequipa. I tried to think of other possibilities. My mind went crazy. I felt tremendous fear at remaining in Cuzco without the group. Members were to be gone several days, meeting with a local spiritual doctor and receiving healings. After Arequipa, they planned to go to yet another city before returning to Lima. I felt sick to my stomach. I stood up to retreat to the bathroom to think and saw a huge travel poster behind my chair that read PUERTO MALDENADO under a large Macaw parrot.

I retreated to a restroom to try to hear what I was to do. The message was clear: "*Leave the group. Go into the jungle for three days.*" I was appalled and terrified even more than I had been.

I left the restroom and returned to the table. I was crying and my body was shaking. Margie noticed my distress immediately and asked, "What is it? What's the matter?"

Through the sobs and heaving, I tried to explain. "Matthew sa-says I have to g-g-go into the jun-jun-jun-gle." Another series of sobs made the words nearly indistinguishable.

"Calm down. Tell me what he said," Margie demanded.

I stared at her. I was numb, afraid, but I was no longer confused. I KNEW what I had to do. However, I had no idea HOW to go about doing it.

I breathed deeply, as she suggested, and waited a few seconds. Then I told her what I had to do and how frightened I was at separating from the group and going into the jungle alone.

By this time Ann, our friend who spoke fluent Spanish and had a degree in South American studies, had joined our conversation. Both she and Margie agreed they would not let me go alone. They also stated that they were not particularly interested in going to Arequipa with the group anyway, and especially not if Matthew was indicating it was not energetically appropriate. They committed to accompany me into the jungle. They further suspected we would be in for the adventure of a lifetime!

We explained what we intended to do to the other group members and were met with mixed reactions. We gathered information regarding where and how to connect with them in three days. Then we left the restaurant to go to the travel agency.

In Peru, you must buy a plane ticket through a travel agency, rather than at the airport. You must buy the ticket the day before you travel, and you must be at the airport at 6:30 a.m., no matter what time your plane is scheduled to depart.

In the afternoon we shopped and repacked, trying to keep our minds off the possible dangers of the next three days.

22

More on Peru

We arrived at the airport at 6 a.m. The terminal was jammed with people and luggage. At least 40 people were ahead of us in each line. Our tickets had to be exchanged for boarding passes. In Peru, it is not unusual to sell more tickets than there are seats on a flight. Nor is it unusual for more boarding passes to be issued than available seats.

For some reason, not logical since I do not speak Spanish, I was holding all three of our tickets as we stood in line. A Peruvian man walked up to me and in perfect English demanded, "Give me your tickets."

Without questioning him or consulting with the other two, I handed him the tickets. Proceeding around the line I was in he took the tickets to the ticket agent. I could not hear what he said because of the noise and angry voices. In a short time he motioned for the three of us to move our bags around and through the throng of agitated people to the front of the line. He handed us our boarding passes and the agent took our bags. We stood mesmerized.

I opened my fanny pack, removed all of my Peruvian money and held it out to the man to take whatever amount was appropriate for the miracle he had just accomplished. He took a couple bills, smiled and walked away without comment. Ann said the amount he took equated to sixty-five cents in American money!

At this point I should probably explain that once in a foreign country, money feels like Monopoly money to me. I do not try to be exact about the exchange rate and such, as I've seen other people do. I simply trust that I will not be cheated and that I will have enough money to do what I need to do. As for the Peruvian man, he was obviously an Angel or an Ascended Master who had temporarily taken a body to accomplish an otherwise impossible task – that of getting us on our way to the interior of the Amazon jungle.

We sighed, relieved, as we finally settled into our plane seats, surrounded by the constant chatter of Spanish. We were fearful, yet excited too. What would we find when we landed? Would Maitreya be waiting at the airport? How would we find her if she wasn't? Would we be able to rejoin our companions in three days? Where would we stay in the jungle?

We were truly entering the unknown. Although we were without hotel reservations, we were filled with many personal reservations! The take-off was uneventful, but the plane began to shudder as the pilot sought to climb to a higher altitude in order to clear the mountains between us and our jungle destination.

The plane was apparently purchased used, from another country. When we decided to read to calm ourselves, we discovered there were no working bulbs in the reading lamps. We also noticed that many of the places on the plane where screws should have been were simply empty holes.

Feeling increasingly insecure, we began focusing on the outside of the plane, calling forth Angels to hold it in the sky and to get us safely to our destination. We worked at concentrating on the beauty of the jungle as it began coming into view, breathing deeply to calm our stomachs and our fears.

The trip, though bumpy, hot and smelly, was short as the landing strip suddenly became visible through the dense jungle foliage. The runway did not look long enough for the plane we were on, but the pilot was apparently accustomed to landing quickly. The airport was small. Only one plane a day flew into Puerto Maldonado.

As the wheels touched down, a large pig raced across the runway in front of the plane and dashed into the jungle. No village or river was visible.

We stepped from the plane into much warmer and more humid air than we had left in Cuzco. We approached the terminal unsure of where to claim our luggage. We also did not know we would need a ride to the actual village, some thirty minutes further into the jungle.

Before we reached the area to claim our baggage, a Peruvian couple approached us and began conversing with Ann in Spanish. The woman worked for another Peruvian airline. The two said they felt somehow obligated, or compelled, to assist us with our luggage and to arrange a taxi for us. They would not accept money for their help, but wished us an enjoyable stay in their village.

The taxi was a large truck with a wooden stake-like fence mounted to the bed. The only seats were benches along the sides of the truck. Any passengers not sitting on the benches had to stand and "hang on," or sit on their luggage.

As we rode along, Ann asked a man who was standing near us about accommodations in the village. He said there was only one hotel that would be appropriate for American ladies. He spoke to the driver, instructing him to stop in front of the "resort." As we arrived at the hotel, which was a cinder block two-story building, and prepared to leave the taxi, our luggage was thrown out to the ground.

As we surveyed the village, we were amazed: It consisted of one dirt street with what felt like four-hundred mopeds zooming constantly from one end of it to the other, stirring up dust. Lining each side of the street were grass and wooden structures, some covered with tin. Since Puerto Maldonado had appeared on the large World map, I had expected something much larger than this village with one dirt street! I sat on the steps of the cinder-block hotel with all of our luggage while Ann and Margie went inside to negotiate lodging. I was wide eyed, my heart beating in my throat.

Almost immediately, a short Peruvian man with a briefcase rushed up to me and began waving a brochure in my face and speaking rapidly in Spanish. I was frightened and appalled!

After several sentences, none of which I understood, I held up my hand to stop him and yelled, "Don't you speak English?" as if I had a right to EXPECT him to understand me even though I could not understand him.

He stopped speaking abruptly and stared at me. Then he replied, "Yes."

"So speak English! I can't understand a word you've been saying!" I was exasperated, more at myself than with him.

He began speaking again, just as quickly in English, but in broken sentences. "Not my day to come to village. Must pick up three American ladies from plane. Take them to my lodge in jungle."

As he spoke he continued to wave the brochure wildly.

I reached for the brochure. He was not asking me now, but directing me. "My man take your luggage to boat. I return in one hour get you. Go next door to restaurant, have lunch and wait me return." He ran it all together without stopping to breathe. I looked down at the brochure hoping it would help me understand his ranting.

Before I could ask, "How did you know to come to pick up three American women from the plane?" the man was half a block away. A much larger man was loading our bags onto a three-wheeled bicycle-sized affair with a wooden platform on the back. I cried as he pedaled away with our luggage.

I did not verbally protest these actions because the first Peruvian had said, "My man will take your bags to BOAT." The night before in meditation I had seen a long skinny canoe-type boat with a grass roof and a motor.

As the man pedaled out of sight, Ann and Margie emerged from the hotel. "Where are the bags?" they exclaimed in unison.

"Well, this man came and said he had been sent to pick us up and take us to his lodge in the jungle. His man took the bags to a boat. They will be back for us in an hour. We are to eat lunch next door and wait for him."

"You let a perfect stranger leave with all of our luggage?" Their voices were less than controlled. "How did the man know to come get us? The hotel manager said there are no phones in this village." Ann's voice was stern. (Cell phones had not been invented.)

I shrugged my shoulders as I handed Ann the brochure, printed in Spanish. I was close to tears as they both looked at me in disbelief. "Let's all go sit down and I'll tell you what I saw last night in meditation and maybe that will help," I offered.

As we were seated at an oil-cloth covered table in the sparsely furnished cafe, I explained about the boat. Since no water was visible from the plane when we flew in, a river was difficult for either of them to accept. Again we prayed internally to be protected and guided.

We ate French fries and waited, occasionally shaking our heads in disbelief that we were actually here and that these seemingly bizarre events were really happening to us.

In exactly one hour and ten minutes – possibly the longest ten minutes of my life – the first man returned. He (Juan) was still carrying his briefcase. In addition he carried a frozen, loosely wrapped, very large fish across his outstretched arms. The odor of the fish was unpleasantly strong.

He spoke quickly and then whistled. Three moped "taxies" responded to his signal. He then told us to get on behind the three sweaty drivers and to "hang on tight." We did as we were told and actually laughed out loud as much to break the tension we were feeling as at the ridiculousness of the situation.

We were much relieved when we saw the river, the motorized canoe with the grass roof and all of our luggage. Juan paid the moped drivers and offered us a hand boarding the boat.

Once seated and motoring up the Madre de Dios River toward Juan's lodge, I began asking him questions. "How did you know you should pick up three American women coming to the village from the airport?"

The only response or explanation he ever offered was, "I heard it on the grapevine." Then I questioned him about a medicine woman, or female shaman in a nearby village. To this he was even less helpful. As we continued motoring up the river I asked Juan if there was an actual Indian village nearby. He merely answered, "Yes." I persisted with, "Which direction is it in and how far from Puerto Maldonado?"

He waved one hand in the air (the one not holding the steering mechanism for the outboard motor). His gesture meant nothing to me. "What direction would that be?" I persisted. He merely stared at me. "I mean, is that south or southeast?" I tried to clarify my question.

"Yes, southeast," he responded curtly.

"And how far southeast is this Indian village?" I questioned.

He shrugged his shoulders and answered, "Four and a half hours up river, but you don't want to go there. They don't like white people to come there."

Maitreya had said she would be 15 miles southeast of Puerto Maldonado. I continued to question Juan, despite his obvious resistance.

"Can you take us there?" I almost pleaded.

"Well, I could, but I'd have to charge $10 each more. It would be waste of your time. It would be more enjoyable for you to take walk with guide into jungle tomorrow. You will be here such short time." Juan seemed quite put out with my questions and continued demand for information. He had no idea how determined we were to go and how much we would have been willing to pay.

I turned to Ann and Margie. "How does he know we are here only for a short time?" I asked in a lowered tone. None of us had mentioned the length of our stay. They both shrugged.

Juan stared at the water, concentrating on keeping the boat in the middle of the very muddy river. He seemed to ignore us as we discussed what he had said. I turned toward him.

"We *really* want to make the trip tomorrow if at all possible. It is very important to me." I stressed my words as I shouted over the roar of the boat's motor.

Juan threw up his hands in relinquishment and obvious exasperation. "You can go for short hike today after you are settled," he retorted almost angrily. "We will cook fish over pit. You be back in time for meal and to bed early. You need get up early to make trip."

The lodge was a circle of large grass huts on short stilts. The eating area was an open air restaurant with a pet Toucan bird, a spider monkey and an animal (similar to a raccoon) the crew had named "Rambo." (The Toucan bit me on the ear the next morning at breakfast while trying to get my fried bananas.)

There was no hot water at the lodge. Showers were buckets with holes in the bottom, suspended by ropes. The water was very cold and straight from the river. Bunk beds covered with mosquito netting were in the hut we were assigned. Pegs on the wall were the only provision for hanging clothes. We decided to keep all of our belongings in our suitcases – zipped up – to discourage insects from crawling in.

The walk in the jungle was wonderful, so quiet and peaceful. The only sounds were those of birds and monkeys. Butterflies were huge and brilliantly colored. Our guide was amusing and knew about medicinal uses of many of the jungle plants.

When we returned to the lodge, other people had arrived from England and there was much activity around the pit where the fish was cooking. Later, when we tried to eat the fish, it tasted awful – muddy and old – just like the river looked and smelled!

We doused ourselves with insect repellent and deliberately sat in the cover of the smoke from the fire. Yet we continually slapped ourselves and each other to kill the insects.

We three went to our hut immediately after the meal, and to bed. The others sat by the fire and sang songs until quite late. Sometime in the middle of the night I went outside the hut to relieve myself and was amazed at the stillness, the quiet and the energy of the jungle.

When I awakened the following morning I learned that Ann had become quite ill during the night and was not up to making the trip to the Indian village with us. She insisted she only needed rest and that we should go without her.

Following breakfast of fried eggs and bananas, Margie and I boarded a canoe for the trip upriver. Several English people decided to take the ride with us. A guide who spoke the native Indian language accompanied us.

I did not question him during the 4-1/2 hour trip, although I did tell him I wanted to get some parrot feathers. Margie and I mostly rode quietly, observing the passing river banks and listening to the talk among the others. The canoe stopped once for lunch. The mixed rice dish that was served had been stored in chests in the middle of the boat. As the canoe glided to a final stop, the guide pointed to a steep sand cliff about 40 feet straight up from the river channel and announced, "We are here."

Amazed, I asked him, "How do we get up there? Do they lower a ladder or a rope?"

"You just climb. Remember, we told you they do not want you here," he reminded me.

I pondered the situation quickly: I had come this far. I would make the climb in spite of my fear of what I would find at the top. Margie chose to come with me.

The sand fell away beneath our hands. We dug into the bank with our fingers to create handholds. We inched our way up the embankment. As my head crested the top of the bank I saw two bare brown feet. Then I saw a very short, wiry man in a burlap loin cloth and a three-cornered burlap hat. He had a canoe paddle in one hand and a long machete in the other. He stared at me.

As I pulled myself up onto level ground, I fully expected the man to either push me back down the embankment into the water, or chop my head off. He did neither. He just stared.

The guide was right behind me. He spoke to the man in Quechua. He introduced the man to us as the "wizard" of the tribe. When he said the word "wizard," the man grinned widely and pushed his little hat back to expose his forehead. A hole had been bored into his forehead to open his inner vision.

The guide told the wizard that I was there to get parrot feathers and asked if he had any. The wizard shook his head and walked away, entering his hut. I looked down at my feet. Discouragement enveloped me. Tiny colored feathers littered the ground where we were standing, evidence that a parrot had obviously been defrocked right at that spot.

Margie, the guide and I began walking up a trail toward an open-air building. Natives were inside their huts peaking out at us through gaps in the walls, whispering and giggling to each other. I could see inside the huts through open doors. There was no furniture, only fire pits in the center of each.

I need to explain here that the night before in meditation I had seen an image of a young Indian woman dressed in a red calico dress. The image was confusing because the dress was obviously one purchased in a store. Also, the woman's hair, although very black and full as would be expected, was expertly cut in layers such as is done in a beauty salon, instead of being blunt cut.

In meditation I was also told I was to return with the long tail feathers of the macaw. These are the most sacred of all feathers to the Indians and are used in their ceremonial attire.

As the three of us neared the building, we observed three women and several small children sitting in the pavilion. The women were weaving baskets, inserting small parrot feathers around the edges of each basket. The woman in the red dress, whom I had seen in my meditation, was perched on the rail of the hut-like building. She and the other women eyed us cautiously.

Our guide greeted the community. (All teachers in Peru had been on strike for a year.) The woman in red had chosen to come to this remote place to volunteer to teach these people so that they would not fall so far behind in their learning during the length of the strike. She told the guide she usually lived in a city. This explained the dress and the haircut. The guide asked her for parrot feathers. She said she had none.

(Before I left the States, I had been instructed by Spirit to take some small polished rose quartz and amethyst stones with me to Peru.) I began passing out these stones to the women and children. I also began playing peep-eye with the children as they hid behind their mothers and the corners of the building. All of us began laughing with the children.

After a very short time the teacher in red asked the guide why I wanted the feathers. As he turned to me and repeated her question in English, I showed her a picture of me from a current brochure. I was dressed in buckskin and had my medicine shields from previous vision quests behind me. I simply said the word, "Shaman," hoping it was translatable in her language.

She grinned widely, jumped down from the railing and ran up a path. She disappeared into a hut. When she emerged, the entire front of her dress was filled with blue, green and yellow parrot wing feathers. When she offered them to me, I asked her in the only Spanish I knew, "How much do they cost?"

She replied by smiling and holding the stone I had given her to her heart. I was moved to tears and gratefully accepted the feathers, trusting they would fulfill the mission Spirit had sent me on.

All of us stood around for a while longer as the English people handed out postcards of the Queen, Buckingham Palace and the Palace guards. The natives were as intrigued as any of us would be if we looked at pictures of inhabitants from another planet!

The teacher continued to watch me play with the children. After a brief time she asked the guide, "How many feathers does she need?" When her question was translated into English, I replied, "All she can spare."

At the guide's words, the teacher jumped down again and raced off up the path. This time she entered the wizard's hut. She emerged shortly with the coveted long red tail feathers of the macaw.

When she offered them to me, I once again asked, "How much do they cost?" This time she indicated that she wanted the other color of stone I had not given out yet. Instead, I reached into my fanny pack and brought out an amethyst, which was set in gold and was on a gold chain. As I placed it in her hand, an energy passed between us. Her eyes lit up and mine filled with tears. At that moment I KNEW I had received what I had come all this distance to acquire and to accomplish.

Margie and I laughed and waved as we returned to the boat and our very hot trip back to the lodge. Accompanying me was a sense of satisfaction: even if I had not met Maitreya at the Temple of the Sun as she had at one point suggested I do during her messages to me back in the States, I had at least successfully accomplished a part of the mission

Margie and I were hot and tired when we returned to the Lodge. The cold, muddy-water shower felt good. Ann had recovered from being ill and listened eagerly to the account of our day's experiences. Following that, I fell into bed – without even eating. I immediately went to sleep.

In the middle of the night my soul awakened me. The vision of Maitreya returned. This time she smiled and said only one sentence, "You are now the woman in the hut."

Even now, years later, I still vividly remember the rush of energy which came into my body at her words. I was aware that I would never see her in physical form. I was also aware that the mission to merge with this aspect of my Oversoul had been completed. Little did I know, though, or imagine what the gift of her knowledge and energy would lead me to next!

23

Working with the Dolphins and Whales

September - December 1989

In September, I spent many hours at my friend Judi's home in Denver. I had met Judi in 1985 when I first began to travel. She was the real estate business partner of my children's godmother, Val. Val and Ray, my children's godparents were two of the first people I was sent to during my travels to tell my story of what was happening to me. The week I arrived at their home Val had planned to go to Las Vegas for the weekend with a girlfriend. Friday night I told them the story. They were shocked and looked disbelieving. Raymond had been one of my ex-husband John's closest friends. They were both firefighters. Raymond was very judgmental about my leaving John and the children. Val left me with him during the weekend she was in Las Vegas. When she returned she said, "If I had heard this story from anyone else I could dismiss it as bullshit, but coming from you, I have to believe it and I know it is going to change my life whether I'm ready or not. She introduced me to Judi, and Judi and I became instant friends. Judi is one of the most loving, generous people I have ever met. Her home had a large basement with bedroom and bath and during the rest of my travels her space was always available to me when I was in the area. I traveled out of her home for four and a half years.

That week in '89, I spent the time bringing order to my possessions, clearing files, giving away accumulated objects and alphabetizing the Namaste library, which Judi allowed me to leave at her home. I also spent a lot of time quietly reflecting on the past year. I felt stronger and more productive every day.

September 30 was the seventh anniversary of my first written message from Spirit.

From October 2 -19, I traveled to the beautiful Pacific Northwest and enjoyed my trip and rest there. I learned even more about myself, as one tends to do when involved in a close personal relationship. I had manifested a relationship in 1986 with a man who lived in Vancouver, WA. He was a close personal friend of my friend David, mentioned earlier. This relationship brought to my attention many things I wanted to know, and I became aware of many things I would like to have ignored. However, once we understand – if we are true seekers – we are called to do something to correct our natures, our attitudes, our environment. The relationship made it possible for me to have someone who cared about me and was willing to come to wherever God had sent me or to fly me to where he was once a month for a four-day honeymoon. It worked well for many years.

In October of 1989 we were all given the privilege to work with the mighty Elohim.

The Elohim are the forces representing the foundations of the physical Universe, which allow "form" to remain in place . . . the laws of physics. The Elohim hold certain Laws in abeyance that govern the experience of physical consciousness. They, of course, work only from the realms of Cause on Solar Levels, establishing force fields in which the final effects occur.

Also, the Archangel Michael was in his Etheric Focus over Lake Louise and Banff, Canada, and opened a retreat to his chelas from his Feast Day, September 29, through October. Archangels represent the Solar Feeling Nature of God. It was an exciting time.

In mid-November, I traveled to Santa Fe. The trip was very interesting, productive, and exciting, but tiring. I went from there on to Sedona, Scottsdale, San Diego and Los Angeles.

Sedona was as wonderful as ever. We had lavish accommodations at a splendid resort, thanks to my friend, Jan. We allowed Spirit to guide our moves and met new people, connected with old friends and enjoyed the beauty of the canyons and their energy.

After two days, we were awakened at 3:30 a.m. by Spirit and urged to leave for California. At the end of a long day, we arrived in Los Angeles and spent time with Jan's daughter.

We also visited the Bodhi Tree, an astounding metaphysical bookstore. I remembered being there years before with Peter, before my attempt to kill myself by jumping off his boat. I had to laugh at how far I had come from that day.

Of all the books there, it both amazed and amused me that Jan was led to *The Green Stone* and *The Eye of Fire*, two books I had been directed to read two years before. The books are true accounts by an English author of a group of psychic people gathered in Glastonbury doing energy work similar to what my supporters and I have been asked to do around the country.

We had planned to do energy work at the library at UCLA, while in the Los Angeles vicinity. However, we somehow mistakenly concluded that UCLA was located in San Diego, so we pushed on south.

The following day we ran into Ann Remick-Barlow at Marine Land in San Diego. A former housemate of mine during the time I spent at her retreat center outside Charlotte, North Carolina, Ann just "happened" to have been sent to San Diego from Charlotte at the same time I was there. Then I knew why Jan and I had not done the energy work at UCLA: I was supposed to do it with Ann!

The work with the dolphin and whale energies in Marine Land was very exciting. We were even allowed to feed these delightful creatures.

The dolphins were fun and entertaining; working with the whales was not what I expected. While Jan and Ann sat in the bleachers watching the whales perform, I stood in a glass hallway above the tank that held the baby whale, Orca. (The scientific name for the species is *orcinus orca*.)

Orca circled the tank and swam directly under me several times. As I started toning, the baby whale began to turn over on its back as it passed under me. Its underside became bright pink as it sent love energy to me and opened my heart chakra. I began to cry.

I felt pretty silly standing there in a public place uttering strange sounds and crying with love and relief! Fortunately, the hallway was empty and filled with piped music, so only the whale noticed the toning. I was truly grateful to have been blessed with such an experience.

The next day, Ann and I traveled to Los Angeles in a car I had rented. We sat on the steps of the library at UCLA and connected with the Dolphin/Whale energies, doing our toning as directed. We grounded those energies of love and peacefulness into a meridian that runs through that area. Again, we might as well have been invisible for all the notice others paid to our presence and to the strange noises we made. (Who knows, maybe we actually WERE invisible!)

Spirit told us the reason I was sent to San Diego first to work with the energies instead of to the UCLA location was that the energies that were to be grounded into the spot were the Dolphin/Whale energies of Sirius. This information helped me to get over the anger about the inconvenience of the extra 400 miles I had had to drive!

Spirit also told us that the purpose of the energy transfer was to avert an atomic explosion that the Spiritual Hierarchy saw as potentially happening on November 21. (I had thought it pertained to possible earthquakes.)

When we asked where the possible explosion would happen, the reply came back, "all over." We did not understand what that meant, but trusting, we continued toning until we were told the transfer was complete. Also interesting to us was that we were doing this trip and the condensed energy work on the days of the Time Warp – November 18, 19 and 20!

After the work was completed at the library, we called Marcus Bach at his home and drove by for a visit. Meeting Marcus in person had been seven years in the making. He had been initially mentioned to me when I first began receiving messages in 1982. Interestingly, he had the original "serendipitous" greeting card still in his files that I had sent him at that time. However, he said the manuscript of the workbook, *Finding Your Life's Purpose*, which I had mailed him when I left Charlotte, had not reached him.

Marcus receives approximately twelve requests a week from people soliciting his assistance with manuscripts. Had I not had this opportunity to contact him personally, it is very unlikely he would have read my manuscript, a copy of which he requested I send him. (Marcus is the cousin of the man from Texas who in 1982 was sent to pay my debts and buy the photo copy machine.)

In connection to my visit with Marcus, it was particularly interesting to me that several things that had happened seven years earlier were now resurfacing in some way. Many of the same people, places, experiences, energies and events were being brought back into my life. When I returned to Judi's home in Denver, I was instructed to turn on the TV. I did so, tuning into a news special about a series of atomic missiles that our government had purchased from one of the leading aircraft manufacturers. The missiles had been placed around the country as anti-missiles, in case of attack. These missiles, it had just been discovered, were linked together by apparatuses assembled with defective bolts, which were already beginning to rust and crack. The government had not paid the $40 million bill, and was refusing to pay until the bolts were replaced with bolts of appropriate quality.

Needless to say, this program clarified why Spirit had said, "all over" when we asked about the exact location of the potential atomic explosion.

Regarding the explosion, about this time in 1989, Dr. Earlyne Chaney, the primary channel for Astara, a Mystery School in Upland, California, experienced a vision indicating that while the rockets were still in the silos, something caused the warheads to disintegrate, triggering an accident causing at least one American rocket to launch and detonate in the atmosphere over the United States. Dr. Chaney saw a radiation leak that would not be picked up by detectors. The vision revealed that the cause of the disaster would not be so much Human error as corrosion or mechanical neglect and the effects of the missiles and their container silos aging. In the vision, Dr. Chaney saw the atmosphere above the United States catching fire, resulting in unbelievable horror and devastation below.

Fortunately for all living things on the planet, something took place that averted this horror. In April or May 1990, Dr. Chaney announced that the danger she saw in her vision had passed.

I want to interject an explanation concerning some of the experiences I had on this trip:

Many times when our guidance or intuition asks that we take certain action, we are not given much specific information as to "why." Sometimes, in fact, the guidance/intuition given us is barely enough to motivate us to attempt the task. But we must TRUST that we will later learn more, or will BUILD OUR FAITH through accepting and doing.

January 1990

I was encouraged by all the changes that were taking place on the planet. I could finally see physical evidence of the energy work that had been accomplished through many of us. Spirit's message to all of Humanity at that time was also very encouraging:

"*Because of your Sacred accomplishments in 1989, great Forces of Light from the Sun can flow through your Solar identity and anchor within the cells, atoms and electrons of form, with which you are also One. For establishing this service, you are cherished throughout the Universe, and your names are known among the Stars.*"

The following message from Spirit to Humanity was even more exciting:

"*It is time for graduation from BS (Being Scared) and BA (Bad Attitudes) degrees, to working on your Masters degree (Making Spiritually Based Decisions).*

"*Before your incarnation into Earth's third dimension, you chose a curriculum, a course of study, if you will. You chose your subjects, teachers and classmates (family). Subjects you may have chosen include:*

Birth Trauma (101)
Only Child/First Born/Middle Child/Youngest Child Syndrome 101
Child Abuse or Dysfunctional Family 101
Incest, Rape, Sexual Molestation 101
Adolescence and Puberty 101
Fear and Guilt (202) Surviving Religion 202
Physical Illness 202
Addictions/Enabling Addicts 202
Abandonment 202
Marriage/Relationships/Divorce 303
Sexuality/Parenting/Abortion 303
Military Service 303
Rejection/Drama 303
Depravation or Opulence 303
Unemployment/Bankruptcy/Business Failure 303
Understanding and Accepting Death 303

"*You chose these to balance either your karma or that of another and to begin to remember who you really are as a spiritual being. When you begin to identify with your Spiritual Self, you are ready for graduation to the Masters Degree program.*

"*Now is the time of choice. Those who choose to identify with their Spiritual Self will begin to have less drama and more peace and spiritual understanding, i.e., become Masters. Those who choose to remain grounded only in material reality and in the acts of competition and conflict will become even more confused and depressed. Their lives will increasingly fill with drama, until they leave the Earth plane.*

"*The first step to spiritual maturity and "knowing thyself" is to begin getting outside your self – to become an observer of your thoughts, attitudes and actions.*

"*Those choosing to enter the Masters Degree program will accept that they are individualized expressions of God operating in the third, as well as other dimensions, simultaneously.*

"*It is time to see your selves as Planetary Citizens and Cosmic Citizens. This will bring a sense of understanding, not only of the greater whole, but also of the events taking place on the Earth and beyond. You will see there is no injustice, BUT there <u>are</u> results of thoughts held in minds (results which* out-picture as the realities we see on Earth).

"Through technology and energy, the World is shrinking. You are a part of a whole Humankind on Earth. Accepting the truth of who you are (a Spiritual Being inhabiting a Human body) will bring joy, spontaneity and co-creation. BUT FIRST IT MAY MAKE YOU MISERABLE AS YOU JUDGE THE PAST AND ACCUSE OTHERS.

"It is time to graduate from the past. It is time to accept unification – accept Earth and her inhabitants as a part of the One Energy.

"Many people are seeking an anchor in your World, a World that seems to have gone berserk. They work to provide financial security, cling to relationships, homes, jobs and patterns of life that, in many cases, are stifling, miserable and debilitating. They do this to have an anchor, an identity, a sense of themselves, a feeling of security. They require sameness to feel secure. And when changes occur, they become very insecure and angry.

"Using attachment as anchors will eventually make individuals – people – miserable or leave them adrift when circumstances change.

"There are no anchors, only a lifeline to your soul through which your soul feeds information and energy to the Spirit that inhabits your body.

"Having a working knowledge of the cord that connects you to your soul, and the ability to communicate with your soul is the only security to remove the fear of death and the feelings of insecurity. The only true sense of peace comes through the ability to communicate with the Higher Self. There is no greater sense of satisfaction than knowing you are in the right place, doing the right thing, in alignment with your soul's purpose.

"The CHOICE to stay attached to objects, places, relationships, the past, sameness and false security IS AN OPTION. However, the time has come for many on Earth to accept their diplomas and to move out of the drama of karma . . . the past."

As other countries open to democracy and spiritual freedom, I am convinced that the energy work we have done and are continuing to do IS MAKING A DIFFERENCE in the quality of life on planet Earth and beyond. This is the purpose I have chosen to serve, and I challenge you to commit to your own purpose.

In this regard, Spirit says:

"Let this time that acknowledges the entrance of the Christ Consciousness into physical form upon your planet, be a time when you enter the manger of your own self to witness the birth of the newness of 'you.' Leave the outer World of illusion filled with its tinsel and glitter and enter into the Presence of the True Light. Remember, children, everything in the outer

World is illusion and will fade from view and become memories.

"You, the Christ 'I AM,' are the Keeper of the Divine Plan of your physical incarnation. To bring more and more of the I AM Presence and a greater conscious understanding of the purpose of this incarnation into your physical being, use the Soul Mantra:
*I AM the Soul.
I AM the Light Divine.
I AM Love.
I AM Will.
I AM Fixed Design.*"*

Repeat the mantra for five to seven minutes to create the vortex of energy.

* (Fixed Design refers to the original Plan for the Soul in this incarnation.)

24

The New Jerusalem, Mexico and Central America

April 1990

Another level of knowing seemed to be opening within me. It appeared directly related to the merging in consciousness experienced during the time I spent in the Amazon jungle and the grass hut in Peru in 1988.

For two months, I had indeed experienced much awareness, on both a planetary and personal level. This awareness was difficult to express in words because it was more like feelings than experiences. For example, while I began to better understand my "purpose," there was a vagueness as to how I would physically <u>act out</u> this purpose. For several months I had felt an energy of completion and finally solidification of some ideas which had been in my consciousness in very vague ways.

About two weeks after my return home from Peru, I began considering going to Mexico, the Yucatan and parts of Central America. However, my physical and emotional bodies were not ready to go then. I did travel to the East Coast and places in between.

About February of 1990, the opportunity came for a trip to Cancun, Mexico City and various cities in Guatemala. At that time I also began to understand the reason for this travel:

For about 13 days, several persons I know were asked by Spirit and the Space Brotherhood (now consisting of 37 different "beyond Earth" civilizations) to participate in the docking of the New Jerusalem (the City of Light). This immense "City" would move into the Fifth Dimension above the Yucatan/Mexico/Guatemala area.

The New Jerusalem is approximately the size of the Gulf of Mexico. It was not possible for this vessel to come into the Third Dimension without wreaking havoc with Earth's electromagnetic fields, gravity, and the rotation and axis of the Earth. Stationing itself above the equator (in the fourth Dimension) would help stabilize the Earth and stop the possibility of the Earth shifting on its axis.

I was told that the docking of this Energy City would affect people on Earth as well. Some would be affected in positive ways; some in negative ways. Everything was to be intensified, both pleasantly and unpleasantly. I understood that many persons would choose not to survive the energies of this City of Light (which are to intensify the Cosmic Christ vibration). Some would create illness, some accidents, others would choose suicide as alternatives to staying on Earth and being subjected to the resulting events.

I further understood that those of us who agreed to take part in the docking of this "City" would act as grounding agents for the energy. You can understand our responsibility if you visualize a hot air balloon being tethered to the Earth by throwing out ropes attached to sand bags. Regarding the New Jerusalem, we were to attach the energy beams from the vessel to the vortex on which each pyramid was built (these vortexes remain from previous civilizations). These pyramids played a part in the docking of various Light vessels, previously, into the fourth and fifth dimensions.

My understanding was that we would be energetically beamed aboard the Ship for instruction and adjustment of our circuits and light bodies. These boardings were scheduled at the time to be non-physical. However, recent visions lead me to believe we would retain memories of the events and return with energies and awareness not possessed previously.

I understood, too, that many other persons had also agreed to assist in the grounding of the New Jerusalem, although they were not aware of it and didn't travel physically to the location. These persons went in their etheric bodies during sleep periods, many individuals required more night time sleep during that time, and possibly naps also.

One morning, I channeled a being named Korton from the Space Federation. He spoke of ways that everyone (not just those of us going physically to the docking) could help adjust to the energies of the New Jerusalem.

Korton suggested that (a) between April 11 and April 28 (1990) people be near water. If that wasn't possible, baths would help. (This was useful in preventing gaining weight, as one attempted to ground him/herself by overeating.) (b) the use of products which would oxygenate the blood, such as organic germanium and Aloe Vera/H2o2. (3) the practice of "even breath" (the in-breath being equal to the out-breath) and breathing as deeply as possible.

Korton further said that as the docking occurred we might experience headaches or lightheadedness, especially if we didn't do anything to oxygenate our blood; we might feel our own heaviness, our own density. He said we might experience tingling around the mouth, the eyes and in the entire head area. This could include pressure behind the eyes, a burning sensation on the soles of the feet, palms of the hands and pressure at the base of the spine and neck. He suggested people use Emergen-C, instead of cola drinks and avoid chocolate (my two last vices), alcohol and caffeine during the week of docking.

Korton explained that the intensity of the new energies might be particularly destructive to the calcium levels in one's body, i.e., bones and teeth. He suggested sources of absorbable calcium. Also that vegetarians might feel the need to eat white and red fish and some seafood – possibly even chicken and turkey (no pork or beef). He also recommended that everyone have carrot and pineapple juice, baked potatoes, corn, bananas, and eight glasses of water a day.

Changes that people might feel because of the new energies included: (a) ringing in the ears; (b) sluggishness (everyone required more rest because their bodies were trying to integrate energy that was restructuring their bodies); (c) strange eating patterns (less food . . . more food . . .) (d) hunger cravings (overeating, attempting to satisfy); (e) change in food consumption because of the molecular restructuring that began about 18 months before; (f) pains in the back of the neck and sacrum; (g) shortness of breath; (h) erratic heart beat; and (i) flu-like symptoms due to the energy breaking up old patterns and blockages.

On the brighter side, I was also informed that most people who were open would begin to experience more visions, experiences of synchronicity, more dreaming – in general, more psychic experiences – as the energy intensified.

Armed with all the above information, I took off for the Yucatan. I first rested in Cancun in a beautiful condo belonging to my friend Carrol who had volunteered to go with me, one of my two traveling companions. The first few days she and I spent many hours out of our bodies. We would arise early, have breakfast, go down to the beach and lay under a grass umbrella to read, two pages later we would be asleep. Just before time for lunch we would both wake up and look at each other and laugh. After lunch we would try again to read and again after about two pages we would be sound asleep, waking again at about 5 o'clock in time to shower and dress for dinner. We could hardly believe we could sleep so much!

When Chris, our other traveling companion arrived from Oklahoma City, we rented a Volkswagen bug and began our energy work.

Our first stop was Tulum, south of Cancun on the coast. I reacted unpleasantly to our arrival. Many large busses full of tourists preceded us. I became very irritated with the aimless and unaware throngs surrounding me, as I questioned, "Why am I expected to do energy work in this crowded, hot environment?"

That evening I had a long discussion with my guides. I explained emphatically that I was NOT happy with these conditions; that I wanted fewer people around me, and lower temperatures.

The following day we left Cancun for Chichen Itza. Because we misread the map, we thought we had a two-hour drive ahead of us. The "two-hour" drive took <u>over</u> five hours! Total darkness, jungle villages, bicycles, animals and speed bumps kept us moving at a crawl.

Irrationally irritated, I mentally griped and protested even more. My inner guide's response was repetitious: *"In the morning you will be glad you have made the drive tonight."* This was nearly impossible for us to believe!

We awakened the next morning in a beautiful lodge near the ruins. This made it possible for us to visit them in the cool of the day with almost no other tourists present. (I had to concede my guidance was right.)

What a pleasant experience! We were awed by the size of the ruins. They are much larger and more sophisticated than those in Tulum.

At this point on our trip, I remembered a recurring vision I had had a few days before leaving for Cancun. The vision had begun with a portion of the sky turning different colors, followed by the appearance of eyes, and then a display of various versions of space craft. Therefore, when the sky began changing and the energy shifted, in the plaza of Chichen Itza I waited excitedly for what was to follow. But I was disappointed when in this time/space, neither eyes nor space vehicles appeared.

The three of us moved on to the museum on our way out of the ruins. There, I caught my breath. There was a large circular object carved from stone and covered with eyes, as if it were the Mayan's depiction of the space ships that observed them from the sky! In fact, when we later developed the slides I had taken they revealed a distinct image of a very large spiritual being standing atop one of the stone configurations beneath the changing sky in the plaza.

My companions and I proceeded to Merida and flew to Mexico City. There we left Chris who had not been able to get a passport in time to enter Guatemala with us. He remained in the care of Luis, a Mexican friend who had traveled with me to Peru two years before. The following morning Carrol and I left for Guatemala City.

We were quite impressed with the friendly people of Guatemala. We were also pleased we had left Mexico City's pollution behind! We met our very friendly tour guide and boarded a bus for our hotel. After a group of Swiss tourists was dropped off at their hotel, Carrol and I were the only passengers left on the bus. At that time, as if guidance had placed him, a man caught a ride on our bus for a very short distance. He immediately began telling us of the central market, its location, prices, etc. He was from Cincinnati and worked for Chiquita Banana, Inc. Later, we went to the market, which covered a city block and was thronged with people. In the midst of all of the confusion, this man walked up to us again, as if it had been prearranged! (Many times on this trip people we needed dropped from the sky, so to speak, or materialized in front of our eyes.)

The following day was a free day for us in Guatemala City. We meditated about what we should do. The message we received advised us to go to the lobby of the hotel; we would then know what to do.

In the lobby, we requested transportation to Lake Atitian. The tour guide suggested we rent a car and drive ourselves. While we were making arrangements for the car by phone, an American woman on crutches approached the tour booth and asked for transportation to Antigua. (Antigua is an ancient city that was the capitol of Guatemala before the earthquake.) The attendant suggested she might ride with us since we would be going through Antigua on our way to Lake Atitian.

The woman, named Barbara, was a charming person from Manhattan, New York. She travels often and alone. We had a delightful chat as we drove along. After she found out we were spiritually oriented, she confessed she felt there was a spiritual reason she had been involved in a plane crash in Denver in 1985. The crash resulted in many months of hospitalization and therapy and was the reason she was on crutches. As we entered the gates of Antigua, a man appeared in front of our car. We had no choice but to stop. He stuck his head in Carrol's window and announced his name was Hugo and that he was to be our tour guide. "I have been a guide 28 years and I am NOT put off in the least by psychic American women!" We told him we would only be there for the morning. He agreed and took over driving the car.

The places he took us included the homes of friends of his who were weavers This allowed us to purchase original work not found in the market. He also took us to a black jade factory in the home of a friend. We purchased black jade, found only in Guatemala and Persia. It was much less expensive than if purchased in the government factory. In addition, we went to a Chinese money changer who was open on Sunday when all the banks were closed.

In Antigua the previous weekend there had been an Easter parade and celebration. We had read about the beautiful floral floats and the carpet-like patterns they made in the flower-and-sawdust-lined streets as they moved along. We lamented that we'd missed all that beauty. And then Spirit created a mini version of the celebration, just for us: Hugo took us to the Cathedral of St. Peter of Beancur and the feast day celebration. As we arrived, one of the majestic floats with St. Peter's statue atop was being carried from the church. A gathering of Indian people attired in their native dress was also attending the festival. Inside the Cathedral, the shrine was covered with letters, crutches, and tributes to the Saint for healing that had occurred there. The energy was phenomenal!

We never did get to Lake Atitian, choosing instead to remain in the charm of Antigua for the rest of the day. Barbara was also relieved to finally understand why her luggage had been lost by the airline and why she had been detained in Guatemala City for three days, awaiting our arrival and her baggage.

The following morning we took a small plane to Flores in the Peten Jungle to view the ruins of Tikal. The weather was good, fortunately, and the flight smooth. (Carrol had experienced my being ill in a small plane a couple of years before when she and I had flown together to psychically locate an airplane that had crashed near Grand Junction, Colorado. She wasn't eager to re-experience THAT unpleasantness.)

A guide, named Willie, met us at the airport. He was driving a brand new Mitsubishi minibus his company had purchased the week before our arrival. He said the previous one had been a 28-year-old, non-air-conditioned Volkswagen van. Willie was Nicaraguan. His father was a congressman in the new government, which took office during our visit at the end of the civil war in Nicaragua. Willie spoke four languages, but he spoke very little English. The van driver did not speak English.

Accompanying us in the minibus were a mother and daughter from

Italy who spoke no English, and Michael, a chiropractic student from Houston, Texas, we had picked up on the plane from Guatemala City. I had been guided by Spirit to ask this man why he was coming to Guatemala. He said he had no idea, but that he just knew he had to come. As we drove to the ruins, I explained to Michael that he had been chosen by Spirit to be the third leg of our triad of energy and to hold the male focus. He would replace Chris, who we had left in Mexico City. Michael was actually relieved to learn the reason he had been sent to Guatemala, and accepted the announcement not only graciously, but eagerly!

I gave Willie a copy of my brochure and explained that we were visiting the ruins for spiritual purposes – to do energy work – and that we were glad the group was so small. He replied that he understood and that he had guided many psychics into the ruins.

At the gate to the ruins, Willie disembarked and requested that the Italian women follow him. When he returned alone, a short time later, we asked him where the women were.

"I have given them to another tour guide who enjoys speaking their language. It is not my 'hobby' to take Italian women who do not know why they visit the ruins. It is better for you to be alone to do your work."

The Tikal ruins dwarfed anything we had previously seen on our trip. Energetically, they reminded me of Machu Picchu in Peru. The Spirits associated with many of the structures were not glad to have visitors to their home. Therefore, we had to be very aware of our footing and hand holds.

Willie managed to keep us either ahead of or behind other groups touring the ruins. At lunch time we were most surprised when we were guided to a grass-covered structure near the ruins and fed a specially-prepared meal of grilled chicken, vegetables, rice, bread and fruit. The meal was served on real plates atop a table covered with a fabric cloth. The forks and spoons were metal. We felt a little like the British we'd seen on TV entering the jungles of Africa with bearers carrying china and tea services.

On the return trip to Flores, Michael read to us about what he thought was our hotel, from his tour book. The hotel "used to be" the nicest in Flores before the lake had risen, flooding the entire first floor and the swimming pool, now beyond use. We were appalled! Surely our travel agent had not booked us in such a place. Michael found he was booked at that hotel. Our driver dropped him off there and told him we would be back for him in the morning.

Fortunately, our accommodations were brand new, having been completed just the month before our arrival. The resort had a purple decor: the umbrellas around the pool were purple as were the table covers and blankets. It seemed almost as if this place on its own lake had been designed with us in mind and set in the middle of the jungle just before our arrival!

Only five people were staying at this magic spot: two European businessmen, one Mexican male, and the two of us. The staff far out-numbered the guests and were most eager to please.

While we were sitting beside the pool, enjoying the sunset, the two businessmen came down to swim. We were sitting under a ledge by a waterfall and thought we were the only inhabitants at the lodge. When the two men dove into the water from above our heads we both screamed. They were amused and shocked also, because they thought they were the only guests at the lodge. They were as pleasantly surprised to see us as we were to see them. They spent the remainder of the evening entertaining us with food, drink and charming conversation. The day after we left, 120 persons were due to arrive at the resort!

The second day in the ruins of Tikal was equally as magical as the first, except for an encounter with a machine gun-toting, camouflage-suited soldier. I was coming off a large pyramid in the jungle on the opposite side from Carrol and Michael. The soldier did not speak a word, but the energy was enough to cause me to nearly lose my breakfast. We had heard stories of Americans being killed and kidnapped in Guatemala the week before our arrival!

The flight back to Guatemala City that afternoon was the roughest we had ever experienced, with thunder, lightning and intense rain. Fortunately, the plane sent to retrieve us was much larger than the one that got us there. I slept through much of the flight, after summoning a number of Angels to assist the levitation. I awakened abruptly to freezing water leaking from the ceiling onto my bare feet. What a shock!

When we arrived back in Mexico City, Luis, my friend from the Peru trip, met us. He took us to the Habanna Hotel, the same hotel he had taken Chris to for the week. He said the hotel belonged to friends of his. Neither the hotel nor its location in the older part of the city seemed right to me.

While Luis went upstairs to get Chris, I remained in the lobby arguing with my guidance about staying in the hotel. My guidance pointed out that it was energetically very important that we stay here on Cuba Street for two nights. We were to work on drug traffic coming from Columbia through Cuba into Miami.

I was really offended. Then my guidance explained that while I had been allowed superb accommodations all during the trip thus far, it was now necessary for me to accept this choice. (I had to agree we <u>had</u> been very well cared for.) My guidance assured me we would be safe in this place (which felt anything BUT safe to me.) I agreed to stay.

During our stay in the country, Luis escorted us to Teotihuacan, outside Mexico City. The Pyramids of the Sun and Moon were much larger than anything we had seen thus far. The Pyramid of Quetzalcoatl was very significant for me in terms of past life memory. Apparently, many of us had extensive spiritual knowledge at that time and have agreed to reincarnate every 700 years as a group to share this knowledge.

Historically, the city began about 200 B.C. and lasted for 1,000 years. It was most densely populated between 450 and 650 A.D. It reached its peak of power and influence around 500 A.D. and by 650 A.D. had begun to degenerate. At its height of power, Teotihuacan rivaled Rome in grandeur and size: 200,000 inhabitants lived in a complexly stratified society. The metropolitan area covered 12 square miles and contained 2,200 apartment compounds. Much of the population engaged in craft activities, many being obsidian workers in some 500 workshops. Obviously, the city was part of a great master plan.

Spirit was proven correct once again. After our first night at the Habana Hotel, we saw a news broadcast reporting the capture of a boat containing the largest drug shipment ever stopped on its way from Columbia to Miami, via Cuba. So, I washed my hair and stayed in the room the second night without complaint. Carrol, who was out of Mexican money, convinced Chris to go out into the city with her looking for a money changer, even though it was after dark. While they were gone there was lots of running, yelling and beer bottles being broken outside the room. I was terrified for them out in this part of the city at night. When they finally returned they told of a man in a car pulling to the curb and asking them what they were doing in that part of town. He was a doctor and his brother lived in Denver where Carrol lived. He drove them to a large elegant hotel in another area of town where they could get money changed and returned them safely to our hotel. I should have known Spirit would take good care of them. Carrol had not told me why they went out . . . I thought they were going out to dinner. If I'd known why they were leaving, I'd have told them I had more than enough Mexican money to get us out of the country. Mexico is the only country I've traveled to where you have to remember to save about $12.00 of their currency to pay to leave the country.

The following day, as we drove to the airport to depart Mexico City, the taxi driver asked me why we had stayed in the Habanna Hotel. He said, "You could not pay me one million American dollars to spend a night in that hotel. It is very dangerous there."

In summary, I felt our efforts to ground the City of Light into the Fourth Dimension and to perform our energy work were completely successful.

25

Homeward Bound, Discipline and Energy Work

May 1990 - And Summer

On my way home to Denver from Mexico and Central America, I stopped in Texas where my daughter, Kelley, was undergoing surgery. Then I took a side trip to Albuquerque, Chaco Canyon, Aztec, New Mexico, and Mesa Verde. There my companions and I grounded energy from the "Ancient Ones" who came to Earth as the Anasazi Indians from their home (now) on Vector One. According to what I have received, a strong connection exists between these Anasazi tribes or cultures, and the Mayans and Incas.

The Anasazi energies were placed on the planet as preparatory energies. When they were no longer appropriate on the surface of the Earth, some were lifted off and returned home and chose to move into the Fifth Dimension within the Earth. The Anasazi contacted me from a location they refer to as Vector One, Two and Three, which they locate energetically between Venus and Jupiter.

For some time after reaching home, I felt overwhelmed by my recent experiences. My increased feeling of stability from the energy was offset somewhat by the intensity and a lack of feeling grounded.

However, the cleaning and yard work I did for the first week after arriving home helped ground all the energy I received on the trip. Then I spent a weekend in the New Mexico Mountains, where I did more physical work to help myself assimilate the energy into my physical body. I also mentally and emotionally processed what the experiences had meant to me personally, and how they related to my purpose and to the planet.

Summer 1990

As summer approached I began thinking a lot about discipline. Jokingly, I stated that the only thing I was consistent about was being inconsistent! Why did I dislike discipline and, therefore, consistency?

I concluded that the words "discipline" and "consistency" aroused feelings of rigidity, limitation and joylessness in me. "Disciplining myself" meant perfectionism and acting out of a desire to avoid punishment or to get praise from others.

About that time I heard another idea that helped me change the way I thought and felt about discipline.

"Discipline" comes from the term "disciple" or "follower." When we follow the dictates of our hearts we are acting as disciples; we are practicing true discipline.

Often when I begin a practice, like yoga or writing down my dreams as a way of getting myself back in line, I start resenting it; through my intention to do something for my spiritual, physical or emotional benefit, I become caught up in the rigidity of adherence and "perfect" performance. I feel dammed if I do and dammed if I don't.

Then I decided on a new approach, that of listening to my body more. For example, if an activity made me feel better, I would do it. If it caused restriction or pain, I would look at the end result, that is, would it make me feel better? Fasting, for example.

Early in the week, fasting made me feel restrictive, but by the end of the second day I felt better, lighter, freer. Some days I felt better staying in bed; some days I felt better getting up, exercising and meditating. Therefore, I resolved I WOULD BE KIND TO MYSELF. I WOULD LISTEN TO MY BODY, MY MIND AND MY SPIRIT.

If the above "rings a bell" with you, GREAT. I'm glad to share it. Another bit of wisdom that came to me: MEDITATE NOT FOR THE EXPERIENCE IN MEDITATION, BUT FOR THE EFFECT IT WILL HAVE ON THE REST OF YOUR LIFE.

July 21-26, I journeyed to Olivet, Michigan, for the Spiritual Frontiers Fellowship International Convention. It was exciting! People were open, warm and receptive – often expressing much love. My workshop, "Finding Your Life's Purpose," and its workbook were enthusiastically received.

Then the weekend before the eclipse of August 6, my friends Jean, Pegi and I were sent to Devil's Tower, Wyoming, from Denver to do energy work. Our responsibility was to activate the communications grid system that connects the Space Station over the Yucatan (The New Jerusalem), to the Inner Earth civilizations.

To accomplish the energy work, we used pictures of the pyramids in Mexico, into which we had grounded with New Jerusalem, together with seven crystals and one piece of Lapis.

I did not understand the use of the Lapis until a few weeks later when Spirit explained that the most beneficial stone to use in conjunction with energy work in the Middle East was Lapis, especially Lapis mined in the Middle East.

The shields were successfully stationed in space. (They were to deflect the energy alignment that would occur in December of that year. The Earth's balance would have been severely affected without the shields.)

Cooperation from Inner Earth was necessary for this balancing act to be successfully accomplished.

We thanked the Space Brotherhood and the Spiritual Hierarchy for their instruction and cooperation in our efforts to prevent destruction. (Devil's Tower, Wyoming, was mountain used in the movie *Close Encounters of the Third Kind*, which my space friends say was no accident!)

The three of us were asked by Spirit to go by way of Mt. Rushmore on our way home to Denver.

The energy of the sculpture, as well as the convergence of several thousand motorcycle riders gathered in Sturgis, South Dakota, for their annual rally was amazing.

We used the mountain's energy and symbology to charge the riders with the energy of World peace and patriotism. (The riders then subsequently took this energy with them to all parts of the World!)

I had never seen so many tattoos or so much black leather in one place in my life!

We buried a crystal at Mr. Rushmore, through which we can continue to transmit patriotic energy in efforts to avert World War III.

On this trip we also sent a lot of peace energy to the Middle East.

(In my Newsletter following this trip, I encouraged those who had a piece of Lapis to (a) take a photo (from the newspaper or news magazine) of Saddam Hussein (b) place the Lapis, which had been energized for World peace, on the photo, (c) meditate daily on the Lapis and photo and (d) leave these two items on their altars for constant peace energy bombardment of the Middle East and its political and religious leaders.)

August 15-16 we traveled to the Grand Tetons in Wyoming to be a part of the Ascended Masters Retreat. There we worked on the energy of World unity.

Following the Retreat we went to Arco, Idaho, to work on the energy at the Atomic Energy Research facility. We also traveled to Washington state and Oregon, where we worked on atomic energy testing, storage and waste handling.

In September, Spirit asked me to review the video of the predictions of Nostradamus. Nostradamus was a French physician, astrologer, mystic and healer who lived from 1503 to 1566. He wrote one thousand predictions in poetic quatrains. The majority of his predictions have been accurate.

Reviewing the video prompted our realization of this truth:

We control the future with our thoughts! We can change outcomes using energy! (Few would have believed, a few years ago, so much would be accomplished toward bringing World consciousness to thoughts of peace and ecology! Much has been done through meditation and prayer!) A situation created in this dimension cannot be solved in this dimension. We must use a higher view and a higher frequency of vibration to solve problems now facing the Earth. Answers can come to us through meditation, by contacting the higher vibrations.

It is a Universal Law: "Energy follows intention." THOUGHTS ARE THINGS. IF WE THINK PEACE AND ACT PEACEFULLY, WE WILL HAVE PEACE. We cannot preach peace while acting in anger, fear and hostility. We must walk our talk. Body language does not lie!

LUNAR ECLIPSE - August 1990

On August 6, 1990, Planet Earth experienced a Lunar Eclipse. At that time a shield was needed in an area of space where it could deflect the magnetic pull of an alignment of planets. The shield was offered by the Spiritual Hierarchy, through the cooperation of the Intergalactic Federation, or Space Brotherhood. The shield was to keep the Earth from severe wobbling and also from further destruction.

The Space Brotherhood, with its advanced computer systems, had calculated the deflection of the energies to the extent that other magnetized devices were to be set up throughout space to deflect the energy. This prevented harm from being done to other systems as energy was deflected from Earth. The Brotherhood's generosity, love and concern for us are immeasurable.

In August 1990, there was a noticeable weakness in the etheric web of Earth. Various clairvoyants viewed this as a dark energy mass, with gas pressure building below the surface. Other clairsentients described it as simply a need to regurgitate, or a feeling of bile building in the system.

Part of the work my companions and I did in the Yucatan, Guatemala and Mexico to station The New Jerusalem in the 5th dimension was connected to this etheric web project.

We also learned that the work accomplished in November 1989 through our efforts to connect the energies of Sirius in cooperation with the Dolphins and Whales was successful. The purpose was to call the government's attention to the defective bolts in the missile silos stored around the United States. However, to date, the bureaucracy's "blame game" has kept the situation from being corrected.

PLANETARY CITIZENS REUNION

September 20, 1990, I was asked by Spirit to fly from Denver, Colorado, where I was staying, to Ashland, Oregon, to attend the Planetary Citizens Reunion on Interspecies and Inter-dimensional Communication. I was told I would be a presenter at this Symposium, even though the coordinators knew nothing was about me or even that I was coming. I argued with Spirit about spending so much money on the flight and the conference fees, but finally scheduled myself to go.

During the flight I was seated next to a young woman who works in the video production department of Apple Computers. I discussed with her a synopsis of the extraterrestrial movie script idea Spirit had given me about children communicating with ET's through their computers. She seemed a bit freaked out, not just by the extraterrestrial idea for the movie, but even more so by how I explained that I had been given the idea.

At the Planetary Citizens Reunion I met many new people involved in planetary work and reunited with others who came in from Oklahoma City, Chicago and Denmark.

Spirit had told me I would be speaking at the Reunion and that I should plan to stay in Mount Shasta for two days following the conference. I wondered how all this could happen since I was not on the conference agenda. The arrangers of the symposium were not aware either, that I was to speak. Nor did I know anyone in Mount Shasta with whom I could stay.

Before the first session of the conference, I became aware that one of the female presenters was not able to attend. I approached Donald Keyes, Director of Planetary Citizens, and explained that Spirit had sent me to fill in for the speaker who was unable to attend. He was relieved to learn who I was and that I was aware I was supposed to speak. He invited me to introduce myself and to talk about my work with the Space Brotherhood and the Spiritual Hierarchy. He then asked me to join Frank Babcock, another planetary energy worker, in a discussion presentation.

The first night the presenters were lined up on the stage. Frank spoke first about the planetary energy work he had been doing for several years. I was intrigued and looked forward to having time to talk with him about his work.

I was so amazed to find someone else on the planet who does what John Hornecker and I do! At that time I had thought we were the only ones! John Hornecker wrote the book, *An Infusion of Light: a Gift From The Pleiades to Planet Earth*. He also travels around the globe grounding energy for the Spiritual Hierarchy and the Intergalactic Federation. I had met John several years before at a walk-in conference in Minnesota.

I was the last person in the row of presenters. When I stood and explained myself, what I do and how I happened to be at the conference, I noticed that Frank had stood and was staring at me with tears in his eyes. He too was relieved to find he wasn't alone in his work.

Frank Babcock and I had no time to discuss what we would present, but Spirit, as usual, knew more about these things than we did. What did not come out of his mouth came out of mine and the attendees learned a great deal about the Spiritual Hierarchy and the Federation. More than 22 years later I still hear from people who heard me speak at this conference.

The last day of the symposium, I sat next to Barbara Thomas at lunch. Barbara is a wonderful artist, weaver, jewelry designer and teacher who offers spiritual and artistic guidance. My son ,Cory, and I had met her in Ben Lomand, California, during our previous travels. You may remember that she and her husband had accepted responsibility as stewards of the natural amphitheatre on top of the mountain outside Ben Lomand.

I shared with her that Spirit was asking me to fly back to Denver, after leaving Mount Shasta, get in my car and drive to Sedona, by way of Pueblo, Colorado, where I was to stop at Port Centauri, a retreat center outside Pueblo. The director of this retreat was one of the primary channels, at that time, for the Ashtar Command. Port Centauri is another of Ashtar's communication stations. Ashtar is the head of the Intergalactic Federation.

I was to do all these things in 48 hours and meet friends from North Carolina in Sedona and share their accommodations. A few days after they were to leave, other friends were to arrive from Denver and I was to stay with them.

As I was leaving the conference center, Barbara stopped me and said, "If you should happen to get to Sedona and need a place to stay, give me a call. We have some wonderful friends there, and I'm sure they would like to meet you and allow you to use their guest room." She did not have the number with her.

The two days following the Reunion, Rachel, my traveling companion from Boulder, Colorado, and I stayed at Frank's home overlooking Mount Shasta. Frank and I finally had time to talk privately and feel how attracted we were to each other. We worked with other members of the Planetary Team to get clarity through discussion and channeling about the next steps to be taken in their project.

When I arrived home in Denver on September 25, I immediately packed again and that same day drove to Pueblo, Colorado, and to Port Centauri. In Sedona, September 27-28, I attended a gathering of individuals from all over the World at NETWORK 2012 (the Light Link gathering). Then I stayed on in Sedona to meet and do energy work with a couple of women from North Carolina.

We worked to connect the New Jerusalem over the Yucatan with Sedona's vortexes and into the Inner Earth civilizations under Arizona and New Mexico.

I drove to Flagstaff to meet friends from Denver. Flagstaff was very cold. My friends were camping out in an unheated shed affair at the KOA. I do not camp out, even for Spirit.

After having experienced the energy at Mount Shasta, the symposium, Sedona and Light Link, I was ready to rest. I checked into a motel in Flagstaff. I washed all of my lingerie and hung items on hangers around the room to dry. I stretched out across the bed to meditate on what I was to do next.

The message I received was, "*Call California and go to the lecture in Sedona.*"

That was a fairly non-specific message. Also, California does not have just one phone number. So who was I supposed to call in California? It wouldn't be Frank because he had left almost immediately after I had to go to France on another energy assignment.

Quite suddenly, I remembered Barbara Thomas' offer, "If you find yourself in need of a place to stay in Sedona, give me a call."

I went outside to the pay phone. The message on Barbara's answering machine informed me they had left to travel abroad. As I started to hang up the phone, I heard a small message Barbara had added: "But if this is bj, call this number and ask for Leslie."

I immediately dialed the Sedona number. I was surprised when a man answered, I expected Leslie to be a woman.

When I told him who I was, he responded, "Where have you been? Barbara called several days ago and said to expect you. I've been concerned about you. Where are you now?"

When I told him I was in a motel in Flagstaff, he said, "Go tell them you don't need the room. Just check out and come on over here. The room's all ready and I'll take you to dinner and we can go hear a speaker named Humbatz Men, one of the World's great Mayan teachers." I was flooded with relief.

The motel attendant was totally receptive and returned my money. I repacked my car, putting all the hangers of wet lingerie in the back seat. I drove to the KOA and notified my friends of my change in plans. They were on their way to Las Vegas. We wished each other well and I left for Sedona.

I arrived at Leslie's, a beautiful house overlooking all of Sedona. I dried my underwear in his dryer, enjoyed a wonderful dinner and attended the lecture. John Hornecker, my friend from Colorado, was seated next to us at the lecture. And so it went. And so it goes in my life when I follow Spirit's guidance...

It seemed that I had a great month-long birthday party, as we celebrated everywhere I went.

26

Working with Frank

Close of 1990 - Early 1991

Following my stay in Sedona, I went to New Mexico where I did some more energy work and some visiting. From there I went to Texas to see my children. Within a week I was in Oklahoma City.

By the time I arrived in Oklahoma, my mail had caught up with me from Denver, and I had received some very meaningful correspondence from Frank Babcock.

I left Denver to drive to Charlotte, North Carolina, and when I arrived there I tried to telephone him. I learned he had already left for England and France, following his spiritual guidance. I was a bit frustrated. Finally, I received another letter and was able to fax him a reply. Several days later we communicated by phone and made arrangements for him to fly to the East Coast to join me upon his return from Europe.

Our travels took us up the East Coast. In Boston we continued the work begun in the Yucatan in April when the New Jerusalem City of Light was anchored. The Space Federation, of which there were then 37 extraterrestrial member civilizations, had begun bringing their ships into closer range of the Earth. These are non-physical ships in the sense that they vibrate in Fourth and Fifth Dimensional frequencies and, therefore, are not visible on radar or to Third Dimensional vision. The reason these ships moved closer to Earth seemed to be to monitor the activities of the planet and its people at closer range. The Space Federation is not willing to allow nuclear war to destroy Earth and her inhabitants and they have spiritual permission to intervene to stop this from happening. These are all loving and benevolent beings. They have the highest good of Earth, her population, and God's Plan in mind. They were on-lining their systems with the government, military and academic computer systems from the ships. They are in position in case evacuation of Light workers becomes necessary.

We had, at the end of 1990, anchored these ships energetically over 35 states and countries. They had arrived at an average of two per day. They came from all 37 members of the Intergalactic Federation, and the crews were intermixing on board each vessel with members from several star systems working together. It is truly an intergalactic cooperative effort. Prior to this time, each ship had a crew from the system that created and owned the vessel. It was a new intergalactic experiment to mix the crews.

As Frank and I traveled, we also worked on averting an earthquake on the Mississippi River. (The energy had become elongated down the river instead of being contained in one area.) We worked to pull much of the energy out into the oceans where small quakes can happen with less physical damage to Human, plant and animal life. We also worked on an atomic energy plant in Mississippi, visited and worked with Mark Ellis, my web master, and did some readings in Birmingham, Alabama, as we moved on to Charlotte, North Carolina.

By late 1990, the planet was still dealing with the possibility of war in the Middle East. Energetically speaking, the Middle East has a gaping hole open into the astral plane. The energy beneath the Middle East, as many of you have seen in your meditations, looks akin to a cesspool.

We had been working to close that astral opening and continued to energetically lance that boil, or drain the cesspool, so to speak. We could see that a brief, intense war might be required to accomplish this energetically. We knew if we were not successful, the entire matter would have to be played out physically, with a war lasting up to 30 years.

We asked people to pray, not just for peace without war, but also for energy transmutation – to call upon the energy of the Violet Flame and the Blue Cosmic Fire of St. Michael's Sword – to accomplish this. It was good to be in North Carolina again. Everyone was very helpful and receptive to the new energy and eager to get on with their own spiritual learning. We did an evening workshop on multi-dimensional realities. By January 2, 1991, I had moved to Frank's home in Mount Shasta, California. The length of my stay there was indefinite. I planned to rest, write (the book on practical metaphysics) and paint.

I had been traveling extensively for six years, following the voice of Spirit, doing energy work, teaching and ministering to individuals and groups – all of this with no salary. I was no longer physically or emotionally comfortable doing this. Neither did I want to rely on credit cards. Instead, I planned to travel only to conferences or cities where expenses were paid.

Frank and I would continue to do the planetary energy work that we had been doing, through out-of-body travel to the necessary locations. I would do a limited number of phone readings. I also planned to write the newsletter periodically and describe my impressions of what was happening energetically.

At that time I recall writing that the shifts that were taking place were increasing the speed at which all things are created. What we held in our minds out-pictured quicker than ever; therefore we could no longer afford negative thoughts.

Spirit had said: *"We must let go of duality. As the polarity shifts to Oneness, so must our thoughts do likewise in order for there to be survival of the Planet and the species."*

And I recall that the alignment of planets on December 19, 1990 – the moon, sun, Mercury, Venus, Uranus and Neptune – could have caused a physical polarity shift had our Space Brothers not assisted us in August by creating an energy shield to deflect the energies of this alignment.

SPIRALS OF ENERGY
By bj King

Quantum leaps, millennium conversions
Spirals of energy, complete within Humans
Mother Nature's plan is served by denizens of the deep
As well as those who sleep for centuries
Before returning to complete a mission
Left wanting in some previous time.
Through quantum leaps, millennium conversions
And spirals of energy, it is done.

27

Swings, Chanting Ceremony, Laws

February-Mid-April, 1991

I often felt like a circus performer, my life being a series of trapeze swings. I was either hanging onto a trapeze bar swinging along, or, for a few moments, in between bars hurtling across space. The first part of my life I hung on to my trapeze bar-of-the-moment for dear life. It carried me along at a certain steady rate, and I had the feeling I was in control of my life. I knew most of the right questions – and even some of the right answers!

But by this time, once in a while as I merrily (or not so merrily) swung along, I gazed out ahead into the distance and what did I see? Another trapeze bar swaying toward me. It would be empty, and I knew (in that place inside me that <u>knows</u>) that this new bar had my name on it. It was my next single thing to do, my growth, my aliveness coming to get me. And I KNEW in my heart-of-hearts that for me to grow, I HAD TO release my grip on the present well-known bar to enable me to move to the new one.

Each time this happened to me, I hoped (no, I prayed) that I wouldn't have to grab a new bar. Because grasping the new one meant that for some moment in time, I had to hurl across space; and I was filled with terror and resistance! It doesn't seem to matter that I had shot across the void-of-unknowing many times before and always made it. Each time, I became fearful that I would miss, that I would be crushed on unseen rocks in the bottomless chasm between the bars. But . . . I did it anyway. I assumed my soul would provide some kind of net that was obviously not visible to me.

Perhaps this is the essence of what mystics call the faith experience – no guarantees, no visible net, no insurance policy. But you do it anyway because, somehow, to continue hanging on to the old bar is no longer an alternative (or maybe to hang on would be death). And so for an eternity (which can last a microsecond or a thousand lifetimes), I soar across the dark void of "the past is gone; the future is not yet here." It is called "transition," its called being constantly in the now.

I have come to believe that this is the only place real change occurs – I mean REAL CHANGE, not the pseudo-change that lasts only until the next time one of my old buttons get pushed . . .

I have noticed that in our culture this transition zone is looked upon as a "no-thing," a no-place between places. Sure, the old trapeze bar was real, and that new one coming at me I hoped was real, too. But the void in between? That's just a scary, confusing, disorienting "nowhere" that one must get through as fast and as <u>unconsciously</u> as possible.

What a waste! I have a sneaking suspicion that the transition zone is the only <u>real thing</u>, and that the bars are illusions we dream up to AVOID THE VOID – avoid being completely in the now (where the real change – the real growth – occurs for us).

Whether or not my hunch was true, it remains that the transition zones in our lives are incredibly rich places. They should be honored – even savored. Indeed, with all the pain and fear and feelings of being out-of-control that can (but do not necessarily have to) accompany transitions, they are still the most alive, most growth-filled, passionate, expansive moments in our lives. Such can be terrifying. Such can also be enlightening, because hurling through the void, we learn to fly! I had landed in Mount Shasta, California, on a trapeze swing in January 1991. Frank, my new partner then, had been riding the bar that I caught. We had settled into a beautiful home with four Angels stationed over the house. The energy of the mountain and the Elementals were fantastic.

And, there was so much information coming through it was difficult to know where to start in my attempt to share it with my friends, supporters . . . and readers.

At that time, many people were experiencing a lot of shock and trauma in their bodies and emotions resulting from the activities of the war (Persian Gulf). Also, the eclipse of the Sun (Jan. 15) and the Moon (Jan. 30) moved us from the Earth's primary reference link of "past experience," to the "future" or the "now." This was confusing for our bodies and our consciousness because our consciousness is accustomed to processing information in relation to <u>past events</u>. Third Dimensional consciousness uses experiences and beliefs as its standard measurement for determining what is real and what is not real. Since beliefs are based on past experiences, they feed the continuous cycle of reruns through our lives, and feed our fears as well. Therefore, this change caused people to feel insecure, their emotions fragile and delicate as the patterns changed in their DNA. In truth, the major pictures of reality, on which the Third Dimension is based, have begun to disintegrate; the new ones not as yet having integrated. So we hang in the middle of that shift. In fact, the whole planet has begun experiencing transformational shock and trauma. Further, an entire civilization is dying (or disintegrating) and a whole new one is emerging (or integrating). And the process is ongoing. The entire scenario pushes people's fear buttons and causes shock and trauma.

The war was karmic. Most people on Earth did not know that the Karmic Board had forgiven, or agreed to balance, the karma of Earth and Humankind. Therefore, most are still determined to live out the karma. As written earlier, the energy of the Middle East looked like a boil, or a cesspool. This energy had to be released in some fashion. Either the people themselves had to wake up to no karma and forgive themselves and each other (pretty unlikely), or there had to be a war. A war was the quickest way to release this energy. The war didn't have to continue, but it did have to start.

As I have stated in some of my writings, there are people on Earth who want off, who are not prepared to stay for the durational changes coming for Earth. The war gave some of them a vehicle through which they could leave their bodies; in fact, people gathered there from all over the World for this purpose.

CHANTING CEREMONY

February 21, about 11 p.m., I received an inner call from the Sisterhood of the Shield to do a drum and chanting ceremony in the ancient tongue. This surprised me because I had not had to serve the Sisterhood during my waking state for more than a year. (I need to explain here that when I went to Peru in 1988, I merged my consciousness with a member of my Oversoul who was leaving the Earth and had held this knowledge, energy and focus for the Earth through the Sisterhood of the Shield. I accepted my position as a member of the Elders of the Sisterhood at that time.) I was told that after the ceremony, if we weren't successful within 48 hours, I would need to go to ask assistance of the giant redwood trees and the ocean creatures.

By Saturday night, I was aware we had not been completely successful and needed help. Early the next morning we left for the California coast with our drum, sage, cedar, tobacco, cornmeal and Frank's crystals.

The energy was deliberately projected from Uranus and was totally male-polarized energy, which would escalate the war. We were already experiencing an energy focus, which the Hierarchy reported would cause symptoms of chronic 13-day PMS. This energy, coupled with that from Uranus, made it difficult for us to stay centered and totally in our feminine selves to transmute this harsher energy.

We arrived at the forest at 3 a.m. before the energy came in. Much of the energy mass was transmuted as it entered our atmosphere through our intention. As the energy started being transmuted and then grounded by the redwoods it was amazing. If you ever saw the movie *POWDER*, you might remember the flow of energy as he was leaving the planet. This energy looked very much like that. It was white, blue and iridescent green. Part of it was taken into the oceans and transmuted by our Sirian friends the dolphins, whales and giant squids. Some had to be deflected back to Uranus.

Overall, we felt the mission was successfully completed, and that the Earth was able to use the energy in the most productive way.

In March, I became aware that the single theme and admonition from the Spirits and the Space Brotherhood/Sisterhood seemed to be that of learning the Universal Laws and teaching them. The Laws are as true today as they were in 1991.

The PRIMARY UNIVERSAL LAW appears to be the LAW of ONE. Every soul, living in physical body, or discarnate (stripped of flesh) is connected to a level of the galactic unconscious, deep within the higher self. We are all part of a great energy gestalt called God, and because we are part of God, we ARE God. The goal of the gestalt is to move energy forward, creating more energy.

If we live harmoniously, we increase our vibrational rate and intensify the vibration of the entire gestalt. If we live in disharmony, we decrease the vibration of the entire gestalt.

Because we are ONE, everything anyone thinks, says or does, affects every other soul.

We are challenged to remember this ONENESS that we forgot when we were born into the third dimension. We are challenged to accept healing of the separation that occurred when we forgot who we were and separated our consciousness from God. We are challenged to restore our memory so we can create heaven on Earth, or return to God.

At that time, I suggested the group I was meeting with in Shasta have a meditation to help people realize their ONENESS; to meditate on God being absolute bliss, peace, harmony, joy, infinite intelligence, all-powerful, radiating boundless wisdom and infinite love.

After the meditation I suggested that all of us continue dwelling on the above. After all, everything we see IS God made manifest, God dramatizing Itself for the joy of expressing Itself. The only way to change ugliness, evil and strife is to visualize "it" as transformed into beauty, harmony and peace. By so doing, we create an energy space so "it" can actually become that which we visualize; we create a new energy matrix for "it" to transform into.

Another PRIMARY UNIVERSAL LAW is the Law of Manifestation. Everything manifested begins as a thought, an idea. <u>Thoughts become things</u>. Ideas and experiences create beliefs, which in turn create our reality. <u>Our current reality is an out-picturing of our past thoughts and current beliefs</u>.

If we are unhappy with our current reality, we must change our beliefs and our behavior. Beliefs can be changed when we first recognize those that are not working for us and begin programming those that <u>will</u> create success and harmony in our lives.

The opposite of visualizing the transformation is <u>worry</u> or <u>concentration</u> on the horror or ugliness of something, like war or AIDS. When you confront or oppose "it," you make a greater need for "it" to exist by supporting the <u>law of polarity</u>; you assist in causing "it" to continue happening. Therefore, VISUALIZE ONLY THE REALITY YOU DESIRE TO EXPERIENCE.

It's often easier to change our behavioral patterns before we change our beliefs, because often, we are not conscious of what our actual beliefs are. Then, as a result of the behavioral change, beliefs also change as new habits establish themselves.

People who do not know, understand or believe the Law of Manifestation find it impossible to believe they create their own reality. They prefer to remain victims.

28

The SE5 Machine Experience

On Sunday, March 10, 1991, Frank and I drove to Ashland, Oregon, to pick up my friend who was coming to visit from Denver.

Jan had attended a weeklong retreat, sometime before, where she heard of a couple in Ashland (Barry and Karen) who were doing energy work with a device called an SE5 machine. The machine had been channeled and was apparently a reproduction of technology available at the time of Atlantis.

On this Sunday morning, Jan had had a session on the machine and offered to "treat" me to a session on it in the afternoon.

Normally, I do not do this sort of thing. However, Matthew, my Eighth Dimensional self, was insistent that a session would be appropriate.

I trust Matthew, but still I was a little skeptical and reluctant because for two weeks I had been in a space of totally examining my belief structures, as well as living with Frank and the energies of Mount Shasta.

This machine is touted as having the ability to change DNA by removing negative beliefs and raising the candidate's vibration to receive and embody the soul in fourteen levels. The process also claims to remove illness in the auric fields, as well as in the physical body. They claimed to use the machine primarily to integrate and seat the soul, or soul star, in the physical body. With Jan, the practitioner claimed her soul star was seated on Sunday, and the following Thursday the Christ Consciousness was merged and seated into her physical body.

The practitioners claimed the process was designed to accelerate one's growth by quantum leaps and with no "fallout" or illness afterward.

When I agreed to the session, a lock of my hair was put into an opening in the SE5 machine. Some DNA information came from this. I lay down on a cot over which was suspended a Meta Form made of metal rods (multi-pyramidal form). The floor of the room was a grid system of copper strips under Plexiglas connected to two crystals, which I held in each hand.

I went immediately into an altered state of consciousness. Barry and Karen sat beside the cot, one on either side. Karen took notes while Barry asked questions about my experience.

I was instructed to open the Soul Center between the throat and the heart. The chakra opened easily and telescoped out into the Universe and into purple and golden-white light in which many geometric symbols moved about.

The symbols were approximately eight inches high and were similar to the complex triangulated form suspended above me.

The symbols entered my Soul Center and took their place within my vehicle, "seating" themselves permanently within my being.

I was then shown a "star chart" of the heavens – of our galaxy. The various geometric forms were in relation to different constellations. I was told that I did not have to intellectually understand the connections, because when the time came to activate them I would remember their significance and how to activate them for the benefit of All.

Then I saw a large "eye," like the all-seeing eye of God on the dollar bill. It came closer and closer and moved inside my third eye. At this point, my abdomen opened and many thought forms and belief systems were drawn up out of my body like thick liquid being sucked out.

Then three cylinders of light, tapered like funnels, were placed into Karen, Barry and me through our soul openings. Throughout the cylinders were symbols approximately 3 to 4 inches high (similar to Hebrew, Sanskrit, Tibetan, Chinese and Egyptian characters) made of gold illumined light. The symbols entered our bodies through the tubes. The three of us were told that the colors, sounds and symbols represented a pattern of information called "dianetic memory" (from Greek DIANOUA = "thought," DIA = "through," NOUS = "soul memory.")

Spirit told us:

"This is information that was hermetically sealed. The seal was broken when your three energies combined and your genetic encoding coming together created a fluid infusium for this information to come into.

"The infusium will proliferate out from the three of you; your containers will no longer be solid. Debris of others' negative thought forms will dissolve when they come in contact with you. New positive thought forms will be encoded to take their place as they come in contact with the energies you will now carry. Negative thought forms will be incinerated and thought

forms of Oneness – Christ Consciousness – will instantaneously come into them.

"You will be able to transfer your consciousness to any part of the planet/solar system through encoded transfer or infusium, to take on Christ Consciousness impregnation.

"The thought forms which you of necessity gave up today were that you would be persecuted or killed for transferring the infusium, spontaneously making great waves of thought forms available to the mass consciousness.

"Part of the symbols is a binary encoding (something composed of two parts) of dialectic understanding of the Universal Law which mass consciousness is ready to receive and understand consciously. Before, you were given only fragments, to be kept secret. You are now in acceptance of the rules of order of the Universe and can transmit them in verbiage the masses will understand.

"**This information can cause mass revolution against established churches and governments – against any form of oppression.**"

Well, that sounded important, but not being one who wishes to cause waves or conflict I wasn't too excited that I might have actually in some moment of weakness before coming to Earth agreed to write about these Laws. ☺ I have since written down what I've been given about the Universal Laws and this information is available in a manuscript called *Universal Laws* available through Namaste, Inc., P. O. Box 22174, Oklahoma City, OK 73123.

Spirit's messages continued:

"Be prepared to see yourselves as energy transformers similar to giant nuclear power plants.

"You will be given hand movements called 'mudras' to use to impart and unblock the consciousness of groups of people in specific areas. Barry and Karen will receive theirs in the Midwest and bj will receive hers in Hawaii. Most likely, these will be given down simultaneously.

"When you do the mudras, further hermetically-sealed information will descend. You must be prepared to be fundamentally confused, as bj has been this week, and not to fear the confusion; to know confusion precedes absolute and total clarity.

"There will be other systems of individuals, with different sets of genetic coding. This information will be set off in a serial eruption over the next six to nine months.

"The draining away and transmuting the negative recess of energy under the Middle East, which was just completed, was primarily important to be accomplished prior to the issuance of that which you now are given.

"Be conscious that you will be brought back together. Meanwhile, be conscious that you are The Third Power. Know only the term 'The Third Power'. You need not know the conscious meaning of 'The Third Power', except as it forms The Trinity."

We were then asked to be still and to take note of the sounds we experienced.

The sounds came as waves, as if through shafts of light. Devices, resembling keyboards of music boxes were illuminated in our heads – small strips, tines, of gold-tinged metal.

As the light beams hit the tines inside our heads, a pinging sound was heard. We were told we would be taught to play these keyboards to cause certain positive things to happen in the environment.

At this point, my Beingness expanded and merged with a huge energy, which Matthew referred to as Maitreya. Matthew joked,

"Isn't this an improvement over the method of transfer used with Saul of Tarsus – it better than being struck blind, temporarily?"

I had to agree. The ceiling then opened and approximately 100 Angels looked down upon us and the music and feelings of love were overwhelming . . .

A few days latter I noticed many of my feelings of fear, doubt, anger and frustration of the week before were gone. However, I was still in a period of deep questioning as to the truth and my part in its dissemination to the masses.

Later, as Jan and I looked through the book, *The Keys of Enoch*, we noticed it was filled with symbols (or keys) similar to those placed in our beings during our sessions with Karen and Barry. (I had been reluctant to purchase or read *The Keys of Enoch*.) Then in the mail that day from North Carolina we received astrological symbols.

We drew the symbols in calligraphy to further institute them into our conscious minds. At that time, I also asked the Universe to get me copies of the symbols of various alphabets.

MORE OF SPIRIT'S MESSAGES

On March 13, the group in Shasta had its regular weekly evening get-together. Spirit's message that night was as follows:

"The theories which are related to the various alphabets (Hebrew,

Chinese, Tibetan, Egyptian and Sanskrit) will begin to come under a great deal of scrutiny within the next few months.

"These various alphabets and their true meaning in relationship to the configurations of the stars, the movement of the planets and their interaction with each other (and especially when applied with sound) are going to create a new level of knowledge that has not here-to-fore been known in the consciousness of beings who reside in the third dimension.

"This information is both digitized and computerized in the storage units of our computers and is stored in several geographic locations in your dimension where it is still hermetically sealed. It is hermetically sealed within various stones, crystals and formations of rock in your dimension.

"As individuals who hold the encodement to unlock this information come in contact with these stones, formations and crystals, and make the sounds, the information will be released to the masses.

"As these sounds and symbols are released into the knowingness and into the consciousness of the masses, you will most likely experience in your dimension much more upheaval: very strong probabilities of revolution, both against established governmental systems, agencies, structures, religious orders and institutions. As these volumes of stored information are released and infiltrate the consciousness of many in your dimension (through a few) there will be more and more individuals who will wish to leave the planet. They will be those for whom "the heat will be too much," so to speak; the heat of conflicting knowledge, the heat of knowledge which will come to the fore refuting that which has been <u>believed</u> as, shall we say, gospel here-to-fore.

"As these conflicting ideologies, theories and beliefs come into current knowledge; the conflict within the individual will be reflected within the conflict of the species.

"As this happens, many beings will leave their bodies through suicide and through continued mass consciousness upheaval – not specifically war. However, in some cases within certain countries, political revolution and unrest will result because of these energies and information.

"So the period of peace is still being pushed into the future. However, the information being released can eliminate a lot of belief structures that have been primarily mythologically created. True fact and physical proof will be brought to the front that will dispute and refute that which has not before been proven, but has been believed by consensus of the masses.

"As ways to explore this information become possible, confusion and hiding of information won't result as it did with the discovery of the Dead

Sea Scrolls; neither will the mystery, and lack of public exposure and release of information to the masses which clouded the unearthing of the Scrolls.

"These new information's will not be shrouded in veils of mystery. They will be much more what we would call blatantly exposed by individuals not currently working in these arenas; by individuals whose integrity will not allow either veiling the information or hiding it from public knowledge.

"Because you are a forerunner – part of the team of individuals who carry the encodement which does release hermetically sealed information – -you may experience a deep-seated anxiety about the potential of the release of such knowledge into conscious mind.

"Consequently, be aware of possible feelings of apprehension, non-specific apprehension, which may begin creeping into your conscious minds, your emotions and your physical bodies. Such may be felt as stress, non-specified stress (stress without a known origin). Allow yourself to understand that this will be from whence comes the impetus for the anxiety attacks. Know also that the way to quell these anxiety attacks is to pursue knowledge, dianetic memory – remembering what your soul knows – and being willing to share that with the masses when the time is correct.

"We wish to say to you this is a team effort, both on our part and on yours. It is a soul agreement to which your souls committed prior to incarnating to assist this planet in her evolution and the species that is now known as Homo sapiens.

"So, be about knowing, Dear Ones, that the evolution is still progressing and is getting ready to take another leap. If it were not explained to you, forthcoming history would record it as "unexplainable." So, be about knowing and understanding. And become willing to remember that which you <u>know</u>, as well as that which you currently hold the keys to unlock for the masses."

ADONAI - The Energy of METATRON

<u>On March 27, 1991, the meditation group received the following</u>:
"The institution of the Christ Consciousness energy into your beingness can, if you are not prepared, be very uncomfortable to your physical, mental and emotional structures.

"Before the actual energy is given in its full-blown reality, your vehicles must be strengthened and the abuse erased that you do to your physical vehicles. The vehicle and the tissue must be strong and the cells must be

completely without fray.

"If we were to give complete voltage of the Christ energy into vehicles not completely prepared, total destruction of your physical form could result. Mental insanity and emotional disturbances, as well as damage to nerves and physical organs, could result.

"If you truly wish to have Christ Consciousness embodiment, Dear Ones, take care of and strengthen your vehicles with nourishment, pure thought, proper nutrition and correct breathing.

"We believe you are all capable, through discipline, to accomplish Christ Consciousness. In so doing, you would serve the masses as has been done before by avatars to the Human race. (And many now will be called forth to be avatars for this race and your species as it moves into the next quantum leap in its evolution.)

"We will be standing by to give you proportionately, and in the increments your physical bodies are ready to accept, a stepped-down version of this energy each week.

April 3, 1991, more information from Spirit:

"The ethers of your dimension are receiving tremendous knowledge and information to benefit either a few, or the masses, depending on how those few who discern and interpret this information accept their responsibility to disseminate it to the masses.

"The consciousness of Humankind as a whole has been rather narrow in accepting any new concept or idea not physically provable.

"We hope Humankind is evolving out of that close and narrow-mindedness so they may evolve into the future we have visioned and thought-projected – that of becoming a multi-level, multidimensional, multifaceted being. This is not possible if they keep blinders on and continue their tunnel vision.

"The mold of the Human species as it is now has been broken. There will be no more reproductions of this particular model. Those being created in the wombs of Humankind are those with expanded capabilities!

"Those now residing on the Earth have the capability of assuming these expanded capabilities simply by desire. Because it is now in the thought form of the species, IT IS POSSIBLE FOR ANYONE who desires expanded consciousness to get this knowledge from the mass consciousness.

"Those of you serving the collective as mystics and visionaries are responsible to discern, interpret and radiate this information when you deem it physically possible and feasible.

"The funds to do this will be presented to you, not necessarily in forms you would suspect or expect, or even find acceptable. In some cases they will be brought by individuals you would prefer not to work with, participate with, or get along with at the personality level. Such is also a part of the Divine Plan because as you experience more and more of Oneness, you will be allowed less and less to differentiate between those you wish to be with and those you wish to exclude. It is not yours to judge who is spiritually evolved and who is not, for this cannot be done at the level of your expertise and knowledge.

"When the thought forms which have been sent forth into the mass consciousness begin to explode in the minds of individuals who have the capabilities to understand them, many new inventions will be created. Many will involve digital communication, phonetic and sound communication, and exploratory devices for inner Earth, spatial and medical exploration inside the Human form and inside the Human mind. A part of these devices will enable Humans to record images of their dreams, to be interpreted at a later time. Other devices will enable individuals who go into meditation to remain at a constant level of alpha without losing awareness. Some devises will make it possible for scientists to see within the Human brain, those parts that react to and refer to different functions of the Human body, as well as to explore time-space from within the mind.

"Other knowledge will relate to the time-space continuum, how to activate hyperspace and the understanding that Humans are NOT the dominate species. Why the mental capacity of whales and dolphins is superior to that of the Human species will also become apparent.

"The less the Human species wars with one another, the more it will see itself as beings riding on a larger organism which is capable of shaking itself and thus shaking off the Human residence. As Humans then explore the mind and other dimensions further, THEY will begin to participate even more actively with those of you who are responding to us and working compatibly with us."

More exciting realizations:

"The Earth, being an entity unto Herself, has requested that the stellar councils act to raise Her vibration in order that She may take her rightful place within the Universe as a Fifth Dimensional vibrational being.

"The councils have granted permission for her to take this evolutionary leap. Therefore, we Humans can either raise our vibrations and go with Her, or "get off Her back."

"Members of the Integalactic Command have taken bodies from the surface of the Earth to help facilitate this process.

"Their job is to implement the decisions of the stellar councils and to act as intermediaries between the members of the mission who have incarnated onto the planet's surface, and those who are serving the mission in any of its many off-planet divisions.

"If you are reading this, you, as a Spirit have very likely incarnated from a distant planet at this time to help with this process.

"Therefore, we – you and I – must remember our status as servants to the Divine Plan. We are here to assure that the decree of the High Spiritual Court is implemented. We are also here to make sure the veils of the Third Dimension are parted so that the Christ Light can enter and accomplish the raising of the vibrations of Earth, Humanity and ourselves. This is the Second Coming."

NIGHT WORKERS
By bj King

The ghostlike quality of dawn's light
Illumines the countryside.
The return of RA's light
Quickens our pulse and pulls us out of sleep,
Back into our bodies to begin another day
Of forgetfulness of selves,
Who have served in sleep
In other realms.

29

Various Needs and Happenings Mount Shasta

Members of the weekly meditation group that formed at Mount Shasta after I went to live there early in 1991 continued to meet and work together.

On April 17, 1991, the group's work was with the extraterrestrial forces, anchoring many additional ships over various World countries, especially over the capitals of most nations. Ships were also anchored over state capitals in the United States.

At the close of that session, this message was received from Spirit:

"The mission you have just accomplished will serve well the Earth, the Spiritual Hierarchy and your individual soul expressions. It is a major part of the plan of God for the salvation of the Earth as an entity, and for the release of the karmic debt of understanding from the minds of the Homo sapiens who now inhabit planet Earth. That which will be given down through these anchored ships will be for the benefit of all."

Meditation group members also worked with space beings from a ship they sent to us. Too, messages were also consistently received from the ENERGY OF METATRON, and occasionally from other beings.

On May 1, 1991, this message was given the group:

"The beginnings of this new millennium create many changes both for your planet and for your people. The most advantageous position you can take to observe and withstand these changes is total and complete flexibility, and clarity of your purpose. Your purpose, of course, is to serve both the male and female aspects of God jointly and individually within your bodies, minds and spirits.

"To have this type of total flexibility requires great self-authority, and

knowing within your self the true soul message at all times.

"It is recommended that your single most important focus be to seek your own divine knowing and inner guidance, and the discernment of the soul and the will of other individuals whom you encounter.

"The ships you have been assisting us to anchor in the Fourth Dimension are to monitor and assist with the transition of Humanity and the evolution of the Homo sapiens species. They bring a great focus of energy and cause great spotlights to pierce the veil of the unconscious. They also illuminate deception and that which is not in alignment with the Divine Plan. As this light pierces the veils and illuminates that which is destructive and out of kilter, so to speak, much upheaval will result. Such will continue and escalate. This is why we say the absolute quality of discernment is the single most important spiritual gift you can activate and qualify within your being.

"In all things, be in total agreement with your soul. This is because it is not productive for your soul, for you as a personality – or as an aspect of the Godhead – to perform functions causing you grief, stagnation, displeasure or frustration.

"It is of absolute importance that you understand and qualify your own goals and desires of that which you enjoy being and expressing. The Holy qualities of the God Self most explicitly resonating through your being to create beauty, harmony and space within the mass consciousness is what is called forth.

"As this production takes place and the quality of life improves, that which has been stagnant and putrefied will need to be transmuted. As this purification reaches consciousness, many 'spillings' will take place that will resemble absolute chaos and destruction. Many people will assemble in masses to disqualify that which is being exposed by the Light that we bring and consciously focus into your dimension.

"As these gatherings take place, the holocaust will happen, but not in the way you have felt from that which has been predicted. Instead, the holocaust will be that of mind, body and knowingness, as all miss-qualified energy – that has putrefied – is expelled.

"When this happens, Dear Ones, know and remember that the absolute focus must be on beauty, order, transmutation and the graceful acceptance of change.

"Further focus should be on the absolute knowingness within your own souls of where it is correct for you to be, what is correct for you to do, and how you can funnel the most God energy into your dimension.

"Separateness will cause you grief. Oneness will call forth power and remembrance of abilities from your soul.

"The newness of life you will experience will astound you, excite you and elevate you within your own soul's consciousness.

"Be of good heart and cheer, because even in that which appears desperate and frustrating, clarity of purpose is trying to erupt from the core of your soul into your conscious mind.

"Guidance is always available when it is asked.

"Renew your commitment to the soul, to the Divine Plan and to the evolution of the Human species. This is your single and primary goal to remember.

"Then you will be able to bring forth the individuation of your promise, of your purpose; of how to escalate, maintain and further the evolution of Divine Principle."

May 1, 1991, Another message from Spirit:

"The Source of all things emanates from within each and everyone of us. It is through these emanations that the gathering of kindred souls will manifest here on the Earth plane. These emanations are drawing together those of like mind and purpose to work together to further the Divine Plan.

"To become at one with these divine emanations, follow the feelings which arise within you, the feelings of attraction or repulsion, or those of questioning. Follow these feelings even though they lead you to unfamiliar places, or have no particular purpose that you can see in the present moment.

"Be aware, too, that while groupings will form for specific purposes, many of those who will join may not be totally clear about what they are to do or why they are there.

"We ask everyone to be patient with those who are in the process of remembering and who find themselves within your presence, willing to work and participate in any way that they can, yet not knowing what that way is.

"One's true purpose is not totally shown to oneself until a certain clarity is reached on the physical plane. This involves a certain amount of letting go of fears and resistances and past concepts or ideas of how life truly is, or how it should be.

"As individuals let go of these resistances, a tendency to follow the divine emanations from within themselves will surface.

"This is a time of great manifestation and clarity on all planes of existence. As this clarity is being attained, each individual will experience the cleansing in a multitude of ways.

"Train yourselves to see deeply within individuals, to see their purpose and intent. From that point of vision you will know who you are to spend time with and who you are to avoid.

"Many of those who belong to your soul group are far away at this time, but they are being drawn to you.

"Stay open to new acquaintances, new ideas; hold true to your clarity of purpose.

"It is our desire that this message be taken deep within your hearts and given to those around you who are of like mind.

THE SPIRITUAL HIERARCHY'S REQUEST

In May, the Interspecies and Interdimensional meeting held in Mount Shasta was very successful with 15 persons from Canada, Colorado, California and Arizona attending.

Committees were appointed to begin creation of an Interspecies and Interdimensional communications magazine and symposium under the Planetary Citizens organization. The magazine's creation was the result of a request from the Spiritual Hierarchy and was to contain information on Earth's and Humanity's transitions. As far as I am aware, the group never carried out this mission.

June 1991

Our 9-year-old copy machine broke down and we desperately needed to secure a replacement. In addition to that, Spirit requested that 600 names be added to our mailing list, persons I had met in my travels during the previous 6 years.

When such requests come from Spirit (they aren't very logical) I always balk and ask a lot of questions before proceeding.

The response from spirit was, *"Your vision is not large enough as yet."* No further explanation was forthcoming, so I again acted on faith and increased the mailing list.

Frank and I also put our beautiful Shasta home up for sale! We needed to do this in order to remove the debt incurred by traveling and to financially continue our Earth work and more travel.

Also, we had been receiving this slogan <u>repeatedly</u> from Spirit: *"JUST DO IT."* We did not have television reception on the mountain in Frank's home, but I later learned this slogan had been picked up by one of the major tennis shoe lines, a beer manufacturer and a line of garden supplies! How intriguing it was to realize that when a thought is placed "on the rings" by Spirit, anybody who meditates can hear a similar message!

The slogan "Just Do It" prompted another thought:

The primary directive we all have – to embody the Spirit we serve – is hard work, but it can be fun at the same time. Meeting and accepting ourselves can be scary, but if we move through the fears and "just do it," our egos will become quiet and the fears will dissipate.

We have the answers within ourselves! The soul will only give us "clues" through psychic readings, not answers. Answers come from within, from experience, from surrender to the soul.

We do not need to "know" anything EXCEPT . . . "the next single thing to do". If you meditate and know "the next single thing to do," that thing will lead you to the - "next single thing to do," like following a thread. Almost no one knows more than that.

Few people see the overall picture or the future in detail, because the future is constantly changing as a result of Human thought and Human choices.

Peace comes only when we surrender to accepting that all we need know is the "next single thing". It is our demand to "know the future in order to feel secure, peaceful and safe" that makes us miserable in the present and fearful of the future.

So, "just do it". Move through the fears and meet and accept yourself. Become acquainted with yourself and your previously "stuffed" emotions, with your fears, desires, wishes, dreams.

Be in the "now" moment, not in the past (regret) or the future (fear). The time to accomplish these clearings was becoming shorter, so it became necessary to "JUST DO IT".

Be where you are. Allow yourself to "in-joy" the sights, sounds, the atmosphere (continue removing clutter from your environment). Surround yourself with people of like mind and with energy you enjoy. The degree of our awakening is in direct relation to the degree of the "now" we are experiencing! Just do it.

Also of interest to me at that time was how many channels were copyrighting their channeling and the various books they were bringing through.

JUST DO IT

Fill Impatience with Persistence.
Fill Discouragement with Determination.
You are not "IN" the Universe,
You "ARE" the Universe. Just Do It!

– Kelley Kay King

THE LIGHT CONVERGENCE

June 22. The Light Convergence happened.

It was another vast galactic window opening, similar to the first Harmonic Convergence back in 1987. At that time, the Convergence released a signal to the Galactic Federation (composed of 27 member off-Earth civilizations – now increased to 37) there was sufficient Earth spirituality to warrant their assistance to redeem the Human race from the Earth throes of civilization under the influence of war and greed.

The Convergence in June 1991 offered everyone the opportunity to experience him or herself as Light, not to merely say "I am a Light Being," or "I am a Light worker". In other words, it allowed everyone's awareness/consciousness to experience itself as light – to move into the Light body.

The time had come upon this planet to move forward into the Light. It was not the time for judgment or salvation, but the time of knowing. Large groups formed all over the planet and people bonded together in Humanity, to believe again in each other as brother and sister, and thus, God.

The Convergence was to create the harmonious knowing of Godliness. This is what people know as THE LIGHT.

As the close of 1991 drew near, people inquired about the "11:11," and its significance.

Each time I had asked my soul about this the response had been, *"This does not concern you."*

Well, nebulous answers are NOT my favorite kind, especially when people expect at least an opinion from me on a spiritual subject or energy condition. So I pressed my soul further for information. The following was received from "The Energies of Metatron:"

"Energy approaches the Earth in spirals. This is a period of time during

which the charge within the spiral attaching itself to Earth is being infused with more Light.

"This energy comes from the Great Central Sun beyond your Sun, is conditioned by your Sun, projected toward the Earth, and anchored in the Central Sun at the core of your Earth. Then the energy spirals back toward the Great Central Sun beyond your galaxy.

"These energies are designed and facilitated by the Source, which permeates throughout and beyond your galaxy, to step up evolution of the Earth, its plants, animals and Humans as well as all life in your galaxy.

"The symbol 11:11 – and it is merely a symbol – was used as a focus for your consciousness. It was designed to spark memory, causing acceptance of a greater focus of these energies into your cells and consciousness.

"These energies affect your entire galaxy and are a part of a much larger configuration of energy transfers which are going on at this time in the Omniverse (the Milky Way Universe and eleven other Universes.)

"It is not necessary to be in any specific location on your planet for this to take place. It will take place regardless of what Humans do or do not do. However, you are capable of using the energies more readily and assisting in anchoring them more comfortably within the Earth and your own bodies if you know and understand more-or-less what is taking place. Knowing will also assist in your own evolution and spiritual growth."

I became aware that these energies were very powerful. Governments, institutions, corporations, religious organizations, and family units all faced crucial alternatives; move to higher standards of rightness, or pass away with the shifting tides.

These energies would not allow deceit. Things, conditions, truths we had tried to keep hidden from ourselves would surface, as would our greatest fears. How successfully we dealt with what came up would determine how successfully we dealt with the next infusions of energy. And the energy would continue to come!

If we learned to work with these energies instead of letting them batter us about, we could achieve great alignment with our souls. Overindulgence in anything (food, sex, tobacco, television, coffee, drugs, alcohol, etc.) would lower our energy vibration and suppress our enthusiasm and inspiration to cooperate with the energies. If we were not managing our emotions, they would manage us, making us vulnerable to breakdowns in our physical systems.

Anger, anxiety and the tendency to judge and criticize would increase with the energy intensity. We would need to look at what we repressed and rejected. What we saw to criticize in others is evidence of what we don't like – or are unwilling to see – in ourselves. To heal we needed to forgive the aspect of ourselves we were projecting onto others. No one is, or has ever done, anything to us. We do it to ourselves!

The energies might force us into extreme discomfort about the areas of our lives out of alignment with our souls. Many of us hold out certain aspects of our lives as <u>not</u> being spiritual, particularly sexual expressions and money. We would need to examine these aspects.

Also, the days of going to church on Sunday (and maybe Wednesday night as well) or meditating occasionally to get a spiritual fix are over!

It became evident that in order for us to be full-time spiritual beings – no matter what activity we were engaged in – we would need to be in a constant state of meditation, in constant awareness of the presence of our God selves. We would need to live spiritually, which means getting "real" – to be honest with ourselves and others.

We either live it or we don't. To be partially spiritual is like being "a little bit pregnant". It is not possible. Our souls eventually demand surrender.

More "truths" surfaced. For instance, the 11:11 cycle of energy meant that everything would be accelerated. Our present age calls for honesty, openness and integrity with our souls. More and more people become telepathic, empathetic. How we are speaks louder than <u>what</u> we "say". We weren't going to be able to hide from our own souls or others.

Our "truth" would be demonstrated in the quality of our lives. If we didn't like that quality, we would need to take a good look at our beliefs. If we "believed" we must live a life of solitude or loneliness (while affirming companionship) we would remain alone. If we "believed" we don't deserve abundance (while affirming wealth) we would remain in lack.

Further, the time of duality was ending.

It seems fitting here to say that much of the work Light workers are being called upon to do must be done energetically, not physically, because of the Earth "systems" These systems exist because scientists and industries have a vested interest in not developing anything that would liberate this planet from economic slavery. Thus, Light workers must be "in the World, but not of the World," as some bright person once said.

Moving into another subject, the Spirits constantly remind us of the changes occurring in our DNA. These changes result from both THEIR assistance and from the way our bodies react to the stress/strain of the energies bombarding the Earth.

As mentioned, Earth has a Central Sun at its core; also a Solar Sun, which is seen in the sky. Beyond this is the Great Central Sun, which focuses energies to this Omniverse of twelve Universes. (Earth is one of the twelve.)

As the Earth prepares for transition into a Fifth Dimensional being, many events are happening, most of which are connected to the interaction of the Earth with these three Suns.

The Source of this Omniverse activating the Great Central Sun, which sends energies through the Solar Sun to the Central Sun within the Earth, is raising the vibration of Earth from the inside and the outside simultaneously. (These radiations also keep the orbits in place.) But the vibrations the Central Sun radiates to the surface and back to the Great Central Sun also cause earthquakes, tidal waves, storms, volcanic eruptions and weather changes.

Some recent weather changes were caused by ships from the 37 intergalactic civilizations that recently anchored over major cities on Earth. This additional magnetic energy in the atmosphere causes many vibrational/weather changes, even though the ships are anchored in the fifth dimension.

Interestingly enough, regarding energies bombarding the Earth, this article appeared in *The San Francisco Chronicle* in 1991:

"The week of June 15th a solar flare, one of the largest detected since regular observations began in the 1840's, sent out a stream of charged subatomic particles that pummeled Earth's atmosphere. Soviet scientists are <u>theorizing</u> that such electromagnetic storms churn the Earth's molten interior and <u>may</u> contribute to volcanic eruptions."

Of little help or consequence are the theories and left-brain conclusions of Humanity. Spirit is asking us to work energetically on volcanic eruptions through already existing volcanoes in inhabited areas, so as to minimize the destruction. Oftentimes, energy can be directed to areas of the oceans and defused.

Earth, as mentioned earlier, is being energetically drawn through the Fourth Dimension into the Fifth Dimension as it transforms itself from the inside out, vibrationally. Although difficult to describe in words, a spin-off of Earth's movement into the Fifth Dimension is the time-space continuum – the action of the ring-pass-not perimeter around the Earth becoming <u>closer</u> to the Earth. For inhabitants of the planet, this results in time speeding up. Interestingly enough, in April of 1991, as we Humans moved from standard time into daylight time, both a noticeable speeding up of time, and a seemingly shortening of the hour, took place. According to the information received from Spirit during the group's weekly meditation on April 17, this happened and was to continue beyond our time-space continuum. We were told, "The adjustment will shorten each hour by approximately 12-1/2 minutes. This will not be discernible by physical clocks, but will be noticed by your consciousness, which is connected outside of the Third Dimension and affects your thoughts and memory storage."

As for the ring-pass-not, the Spiritual Hierarchy erected it to prevent the pollution of Earth from spreading and affecting other members of the Solar System.

The tightening of the "ring" and the vibrational movement of the Earth toward the Fifth Dimension is forcing the lower astral realm (the lower fourth dimension) into the Earth's current dimension. Consequently, Earth's population is being affected because the lower astral realm is the home of spirits still holding to physical individuals and/or situations; wayward spirits who have not successfully made their transition into the Light; spirits who are possessing and interfering with the lives of embodied beings because they (these spirits) still have addictive needs served only by possessing bodies of physical individuals addicted to drugs, alcohol, food, sex or power.

As the Earth moves toward the fifth dimension, it must maneuver through this abyss of chaos. How difficult this may be for both the planet and Humans depends partially on Light Workers' abilities to assist in clearing the astral plane. Calling on Archangel Michael and the Band of Mercy (Angels whose job it is to escort souls to the Light) to bring the lost and wayward Spirits into the Light is an effective way to do it. Also, using the symbols – the symbols being given to raise and alter vibrational frequencies and situations – is another way.

DREAMSPELL PLAN

Another Plan related to redeeming the Human race was the Dreamspell Plan suggested by Jose Arguelles and Spirit. This would move Humanity to a common standard of time during an eight-year conversion starting July 26, 1992, and ending July 26, 2000. It would introduce a galactic culture and the 13-moon calendar. The calendar measures the solar year according to thirteen perfect months of 28 days each.

I found this information very interesting because Spirit had been pushing me to understanding the lunar aspect of the zodiac calendar since the first of 1991.

I also found these suggestions by "Dreamspell," interesting: "Realize we are controlled by the way we have been taught and told to relate to the phenomena of time.

"Turn off your TV sets. Get back to primary KNOWING. Do this with your family and your loved ones . . . "

I had been living pretty much without time the past year when my watch exploded upon my arrival in Mexico to anchor "The New Jerusalem." Of course, I had the advantage of living outside the normal day-to-day world, most of that time.

Also in June, a friend called me from Oklahoma to tell me this true happening:

A couple with a three-year-old brought home a new baby. From the first day the baby was home, the older child asked to be left alone with the infant. However, fearing sibling rivalry, the parents were very leery. Finally, they agreed to the child's plea. As they listened on the intercom, they heard the three-year-old say to the newborn, "Baby, tell me what God is like. I am beginning to forget." Chills!!!!

WHAT WE CAN DO

I continued working consciously to block the storage of nuclear waste in the caverns of New Mexico and to awaken scientists and the President to the idea of transmuting this waste, WHICH IS POSSIBLE. There was now, also, another person assisting in the procedure, working in the plant in Colorado (where the waste accumulates.) Years later a group of us met in Denver and focused the energy of jimson weed all over Rocky Flats. Spirit had revealed that jimson weed feeds on contaminated soil and leaches out and transmutes the toxic elements.

It took two years for the idea to enter the minds of scientists at Washington State University where they hybridize certain plants with the enzymes from a rabbit's liver to create plants that would do the same thing as the jimson weed. The idea was planted and now is a reality.

Burial is NOT the answer to this nightmare man has created and Spirit assures us that burial in the salt caverns would be disastrous. Spirit further tells us it is possible to neutralize atomic waste through the addition of diozonian phosphate. The molecular structure can be changed to create a non-toxic substance.

I remember a talk I gave in Charlotte, North Carolina. A man in the audience told us he had previously worked for EXXON developing a formula for detoxifying nuclear waste. He stated that the company now has the formula, but is shelving it to keep the price of fossil fuel up!

It is amazing what greed can do! What price ignorance or "progress" if we lose the planet and our souls??

Individuals can still help with the effort to block storage of nuclear waste by meditating on it. Ask your soul to project the answer to this situation into the hearts and minds of our leaders and scientists. Ask for help in stopping nuclear weapons testing and stockpiling.

Also, project with me the transference of monies and energies now being used for the wars into environmental issues. We and the government have the resources and abilities to solve these problems if we ask for spiritual guidance and intervention.

We are in control, <u>but only if we wake up and use the spiritual power and energy we can access</u>. <u>We must release and give up our fear of being powerful and responsible</u>.

Many of us misused these abilities in past lives, and need now to clear that memory from our DNA. (The "Cellular Release Process" tape, available through Namaste, can help with this.)

Ask yourself <u>continually</u>:

WHAT IS THE NEXT SINGLE THING FOR ME
TO DO OR KNOW, FOR ME TO BE IN A STATE
OF DIVINE GRACE?

Do this thing, then ask again.

WHAT IS THE NEXT SINGLE THING FOR ME
TO DO OR KNOW, FOR ME TO BE IN A STATE
OF DIVINE GRACE?

30

Moving On

Mid-1991

In June of that year I began feeling very uncomfortable in Mount Shasta. My body, which had been fairly relaxed all winter, began aching. I felt annoyed and unsettled for no apparent reason. Also, circumstances concerning my relationship with Frank and the community began irritating me, although these situations were actually the same – and in many ways better – than they had been for months.

At this time, my "logic" came up with pretty good arguments: "This is the most beautiful time to be in Mount Shasta. The snows are finished, and the flowers are beginning to bloom. Frank loves you. This relationship works. He understands you, and you are well cared for and protected in this environment."

However, my soul had other reasons as it whispered, "It is time to move on. Your vision is not yet large enough."

The argument was quite irritating to me. Being a Libra, I weigh everything – all possibilities and probabilities – and examine how my choices may affect everyone else in my life. In doing so, I have what some people feel is an advantage in that I have learned to project myself into various physical locations to see if they "fit" before I leap into the void.

There is a place within me where I take statements to see if they are my truth, or if they are appropriate for me. Everyone can learn to do this. Everybody has this capability.

However, after weeks of inner argument, I knew I had to leave California. I did not know where I was to go, but I knew that I was to go alone. And I knew I was to go to a place centrally located in the United States where I knew few people. These were my only clues (my soul was very vague with its instructions on my move).

Later on, I realized that one of the reasons I had to leave Mount Shasta concerned what I saw as a psychic net of energy being dropped over the region. Many similar nets were being put into place over some of the major energy vortexes of the Earth – locations that are normally gathering places for spiritual seekers.

The purpose of the energy nets was to make soul communication difficult; to make it possible for the imposters to connect themselves to seekers, as their guides; for the pretenders to find channels for their energies.

I recognized these imposters as part of the "dark force." They were aspects of energy and parts of souls that had forgotten they are God and were standing in the shadows. (See the Chapter on Discernment for more on this.)

Then in July I flew to Denver to work again with Barry and Karen and their radionics machine.

My basic purpose for going (other than enjoying friends) was to release more symbols into the Earth's etheric, which we did together.

These symbols are necessary to activate the waiting star seeds within the DNA of Humanity. These symbols carry concise symbolic content of "meta-conceptual information". This information includes inventions and systems necessary for the continued evolution of Earth and Humanity.

This information teaches us more about our own nature and purpose upon Earth. According to Spirit, it is like issuing a "cosmic news release." The availability of the symbols and activations will further enhance the knowledge and energies available for us in our evolution from Homo-sapiens to Homo-universalis.

These symbols were different from those previously released into the Earth's etheric. These were much larger than the small golden ones. They were similar to the ones at the bottom of the ocean as seen in the movie *Abyss*. They were winged, or butterfly-shaped, brilliantly lighted and graceful, almost like large Angelic or Devic presences.

After being in Denver for two weeks, Spirit suggested I stay another ten days while Frank went through a soul-clearing process, for which he needed to be alone.

The third week, Frank completed his processing and drove my car to Denver to join me. We each went through several clearing processes with a wonderful counselor, Kathleen Buchenauer, who practices "Circles of Life" release techniques.

After the counseling, Frank and I drove to South Central Texas to check out a possible relocation site. We went to New Mexico to visit friends and to Sedona to have our "batteries charged." We also went to Tucson to visit the site of a symposium. By the time we got back to Shasta, we had driven 5,000 miles.

During the trip, through communication with our souls, Frank became aware that we needed to separate for several months. This corresponded with my earlier feelings that I HAD to leave California. For me, the trick here was to ask the "right" questions! So I requested that the Universe "show me the next step; show me clearly!" Several options were presented. I "felt" each one carefully, weighing the pros and cons. Since the two priority items at the top of my "list" are <u>always</u> FREEDOM and FLEXIBILITY, the soul suggested that I pack my car and that Frank call a moving service, even though we did not know where I was headed.

By the time the car was packed and the movers had arrived, the phone rang. Friends in Albuquerque, New Mexico, were calling to say they had been asked in meditation that morning to offer me a condo they had in Albuquerque rent-free for nine months. "If this would serve you in some way," were the words they used. I laughed and cried as I gratefully accepted their offer. I moved into their beautiful vacant, furnished condo. I was extremely appreciative and felt especially blessed to have that sacred space as my next home. I worked on further writing and on my paintings. Frank wanted to sell his house and go to Hawaii. He summed it up this way:

"The last ten months with bj have been a time of happiness and a time of growth. In July 1989, I completed my 'contract on Earth.' I chose to stay in body and was put back to work. I had some difficulty being in this dimension, and a short time ago realized I was digging myself into another pit. With bj's help and understanding and my strong determination to turn this around, I went to work.

"In the last few years I had in my eagerness to serve and with unquestioning faith, unknowingly sometimes opened myself to the influences of clones (beings from the astral plane impersonating high spiritual entities). Because of low self-esteem I have misinterpreted some of the information I have received.

"While bj was in Denver, I progressed to a point that started freeing me from the blocks I had set. During our sojourn through the Southwest, with bj's help, I began to merge with my Oversoul.

"At this point I need to re-evaluate what I have received from other beings, and most importantly, complete the merger with my Oversoul. For this I need to once more temporarily become a hermit. bj also needs time alone. So, for a time, we will be physically apart.

"I will go back to Kauai where I began to claim my power in 1987. This time I will complete it and move on to the next step."

Obviously, I had to change the nature of my relationship with Frank. This was all difficult and exhausting. For example, the day before I planned to leave Mount Shasta, some friends were driving my car to pick up the newsletter at the printers. A drunk, uninsured motorist with an expired driver's license struck the car, damaging the entire passenger side.

I was devastated! How could this be happening to me? I had a deadline, a time when my soul had stated it was appropriate for me to leave.

For several hours I stewed, fumed, cursed and fretted. Finally, after releasing the anger and frustration, I became quiet, went inside and LISTENED.

"*This is not your lesson. All systems in the car are intact. You will not be inconvenienced. You are still to leave as scheduled.*" My soul was explicit. However, the person who hit my car could not be located from any of the addresses he gave. The responsibility then for repairing the vehicle was shifted to my insurance agency in Denver. The agent assured me the car could be repaired in Albuquerque with no difficulty. So I left as scheduled.

Three hours after I arrived in Albuquerque, the insurance agent called to say he was getting me a new rental car and making immediate arrangements to have my car repaired. As soul promised, I was not inconvenienced.

The condominium was lovely. Located on the eastern edge of the city, it provided a view of the Sandia Mountains from the living room! The space was light (many windows and skylights) and cheerful with Jacuzzi and fireplaces. Everything I needed was within a five-minute drive.

I was soon fully settled and feeling very comfortable, productive and blessed. I also soon became aware that the southwest sunsets from the back patio were awesomely inspiring. (I must include here a local joke about the area – if you learn to spell "Albuquerque," you get to live there!)

A short time after I arrived in New Mexico, my children from Lubbock, Texas, drove over to celebrate my fiftieth birthday. We had our best time together since we separated in 1979. I was so pleased to be living much closer to them.

From my new location in Albuquerque, I now planned to travel to a different area once a month to speak, and perform readings, initiations and clearing processes.

I might add here that I felt again like a circus performer and the trapeze bars: I had just leaped once more into the void and caught yet another trapeze bar with my name on it, requiring a relocation. (Friends have learned to "pencil in" my location in their address books.)

AN EMBRYO AND A NEW GRAIN

For months in meditation I had been seeing an embryo forming in the center of the Earth. Since no one else I know had mentioned seeing this infant, I did not mention it. (This silence was similar to when I first began seeing The New Jerusalem moving into our etheric. This was before my companions and I helped ground it in the Yucatan in 1990. I had thought if the ship really was as large as I perceived it to be, everyone who was psychic would have seen it and been talking about it.)

During the session I noticed the embryo stirring and it asked to be birthed through my body. At that, my breathing deepened, my body began to arch and the birthing process began. Interestingly enough, I had had my two physical children by Caesarean, so I had not experienced this more natural form of childbirth, which involved a great deal of breath control.

When the infant was born I was told by the Mother Earth that its name was HOPE; that its birth represented Humanity's turning the corner into the Golden Age. (At that time I understood there were enough souls [*The Hundredth Monkey*] who were aware and awake for the Earth to feel hopeful about its survival and transformation into a higher vibrational planet.)

We were then asked to bring into the etheric of Earth the thought form of a new hybrid grain that would grow virtually without water (to solve world hunger). We were also asked to instill this thought form into the minds of scientists in the Agricultural Experiment Stations at the University of Texas, Texas Tech, Texas A&M and three agricultural schools in Idaho. As the extraterrestrials were giving the information, they reminded us that no "wild" corn grows on Earth; that it, at one time, had also been a gift from them. The new grain would be a hybrid of grains we already know. When I saw it psychically, it resembled corn leaves and stalks after they are dried. However, the heads of the grain looked more like sorghum or maize than corn.

The new grain would resemble "quinoa," which is grown high in the Andes Mountains of Peru. The extraterrestrials said that when this grain is grown and ingested physically, like quinoa, it opens spaces within the cells of the bodies of those who eat it so they (the bodies) can hold more Christ light. This grain would fulfill the biblical prophecy "the last shall be first." Those who are now starving would be fed. I still have not read of this new grain actually being hybridized. Sometimes it takes years for an idea that is planted on the rings of our planet to be picked up by scientists and researchers.My daughter wrote the following poem for my birthday (September 1991):

WE ARE ONE
By Kelley Kay King

We are One And One are we, Although we dwell here Separately.

We came to Earth
By magical birth
To savor her beauty
And heighten her worth.

But, greed and stupidity
Led to loss,
If only we knew
How huge the cost.

To save our planet
We ALL must try,
Not just to watch
And let her die

For we are One
And One are we,
Although we dwell here
Separately.

31

Prejudice and Judgment

October 1991

I want to share one of my experiences I call "Prejudice." I want to share it because it is so important that we give up prejudices, judgments, deceptions and self-deceptions.

The new energy which began coming in November 11, 1991, put these thought forms "in our faces," so we could confront them, correct them and release them. (If we don't confront them, they'll surface later in far less pleasant circumstances. <u>And this is just as important now as it was in 1991</u>.)

I was barely settled into my new home in Albuquerque when it was time to go to Denver for a week. Shortly after, I spent ten days in Spokane, Washington, and Coeur d'Alene, Idaho.

Since I did not yet know anyone in the Albuquerque area I could call upon to take me to the airport, I had to take a taxi. As my hands flipped through the pages of the telephone book, I became aware that I was holding an "opinion," a "prejudice," a "judgment," somewhere in my consciousness concerning taxi drivers. This judgment conceded that I assumed taxi drivers were uneducated people (which also meant boring) who could not perform more meaningful work. This was the reason behind my bigoted decision to not talk with the driver on my way to the airport. I wanted to just sit back, relax, gather my thoughts and read *Writing Down the Bones* by Natalie Goldberg, which had just arrived in the mail from a fellow writer in Charlotte, North Carolina.

I climbed into the taxi and was beginning to lose myself in my book when the driver interrupted me.

"Do you want to take the long route or the short route to the airport?"

"What's the difference?" I asked.

"Four dollars," he replied.

"I want the less expensive route, but I want to be on time," I stated rather emphatically.

"What time is your flight?"

"5:10."

"OK, we can make it," he stated, adding "that's what I thought you would say."

He turned around in his seat and started the engine. The vehicle was a white Chevrolet, an older model. The seats were black plastic. The floor mats had been recently vacuumed.

As we pulled gently away from the curb, I went back to my book. However, as we rounded the first curve on the way out of the small subdivision, he began his interrogation.

"Where you headed out to today?" he questioned, all the while watching traffic with one eye (and his body) and watching me in his strategically positioned rearview mirror with the other.

"Denver tonight and Spokane, Washington, tomorrow." My reply was as succinct as possible, as I didn't want to converse with a taxi driver about the weather or any other Third Dimensional, meaningless subject. I just wanted to relax from my lively morning trip preparation, drink my Classic Coke from its cold red can and munch a handful of salted nuts I had grabbed as I ran out the door. All of this would suffice for breakfast (which I had skipped) and lunch too, since it wouldn't be served on the flight. (I ignored the sign on the cab's window that read, "No eating or drinking in this taxi.")

"What will you be doing in Denver and Spokane?" The male voice interrupted my reverie.

"Speaking." My reply was short and quick.

"What is your subject, if it's not too personal," he inquired.

I sat very still for a few moments. I was quite annoyed, yet curious at his persistence. Since many fundamentalist Christians still have a negative reaction to my work, I searched my mind, brain and Higher Self simultaneously to find words that would say just enough – yet not too much – about who I am, what I do and the nature of this particular mission.

"Spiritual creativity," were the words I formed and enunciated.

"Spiritual creativity," . . . (pause) . . . "Yeah . . . that works. I understand that. Yeah, that's good. I like that. Will any part of your talk be channeled?"

An electrical shock went up my spine. I sat up straight in my seat and looked directly into his eyes in the small mirror.

"Yes, yes, as a matter of fact it probably will be. Why do you ask, that and what do YOU know about channeling?" The words fell out of my mouth all over themselves. I felt a flush spread over my face. My most recently uncovered judgment and prejudice were confronting me so quickly and blatantly! I began laughing loudly and somewhat uncontrollably.

"What's the matter?" he questioned. "What are you laughing at?"

"Me," I confessed as I dug through my purse for a tissue to wipe away the tears and blow my nose. "God would not dare send me an unenlightened taxi driver..."

"Probably not, considering who you are," he rejoined. "You're from Texas, aren't you?"

He continued his inquiries as he maneuvered the old cab through the late afternoon traffic. He didn't give me any opportunity at all to ask, "What do you mean, 'considering who I am?'"

"Yes. How did you know that?" I was a little taken aback by his observation.

"Because of your accent. You've tried to overcome it, during your travels, obviously, but it's still there. Leave it alone. Let it come through. It's charming. Don't hide your roots."

By this time I was beginning to feel a little defensive. As a result, I decided to take an offensive position in the conversation and began asking my own questions.

"Where are you from? Have you always lived in Albuquerque?"

"No," he answered, "only since high school. I'm from a place about forty miles southwest of here. I rode the bus here because it was the closest high school. Later, I went to work for an international construction firm and traveled as a foreman building bridges and structures in a lot of foreign countries.

"I guess it was God's way of getting me to be planetarily literate," he went on. "I learned a lot about different cultures and how to function in strange circumstances and be peaceful with whatever happened to be going on around me.

"I moved here a few years ago when I quit traveling. I came here to go back to school."

By now my curiosity had me sitting forward on the seat. I could feel my own skin. I was aware of moisture, tension, pleasure, a sense of excitement and pain. I pursued my questioning.

"How do you happen to know about channeling?" I inquired boldly.

"I've dated several women who were into that, and they took me to hear some people channel. I found it fascinating, so I read up on it some and listened to them tell me about what they were learning," the man responded.

"What are you taking in school?" I asked fast before he could resume his position as questioner.

"Creative writing and English. I've got some stuff I want to write about as a result of my travels and I butcher the language pretty badly. So I thought I should see if I could learn something that would help me."

"Have you seen this book?" I questioned, holding up, *Writing Down the Bones*.

"No. No, I haven't," he answered, looking at the cover as I held it up to reflect in his mirror.

"Why are you driving a taxi?" I pushed tactlessly.

"Oh, I'm coasting. When I quit construction, I wasn't sure what I wanted to do so I decided on this. It gave me time to think and the schedule made it possible for me to go to school."

"What do you do for fun?" he suddenly threw at me before I could verbalize my next question.

"I paint." The words dropped out of my mouth.

"How about you, what do you do for fun?" I slung the question at him before he could ask another.

"I dance. I usually go dancing three nights a week," was his reply.

"Really?" I said. "What kind of dancing?"

"Country-Western." He watched for my reaction in the mirror.

"I used to do that, about 10 or 12 years ago. I dated a fellow who loved to dance. I really enjoyed it. Good exercise, too. Interesting. My guidance has been pushing me to take up dancing again even if I only dance for myself at home. My daughter, 22, who lives in Lubbock, loves to dance country and western. She goes several times a week. She's been visiting me recently and is also psychic. She said she saw me going dancing again." I was nearly breathless, saying far more than I had intended to reveal.

"My name is Dave Bob, and yours is?" He left the question hanging in the air between us.

"bj," I answered.

"B. J. like the initials?"

I could feel the next question coming: "What does that stand for?" the same response almost everybody makes when I say, "bj." I took my brochure from my briefcase and leaned over to lay it on the seat beside him when he asked the name of the airline I was traveling with.

"Continental," I said quickly, diverting him from the previous question. At that moment I didn't want to explain that the initials stand for the name of the previous entity who inhabited this body. Nor did I want to explain that, almost as a standing cosmic joke, they also stand for "before Jovanna," the cosmic entity who now has primary control of the body. I wasn't about to explain that "bj" is used simultaneously by at least twelve members of the Oversoul, from various vibrational dimensions, who do not have ongoing physical bodies of their own.

We pulled up where he was to let me out at the airport. Jumping out of the now stationery vehicle he stuck his head back through the door and grinned with his whole face.

"That will be $17.50 for the first leg of your journey. You can leave the money on the front seat if you don't need change and I'll get your bags."

I rummaged in my purse for bills. I placed them on the seat along with a copy of my *Finding Your Life Purpose* workbook. I also exchanged the brochure I had previously placed on the seat for one that did not contain my Albuquerque phone number, and stepped away from the cab.

"Thanks for being so prompt and getting me here on time," I yelled over the noise and flow of terminal traffic.

"You take care and tell 'em how it is when you get up North," Dave hollered back, waving his massive hand and grinning broadly. He got back in the car and pulled away from the curb.

As I stood near my bags, watching the old cab gradually disappear, I felt a bit dazed. I handed my ticket to the ticket/baggage porter without a word. It seemed much like I had just stepped out of a time warp.

I tipped the man who took my bags as he returned my ticket to Denver, but did not grasp the words coming from his lips. I entered the terminal through automatic sliding doors that required nothing from me, beyond being present.

Down the corridor I consulted my ticket jacket for the gate number. C-8 to the right. A few minutes later I automatically zipped open my bag and briefcase, slipped off what I jokingly call my "Wonder Woman" bracelet and dropped it into a plastic container. A moment later I passed through the electronic device undetected.

Retrieving my bags, I donned my symbolic metal armor and proceeded to the designated gate. Subconsciously, I noted the location of seated smokers and moved to a suitable location. Sitting down, I retrieved my reading glasses and my book. I reran the taxi ride on my mental screen, to deliberately record the details and sensory experiences in my long-term memory, so I could retrieve it at some future writing time . . .

Once again I became absorbed in *Writing Down the Bones*. The words seemed to have been written by my soul just for me! As I completed each brief chapter I thought of more and more people with whom I wanted to share the book and the wisdom it contained. My mind was eager and my fingers itched to write. I pulled the small brown-flowered journal, recently acquired, from my leather bag. I began jotting down impressions of people around me and feelings I discovered within myself. As I did so, I noted how confident I felt, my hair freshly cut and set, my nails recently done. My outfit, enhanced by the addition of a yarn and shell necklace and earrings I had designed myself, augmented the feeling. I knew, too, that the Earth green of my clinging cotton top and long, flowing skirt accentuated the more positive points of my figure.

Continuing my inventory, I appreciated the stunning Chinese tie-dyed silk scarf I had deliberately grabbed from my closet the last moment before departure. Its fall colors drew together all the shades of my outfit, from the rich brown of my riding boots and the creamy leather of my bag, to my shells-and-feathers necklace – even my copper hair. Also, the beautiful taupe leather coat draped over my shoulders brought the energy of Mary Jo, my adopted Mom, symbolically around me. The coat had been a gift from her.

I felt "together" and totally ready for this trip and the adventures it would bring. This assuredness was in spite of the nagging feeling I'd had from the beginning; that the end of the trip would turn out differently from what I supposed or planned! I left my options open (and had thrown in extra lingerie just in case.)

I began an inventory of my bags: meditation tapes, blank tapes, workbooks, brochures, teaching materials, tape recorder, painted greeting cards, and enough coordinated outfits for at least ten days.

"Now boarding flight for Denver through gate C-8." The announcement interrupted my inventory as I reached "lace underwear." I moved through the slanted runway with my carry-on luggage and onto the plane.

The captain was cheerfully greeting passengers as they boarded. Psychically checking out his body, I felt very secure as I noted no drugs or alcohol in his bloodstream. That he had the hots for the stewardess next to him amused me, but did not concern me. The two would be far too busy during the flight to have any time or opportunity to fulfill the desire I could feel in their bodies.

I deliberately closed my aura and disengaged from theirs, having obtained only the information necessary for me to feel safe. I apologized to their souls for the psychic intrusion, moved to my seat and settled in . . .

"I hope no one else is assigned to this row," I thought to myself, "so I can read some more and let my mind wander. I might even write some."

"Looks like this is my seat. Hi. How are you?" A cheerful young executive type with reddish hair and close-cropped beard greeted me as he began stowing his coat in the compartment above the seat. He eased into his place, adjusting the seatbelt over his small paunch.

I noted his name on the briefcase he laid on the seat between us. As I did so, I checked a mental list of names (in my head) of persons unknown to me but who I'd been told I'd meet in the future. This list is added to, periodically, by my soul.

When I meet a person whose name is on that list, I know I will be given a message for him or her during a conversation. This man's name was on the list . . .

I picked my book up, but remained aware of my row companion. I also prepared to be interrupted.

The young executive opened his briefcase and retrieved several papers to look over during the flight. Letterheads on the paper revealed he was an environmental specialist.

"Interesting," I mused to myself as I made more mental notes of his well-polished shoes, immaculate nails, gold watch, polished cotton subtle mauve shirt and muted multi-toned tie. My internal computer picked up that he was happily married, had young children, and that his wife bought his clothes. I also knew he was good at his job, but that he wished he was doing something different.

I went on with my reading, underlining various passages. He became absorbed in his papers, almost like a school teacher grading an exam.

He began chuckling and rubbing his forehead while shaking his head from side to side.

"I can't believe how people write," he declared, "especially when they are trying to impress you. Why can't they just say what they want to say, just like they would talk?"

I stopped reading, held my place with my finger, shoved my reading glasses up on my head and turned toward him, acknowledging his obvious need to engage in conversation.

"Have you read this?" I asked, exposing the cover of *Writing Down the Bones*.

"No, but I've read a lot of books about writing," he answered.

"So have I. As a matter of fact, I am a writer, but something about the energy of this book is different. You might want to get a copy," I suggested.

"What do you write?" he asked.

"I write about feelings, spirituality, metaphysics, stuff like that," I replied. I hedged a little, couching the truth in words I thought he could accept, yet might challenge him.

The plane's intercom began blaring the captain's message that we would remain on the ground for thirty minutes before take-off because of a backup in air traffic at the Stapleton Airport in Denver. "Damn." The young executive banged the lap tray with his fist.

The words over the intercom kept coming: "You may deplane briefly if you need to call ahead to notify anyone of your change in arrival time. Please return as quickly as possible in case we get clearance to depart sooner. Thank you for your patience."

I deliberately projected my consciousness to Denver to see if I needed to deplane to call Jan who was meeting me. However, my feelings grew calm and I knew I didn't need to do anything; everything felt in order.

"By the way, my name is Bob – Robert. What's yours?" the young man asked as he returned the papers to his briefcase.

"bj," I responded, as usual checking his mind and aura and waiting for him to form the familiar question.

"What do they stand for? Why do you choose to use initials as your name? I once had a man interview for a job whose name was a five-digit number! He was pretty weird." The young executive ran the sentences together without waiting for an answer from me.

"It's a long story," I offered. "I'm an artist and a writer and a lecturer and counselor, and the name seems to fit who I am and what I do. I use lowercase letters with no periods to sign my paintings."

"But, about the longer story. I'd like to hear that," he responded. It was as if some cosmic force were encouraging me to reveal events that might prod this conservative – yet very creative man – to leave the security of his stressful and unrewarding job to do his soul's work.

"What's the name of the book you've written?" he prompted.

"One is a workbook for finding your life's purpose. The other is a book of poetry entitled *Old Loves are Seldom Finished*. Life purpose is usually what I talk about in my lectures. But the subject seems to be adjusting itself to spiritual creativity, or using the spirit of creativity to find your life's purpose," I revealed to him and to myself simultaneously.

"Well, it looks like the Universe has arranged extra time for me to hear your story, so we might as well sit back, relax and take advantage of it and enjoy ourselves. Want a beer or a glass of wine?" he offered.

"White wine would be good, thanks."

As he ordered, paid the stewardess and arranged the drinks, I stowed my book, pen and glasses into my briefcase. I accepted my mission as storyteller and smiled at him (and privately to myself). I took a deep breath and began the story I'd told hundreds of times before . . . how I became bj.

Some days later, on my return flight from Denver, Spokane and Coeur d'Alene, I thought ahead for a moment. I reasoned that I would have one hour to get to my house, jump into my car and arrive at the post office to pick up my mail. I would get a good start on the correspondence before company arrived from out of town the next afternoon.

I programmed that I would find a cab immediately after I retrieved my luggage at the airport.

When I arrived, one taxi was in the drive as the porter carried my bags to the curb. As soon as I walked up the driver, who had been negotiating with a foreign-appearing gentleman, turned her head, saw me and began backing up the driveway to pick me up.

Upon entering the taxi I explained my hurry, to which she immediately asked what I did professionally.

As I attempted to give her an explanation, she began telling me about herself.

She had three degrees, one in political science, one in journalism and one in photography. Her most recent job had been with NATO.

Information began pouring in immediately from her soul, suggesting she was preparing to leave Albuquerque for New York to become a photojournalist for the Associated Press.

When I related this information to her, she was shocked at it coming from a stranger. But she confirmed that these events were already in motion in her life.

Upon arriving at my condo, she thanked me and asked for a copy of my *Finding your Life's Purpose* workbook. I was able to get one for her and still arrive at the post office before closing time.

In conclusion, I'll repeat what I said at the beginning of this chapter, that it is time to give up prejudices, judgments, deceptions and self-deceptions. These will come up in our lives so we can confront them, correct them and let them go.

If we do not do this, down the road in our lives we will be faced with the same issues, and they may even be more difficult then.

NEW CONSCIOUSNESS
By bj King

A new consciousness
Is creeping across the old, Engulfing it
As an antibiotic wiping out a dread disease
Of limitation
Stagnation; Expansion of consciousness
To include all races, all sexes,
Liberation to face
A changing World
With new awareness of problems created
By the changes,
Problems that cannot be solved
By men, by women, alone
But can only be surmounted
By men and women
Side by side.

32

Rewarding Work and Contemplation

While catching up on the correspondence and other chores about the place prior to my next journey, I reviewed some of the experiences of my just concluded trip to the Pacific Northwest.

The ten days in Spokane and Coeur d'Alene had gone very well. I had been warmly received.

However, I'd had to make some changes to my original plans. For example, the home where I had been scheduled to stay was not available. Since by that time I had become accustomed to being flexible, I just assumed that Spirit had had good reason for arranging different accommodations for me.

On the second day of my visit, a 12-year-old boy in the home where I was staying called me aside privately and questioned, "Do you realize that I am the reason you are here?"

"Yes, please tell me why you think that is true," I responded.

"Because I have been praying to God to send me someone who could answer all my questions about spaceships, extraterrestrials, where I am from and why I am here," he exclaimed excitedly.

I laughed in amusement at the Spirit, while assuring the young man that I was NOT laughing at him. "Please ask your questions," I then said. "Your soul is ready to respond."

We talked for several hours. I introduced him to his guides from his Oversoul and through a guided meditation they took him on a tour of his home planet.

I was impressed with this boy's sincerity, lucidity and openness. I had the feeling that many of our young people are beginning to look very deeply into why they are here and where they came from.

Many miraculous things, too personal to the clients to mention here, happened during the trip. I also continued my work with the Atomic Energy plants in the Pacific Northwest.

A few weeks following my stay in the Pacific Northwest, I went to Alabama and North Carolina. This was very enlightening and enjoyable.

SPIRIT COMMUNICATIONS

I was home alone a few days before Christmas when I received these intriguing Truths from my Oversoul;

"Co-creators of World peace will be those individuals whose hearts are well connected with their minds. In so doing, their minds become connected with the One Mind, thereby causing a SYNERGY of such proportions that war is an impossible thought; conflict is an impossible thought. Each individualized expression becomes the expression of God.

"Synergy is when the whole is greater than the sum of the parts added together; when the result does not appear to have been able to be created by that which went into the process; when Divine Grace is combined with Human activity in the process of regeneration.

"Truth comes. It is not first known, then embodied. Truth is embodied, then realized. This is true self-realization, or God-realization. The Truth is fully known when a thought becomes so strong, a desire so great as to become a reality; it has first become a Truth for the individualized expression of God.

"Make the mind a vacuum. Connect this vacuum to the Mind of God. Become the embodiment of the flow between your mind and the Mind of God. Know the reality of the relinquishment of your free will to that of the Source and then you shall know true freedom, true creativity, TRUTH.

"Be not afraid to share the Truth which is known to you by its embodiment. Be wary of sharing an intellectualized truth, for you will be as one beating a dead drum.

"Be wary of spouting an intellectualized faith, for those who seek can see the skeleton behind your faith. If this faith is not walked and lived, the image you project will be that of a ghost, an illusion of faith. None will draw forth to follow your example, but will shun you as a false prophet, a builder of empty temples to the false God of the intellect.

"Tread lightly upon the Earth, leaving only footprints in the hearts of others which permeate the love within each of them and draws forth their *best, their God selves.*

"Take note to understand your true purpose as a co-creator of beauty, expresser of love, a spokesperson of embodied Truth.

"Find that part of self which fears rejection and confront it. Remove all fear by asking your soul to remove all fear.

"Find that part of self which will not be denied and you will find God.

"Know yourself by introspection, listening, patience and gentleness.

"Understand the physical form as a cloak you wear for the covering of your soul's individualized expression. Know that you will remove it and move on to a greater reality, but you shall not die. That which you embody as Truth lives on. That which you preach, but do not practice, will be as shackles on your Selfhood even after the physical body is gone. Your individualized expression (your body) is an aspect of God. Handle it as such. Revere it, but do not idolize it. Understand its importance as a vehicle to be used, but do not abuse it. Realize its importance as a vehicle through which God can express Itself to others."

CHRISTMAS HOLIDAYS

I chose to spend Christmas Eve and Christmas Day, 1991, alone, which took active effort on my part. I needed introspection and assimilation.

Christmas brought many things to mind. For example, tradition: which to keep, which to let die. Churches: what do they represent and why do they survive? Jesus: why did he come and why did he leave by way of the cross? Why do Christians keep him on the cross instead of interacting with Him as if He were still alive? How could one life make such a meaningful difference for so long?

And more questions surfaced: What are we seeking when we agree to continue making the effort to get together with our families when we feel no connection, no joy in so doing? Why are we afraid, instead, to be with the people we enjoy? Why do we fear being alone? Should I be willing to continue making the effort to communicate with individuals who do not respond and demonstrate no interest in maintaining a relationship with me? Do I want to continue seeking a primary male/female relationship?

All this was a lot to contemplate. I learned a great deal and enjoyed my own company and that of a good book, *Fire in the Belly* by Sam Keen. It helped me understand more about the confusion regarding male/female roles and the conflict between the sexes. Since coming to Earth from the ship in 1969, I had been quite perplexed about these subjects.

On the ships we have only mental and spiritual bodies and are more androgynous (having the characteristics of both sexes in balance). We do not have emotional bodies. We DO have feelings and thoughts, but we see ourselves more as our role within the soul or as soul assignments. This is our primary focus. Our relationships are based on cooperation to accomplish the assigned task and are spirit based rather than emotion based.

As I read, painted and worked my way through New Year's Eve, I became much more aware of the need for balance between work and play in this life. I read a quote, "A well-rounded life is like a safety net under you. It allows you to do fancier tricks on the high wire."

This quotation made me think about the way we flow in life, grabbing one trapeze bar after another, taking risk after risk in order to reach our goal of remembering God . . .

Also, several visitors during the week prompted me to repeat my story of leaving Lubbock, Texas, in 1979, plus the events leading to my opening to the whisperings of my soul. Each time I told the story I became amazed at the faith I displayed in following guidance – just since I began listening to myself! (Right here I can say in all honesty, if we never take time to review our progress, we do not grant ourselves recognition for what we have accomplished or overcome!) A review of our past is often useful if only to remember we are making progress.

Another truth came to me during the holidays, which I spent mostly alone. It was that, energetically, the days of going to church on Sundays (and maybe Wednesdays also) or meditating occasionally to get a spiritual fix are over. We must become full-time spiritual beings, no matter what activity we are engaged in.

We can no longer afford to be in anything LESS than a constant state of meditation, a constant awareness of the Presence of our God-selves. To live spiritually means to get "real," to be honest. We either live it or we don't. To be partially spiritual is like being "a little bit pregnant." It is NOT possible.

During those holidays I also read the fascinating article, "Talking to God - An Intimate Look at the Way We Pray," an article that, amazingly, appeared in the January 6, 1992, issue of *NEWSWEEK*.

Up to then, nothing physical, other than the fall of the Berlin Wall, had given me more evidence that a shift WAS truly taking place resulting from the energies being given the Earth and Humanity!

Daily I felt more and more impressed to commune with the Creator, to honor creation, to be a co-creator, to recognize I AM THAT, I AM. I wanted to understand that I was both a part of the problem and a part of the solution because I was capable of contributing to the solution.

Also, praying "to" God or Holy Mother/Father God "felt" more and more like separation. It did not give me the same feeling that accepting Oneness and responsibility (my ability to respond to my soul and act accordingly) gave me.

I felt too, a need to recognize SPACE as ENERGY, and not a void between solid matter.

I experienced the terms "channeling" and "channeler" diminishing in relevance to my goal. Recent contacts had forced introspection, as more and more people asked, "What do you do?"

The word "mystic" kept replacing "channel" in my mind as a form of reply. But then I was confronted with the question, "What is your definition of a mystic?"

Some definitions emerged: "A person who seeks communion with God through contemplation and self-surrender." To "channel" seemed to imply opening to a flow of something other than Self. It felt different from embodying and "being." A mystic seeks to "be" an expression of God. I felt it time for me to merge with, "be," embody the soul, and admit that I AM THAT I AM is God.

There was indeed much to digest as the close of 1991 approached. I recalled the energy work we had done during the year to unlock hermetic seals on information that would make it possible to release facts and details previously withheld from the public. Evidence that this was so are the Dead Sea Scrolls, the Bruton Vault, the caves of the Wingmakers in New Mexico and the chambers beneath the Sphinx. Although the response had only been simply to question how old the Sphinx really was, as well as the continued blockage of the entrance to the Bruton Vault under the church at Williamsburg, Virginia, progress WAS being made.

ENERGY WORK ON THE CITY OF LIGHT

Time seemed to pass more and more quickly and I was shocked when the new year of 1992 began.

Early that month, three of my close friends and I went to Mexico to do "cosmic energy work." We worked with the entities (crew members) aboard The New Jerusalem, the massive energy Light merkabah we helped anchor in 1990.

Our work in January was to bring the energy rays up through New Mexico, Colorado, and Wyoming to strengthen the energy meridian that Spirit referred to as "presently deficient." The work was to delay – and hopefully prevent – the earthquake expected in the Rockies in 1992.

During our last day there, we received a "bonus of energy," so to speak, and were asked to assist to create an etheric border against nuclear weapons around the United States.

The New Jerusalem contains representatives from all 47 extraterrestrial civilizations who are assisting in the transition of Earth and the evolution of Humanity. Put another way, these members are helping to prepare Earth for her transition into a higher vibration. Members of this Intergalactic Federation monitor and adjust the energies of Earth's overall grid system.

The New Jerusalem is situated in the middle of the Nasca Ley Line. This Line runs northwest by southeast through the Andes Mountains at Machu Picchu and the Pyramids of Sun and Moon, south to Mexico City, up through California, across Mount St. Helens, and into Alaska.

Ley lines are magnetic grid lines within and above the surface of the Earth. They reach around the planet. These lines are the reason an earthquake in one sector of the Earth can cause a corresponding earthquake on the other side of the planet.

While ley lines are not the same distance apart, they do follow a dodecahedron grid system upon which this planet was originally formed. These lines are not always in perfect alignment, nor are they stationary. Some are fluid. The lines provide portals of entry for interstellar vehicles. The extraterrestrial beings understand how to utilize this energy and how to ride upon the energy waves after entering the Earth's atmosphere.

> **"If the spiritual life means anything, it means living more gently, mindfully, compassionately, and freely; it means, perhaps, finding a way to live lightly in a difficult World."**
>
> – Andrew Campbell

33

Choice

A short time after getting home from Mexico, I began hearing the same words, both when falling asleep, waking up, and in meditations. The words were, "Oldsmobile Cutlass Supreme."

"What a strange thing to get in meditation," I thought.

When these kinds of messages come to me, I often think I have tapped into a radio or TV frequency, instead of a spiritual frequency. Also, in this case, since I was not seriously considering trading cars (even though my car had lots of miles on it), I ignored the message for a few days.

About this same time, I received some coupons in the junk mail. I never look at coupons, but, for some reason, I opened the envelope and read each one.

One coupon was a $500 check toward the purchase of an Oldsmobile if bought at a specified local dealership. Because this Oldsmobile thing in meditation was getting repetitious, I stuck the coupon in my purse. (I do pay attention to repetition, regardless of how illogical the messages.)

A day or so later upon awakening the message, "Leave to look at the Oldsmobile Cutlass Supreme at 2 o'clock today," was so strong I dressed to go to the dealership. I also had to come to grips with my feeling that I needed to be writing and packing for the trip to Hawaii, more than I needed to go to a car dealer!

It is helpful for readers to know I would rather clean a cesspool than shop for a car. Most car salesmen I have met have been obnoxious and condescending. Also, I know little about cars, except how to put in gas and where the Jiffy Lube is located. Further, I seem to get more deeply in debt each time I trade cars, since I do not accrue any equity before running up lots of miles and needing to trade again. In the car business I am known as "upside down in my car." I did understand, through past experience, though, that I should arrive at a dealership in a clean car, so I had my car washed.

The first car wash was blocked by a tank truck filling reserve gas tanks. I was given a rain check and sent to the next station that would honor my purchase.

The second station was cleaning their car wash, but they did give me another rain check for the next closest station.

The third car wash did clean my car, but it took thirty minutes. By this time, as you might well imagine, I was curious and asked myself "Why leave at exactly 2 o'clock and spend all that time going from one car wash to another?"

I drove to the dealership, pulled in and parked my car at the front door. As I was getting out, a man in a golf jacket and baseball cap was getting into the car next to mine. He spoke and smiled. I returned the greeting and headed for the front door.

The door was LOCKED.

Although I had been able to maintain my sense of humor and interest through the three car washes, they now vanished. I began complaining about being sent on a "wild goose chase."

I returned to my car, preparing to return home to "purposeful activity."

The man in the baseball cap was now getting out of his car. Turning to me he asked, "Can I help you with anything?" I had not recognized him as a salesman because I had never seen one in anything but a suit coat and brightly colored tie.

"I want to look at a car, but I guess they are closed," I responded.

"I'm the only salesman here today," he explained. "We work on a volunteer basis on Sundays and it's been slow, so I decided to close and go home. However, if I can help you, I'll be glad to reopen. What can I show you?"

"I want to see what an Oldsmobile Cutlass Supreme looks like," I answered. (I was thinking to myself that he probably thought it strange I knew exactly what I wanted to see, but didn't know what it looked like. However, he didn't seem to notice.)

He reopened the front door, brought out some keys and pointed the way to a row of automobiles.

Few of the colors appealed to me, but I did choose a light metallic gold one to drive. He backed it out, described some of the features, and handed me the keys.

"Drive it around for a while and I'll wait here for you," he said, closing the car door.

I was surprised – and impressed – that he did not insist on going with me, to talk constantly, as had happened to me before. Then I thought maybe this was another prejudice I would be able to change, or relinquish, through a new experience!

I drove the car only briefly, since I was sure it was not the right car for me, and returned to the lot.

"How do you like it?" he inquired.

"It's nice, but just not what I need," I responded. "If I were going to trade cars, I would need to get one with lumbar support in the seat because I drive a lot of miles cross-country."

"We only have one in that model with lumbar seats. It's this 1991 burgundy demo, fully loaded," he offered.

I looked at the red car and thought, "Nothing red appeals to me except red flowers. God would not expect me to drive a red car!!!"

"I'll try it," I heard myself saying. He again gave me the keys and said, "Take your time," as he closed the door.

The car felt much stronger, the seat was wonderfully comfortable and touched my body in all the right places. The sound system was outstanding, too.

As I drove the car, I noticed that the message from my guidance was very clear: "This is the one." I couldn't imagine this to be true! I drove back to the lot. This time the salesman asked, "What do you think?"

"I like it OK," I said, "but I'm not crazy about red. I don't like so many gadgets either, but if the price is right, I'll buy it." Again I couldn't believe what I was saying!

"Why don't you take it home, drive it tonight and make sure you like it, bring it back tomorrow, and we'll see what we can do about figures," he suggested.

Since I didn't plan to trade cars, I hadn't called for a payoff figure. "I'll get the figures tomorrow before I come back in," I offered.

The man put the dealer tag on the car and handed me a $5-dollar bill to buy gas, since the tank was low.

"It would help my records if you would get a cash receipt," he said. "What kind of deal would you like to make on this car?"

"What I can do is trade my car, which is mortgaged, give you no money and have a payment of not more than $300." (I quickly heard his question almost in retrospect and corrected myself by saying, "What I would like is...")

I left my car keys with the man and drove away. Then I realized he had not taken my full name, phone number or address. This amazed me!

The following morning I called the bank in Colorado for a payoff on the loan. When I called the salesman to give him the figures (hoping this would speed up the time required to complete the purchase after I arrived) he admitted he had already acquired this from information he'd obtained from my glove compartment! Again I was impressed! When I arrived at the dealership, the salesman introduced me to the finance manager who took me to his office to complete the deal. I became very observant about my lack of emotional involvement to the idea of buying a new car and what this man might think about me and my financial condition.

When we were seated in his office, the finance manager leaned back in his chair and stated, "You are offering me a real challenge here."

"Yes," I replied knowingly. (I was thinking, "If he only knew . . .")

"What kind of work do you do that you put so many miles on a car?" he questioned. Before coming to look at cars, I had made a decision that regardless of what I was asked, I would be direct and honest.

"I have a very eclectic profession," I heard myself say. "I am an artist, a writer, a motivational lecturer and a spiritual counselor. I travel a lot by car. Since I usually have very little notice about where I am going, flying is not always financially feasible."

"What kind of motivation?" he inquired further. "Do you know Tony Robbins? I'm on the third series of his tapes."

"Yes, I do know of his work, but I've never met him personally," I admitted. "He and I are sort of in the same business, the God business."

"Are you Christian?" he asked with some concern rising in his body.

My guidance whispered, "Say yes," so I did, but I added that my organization was non-denominational.

"How did you feel about the car you drove," he questioned, seeming to try to move the subject back to business.

"It was much stronger than the first car I drove," I replied, "but there is something not quite right about the front end. It needs to be aligned or have the brakes checked. The person who has been driving it seems to wish he were doing some other kind of work. He has a few psychological problems, nothing serious, and seems to have a lower back problem . . . But, I apologize. You didn't ask me about the person; you asked me how I felt about the car."

"No, he said, "that's fine. I find what you have said very interesting because I'm the one who put all the miles on that car." I wanted to be swallowed up by the floor!

He got up out of his chair and closed the door to his office apparently deciding that our conversation was best not overheard or interrupted by others.

Overcoming my embarrassment, I leaned a little forward and looked right at the man. "Let me clear something up for you," I offered. "I did not choose your dealership by accident. I meditate, and in my meditations for a while now, I have been hearing 'Oldsmobile Cutlass Supreme.' Yesterday, I received the message that I was to leave my home at 2 p.m. and come to this dealership . . ." I proceeded to summarize the events of the previous day.

Then he began explaining that I was "upside down" in my car, and that leasing would be better for me than buying. He was very patient. He was not the least bit condescending, but honestly tried to help me understand. He, of course, did not know that I had been in banking for 18 years and worked in installment loans, so I just listened.

As he continued explaining that it was not that I had made bad "choices" – they had been logical "choices" at that moment – the word "choices" began lighting up energetically in his speech and put me on alert.

When there was a pause in his speech, I interjected, "Last night, just before going to bed, I began reading a book, which has been on my bookshelf for sometime, called *The Choice*. It seems to have something to do with you. I just finished reading it this morning at 2:30. Did you make some kind of choice in your life three years ago which dramatically changed it?" I felt compelled to ask him.

The color drained from his face. Then he confessed, "Yes, yes I did. I made such a choice. I was married to a doctor and my marriage was very bad. I went on a fishing trip one day and never returned. I later met and married a wonderful woman who is now my wife. My life changed dramatically. Someday I want to change it again. I want to quit what I am doing and write . . ."

Chills covered my body as I recalled the story I had read the night before.

"The book, *The Choice*, is about Mark Christopher, an insurance executive living in the east," I said aloud. "Christopher's peers had labeled him 'Mr. Success.' Then he had suddenly made a decision to quit his job as an affluent vice president and become a writer. He made the decision after becoming aware that he did not have a personal life because he gave all of his time to his job.

"He made the choice," I continued, "in favor of his dream and his family and left the corporate world. He wrote a book on success, which became a bestseller, and he was given a very powerful example of communication and success beyond logic."

I went on, "I'm here to tell you that when you made that decision three years ago, you made a decision in favor of yourself and your soul. In approximately twelve years – possibly sooner – you will be given another opportunity to make such a choice. The choice will be to leave your profession at that time, and to do something that your soul refers to as 'graphic,' something that has the potential of having 'planetary significance.'

"That is all I am given to say," I stated, "but it is important for you to have the information now so that when the time comes, you will know you are making the right decision. You will also have time to plan for the change of lifestyle. You made the correct choice three years ago," I concluded.

Having completed the message I had been asked to deliver, I arose from my chair to leave. "Don't worry about the car deal," I told him. "I probably wasn't sent here to buy a car, but to deliver this message and I feel complete with that."

"Thank you for coming in," he said as he took my outstretched hand. "I will continue looking at these figures and see what I can do. Don't discount the fact that you are supposed to get into another car," he advised.

"I don't doubt that I will, since this one has so many miles," I smiled as I left his office.

As soon as I arrived home the phone rang. It was my friend Ann from Oklahoma City.

"Did you make it through the car deal?" she inquired. Since I had talked to her just before I left for the dealership, she knew how much I had dreaded the encounter. She had also enjoyed a big chuckle out of my "cleaning a cesspool" remark.

"Yes I did, amazingly enough. It was very pleasant and seemingly not so much about buying a car as meeting the finance manager and delivering a message to him about a book I read last night," I explained.

"What book is that?" she asked innocently.

"*The Choice* by Og Mandino," I replied.

I heard a definite intake of breath on the other end of the line, then Ann burst out, "My gosh! I've got those tapes lying here in front of me on my desk, along with his *Mission Success of the Anthology of Achievement* tapes and a paperback copy of that book. I was just getting ready to send them to a friend in Tulsa, but I think I am supposed to send them to you instead so you can give them to that young man." She was nearly out of breath as excitement mounted in her voice.

I mailed the tapes and the book to the finance manager the next day.

"We must live with the consequences of our choices."

34

Kauai, Hawaii

January – February 1992

The day my friends and I had returned from our trip to Mexico after completing our "cosmic energy work" on The New Jerusalem in January 1992, a ticket, which here-to-fore had been non-changeable and in someone else's name, <u>became</u> changeable and manifested in my name for my trip to Kauai, Hawaii.

After returning from the Oldsmobile car dealership, I began packing for the trip to Hawaii. About 9 o'clock in the evening my entire right side began to draw up as if I were having a stroke. The pain was excruciating. I lay down on the bed hoping the pain would pass. Shortly, the phone rang. It was a psychic friend in Denver who was to meet me and my traveling companion in Hawaii for one of the four weeks we were to be there. She called to see how I was doing and if I was packed and ready to go.

"No, I'm not. I'm in terrible pain." I explained what had happened. She immediately tuned in to me energetically and asked, "You know those people where you come from are the short, slight people?"

"No, Venusians are tall, usually over six feet, sometimes even seven feet tall."

"Well, some female spirit is standing by your bed who is short and slight of build. She seems to want to talk with you," my friend explained what she was seeing.

Suddenly I remembered when I moved from Mt. Shasta to New Mexico a book had materialized in my book boxes that I did not own when I was in California. The book was the autobiography of Georgia O'Keeffe. I had read the book and felt very connected to the woman who was one of the most well-known female American painters. She had loved New Mexico and after her husband's death she had moved from New York to Abiquiu, New Mexico, and made her home there until her death.

"Ask her if her name is Georgia," I suggested to my friend on the phone.

"Yes, she's nodding her head."

"Ask her what she wants."

"She is offering to help you paint."

I immediately began to cry and argue for my limitations. "I'm not a trained artist. I'm not worthy of having someone like her help me." By then I was actually blubbering and the pain was not subsiding.

"She says you know how to put energy in the paintings and that is the most important part. She can teach you to paint, but she would have a hard time teaching anyone how to put energy into their artwork," my friend relayed Georgia's message.

"I think she should find someone who really knows what they are doing artistically," I continued to argue ungraciously.

"She says she really wants to help you as you are someone who wants to paint and make a difference energetically."

I finally quit arguing and humbly agreed to be available whenever she wanted to help me. I later learned that Hawaii was one of Georgia's favorite experiences. She had been paid by Dole Pineapple Company to paint the pineapple plant. She became so distracted during her time in Hawaii that she never did the painting while she was there. They later mailed her a plant and she painted it for them after she returned from Hawaii.

Georgia doesn't paint through me, but when I get stuck working on a painting, I can feel her encouraging me and making subtle suggestions. I am extremely grateful for her help.

I looked forward to visiting Hawaii, since I had never been there. But more than that, I felt the trip would cause a life transformation to take place within me. During the holidays at the end of the year, I had consciously committed myself to another level of evolution. At the time I had no idea that we would eventually have an additional Namaste Creativity Retreat Center on Kauai or that I would be given a way to travel there for two weeks every year to paint.

Things were happening very quickly by the time of the first trip to Kauai, February 1992. My soul was stretching at a rate that caused my body to experience some strange feelings. I felt sure that many others were having similar experiences, since everybody is affected by the same energies.

One night after I arrived in Hawaii, I was awakened by a gentle rain on the roof and the noisy refrigerator – or so I thought. Then I realized it was a full bladder that had actually aroused me. I threw off the blankets. My feet touched the bare, wooden floor, damp with excess humidity.

Through the darkness I made my way to the bathroom. As I opened the door to the combined closet, dressing area and bath, a 200-watt bare bulb of light streamed into my face. The bulb was left on deliberately to defray some of the humidity in the closet.

The brightness caused my pupils to dilate and an instant headache ensued.

Body relieved, I crept back through the darkness to the damp, but still warm bed. The soft, gentle rain continued touching the roof. I closed my eyes and waited for rest, but try as I might, my thoughts refused to return to the oblivion of sleep and I couldn't relax. My head throbbed, my body ached and thoughts raced through my now activated brain . . . tropical Hawaii . . . warm sun . . . beautiful beaches . . .

So far, our first week stay had been rain-soaked and we'd barely glimpsed the sun. We'd had to run countless errands, trying to convert our rustic one-room cabin into a semblance of a home. We were constantly cold and back then no stores were available to buy a sweat suit. Everyone had assured us, "Once you are in Hawaii all you will need to wear is your bathing suit," Yeah, right. They must have been here in August I groused.

The lush green surroundings of our temporary domicile in the mountains of Kauai (the Garden Island) could not have contrasted more with my condo in the desert of Albuquerque, nor my cabin mate's beautiful home in Denver.

I became aware of one thing, though: It only takes a few days for Humans to create new patterns, habits – even temporary ones – and routines that make them feel comfortable in totally new and foreign surroundings!

My thoughts became repetitious as I struggled to return to sleep. I didn't want to wake Jan.

"I had a farm in Africa . . . I had a farm in Africa . . . I had a farm in Africa . . ."

The words "Out of Africa" had been haunting me for days. They were so strong in my mind, and we had become so telepathically connected in such a small space, that Jan had actually stated them aloud earlier in the week. In fact, as she had uttered them, both our energy fields opened and floods of warm, loving strength and power swept over us starting at our crowns, opening our emotional energy bodies to joy and excitement.

We both recognized instantly that we had joined the ranks of a special order of people, people who "do" and "live," rather than just support or watch others; people who report their "beingness" through words, sounds and images to inspire others to "be," rather than just "watch," or simply exist. My friend, Jan, was a sculptor who was beginning to paint and write.

But the line "Out of Africa" continued to haunt me. (Later, I would remember these words were from the movie Out of Africa. And I would recall Isak Dinesen's book, *Out of Africa*. I would also remember Spirit's words:

"Because of the vibrations of the book certain people will have an energy reaction when they hear or read the words, 'I had a farm in Africa, at the foot of the Ngong Hills.' These people are forerunners for the race of the new Human. These people have adventures that others only dream of. They pave the way for Human beings in the World of fear . . . "

This message didn't make much sense to me then, since it seemed I often <u>felt</u> fear. But then I realized that although I felt fear, I still moved forward <u>through</u> the fear to the adventure of living, as do many of you. At the time, I had to <u>assume</u> that was what Spirit was indicating in the words, "Out of Africa."

There in Hawaii, my nights were filled with conversations and images just beyond my conscious awareness, no matter how hard I struggled to grasp them. And then one morning the images and dialogues seemed much clearer.

The first conscious memories to surface were of Betty Jean as a toddler, hiding under a coffee table. Her parents were fighting, yelling and throwing dishes and ashtrays at each other. Then memories of being sexually intimate with her great-grandfather were remembered in great detail.

I remembered Betty Jean's life in her ninth year (which cleared up that gap in her life for me). She was in the third grade, happy, productive and popular. She was in a new school facility and had just been chosen queen of the third grade class.

Her folks were no longer renting a house. Instead, the family was living in an "owned" home for the first time in her life, a home that had been built by her grandfather.

One day her brother, three years older than she, walked home from school, 1-1/2 miles across a cotton field. His parents told him that they were going to move to Fort Worth, Texas, the next day, that his father was changing jobs and that their home would be sold. This move, along with having to give up her pet dog, put Betty Jean into shock for nine months, as I wrote earlier.

The family returned from Fort Worth and lived in rental houses until Betty Jean was a senior in high school. Then her father came home from work one day and announced he had bought them a new home. He had done this without even consulting her mother!

When her father took the family to see the house, the three of them were shocked: the house had only one bedroom!

Her father explained that since she and her brother would be getting married soon, he and her mother would need only one bedroom. (At the time, neither Betty Jean nor her brother was dating anyone they would consider marrying.) The entry hall became Betty Jean's bedroom, the dining room her brother's.

Within two months, both Betty Jean and her brother were married and on their own.

Betty Jean took employment as a bank teller. Her father said being a bank teller was perfect work for a person who "wasn't going on to college." He was also pleased that, at that time, banks closed at 3 p.m., which would allow a woman to work and still pick up children from school. It would also provide plenty of time to prepare an evening meal before her husband's arrival.

As I recalled these memories, I began to better understand why Betty Jean had had the attitudes and feelings she displayed, and also why she had married so early in life.

Aside from my puzzling over the conversations, images and memories that filled my nights, I did a good deal of writing and painting during our stay on the island, as did Jan.

We also connected with a group of spiritual beings referring to themselves as "The Founders" (another name for "The Elohim") the "Creators," you might say, of Earth and its species.

Then during the last few days of our stay, our friend Kathy joined us from Denver.

An interesting event took place about this time.

Sometime before this trip to Hawaii, an acquaintance had sent me an envelope of ash. This person had visited Sai Baba in India and acquired the ash, which had materialized from Sai Baba's finger tips. The day the ash arrived I had also received a group picture of Baba and the people with whom my acquaintance had traveled.

I took both the ash and the photo with me to Hawaii. I placed the ash and the picture on the nightstand beside my bed in our one-room cabin.

After Kathy joined Jan and me, she asked me about Sai Baba and his abilities. I explained what I knew of direct precipitation. "Have you ever tried it yourself?" she asked.

"Yes, several years ago, using the meditation from the book, *St. Germain on Alchemy*," I said.

"With what results?"

"Well, I couldn't do it. I tried for seven days and my palms would get hot and tingle, but nothing materialized, so I quit trying. I figured God supposedly created the World in seven days so that seemed long enough to try."

"What were you trying to create?" she persisted.

"An amethyst. St. Germain suggests you first try to bring an amethyst, because he has lots of amethysts he is willing to drop through the causal plane to anyone willing to practice alchemy. Besides, I've always loved purple and amethyst.

"In the meditation, I envisioned an inch-long, faceted, oval amethyst. I was always jealous that my brother's birthday was in February and his birthstone was amethyst and mine was sapphire, which I don't care for," I finished lamely.

"It is actually interesting that I never did pursue it again, because something unusual did happen."

I continued sharing my story with Kathy, remembering that the week after I had given up trying to materialize the stone, I had been in Denver teaching a workshop on manifestation through affirmation and visualization (a different technique). I hadn't included precipitation because I had not been able to accomplish it myself. (I only teach from my own experiences. If I can't do it, I don't teach it.)

I went on, "At that time, I didn't tell anyone I was even trying the experiment, because I assumed they would think I was crazy."

Kathy was listening intently.

I told her how when I awoke the second day of the workshop, three unfaceted, purple stones lay on my bedside table. I still hadn't mentioned any of this to anyone, but I did take the stones to a rock shop later. The man told me they were not amethyst, but fluorite. So I still figured I couldn't materialize.

Since these purple rocks weren't of the variety I held as my intention I had really never given myself credit for co-creating. At that time, though, for the next several weeks when I meditated, I saw a large blue, pear-shaped, faceted stone in my third eye area.

Two weeks after the workshop, spirit had asked me to go to Sedona.

After my arrival, I had been directed to a large crystal store in Cottonwood, a little town west of Sedona.

I recalled that when I walked into the white wooden church structure, the proprietor, a little East-Indian-looking man with dark skin and a long white beard, had come up to me and looked right straight into my soul with the most penetrating black eyes I had ever seen.

In his heavily accented voice he declared, "I have some stones that belong to you."

At that time, I thought that was the most novel new age sales technique I had ever heard, so I said to him, "Really! What do they look like?"

The man led me to a table in the back room, which was more like a closet. A small piece of black velvet was on the table and on the velvet were four stones: one, a pear-shaped blue topaz, two pear-shaped amethysts and a one-inch, oval-faceted amethyst exactly like I had been holding in my matrix.

Kathy drew in a breath as I told her that a jolt of energy had coursed through my body then, and I was instantly aware that I had co-created the stones. "But I had not been brave enough, or patient enough, to allow them to actually materialize in the palm of my hand," I explained.

"What happened then?" Kathy breathed.

"I asked how much they were," I said. "I had priced the topaz in Oklahoma City and Denver after it had begun appearing in my meditation, so I knew that it was worth between $400 and $600."

The man picked up a pencil and a piece of paper and began figuring.

"What did he say?" Kathy asked excitedly.

"The figure he gave me was $285 dollars," I recalled, "and you know, I had exactly $285 with me at that time. I'd been saving it to make a $300 payment on my van. The payment was due the next day."

"Did you give it to him?" Kathy's eyes were big again.

"I said to him, 'how do you know how much money I have?' And do you know what his answer was? '<u>I don't know</u>. That's just what Spirit says I am to charge you for the stones. They are worth a lot more than that.' He told me that quite defensively."

Kathy was waiting for me to continue.

I told her that I had let the man know I was aware of that, but that $285 was all the money I had. I also had told him I needed that money to make a car payment.

The man came back with the fact that he only knew the stones belonged to me and that he was being asked to sell them to me at that ridiculous price. He said I'd have to make up my own mind if I wanted to buy them or not.

"Did you buy them?" A slight smile of wonderment was on Kathy's face.

"Well, I thanked him and left the store in complete confusion," I told her. "But the next day, on blind faith, I went back and bought them."

Kathy was still listening intently as I told her about the thoughts of doubt and how illogical but intriguing and amazing it all was that had crossed my mind as I left the store. I had thought how ridiculous it was to even think that I would be asked to do readings there in Sedona for others and thereby make enough money for the van payment. After all there were so many psychic readers in Sedona. When I left the church/rock shop after buying the rocks I went to the Airport Restaurant. When I opened the door a very flamboyant woman came out followed by her friends. She grabbed me and asked, "What took you so long? We expected you hours ago." I assured her she had mistaken me for someone else. She assured me that Spirit had described me and told them to wait for me at the Airport Restaurant and that I would read for them. They were in town from New Jersey. At that time I charged $50 for doing an hour-long reading. There were six people in her party. They invited me to do the readings in their rooms at the Sky Ranch Lodge and gave me a bed for the evening. The next morning I was free to leave Sedona with the stones and my van payment in my pocket.

Kathy stirred my memory with her interesting questions. I recalled that the following week I had been back in Denver and had heard of a woman who did Angel drawings of a person's personal Angelic presence. I called her on the phone and arranged for her to do a drawing of my Angel and to deliver it to me in four days.

I shared with Kathy that when the colored pencil drawing was delivered, the Angel, which she had drawn only from knowing my name and birthdate, wore a headband over her third eye, portraying the stones that had manifested for me placed exactly as the man had laid them on the black velvet. Once again I had received confirmation that the stones were mine, as the chills had gone up my spine.

I finished the story and looked at the concentrated expression on Kathy's face.

"I'm being told you are supposed to try direct precipitation again," she said.

A surge of energy went through my body in confirmation of her statement.

"OK, but I don't need any more stones. I need something I can convert to money to pay my debts," I replied.

After I had finished sharing my story, Kathy and Jan left the cabin to use the public telephone in the lodge. While they were gone, I went into meditation and tried to remember the exact details of the alchemical formula for direct precipitation.

A vortex of blue energy began gathering around my body. I could feel beams of white light coming directly into my palms. The tingling began.

I waited, then I repeated the directions, this time creating the matrix for gold coins, which I thought would be more negotiable than stones. I felt my palms grow heavy, as if leather chamois-skin bags of gold coins had been placed in my hands etherically. I could even psychically see the bags and leather thongs that gathered them together to close their tops.

I was concentrating so deliberately that I nearly left my body when it 'startled' suddenly at the words of "The Voice." (That is what I called the Spirit that seemed beyond my soul – like the voice of God.) The Voice said, *"What will you do with them?"*

Surprised by the question, I was briefly at a loss for an answer. I declared, "I will pay my debts with them."

"What will you do with them?" came the question a second time.

I felt like saying, "I SAID I would pay my debts with them!" Instead, I repeated quietly, "I will pay my debts with them."

"Then what will you do with them?" The Voice asked, as if insinuating that there would be a continued supply.

"I would travel to wherever you want or need me to go to do the work of my soul," I responded.

I experienced what seemed to be a very long, pregnant pause. Then The Voice spoke once again with one word: *"Zimbabwe."*

I felt my heart respond.

"Yes, I will go if that is what it takes to manifest what I need to pay these debts."

The energy gradually subsided and the heaviness in my hands went away. I felt drained, confused and exhilarated.

"I had a farm in Africa . . . I had a farm in Africa . . . I had a farm in Africa . . . ." The words from *Out of Africa* had bothered me for days. It occurred to me Zimbabwe is in Africa. I did not want to go to Africa.

But I was still confused by the message. How? When? Why? Why would I need to go to Zimbabwe? When I had turned my life over to God in 1982, the worst fear I had was that God would ask me to go to Africa as a missionary.

Here, I had just agreed to face my worst fear!

(A month or so later I learned that a friend and I have aspects of our Oversouls in Africa. She will go to Zimbabwe, with a crystal to pick up the energies from my soul, which have been stored there for a very long time.) I never had to go to any part of Africa other than Egypt.

When Kathy and Jan returned to the cabin, I told them of my experience. Kathy responded that she had recently read the book, *The Power of One*, which was set in South Africa, and which she felt I was supposed to read.

On March 4, Spirit asked the three of us to go to Kee Beach on the northern most end of the Island of Kauai. There we were directed to walk up the mountain to a waterfall flowing out into the ocean from a fresh water source inside the mountain. We were then asked to tone and to ground seven additional rays of energy being offered by "The Founders" to the Earth and Humanity.

The gift of these rays was dedicated to the evolution of the planet, animal and Human species. (A separate chapter on these Rays has been included in the book.)

And yet another interesting wonder happened to us.

During the last two days in Kauai, Jan and Kathy were told it was time for Jovanna (bj King BEFORE I entered Betty Jean's body in 1969) to be completely in the physical body.

They did energy work to accomplish this.

The only time I, Jovanna (bj King) had been totally in the body energetically, was in November 1979. At that time, Betty Jean and I merged completely as we moved from Texas to Oklahoma City.

Then, later, the emotional pain of that move, the abandonment trauma caused by Ed's death, and the subsequent return of my children to Lubbock to be with their father, impelled me (Jovanna, bj King) to move outside the body. Since that time I had been operating it more or less by remote control.

The day after the merging, Jan and Kathy went on a boat ride up the Na Pali Coast to see the dolphins, whales, sea turtles and mountain goats.

I (bj King) was asked to remain alone at the cabin. At that time, I wrote the following:

Today I feel very dense (as the density of gold, rather than flesh) and very boring, very Human and <u>very</u> flat (as flat as Wiley Coyote after a safe drops on him). I feel as if I have become two-dimensional, if not maybe only one, for yesterday I agreed to become fully Human, fully in this body.

The greed that Humans have to satiate their bodies is fully understood by me today. They must do something to overcome the "flatness" of this experience. They would be tempted, no doubt, to do drugs, drink, cause drama of any sort – resort even to violence or excessive sex – to change this feeling of flatness; to know for certain they are experiencing their bodies and emotions, if they do not know of their Spirit.

I see they kill and destroy their bodies so they will not have to be confined in them. I see some of them exercise religiously and excessively to strengthen the bodies and their awareness of them. I also see some have begun to meditate to move beyond their physical bodies, to experience other dimensions.

To capture the mind and Spirit and to confine it to only three dimensions of experience is a travesty of the possibilities.

The thought to escape the body by going to sleep is strong, yet last night it was not allowed by the soul.

Twelve hours after confining myself to the physical, I awoke feeling just as dense and just as tired as when I went to sleep. The body ached, because it had not been left in peace, as it usually is. I felt full, like an overstuffed sausage skin.

To only suspect there is a Source, to only suspect there is a soul, yet to not have that connection – that communion, that knowing through communications – causes this feeling of density, this feeling of helplessness in Humans.

I can understand they seek religion to try to find answers to the question, 'Isn't there more than this?'

The feeling bodies have to shut down or be exploited by over-stimulation to cope with these feelings of density and flatness. Otherwise, conscious connection to the soul must be sought and accomplished.

The waves of sadness return . . .

The waves of hopelessness return . . . The wish to sleep returns . . .

The wish to escape the body returns . . .

I choose to meditate, to reconnect consciously with all levels of my soul. During the meditation I was asked to feel gratitude for the body, to feel gratitude for the feelings of density.

I found agreement to feel gratitude difficult and asked the soul to explain how to create gratitude. The following information was given:

"*Gratitude*"

"*Gratitude is the hallmark of an enlightened soul. Gratitude is related to recognizing past thoughts, words and deeds have created the present. The* present and future are created by our thoughts and attitudes.

"To foster an attitude of gratitude, we foster a positive future for ourselves and the World.

"Gratitude for what is and what possibilities lay in the future actually are seeds planted for the future.

"When we learn to express gratitude consciously and sincerely, we plant seeds that can then be nurtured with thoughts of joy, love and action.

"When we do not deliberately cultivate seeds of gratitude, the seeds of the mass-consciousness (which are primarily weed-producing seeds of greed, resentment, lack and animosity) will grow to create our futures.

"If we work <u>daily</u> toward seeing things with new eyes (which means not taking anything for granted, but living with gratitude), we create a space within which positive changes can take place.

"If we can begin to be more and more conscious of the relationships and complexities of what we know now, we can help to release gratitude.

"When we look at a plant, such as a rose, we can superficially think, 'that is nice,' or 'that is pleasant.' Or we can ignore it completely and concentrate on some area of our lives that isn't working well.

"Or we can stop and actually SEE the rose, appreciate its beauty, its aroma, its color, the shape of the petals, and even discern how it grew.

"We can analyze this information: Where did the seed come from? From whence came the life within this seed?

"We can be conscious and recognize that from a small seed came this bush, its branches, stems, leaves, buds and then the rose.

"We can discern the Law of Cause and Effect.

"We can recognize the association and combination of the seed itself, which means because of Universal Law, a rose seed produces a rose. The soil, water, time, sunlight and the Law of Photosynthesis all cooperated to create the rose that we are observing.

"This data, combined with the synchronicity that caused us to be in this very spot to observe the rose (which will last only a short time in its blooming state) creates an atmosphere in which gratitude will flourish.

"This process of practicing consciousness results in a well of gratitude springing from within us as we deliberately recognize the Law of Cause and Effect, Photosynthesis and Synchronicity, all of which created this event and the rose.

"As conscious persons we can look at all things as if for the first time. And in so doing, we see past, present and future simultaneously (seeing Cause and Effect).

"Gratitude comes from a synthesis of mind and emotions relating to a specific idea or process. It gives wings to the everyday cares and events of life.

"In gratitude, we can stand outside our ego limitations and thereby be free to function as a part of a group or larger whole. And we can recognize our Oneness.

"Gratitude changes our focus from the ego-centered personality and its mental images, desires and physical awareness's, to the mental images, desires and awareness of other persons, situations, and the Oneness. It provides us the ability to see and interact with them on a non-personal, less judgmental and synthesizing manner.

"There are events in our lives for which we find it difficult to feel or experience gratitude.

"Gratitude for our experiences, whether they be 'good' or 'bad' presupposes that we first recognize what is and see some purpose or some lesson in the experience.

"If we are ego-centered and a situation is unpleasant, we may ignore or move away from it, for our own comfort. Or, we may aggressively act against the situation, adding to the inharmony of ourselves and others.

"If we are conscious, and thereby in a state of gratitude, we can realize the situation is a process, with the individuals involved actors in the process.

"We can be grateful for all that helped present this drama for us to see. Situations then become challenges.

"We can then allow ourselves to be somewhat detached from the circumstances and from our emotions long enough to:

"Change our focus to something more beneficial; hold a clear space energetically, enabling the confusion to lift ourselves and others; use the situation to teach ourselves another way to relate; discern the facts of the dilemma, process and then make a decision. This kind of decision is based on discernment, rather than allowing an ego-based reaction, which is a reaction founded on fear or defense. Without gratitude, we tune into the events themselves, have a personal reaction, and by our thoughts and energies actually increase the situation.

"By learning the practice of gratitude we assist ourselves and others with planting seeds of growth, which do not have to be painful. Gratitude for the experience, because of what we learned, releases us from past limitations and allows us to move forward. Gratitude also allows us to plant new, more deliberate seeds for fun and positive future experiences.

"When we are grateful, we are not focused upon ourselves, but upon that for which we are grateful. We see more clearly and act more purposefully when our minds are directed outside ourselves and outside our own environment.

"We can become aware of a new set of priorities and seek to cooperate instead of oppose. We can see from the point of view of others.

"There is so much pain in the World. We can either be a part of the problem, or a part of the solution.

"We are a part of the problem when we:

"Focus on the pain of others.

"Focus on blaming something or someone for the situation.

"Refuse to recognize there is a problem.

"React without giving ourselves time to discern and respond.

"We are part of the solution when we:

"Do something positive to correct the situation.

"Focus on sending love to persons or situations.

"Radiate joy out into the Universe.

"Treat nature respectfully.

"Reduce our level of greed.

"Teach others only by being a demonstration.

"and an example of actualized truth and love.

"We must first be grateful for the differences in individuals, groups and nations. (This can even affect economic and political situations.) We must recognize that difference enriches our lives, stimulates thought and growth, and affords limitless possibilities. Out of difference comes the production of products, which give us choices and variety.

"We can be grateful to other persons, groups or nations if we:

"Recognize our dependence upon others for food, technology, money, skills, manufacturing, etc.

Accept our interdependence with the Earth and others for survival.

Desire to enhance that in others, which is for the common good.

Assist ourselves and others to eliminate that which is not for the common good.

Recognize we are one common species riding on the surface of a living organism : THE EARTH.

"If we can see the beauty in difference as a part of the truth of Humanity, we can be grateful for what exists and desire to enhance all possibilities in all persons.

"We can enjoy our relationships and friendships by recognizing the process of Cause and Effect. This process has brought us to our present circumstances, and has helped us evolve to our present state as a species and individual achievements.

"Recognizing that our present state and that of our friends is what has brought us to this point, we can willingly want to assist ourselves and them in their growth in the most painless way possible. We can recognize that it is the Universal Law of Cause and Effect that has brought us together and we can choose to enhance the experience.

"When we free ourselves and others from limiting thoughts, attitudes and judgments of the past and seek new insights, we free both of us to move toward an expanded future, released from limitation.

"We can stop holding others back by simply <u>not</u> attaching labels to them. Labels encourage us and them to remain static. We interrelate with each other on so many intricate levels – even on the level of unspoken thought.

"We must be willing to recognize the beauty in others and enhance it by gratitude, gratitude toward another struggling member of the Human species, a spirit in Human form. That way, we can both become more of what we already are.

"Lack of gratitude, of awareness of the complexities that make a person beautiful, puts fences around each of us. These fences give the illusion of providing safety. However, in actuality they take away from both of us the freedom to grow and perfect our characters, to accomplish our missions.

"We cannot force gratitude nor make it happen. But we can practice the thought process of recognition and analysis, which will allow it to happen.

"The realization of some truth and its relationship to us comes first (the Cause). Then, we feel it and the movement of energy outward from our hearts (Effect).

"As we learn to discern facts and to analyze them (become aware of Causes and Effects) pure gratitude will come through us as an effect of learning Universal Law. THIS IS REALIZATION."

35

Lady Venus' Instructions

After my return to Albuquerque from Hawaii in early 1992, the memories, images and dialogues, which began stirring there, continued at an ever-increasing rate.

I finally began to have prior-to-Earth memory, remembering WHO I had been, and WHERE I had been before I accepted the mission to come to Planet Earth.

The veil was lifting at last. I was also beginning to remember some of the conversations with Lady Venus in 1968 on the Venusian ship before I decided to enter Earth life.

As I tuned into the Lady's words, much of the sequence and happenings of my life as Jovanna, Betty Jean, and now as bj King, with full custody of the physical body, began falling into place. I was seeing a pattern and meaning to the events, which heretofore had seemed to be merely random happenings.

I could see myself on the Ship, sitting before Lady Venus. She was already talking, as I tuned in, her voice so filled with love for all Humankind: . . .

"Second child, a male, born 1973 . . . he is three . . . the female body . . . will undergo removal of certain organs . . . will help establish freer vehicle . . ."

The message grew stronger.

"Just prior to the operation on the body, an adult male will be brought into the life of you and Betty Jean. This is a man who is nearing the end of his time of embodiment upon the Earth. This will not at all be obvious to this individual, nor to anyone around him. This man is playing the role of a priest within the religious faith to which Betty Jean and her husband belong. This man is a member of your same Soul family.

"The initial reaction to his entering your and her life will be rejection, which is appropriate. You and Betty Jean will become close friends of his wife and later, of him. He will serve as a catalyst and challenge, both for spiritual and intellectual growth. He will help with what in mythology is called the 'sorting of the seeds.'

"This man will assist Betty Jean recognize who she is without the use of drugs. He will help her understand that she creates her own feelings and therefore can be in control of them. He will aid her in realizing that her feelings are not brought on by others as she previously believed, but are controlled from within herself. He will teach her that feelings are not to be judged as good or as bad; that feelings just "are" and that they are to be honored. He will help her know that feelings can be examined and responses chosen before reactions occur. And that they can be lovingly controlled without being denied.

"This man will also teach Betty Jean that she has choices and how to find her self-worth and power without losing her femininity. He will teach her the true value of her femininity. And he will teach her that within herself she has both feminine strengths and masculine strengths.

"During this process, Betty Jean will learn to use her feminine strengths and virtues, as well as her masculine ones. In the Myth of Psyche, which you are destined to live out in this body and timeframe, is called 'Gathering the golden fleece.'

"Betty Jean's true freedom and your opportunity to use the body more fully will begin with her mother's death in March of 1979. Her mother will die after experiencing two heart attacks within one week. The same day her mother dies, the priest, whose name is Edward, will leave Lubbock with his family and move to another area called Oklahoma City. He will be in the process of leaving the priesthood as one of his final statements of revolt against the organized church. His experience is that the organized church is becoming more and more a business venture, and less and less a ministerial vehicle on the Earth plane. He will be subconsciously preparing for his departure from the physical plane, although he will not be aware of this at the mental or conscious levels.

"One of his last acts for the benefit of the Oversoul will be to develop an intimate correspondence with the corporate being that you and Betty Jean will have become. The purpose of this will be to deliberately cause that being to be aware of her love for him and her desire to have a life that is more spiritual, creative and reflective. Through this supportive correspondence, he will serve to open Betty Jean (and you) to past childhood memories for your benefit. These memories have been blocked from her psyche and will be very difficult for you to retrieve unless they are drawn forth into her conscious memory before she leaves the body and rejoins the soul.

"Her love for him and the dream of having a more creative, intellectually stimulating and spiritual life will eventually draw her and you away from the limited lifestyle, which she is now living, to Oklahoma City and away from Lubbock. You will take the children with you when you initially leave Lubbock.

"When this relocation takes place, you will gradually be given greater and greater control over all aspects of the physical life. Shortly after arriving in the new location, Edward will leave his body through death and return to the Soul. The children will return to Lubbock to be raised primarily by their father, for karmic reasons, which we have explained to you previously.

"At this point, you and she will feel totally abandoned. This is, however, a necessary part of the transition. If he were allowed to remain, he would not be fulfilling his contract, and Betty Jean would continue to live in his shadow as his helpmate and not be pushed to develop herself. You (bj King), however, as you later develop your telepathic abilities within the body, will be able to communicate with him.

"It is necessary for the two of you to live through these events together in order that the new matrix for the species may be appropriately created. I spoke of this earlier.

"You must be left in isolation in order to become aware of 'roles.' All of the 'roles' Betty Jean has played for others and for the society must be given up, or at least examined for what they are. A decision must be made by both of you as to which ones will be healthy for you to continue. She must at last see that she is NOT her 'roles,' but a spiritual being AGREEING to be in a physical Human body TO PLAY roles.

"The consciousness, which the two of you are, must reclaim its feminine spirit from all of the causes and people to whom Betty Jean has given it. This process will be escalated by two things: one, the remarriage of her father and two, the offense the Bishop of the Diocese will take to her actions. The Bishop will be so offended that he will demand she refrain from taking communion in the Episcopal Church. This will remove her from her dependence on the church and on the church leaders as intermediaries between her and God.

"And almost all of her so called 'friends' and 'family' will turn against her (and you) or avoid you. This will be in judgment of your (the corporate entity you both have become) leaving her husband and giving up the children for their father to raise. All of this will add to your feelings of abandonment. However, it will also make you look closely at your roles and the true meaning of friendship.

"You will go through a period of deep introspection prior to returning to the banking industry. This will be for the purpose of healing memories. You will reclaim Betty Jean's spirit from its 'roles.' You will also begin to forgive and consciously forget everything that stops her growth and diminishes her happiness. This period will take several years. (In the myth of Psyche, this period is referred to as 'filling the crystal vessel with the water from the fountain of forgetfulness.') It will be one of the most difficult of the challenges that you will face and, as I have said, will take several years.

"The following few years will be very trying, financially, mentally, emotionally and spiritually. Less than two years after you reenter the banking workforce you will be required to leave, in order to do the outward spiritual work that you are being sent to do. The events that will cause this conscious opening to happen are as yet undecided. But their acceptance by your psyche will be difficult and you will feel as if you are (by Earth standards) 'going crazy.' However, you will simply be beginning to open telepathically to hear the Soul.

"During this same period, you will encounter several males. They will be brought to you deliberately, so you can work with them in order to get in touch with your deepest feminine self. This is necessary so that you may transform what Betty Jean considers her mistakes and painful memories into creative adventures. You will, therefore, confront all of her fears related to males; that is, her fear of being controlled, fear of abandonment, and fear of financial insecurity. This period of the life will feel like a proverbial 'hell' and in the Myth of Psyche it is literally called the 'Descent into Hell.'

"Because you and Betty Jean chose the way of spirit, creativity, passion and erotic love, you will be risking the life in order to sustain it, not only for you, but to create the matrix to change the rules for all of Humanity.

"You will rediscover an ancient but long-hidden way of thinking, being, doing, loving and living. This ancient way can free men and women from their unhappiness so that they can become the persons they were created to be.

"In order to accomplish this task, though, you and she both will have to be willing to fail, to lose everything for the sake of love - - even her heart's desire, the man she wanted. But in doing so, you will have claimed wholehearted, whole-souled womanhood for yourself, and will then be free to integrate yourself totally with your maleness. As you are moving through this integration you will be brought other men with whom you will have *relationships, as you learn more about maleness.*

"Eventually, we will send another member of the Soul, Jovan, your counterpart, to be embodied into a willing form to join with you to form the matrix for the new male/female relationships on Earth. This relationship will create the new reality of men and women living a shared Humanity in ever-increasing spiritual, co-creative and erotic love.

"Only through a new matrix formation, by one who DARES to descend into the depths and bring into consciousness the immortal beauty of being woman, can men be restored to the true power of their masculinity.

"Men are now living from a false power of maleness, a power of authority 'over,' rather than power 'for.' This false maleness exalts armed might, control and subjugation. It uses violence as its twisted system of 'justice.' It is a maleness born out of fear and it is false to the original form of maleness, which is a force to externalize creation. It is maleness without balance, without the true feminine, the femininity of creation.

"The patriarchal society on Earth has debased Human sexuality and the feminine. It has turned the holiness of erotic love, physical love and true love into something bad, something to be feared, controlled - - something opposed to spirituality.

"Erotic love, true love, which is in truth the creative force moving through Human form, has been turned into an anathema of its original design. Patriarchal society's control of the church has taught that individuals are born in sin, rather than out of love. In an attitude of overwhelming arrogance, woman have been designated as the source of evil and the cause of man's infidelity to the Spirit. In truth, however, it is man's connecting with his own feminine essence within that leads him to his Soul, and back home to the Source.

"When a culture denies the worth of the feminine, restricts the development of the true masculine and debases Human sexuality, terrible things happen between men and woman. This has happened on Earth. And, because man and woman together form the basic unit of all society, terrible things are happening in the World as a result of this imbalance.

"Without true love, the sexes are at war. They are disunited and all Humanity is disunited with them. Without consciousness of the worth of the feminine, man cannot be man. And without consciousness of the worth of the masculine, woman cannot be woman. They are doomed to live life as only a part of the person they are capable of being. Men and women experience a deep sorrow, an indefinable longing so great that it is impossible to love themselves or others. They do not understand the source of this

grief – – a grief for the repression and killing off of a part of themselves – – a longing to reunite with their opposite self.

"This longing is what pushes men and woman continually, yet unsuccessfully, to seek physical union with someone of the opposite sex. It is this hollowness they try to fill with belongings and food. It is this longing that drives them into addictions in an attempt to quiet, forget or stop the yearning.

"Yet men and women will never successfully accomplish this union until they first accomplish it within themselves, independently and individually.

"True love is the power that unites the sexes without destroying the identity of either individual. But this form of love can only develop between equals.

"At this time on Earth, the male-dominated society does not foster this form of love. It fosters control. It fosters men and women playing roles, which have been assigned to each sex, in order to control.

"We are not advocating that women should become like men, or behave like men, or that men should become women, or behave like women. What we are endeavoring is to create a form that is more in alignment with the original design, wherein both sexes understand they contain both the masculine and the feminine. From this understanding they each would actively utilize both for the benefit of the entire species and not just for their own good or to control others. This will not be corrected overnight, but it will not be corrected at all unless a few beings agree to go to Earth to create the new form, the new matrix.

"When the primary unit of society – man and woman – is rebalanced, rooted and grounded in the truth of love and their sexuality, civilization can also be righted and the evolution of the original intention of Human nature can proceed. Sexual love is a gift of Spirit.

"Approximately three years after the relocation, you will be given primary custody of the body and Betty Jean will leave to reenter the Soul.

"Upon entering the Earth plane you will not remember our conversations of this time. This is in order to neither confuse you nor to cause dread and fear in consciousness during the upcoming events.

"After the deaths, and a few months prior to the timing of Betty Jean's leaving, you will go through a series of events that will open you to direct telepathic communication with the Soul, as we are doing now. You will receive information that will be relevant to your life and mission at that time.

"However, you will still not remember until 1991 Earth time, that prior *to entry you were told these events would happen. Your memory will then return gradually. You will remember when it is time to write these memories in book form for the benefit of others.*

"When others read what you write, it will awaken memories of their own entries into the Earth plane. There will be persons within the masses who will be ready to read of your willingness to assist in the evolution of Earth and of Humanity."

And with that Lady Venus stopped the telepathic communication within my consciousness as suddenly as she had begun . . .

I was overcome with awe, appreciation and gratitude as patterns of my experiences on planet Earth began to fall into place with new meaning. Waves of indescribable love washed over me for Lady Venus, my Cosmic Mother.

Her explanations, my experiences, the challenges I had accepted in coming to Earth, "You will remember when it is time to write these memories in book form," all tumbled about within my consciousness like leaves on a windy fall day. The awakening that began in Hawaii was indeed continuing.

36

Serendipity

Spring 1992

After returning home from Hawaii in early spring 1992, I was still having difficulty and became very depressed. I felt somewhat frustrated because I had followed Spirit's obvious promptings to go to Mexico and then to Hawaii. And I had abundant evidence that the energy work I was doing was making a positive difference in the World. So why was I feeling like this?

As a few more days passed, I realized my body was in shock. The trauma was the result of my RELIVING some of the events of my earlier life as I endeavored to write a chapter of this book.

When the body goes into shock, the etheric web separates itself from the physical body slightly. This causes an energy crack and makes it impossible to hold a charge of energy. Later, when I would see people in shock I noticed their energy field shifts about twelve inches to the left. I have no explanations why twelve inches or why to the left, this is just the way it appears to me.

I received homeopathic medication for the shock and began feeling stronger and less depressed.

When I had reached home, my answering machine contained several calls from a woman named Gilda who had been referred to me by people in Georgia.

When I could not reach her by phone after several tries, and could not recall anyone I knew personally in Georgia, I began opening mail.

A letter had come from Marianne, a woman I had met two years before at the Spiritual Frontiers Fellowship gathering in Michigan. She had come for a reading in December 1991.

During the reading her soul kept mentioning "Duluth." She and I assumed this meant Duluth, Minnesota.

I continued with the mail.

A few days later, my friends Hal and Marian, their friend Dean, and I had lunch together.

During the meal, we discussed two parcels of land near Albuquerque, New Mexico, which Dean had purchased several years before at the request of his soul. He had been told the land was to provide future landing sites for extraterrestrial ships. He was to eventually divide the land into sections and sell them to others of like mind.

There was a plan to form a spiritual community, at least on the western acreage.

The brochure about one of the land parcels Dean showed me included photos of Indian ruins close to the property.

A jolt of energy hit my body. I knew I was to visit the property and I mentioned this as a future possibility.

When I returned home after lunch, the phone was ringing. It was Marianne. She had been at lunch with Gilda! (The two had met, quite by chance, in the lobby of the La Fonda Hotel in Santa Fe the winter before when they had each arrived there from Michigan and Florida.)

During their conversation at lunch I was mentioned, although neither woman was aware the other knew me.

When Gilda learned that Marianne knew me, she excitedly retrieved the postcard that had been sent her with my number on it by her friend in Georgia. A blast of energy charged up Marianne's arm when she saw the postmark on the card: "Duluth, Georgia."

I soon learned that Gilda lived in a mobile home on land adjacent to one of Dean's parcels. When she invited me to her home for the weekend and I accepted.

As she drove me to her place, Spirit asked me to go to each of the three Indian ruin sites surrounding Dean's property. It was time for ships to be anchored. Gilda agreed to assist me in anchoring the energy.

The next day we went to each of the sites. Beams came down from three beam ships from the fifth dimension. These three ships were the anchoring vessels for an enormous merkabah (light vessel) in the seventh dimension. The merkabah was called Metatron Transport.

On the following morning (Sunday), Spirit suggested we drive to Santa Fe to visit the Inn of Loretto Chapel. The Chapel has a miraculous winding stairway. I had visited the chapel many times, with no strong energetic experiences.

We were told that Gilda had an aspect of her Oversoul (who had been one of the original nuns) to incorporate with her.

As we sat in the Chapel, I was surprised when a spiritual sister (who had also been a nun) from my own Oversoul joined me energetically! Apparently, she had not been prepared to leave the other nun until it was time for them both to leave together. After the weekend trip, I was home for a short period. I was still quite tired and somewhat depressed. But I had promised to visit my adopted mother in Oklahoma City for her 80th birthday.

Before leaving on that journey, I had mentioned to my daughter Kelley that international travel was exhausting, energy-consuming, assaulting and insulting to the physical and emotional bodies, among other things. Kelley then ventured to say that many people would love to have the lifestyle I was living and suggested I needed a change of attitude! She recommended I look at my life as more of a "permanent vacation."

I decided to take her advice and left for Oklahoma City for two weeks.

The weeks stretched into four. I spoke in three different cities in the area.

One of the interesting events included going to Norman, Oklahoma, where a Ray of energy was anchored into the stadium where Ross Perot was scheduled to give the commencement address the following evening! Ships over Lake Hefner, Founder's Tower and Rose State College were also anchored. The ship over Guthrie, Oklahoma, which I had helped anchor there in August 1991, moved out and relocated over Minneapolis, Minnesota.

Yet another interesting incident during the four weeks was related to a reading I was doing for another psychic. She had asked, "Have you connected with Clark since you arrived in Oklahoma City?" I had met Clark in 1986 at the Marcel Vogel Crystal Workshop outside Reno, Nevada. (At the same conference I met Margie, another member of my Oversoul who took me to Peru three years later.) I was surprised that the psychic knew Clark. (He is an acupuncturist who was living in Boston when I met him.) She said when he heard I was in Oklahoma City he asked that I call him. He and I met for dinner and while we were eating I kept seeing the spiritual image of a big black dog next to him. It finally became so distracting that I asked him if he had a dog.

"No," he replied, "Well, yes, sort of. There is this large black dog that has been hanging around outside my office."

I then told him that the dog was a very special dog because it was an embodied being from Sirius who could assist him with his practice, if he'd listen to its suggestions. He thanked me for the information. He did not behave as if my remark was strange (for which I was grateful). Later, he said Spirit suggested he treat me with acupuncture. The following morning while he was working on me, the dog physically appeared outside the office window. Clark had not seen the animal for several days.

The next day I had another treatment. When the needles were inserted I was left to "float" with the music while Clark left the room to attend another client.

He returned shortly and said, "bj, the dog says I am to ask you about the patient in the next room."

I immediately tuned in to the woman and discovered she had been under severe psychic attack for quite a long time. The attack was negatively affecting her health. I described what I saw. Clark told me he had also been receiving similar impressions.

He and I did the Prayer of Exorcism.

I deliberately called forth the Arch Angel Michael and the Band of Mercy to enter this person's body and to remove any invading entities and to take them into the Light that they can continue to grow and proper. I triple sealed this individual's body against any further invasion by other entities.

Then he removed my needles and returned to the other patient. As he entered her room he asked her how she was doing. She responded that for the first time in a very long while she could feel energy moving through her abdomen, which had been blocked.

Clark told her about the prayer he and I had done. She responded, "Would you ask the woman who prayed with you to come in here so I can thank her?"

As he opened the door on his way to get me, I was in the hallway moving toward the bathroom.

"bj," he'd said, "when you finish, could you come into this room for a minute?"

When Clark went back into the patient's room she said, "bj! Is that bj King?" Then she began to cry.

Through her tears she explained that she had met me about eighteen months before when I'd given a talk at a Silva Mind Control group in Oklahoma. She said in her meditation the night before, her soul had suggested she get in touch with me, but she had not known how to reach me.

She was totally amazed that her Spirit would have brought me to the same clinic and placed me in the next room at the same time that she was being treated. She was even more astonished that the dog would have told Clark there was some connection to be made between us!

Following my treatment I was asked to proceed to Hot Springs, Arkansas, and to Birmingham, Alabama, by way of Memphis.

In Memphis, I stopped to work on the New Madrid Fault Line that runs parallel to the Mississippi. The energies had built up again creating the potential of a severe earthquake. The Space Command, through my Human permission and in alignment with the Universal Law and Divine Plan, did what looked to be energetic stitching in more firmly sewing the crack together.

At that time the Earth was experiencing approximately nine earthquakes a week. To remain within the Divine Plan we were allowed to transmute certain areas, but not others. (Apparently, it was karmically correct for certain areas to experience these catastrophes.)

I drove on to New Orleans to work on the lower end of the Fault Line. I also assisted the Space Command to anchor ships over the NASA bases in New Orleans, Houston and Austin, where I spent a few days vacationing.

I spent three days in El Paso. There were massive electrical storms, as seven ships were anchored over the Texas-Mexico border. (This anchoring would influence efforts to stop the underground burial of nuclear waste. It would also enhance the trade and employment between the two countries.)

While there I stayed with Ann Remick-Barlow and got to see her friend Barbara. The two women had recently co-founded the International Institute for Attitudinal Healing. They now work with people (many young people) with horses and cats to accomplish healing in Los Cruces, New Mexico.

While I had visited many attitudinal healing centers during the seven years I'd been traveling, I had never felt energetically connected to any of them. However, when Ann handed me the business card on their "Institute," a jolt of energy hit my body.

At that moment an understanding came of what the Master Jesus meant when he had appeared to me back in the early '80s. (He had said then that I would be the energetic catalyst for the creation of twelve attitudinal healing centers around the World.)

I realized that He had meant "the healing of International attitudes!"

(When the Master had appeared, I had assumed He meant individual attitudinal healing, such as with individuals who have terminal illnesses.) The Master Jesus recognizes that we, as a species, and the Earth, as an organism, have an illness that will prove terminal unless we change our attitudes.

At that time, Ann and Barbara did not know the future vision of their center. They proceeded on faith that the information would be given them. The addition of horses came later. I acknowledged and admired their beginning.

I too had traveled to ground energies, even though I had not had the benefit of the full vision.

Very often Humans are called to move forward – with little information – toward a goal that is not totally defined. As you can see, it is as if I was pulled along energetically from one serendipitous event to the next. As we meditate and ask for daily guidance, we follow that guidance and move from one clue, one connection, to the next with faith and trust in the process.

Upon completing the seven-week trip and arriving back in Albuquerque, my speedometer registered 3,000 miles! Yet I was not as tired as usual after such a long drive. (My change in attitude before I left must have helped!)

For several days I was so much at peace. I stated to myself, "I want to <u>always</u> continue to feel peaceful, no matter what events are happening around me."

Almost immediately, both of my children called in the midst of personal crisis. I remained calm and peaceful. We prayed together and the situations resolved themselves.

That afternoon I turned on my computer (which had been working perfectly for two weeks, since its return and reconnection). "Hard disk failure" came up on the screen. (Such a message can strike fear in the heart of any computer operator.)

I lost my peaceful feeling, briefly, and said every ugly word I knew. Then I chose peace and calm and went to lunch.

During lunch, I met a woman who knows a man who teaches about computers at a university. She gave me his name and I called. He came and repaired the computer, but he had to take it with him for several days. The fee was minimal.

It was a real test for my conscious decision to remain peaceful, no matter what!

Serendipitous and Synchronistic events increase in our lives when we live with:

A. Great expectations

B. Great sublimations (to hold elevated, lofty or higher thoughts); to keep our minds on that which we want, instead of worrying.

C. Great observations (staying conscious of all that is going on around and within us, and observing messages or intuitions from our Oversouls).

37

Willingness and Trust

Summer 1992

One day in the early summer of 1992, I was cleaning the guest bath in my condo when a porcelain-framed calligraphy, hand-painted with butterflies, fell from the back of the toilet and hit the bathtub. A corner broke off the frame.

I glued the piece back and placed the frame back on top of the toilet. The calligraphy read, "God gives the best to those who leave the choice to Him."

A while later, when a friend who was visiting me sat down on the toilet, the same framed object flew off the back of the toilet and landed in the bathtub. This time the frame broke into hundreds of pieces. She was startled and very upset.

I had been praying for clarity. While picking up the pieces, the message came through that I was no longer to believe what that calligraphy stated because it was not truly expressed in accordance with THE UNIVERSAL LAW OF CO-CREATION.

To match the Law, it should have read, "God gives the best to those who state their desires, release the WAY and the HOW it is to come to them, and proceed mentally, physically and emotionally toward their goals." I had the opportunity to work on this a short time later when my soul asked me to put my belongings in storage and to travel for a year, staying in the homes of friends.

I checked my body and emotions to see how this felt. It felt AWFUL!

I then concluded that it was important to be WILLING to travel, but that I felt I could be more effective, more productive and more at peace if I had a home base where people could contact me.

I stated this to my soul. Almost immediately, the owners of the condo in which I had been living received messages from their souls to the effect I should begin paying rent; that prosperity would increase to match the increased expense. They requested $500 a month, plus utilities.

I did not see how I could pay that amount, but I also knew I did not want to move. I knew too, that I did not accept going back to being homeless. I was no longer willing to lower my standard of living in order to serve my soul. I believed I could do both.

Then in my heart I heard, "You can pay $300 per month."

When I explained this to the owners, they agreed to accept this amount for the summer, until my prosperity increased, enabling me to pay an amount closer to $750, the amount the condo normally draws. The day after I made the commitment, a check for $1,000 arrived in the mail from someone in California I didn't know well. It was enough to pay the rent for the summer!

While putting these two events together in my mind and seeking more clarity regarding the LAWS OF MANIFESTATION, I concluded that Humans are meant to be prosperous.

I further concluded that God (our Oversoul) does not expect us to suffer to do what we came to Earth to do. We must, however, KNOW our desires, STATE them, and BE CLEAR about both our "bottom line" and "upper limits" of acceptance. How little are we willing to settle for? How good can we allow our lives to become?

In early September I spent two weeks in Colorado and Minnesota. On the drive to Colorado, I visited Ghost Ranch near Abiquiu, New Mexico, the area where Georgia O'Keeffe lived for many years of her life. My friends arranged a tour of her home as my birthday present. I felt energetically and emotionally overwhelmed (very positively) to be in the space where she had spent so much of her life, where she had been so happy and content.

Once I was in Colorado, my friend John Hornecker, who does energy work similar to what I do with the Hierarchy, joined me to perform energy work requested by the Hierarchy. It is always easier to do energy work when there is at least one male and one female body to send the energy through. We went into Aspen to be used during the Wind Star Symposium and to release more of the pressure that continued to build under the Rocky Mountain Fault Line.

Working to stabilize fault lines is part of our commitment. While in Minneapolis I had also worked, on the upper end of the New Madrid Fault

Line. These areas were two of the few we had been allowed by Karmic Law to adjust. We do this by (a) presenting our physical bodies to be used as conduits and (b) by giving Human permission to the extraterrestrials to override the LAW OF NON-INTERVENTION, AND THE LAW OF FREE WILL, to release the pressures and energetically pin the fault lines together. One species is not allowed by spiritual law to intervene in the life of another species without being asked to do so by someone within that species. This is one of the major reasons we, as extraterrestrials, have agreed to come to Earth to impersonate Human beings to the best of our ability.

Other friends and I have worked on the lower end of the New Madrid Fault Line, from Memphis and New Orleans, several times.

However, there were certain events we were not allowed by Karmic Law to change, such as the hurricanes that later hit Florida and Louisiana, and the one in Hawaii in 1992.

Energy continually builds, which results in cosmic changes taking place on the Earth's surface and within.

IT IS IMPORTANT TO NOT ALIGN OURSELVES WITH PREDICTIONS OR MAPS OF PREDICTIONS. This is as important now as it was then, because doing so adds to the problems by <u>strengthening the thought forms</u>.

Instead, it is important for us to listen and to know when we are allowed by Divine Law to change circumstances ENERGETICALLY.

We are not helpless! <u>We are co-creators. We created and can change these circumstances with thought and energy!</u>

Getting back to my travels to Minneapolis, I shared a seat on the plane with a man who works for an international company. He asked me if I was involved with the Human Potential Movement after observing the book I was reading. I don't remember now what the book was, but it was obviously one of Spirit's "plants."

After the two of us had talked for a while, he told me his company had just rewritten its purpose statement – "to liberate the Human spirit."

I got goose bumps on my goose bumps . . .

Something else I want to share about Minneapolis:

One night during my stay there, I went to sleep and reported (in my energy body) aboard the Venusia. (This is the Mother Ship I left to join Betty Jean's body in 1969.) Each night (although I am in a physical body), I had worked in my etheric body aboard the Venusia, adjusting the percentage of each Ray coming to the Earth. I was part of a crew, yet my work was done independently. When we work aboard the ships we more or less become our job. We don't think of other things. We think of ourselves as our assignment. We are unlikely to develop emotional relationships with other members of the crew.

On this particular night when I arrived aboard, I was told to return to my body; I had been <u>reassigned</u> to THE NEW JERUSALEM, effective the following night. (The New Jerusalem is the giant energy merkabah "City of Light." Some friends and I helped the Federation anchor the New Jerusalem above the Yucatan in 1988.)

A City of Light Merkabah is a light vessel, non-physical, composed of the individual merkabahs, or light bodies, of those aboard or included. The work I was given to do in my new assignment required me to be a member of a council that makes and acts on decisions affecting this entire Universe and Galaxy, not just that of Earth.

My job on this light ship is very different from what I did on the Venusia. When I went aboard, I totally lost my sense of identity and became a part of a group mind that functions as one entity.

In the morning when I returned to my body, I found myself disoriented and had trouble regaining my sense of separate identity and remembering who I was. It took several weeks for me to adjust to this new routine.

My daughter called one morning and asked how I was.

"I'm having an identity crisis," I told her.

"Oh, I can help you with that; you are my mommy," she quipped. We laughed together, remembering her telling me this in 1979 when she was 10. At the time I was going through the merger with Betty Jean and taking on more and more galactic responsibility without realizing Third Dimensionally what was really going on.

Getting back to The New Jerusalem, our main focus aboard ship at that time (1992) was to merge two of the twelve Universes in this Omniverse. This was to make it possible to bring in a thirteenth Universe as the twelfth. The thirteenth Universe contained most of our home planetary systems.

Making the thirteenth Universe a part of this Omniverse was a very Humanitarian act on the part of the Spiritual Hierarchy. Those of us serving aboard the ships were never allowed to go home to our planets of origin since they are outside this Omniverse. Therefore, many of us felt abandoned and isolated, as if we had been dropped off and forgotten by our own people.

Although I was allowed to go home to Venus, the portal through which I came into this galactic system. I was not permitted to go to Nova, my home planet, because it is outside of this Omniverse.

Many of us who answered the call to come to Earth to help Humanity's evolution came from outside this Omniverse. It was never expected, however, that we would have to remain so long away from our homes.

Nevertheless, we committed to continue our Earth-life incarnations for as long as it takes for the planet to ascend. If the move to the Fifth Dimension has not been completed before the end of our current incarnations, even those of us who are already 'walk-ins' will be expected to rescue other bodies no longer wanted by those currently in them and start another life as an adult when these bodies we are now in die. We would need to walk into other adult bodies, because it would take too long for us to reincarnate though the birth canal and grow up.

When this Universal merger is complete, many Humans on the Earth will have more contact and memory of our planets of origin and feel less lonely and abandoned.

It was a tremendous energetic feat to even consider merging Universes, let alone bringing another Universe into an Omniverse! I was told that this was an experiment that had never been tried before! When I first learned of the possibility, my initial reaction was one of disbelief! "How could they even consider such an enormous task, simultaneously with up-scaling the energy of the Earth herself?"

The opinion of the Hierarchy was, however, that the workers who volunteered to come to Earth to help were growing weary. They needed reassurance and assistance from their families of cosmic origin.

When the above was explained to me in that way, I understood. I also felt the need in my own self and I knew that if I felt it, many others felt it too. In fact, for several years, many people's responses to my newsletters had been that what had been happening to me was happening to them as well.

MY BIRTHDAY

On my September 28th birthday each year (the date Betty Jean was born), I usually celebrate by doing two things: I allow myself to write poetry, and I honor the anniversary of my first acknowledged message from Spirit. That year (1992) was no exception.

I reread that first message.

That day Spirit had said to me, *"Take this opportunity to reflect ... what do you really want to do? Where do you really want to be?"*

Ten years later I found it fascinating to look over the list of six items I had written then. It was equally fascinating to realize that I <u>really was doing all of those things on the list</u>, but not in any way I might have imagined 10 years ago!

While I did not list "traveling" as one of the items, I have done a lot of that in the past few years while accomplishing four of my listed desires. "<u>I want to do</u> something that helps people communicate . . . something creative... something I can't be fired from . . . to teach . . . help people to self-actualize."

HOLD ONTO YOUR VISION
By bj King

Roads to our dreams
Are paved with "if onlys,"
"Might have beens"
And "somedays,"
Cluttered with detours,
Roadblocks and potholes
Of forgetfulness.
Caught up in survival
We forget
The dream, the vision
In favor of compromise
And lack of faith
In our worthiness.
Those who hold their dream
In spite of the odds
Are the victors,
For the vision appears
In Third Dimensional reality
If held intact.
Remember your dreams;
Move toward your vision.
It will be there.

MY VISIT TO OREGON

Soon after my birthday, I went to Oregon for a few weeks. Being there was a delight. I was very well received, due in part to the PR work of my friends Robert and Deborah.

Much synchronicity happened during the two weeks I was there. For example, Robert had had a disagreement with the woman who owned the bookstore where the workshop was going to be held and, therefore, had been avoiding her.

On Saturday, the day before the workshop, we took the light rail to the Saturday Market in downtown Portland. The Market was a little like a big arts and craft show. (Spirit has such a sense of humor.) Of course we ran into the owner of the bookstore and another workshop presenter who had just rented the room next to the one we would be using.

As it happened, I had given a talk in that same room just a week before. To brighten up the place, Robert had purchased twelve lovely potted mums. He had also bought an off-white reclining rocker (at a thrift shop) for me to sit in while I spoke and led the workshop. It was an attractive chair and very comfortable.

The woman who owned the bookstore confessed that she had been using the plants all week, as well as the chair. She was thrilled when we told her we would leave the flowers for her when we finished the workshop. (We gave the chair to a friend of mine from Charlotte who had just moved to Portland to attend the Naturopathic College.)

The owner of the bookstore was totally gracious when we met her at the Market.

On the Friday before the workshop (on Sunday), Spirit woke me and suggested that the workshop be videotaped in addition to the audio taping Robert had arranged.

Since Robert had paid $350 for the audio taping, I was in no humor to hear about the potential expense of this additional idea from Spirit.

I told Spirit, "I have no idea how to arrange that on such short notice, and I'm not going to ask Robert to do more than he has already committed to do. If you want it on video, send someone with a camera to do it."

At 1:30 that Friday afternoon, the sound man called and I happened to answer the phone. He asked me if I had any objection to his videotaping the workshop in addition to audio taping it!

I broke into laughter. Then I told him what I had heard that morning from Spirit and acknowledged his having listened so well himself! He was impressed, since both he and his wife are metaphysical.

Robert, who had chosen that company from the yellow pages, was a little spooked by all the synchronicity.

A week before I left for Oregon, a friend I had met in Albuquerque had called to say her ex-husband telephoned her from Portland and gave her the name and number of the coordinator of the UFO activities in Portland. I reached that coordinator by phone, and she invited me to speak at their meeting that week. About sixty people attended.

As a result of that talk (which was supposed to be two hours, but lasted four) two other "group readings" were arranged. (A group reading is one in which each person present is allowed to ask two personal questions.)

One of the women who attended had just driven back to Portland from Guatemala by way of California. She stopped to visit a friend who gave her a copy of the Namaste Newsletter, which she had just received in the mail.

Jackie was scheduled to attend an astrological gathering being held on the Sunday I was speaking at the UFO gathering. However, her meeting was canceled, so she and the friend she was with decided to come hear me. Until they entered the room and saw more newsletters on the table, neither of them was aware that I was the person speaking!

Jackie then invited me to perform a group reading for 15 of her friends at her home. When the people arrived, a similar experience took place.

One of the young men in the audience did not know who he was coming to hear, but he received the Newsletter (secondhand) from a friend in Buffalo, New York!

It is truly amazing how Spirit brings people together when it is time for them to meet, or when certain messages and energies need to be exchanged or delivered. Years later I am still meeting people who were in the audience that day at the UFO lecture.

There were more private sessions generated out of these meetings than I had hours to do!

One more thing that happened while I was in Oregon:

For thirteen years, I had worn a gold nugget cross – a crucifix-type cross. I had it made by melting down Ed's and my wedding bands after his death.

Some months before the trip to Oregon, when we began working on the changes for the idea of churches no longer being focused on the crucifixion, but rather on the concept of ascension, Spirit had asked me to symbolically cooperate by having the cross melted down and reformed. They suggested a Maltese cross – an even square – with a large, dark amethyst set in the center.

Of course, one of my usual responses is, "Do you have any idea what that would cost?" The question was met with silence. I was very sentimentally attached to the cross. After repetitive suggestions from St. Germain, I finally became "willing" to have the cross melted down IF it could be done in a manner I could afford. Of course. I thought I could put it off because I knew I couldn't afford either the additional gold it would take or the stone for the middle.

A few days later, a couple I did not know well, came through Albuquerque to spend a few days with me. I did several hours of spiritual work for them, plus a phone reading for a friend of theirs in Portland.

After the work was done the man announced they wanted to barter my spiritual services. I was furious. When I had met the man before in Mt. Shasta all I had known about him was that he was a poet. I certainly didn't need $450 worth of poetry.

"What did you have in mind to barter?" I said, probably through clenched teeth.

"We wholesale gems and minerals to New Age stores," he replied.

I knew instantly that St. Germain was calling me on my willingness to have the cross made.

"Let me see what you have," I offered.

The man went to his van and came back with a tray of faceted stones. Of course the amethyst I needed lay in the center of the tray.

"I'll take that one," I pointed.

"What are you going to do? Are you going to make a ring out of it?"

"No, a cross," this time I was definitely speaking through clenched teeth.

"What kind of cross?" he inquired.

"A Maltese cross."

"Who will be making it for you?"

"I don't know yet. I have to melt down a gold nugget cross and have it transformed into the Maltese cross with this stone in the middle." I pulled it out of my shirt and showed it to him.

"I have a friend in San Francisco who is a wonderful goldsmith. If you give me your cross and any other gold you have, along with the stone and a drawing of what you want, I'll take it to him and then when we meet again in Portland in two weeks we will get together and I'll have it for you."

They just "happened" to know a goldsmith in San Francisco who could do the gold work. They lived in Bellingham, Washington, and were on their way to Florida from New Mexico and then would make their way back across the south to California and back to Oregon in two weeks, when I was scheduled to be back in Oregon. I did not know these people from Adam and here St. Germain was expecting me to give them the cross I was sentimentally attached to, two other gold rings and the amethyst I was bartering for. I was clear that I had been called on the "deal" I had made with St. Germain, that I would do it when I could afford it. Now I could afford it financially because of the barter, but could I afford it emotionally? They took my gold cross and the stone with them. When I arrived in Portland to do my workshops and readings, the couple delivered the new cross to me on their way home to Bellingham, Washington!

Again, all that was required of me was willingness and faith . . . (I hope I don't make this faith and willingness thing sound easy.)

This symbol (the Maltese cross) has many positive meanings, including the balance of male/female energy and bringing Spirit into matter. More symbols are explained in St. Germain's book *Alchemy* as channeled by Elizabeth Claire-Prophet.

In closing this chapter I need to say that one of the reasons for my trip to Oregon was to give the extraterrestrials permission to energetically "cap" the Trojan Nuclear power plant. The plant was located about 40 miles northwest of Portland and was in grave danger of contaminating that entire area.

The energetic dome that was put in place looks much like those that cover anniversary clocks. (Incidentally, the plant shut down operations a few months later.)

Giving permission to the extraterrestrials to energetically cap such plants has successfully resulted in physical closure, or of limiting activity in some of the plants. But neither of these actions solves the question of what to do with the waste that is left!

However, I am reminded of the article entitled "Nuclear Waste Breakthrough" I read in the Wall Street Journal earlier this year. It seems a biochemist, Paul Jackson at the Energy Department's laboratory in Los Alamos, New Mexico, discovered that jimson weed eats and digests plutonium without killing itself in the process.

In addition, the weed has a weird affinity for "pink water," a troublesome liquid left over from machining explosives that trigger atom bombs.

It isn't certain exactly how the weed separates plutonium and pink water from the rest of the sludge. But the weed removes not only the plutonium, but also the cadmium, boron and copper from the water it ingests. The metals are concentrated, then bound by a protein compound to the plant's cell walls, protecting it from the poison.

Of course, once the weed has eaten radioactive material, it too becomes radioactive. That causes a smaller problem: where to store the jimson weed!

It would be good to visualize nuclear power plants and other areas relating to nuclear power and waste, being planted in jimson weed and these new plants. Also, visualize an energy the color and consistency of Pepto-Bismol pouring down over the plants and waste. (Further, see the scientists in these locations accepting the telepathic inspiration for the solution to the problem!) Since the time this was originally written the scientists at Washington State University have hybridized several plants with enzymes from the liver of a rabbit to create plants that consume contaminated soil and transmute the contamination.

"Obstacles are what we see when we take our eyes off the goal."

38

Opportunities and Fun Working With Energies

When I returned home to Albuquerque from Oregon and went to the post office for my mail, the woman handed me about twelve pieces.

"That can't be all of it," I commented.

"I don't know what to tell you," she said rudely. "That's all there was in the box. You will have to check with your carrier."

I left feeling very frustrated. I grumbled to God that I thought this was grossly inefficient on the part of the Universe to waste two days in which I could have taken care of the mail during the weekend.

When I arrived home the postman had already come. Flags on the neighbors' boxes were down, and my box was empty.

I unloaded my groceries and continued fussing with Spirit.

After about 20 minutes, the doorbell rang. It was a substitute carrier with my huge box of mail!

"I understand you came to the post office to pick this up, and I had it in my truck," he explained. "When I saw your car, as I was leaving this area, I realized you had returned from your trip and I thought I should bring it back by."

I still don't know how he knew I had been to the post office. And I was too stunned to ask! This level of manifestation and being taken care of by the Universe I could definitely tolerate . . .

I had rearranged my condo after coming home from Hawaii. At that time, my energy body would no longer tolerate either the limited space or light in the small guest room I had been using as an office. Therefore, I made my living area into an office/studio, providing much more light and space in which to work. (This move must have helped create a spiritual center out of my condo because fourteen different groups of people stayed there in eight weeks!)

Shortly after I arrived back in Albuquerque I received a call from a woman I had met once and read for in Oklahoma City. She said Spirit was asking her to arrange a one-woman art show for me in Oklahoma City at the Marriott Hotel in December. I was thrilled and amazed that Spirit was so specific in asking people to assist me, especially people that I hardly knew.

I began painting daily in order to accomplish a large enough body of work for the show. In three days I accomplished a great amount of art work, including five paintings. All of it was in addition to unpacking and sorting the mail.

When I was ready to take the paintings to be framed, Spirit told me to take just four of them. Logically, I could not understand why I wasn't taking all five.

When I arrived at the framers, a sale was in progress: forty percent off if you had four paintings framed at once. However, this did not explain why I was supposed to have only four paintings be framed instead of five.

I continued painting – 16 hours a day. By the end of November, I had eighteen framed paintings, thirteen matted, twenty-three matted miniatures, forty-three sets of stationery, fifty-two bookmarks, and 350 greeting cards ready to take to the art show in Oklahoma City. (It is astonishing what we're capable of accomplishing when we stay focused and create goals for ourselves.)

By the end of the month I needed a framer who would work inexpensively and fast to frame my paintings. Spirit suggested a name from the Yellow Pages.

When I called, the man was very personable and accommodating. Both he and his wife were interested in metaphysics. She worked in a mental health hospital. At the time, it was possible that I might be able to teach her to do exorcisms on some of her patients . . . opportunities to serve . . . People coming together when the time is right . . . and so it went . . .

During the month, Frank, with whom I had lived in Mount Shasta, came into town. He had sold his home and was in town to arrange to have his belongings shipped to Arizona. When he arrived, it became obvious that the fifth painting I had not framed was his! (We took it to an overnight framer so he could take it with him in his car when he left Albuquerque.)

We had a great visit. Also, I love to dance but rarely go because of the cigarette smoke. However, we found a wonderful non-smoking restaurant with a piano bar and two dance floors, one for smokers and one for non-smokers. The musicians played all the old songs that are so great to dance to. We also sang along with the music. Fun!

Sometime in here I began noticing a large energy for another potential move at the end of December, even though I was not given any specifics. I had been very happy and productive living in New Mexico. It seemed to be the crossroads of the World, if the number of persons coming through was any indication! However, if Spirit had a better idea, I was open to suggestions.

During most of November I remained in isolation in order to paint for long hours each day. Being alone gave me a lot of time to think and to listen. Also, starting a few months before, I had done more Bible reading than I had done at any time since I left the Episcopal Church in 1979.

Too, Matthew, my Eighth Dimensional higher self, told me he had been on Earth as the apostle Matthew. He challenged me to read the book attributed to him and to write a commentary on <u>his</u> opinions about what had been written.

I had thought a lot about what Jesus meant by "becoming as little children," and the difference between "child-like" and "childish." Being "born again" and the story of Christ's birth had also been in my thoughts.

As children, most of us were open, curious, easily excited and involved with life every waking moment. The thing we did best was to grow. We grew because of – and in many cases, in spite of – what was going on around us.

And we used our imaginations to create. We were eager to believe and quick to forgive. We were interested in almost everything around us and afraid of almost nothing. We knew how to play. We had not as yet learned fear and shame.

I concluded that being "born again" did not mean we were to rededicate ourselves to the theological and dogmatic beliefs of another person or persons. Rather, being born again meant to reclaim our essential innocence and honesty, our fearless interest in and openness to new ideas, and our eagerness to trust life enough to let our love for it drive away our fear of it.

Another thing I had thought about was the "Star of Bethlehem," which happens to be the name of Ashtar's Command Ship. In the Bible, we read that the star moved to lead the "wise men" to Jesus' location. And then I thought, "Why have people remembered and praised Jesus? Even those who do not consider him the "son of God"? Was it because he lived in total dominion – total authority – over conditions? He lived an exemplary example of how life <u>could be</u> lived in a state of One Presence. He overcame all obstacles – even death.

His story represents the evolution of the Human mind coming to a point of accepting itself as divine. He stated, "Greater works than these shall you do – "

In Jesus we see Universal Reality seeking Universal expression. As he "walked his talk" he encouraged others to consider what they could accomplish if they developed their potential.

And then I had another thought: "Someday I will have time to write all the books and screenplays that go on in my head. There are so many ways these ideas and experiences could be expressed in fun and readable stories." However, right then, there weren't hours in the day to answer correspondence, talk with people, paint, write the newsletter and travel.

And soon it was December and time to gather up all my paintings for the art show in Oklahoma City.

A couple weeks before, a woman had called to request I speak to their group of about 40 persons at the Shaffenburg Psychic Research Institute in Kingfisher, Oklahoma. This date was the same evening the art show was scheduled!

Kingfisher is about thirty miles northwest of Oklahoma City. Because both events felt important, I agreed to rush from one to the other.

Later that week we learned the room in Oklahoma City where we planned to hold the art show wouldn't be available for another week!

I felt that because I had been WILLING, Spirit rearranged the schedule so events would move more smoothly.

The art show was a success. The occasion attracted many people I had not seen in years. This resulted from one of the cosmic purposes for the show: affording people who attended the opportunity to meet each other. The other purpose was to expose those in attendance to the energy of the collective paintings. The synchronicity was amazing. While I was in Oklahoma City, we anchored eight Saturn ships over the city. Because the ships came so close to Earth, they caused the most severe thunder and lightening storm and blizzard the people there had ever seen!

ENERGIES

The energy that came in to Earth December 26, 1992, actually struck Oklahoma December 24. It poured around the Earth like the old Sherwin-

Williams paint commercial.

The energy seemed to have created quite an opening. The image I saw was an office door whose upper half was covered with frosted glass. The words printed on the glass read, "Purchasing Office." This image told me we could (energetically) walk into this office and place a listing of what we desired for ourselves on the desk. We could also place a list of desires for a collective Humanity, or desires for Earth, on the desk even if no one was sitting there to receive them.

It was extremely important at that time that everyone hold a very clear vision of what he/she desired. This energy was all about receiving what we desired!

The energy was to shift again on February 14, 1993, and the door would close. Between February 14 and March 30, the "Purchase orders" were to be processed.

On March 30, 1993, the energy flow coming in was to cause physical manifestation of that which we were holding in consciousness.

It was my impression that the energy shift on March 30, would also set off what had been prophesied as "The Rapture." The Christian interpretation of this seems to be that those who are "saved" would be lifted up to Heaven.

My impression was that those who were "awake" – those who knew they had a soul, who recognized they were spiritual beings behaving as Humans, rather than Humans trying to become spiritual – would remain with their bodies. Those who were still asleep – who had no conscious awareness of Spirit – would begin being lifted or "beamed up" into the Oversouls. Higher energy replacement aspects of the souls would then "walk-in."

I felt that we had reached critical mass in terms of negative energy. It was now time in evolution for the "major shift" that had been predicted to take place.

This tremendous influx of energy would change many things positively. It would also create more chaos. For example, these "walk-ins" would not have the same advantage as those of us who had longer periods of co-habitation in the body before the original inhabitant departed to return to the Oversoul. Therefore their integration and awakening might be even more traumatic than ours had been! This meant that facilitators, body workers and counselors who understood the concept of "walk-ins" would be greatly needed.

CHURCH DECEIT

I (as well as others I'm aware of and know) had been working with the Saturn Command to disclose the deceit upon which the Catholic and Christian churches are based.

On a visit to Rome, my friends Hal and Marion placed crystals inside the Vatican. The crystals made it easier for us to continually ground energy in the Vatican and to infuse thoughts in the minds of Cardinals and the Pope. And, apparently, changes ARE occurring.

To illustrate, Hal and Marion brought me a hand-carved, wooden rosary from the Vatican when they returned from Rome. I wore it around my wrist for two days, rubbing it constantly to send energy to the Vatican.

On the second day, the cross bar fell off and a tremendous jolt of energy hit my body.

"What in the world was that?" I cried out. Then I stopped what I was doing and lay down to meditate.

As I became quiet I traveled etherically to within the Vatican. I saw something that looked as if someone had opened a trench down the middle of the floor with an old-fashioned can opener. The rent left very ragged edges. Coming up through the floor was a gigantic fountain of brilliant white light, resembling Old Faithful. Since then, I and others have been visualizing this light growing stronger and stronger. And it is happening. For example, in the past the church has paid out hundreds of millions of dollars to settle lawsuits when priests were found to have molested children. (The Vatican reportedly faced a $92 million deficit in 1993.) By 2007, the figure was into the multi-billions.

Later, the Pope agreed to comply with laws about reporting incidents to authorities and to cooperate in investigations. An agreement was also reached to prosecute the guilty in public trials, to relieve alleged offenders promptly of ministerial duties and to refer them for medical evaluation. Further, officials with the church committed themselves to reach out to victims and their families, communicating "sincere commitment to their spiritual and emotional well-being."

About this same time, several well-known TV and movie celebrities attacked, on public television, the underhanded ways the Catholic hierarchy had operated in the past.

One thing we were working on was to change people's belief that the priests, and especially the Pope, were infallible; that, therefore, their opinions and interpretations must be honored more than those of the individual. And this change is happening!

About mid-1992, the Pope admitted that the church had been wrong in its treatment of Galileo and apologized in a public confession. Although progress seems slow, prayer and energy-work DO MAKE A DIFFERENCE.

A few years later, I was assigned to etherically go sit beside the Pope's bed while he was sleeping and to insert images in his dreams of the Holocaust and the Spanish Inquisition. During his first Easter message after I began my assignment, for the first time in recorded history, the Pope admitted the fallibility of the Church by publicly asking God's forgiveness for church officials knowing what was happening in Germany in the 1930s and 40s and doing nothing to help with the situation. The second Easter, after I started my work with his consciousness, in his public message Pope John Paul asked God's forgiveness for the atrocities committed during the Spanish Inquisition.

39

Charlie

December 1992

For several years, I had been told that Jovan, my male counterpart from the Venusia ship I left to come into body in 1969, would eventually "walk in" to a body. He would join me to do the work of grounding the energy of the Goddess Psyche and Eros, to create a pattern for balanced male/female relationships. This would help end the war between the sexes on Earth.

Of course, as many of you know, when Spirit says "soon," it may mean many things, and not necessarily "soon" as Humans know it, since in Spirit's dimension there is no time as we know it.

In September 1991, I was told Jovan had merged with a body in Oregon. I did not know the person chosen, other than by reputation. When I checked the body psychically, I found a heart condition and cancer cells. I explained to the soul that I was unwilling to mate with another person who had a heart condition (after experiencing the death of my fiancé in 1979 by a heart attack).

Jovan returned to the Venusia, and we continued to work together at night.

In July 1992 Jovan merged with the body of a man who had been a friend of mine for several years. This was only a temporary situation, since that person was in a state of merging with a larger expression of his soul.

The merger with Jovan became inappropriate. Again I was disappointed.

After I was transferred from the Venusia to the New Jerusalem merkabah in September of 1992, I was unable to connect with Jovan's energies. Even though we do not form emotional or sexual relationships aboard the ships, we are close to those members who are projected from our own Oversouls.

I felt very abandoned and isolated. In fact, by November I had begun feeling extremely depressed. At that time I wrote the following:

JOVAN
By bj King

Oh, Jovan
My heart seeks you now
As it has not here-to-fore.
Separated by time and space
By day
We flew together
By night Always reserved
Always practical
Always efficient.

Then you came to Earth
Briefly in bodies.
We rejoined
As we did in eons past.
Briefly, ever so briefly
We touched
And spoke
And loved
As Humans.

And again you are gone,
Again separated
By time and space,
Though not our hearts
Our souls still
Act as one.

So little understood
In Human terms
Is our plight,
For they recognize not
Separate selves

bj King

Joined at the soul
For eternity.

I entreat you
To return to me
In Human form
For I suffer loneliness
As a mortal
Encased in this skin
With only brief reprieves
While the body sleeps.
And now the mission of the soul
Separates us even then,
This new assignment
Keeps me from your side;
Even when the body sleeps
I cannot come to you
Even briefly.

Oh, Dear One,
I cry from loneliness
To leave this place
And this mortal form
To fly with you again.
Unless you return to be with me in flesh
The shallowness of this life
Engulfs me.

I have no one
To speak with
Who understands this pain
Of separation
From my self.

I work for peace,
Create beauty,
Share what I feel.
I understand
And wait . . .

> For you to reappear
> In Human form
> To join with me
> In Earth's illusion
> Of flesh
> And mortality. I wait . . .

On December 9, 1992, a few days after I arrived in Oklahoma City for the art exhibit and to speak and do readings, my hostess invited me out for dinner at a nice restaurant. She also asked if I would accompany her to hear a friend play the piano at a piano bar in the restaurant. I was to speak in a suburb of Oklahoma City that night to a friend's meditation group. I normally stay after the talk and meditation to answer questions the audience might have. But she mentioned she wished we could have dinner in order to become better acquainted. She was the mother of the acupuncturist I mentioned before. The one I had met at a retreat outside Reno, Nevada, years before and I did not really know my hostess. I heard myself agree to be back in the city to go with her by 9 p.m. instead of lingering longer to answer questions.

When we arrived at the restaurant, the kitchen was already closed, but since she is a regular there the cook agreed to make us salads to eat at the piano bar. She introduced me to people she knew and to the pianist, telling them I was her guest from Albuquerque. The pianist is most talented and versatile, and "ego-less" enough to play for just about anyone in the audience who wants to get up and sing.

As I surveyed my surroundings, I noticed a tall man with gray hair and a beard sitting on my extreme right. Next to him sat a most attractive lady, next to her another man. My hostess was next, and then me. As the pianist began playing, the attractive woman got up and began singing. Her voice was beautiful, and obviously professionally trained.

After a song or two, she took her seat. As she did so, the tall, gray-haired man gave her a side hug around the shoulders. Then he got up to sing. I "assumed" the two were together.

I had observed that when the tall man was not singing, his aura was about 1-1/2 inches from his body. When he opened his mouth to sing, his aura expanded to about four feet in all directions and was gold, white and green. Further, when the energy and emotion of his voice hit my heart chakra, I began having what felt like a pleasurable anxiety attack. Fortunately, he closed his eyes while singing and I was free to put my chin in my hands and rest them on the table to stabilize myself while I listened intently to what he was singing.

His first song was "My Funny Valentine." The second, requested by a voice coming from several rooms away was "Amazing Grace." This was pretty unusual to be requested in a lounge, but it was a direct signal to me from Spirit to pay attention to what was happening. ("Amazing Grace" is one of the pieces of music we use to ground the Christ Consciousness vibration. Others are "Danny Boy," "Green Sleeves" and "Rhapsody in Blue.")

Of course, when the man began singing "Amazing Grace," my whole body – and his – began radiating the Christ Consciousness out into the lounge.

As the tall man concluded his songs, the pianist took a break. The woman who had sung before him came over to where I was sitting. The tall man vanished out a side door, and I thought he had left. Actually he had gone to the restroom, which was out in the hall.

The woman introduced herself as Mary Kay, a friend of my hostess, and said, "Well, you have accomplished quite a feat."

Not understanding what in the world she meant, I asked her why she was saying that. She quickly replied, "You have stolen Charlie's heart with just your presence."

"Who is Charlie?" I inquired.

"The man who just sang to you," she answered. "When you entered the lounge and sat down, he turned to me and said, 'Now that is what I call a VERY attractive lady. I wish I had nerve enough to speak to her, but if she's from Albuquerque that would be a dead-end street.'" Then the woman asked, "Would you be insulted if he came over and introduced himself to you? I can assure you he does not pick up women when he comes here to sing. He has one beer, then he drinks ice tea and he never takes anyone home with him. You can believe whatever he says to you."

"I would not be insulted if he wants to come over. I would love to meet him. He has an amazing voice." (I wanted to add, "Not to mention a phenomenal aura when he sings.") The woman returned to her seat.

Charlie, the tall, gray-haired man returned from the restroom, then returned to the bar for his iced tea. He told me later he was trying to get his nerve up. He was not aware that Mary Kay had been over doing PR for him in his absence.

When he walked up to me a short time later, he greeted me with, "Hi. My name is Charlie Burns. I understand you are from Albuquerque."

"Yes," I said. "I am here to have an art show on Saturday at the Marriott."

I was not willing to mention what else I do.

"I hope you don't think me forward, but I would love to take you out to lunch or dinner while you are in town. Here's my card. Please give me a call if you have any free time," he offered.

We chatted for a few more minutes, and I told him how much I enjoyed his singing. He then said again, "I hope you don't think I'm being too forward. I don't usually behave this way when I first meet someone, but I'd love to have you move around and sit with me."

My hostess had become engrossed in conversation with the man sitting next to her, so I did not feel as if I were abandoning her by moving. I did, however, mention to Charlie that there were no vacant seats next to where he had been sitting. To that he replied, "I would consider it an honor and a privilege to stand behind you for the rest of the evening if you would sit in my chair."

I thought, "What an interesting thing to say, but I did ask God to bring a Southern gentleman." The thought made me smile.

I could not refuse such a gallant offer. Also, the man seemed to be truly sincere and shy. I moved and he stood behind me with one hand on my right shoulder except when he was singing.

The next song he sang was "Wind Beneath My Wings." This is my daughter Kelley's song to me!

As the piano player was announcing his last song, Charlie told me he wanted very much to dance with me.

"I hate to point out the obvious, but there is no dance floor here," I pointed out.

"If you will dance with me, I'll make one," he replied and began moving tables and chairs to create space for us.

As I moved into his arms it felt so natural and right it both amazed and startled me. Since I have been on the planet, Earth and Earthlings have felt "foreign" to me. This man's presence was the closest thing I had experienced to the vibrations of "home." (Later, when we had his astrological chart done, we found he has eight planets in Venus!)

We said good night and my hostess and I left.

I found it difficult to get Charlie out of my mind most of the night and could literally "feel" him thinking about me.

The next day I was doing readings at a doctor's office and when my 11 a.m. appointment canceled, I called Charlie's office number. His secretary answered, and when I explained who I was and that I wanted to leave a message for him about lunch, she said, "Oh, yes. He left instructions that

I was to take down every word you said if you called." I left a message requesting that he call the doctor's office with information about where I could meet him and at what time.

When my next client had gone and I checked the machine, I found a message from Charlie stating that he would prefer to pick me up, rather than have me meet him in a public place. I was again impressed by his manners and consideration. (Again I remembered having asked the soul to find the body of a "Southern gentleman" for Jovan.)

Charlie took me to a very nice, quiet restaurant. Inside, we were directed to a small corner table with an L-shaped booth and one chair. I sat in the booth and he occupied the chair. I became aware immediately that the energy of the seating arrangement was wrong for me. I tried to find a way to express this to Charlie without mentioning "energy."

"Would you mind moving to this side of the table?" I asked. "This arrangement feels very awkward to me."

He gasped. His eyes became as big as saucers. "Do you do this very often?" His words came out as big as his eyes.

"Do what?" I said, puzzled. "Be forward and ask for what I want? Yes, nearly always."

"No," he exclaimed. "Read people's minds!"

"Well, yes, as a matter of fact I do. It's more or less what I do for a living. I'm a professional mystic. Many people call what I do psychic," I explained. "I try not to do it unless a person comes, sits in front of me and pays me to do it, but if a person is projecting a thought strongly enough, and I am sitting in his or her energy field, it is pretty difficult not to pick up on it. I'll try not to do it in the future. You don't have to monitor your thoughts because of me, honestly."

"That's exactly what I was thinking: *I want to sit on the couch closer to her, but I don't want her to think I am being too forward,*" he confessed.

Charlie was very quiet for a few minutes studying both me and the menu. Then he explained that he was a member of, and a soloist in a charismatic, fundamentalist Christian church. He had already told me the night before that he was an insurance salesman. God was practicing her sense of humor again.

At this, my heart sank and I began mentally fussing at my soul. All my prejudices regarding fundamentalist religions began surfacing. We ordered the same lunch, and he asked me if I had always been psychic. He also asked me to explain how I happened to believe the way I do ,and how I began doing what I do. He said that his church taught that psychic and occult activities are demonic.

I gave him Webster's definition of occult: That which is hidden from sight. He confessed he had never bothered to look it up, but had simply accepted the church's definition as his own. I began to tell Charlie my story. As I talked he seemed to relax.

After lunch he dropped me off at the doctor's office. I invited him to attend the art show at the Marriott the following day, Saturday. I did not expect him to come. However, "reading" his feelings was difficult because so much had been offered him in such a short time. His mind was filled with more thoughts than he could sort and file. To believe me, he would have to overcome much of what he had been taught.

That night I again had difficulty sleeping because I was thinking about him, could feel him thinking about me and I was a bit anxious anticipating the art show.

Saturday morning, Charlie arrived at the show about fifteen minutes after it opened. A great warmth for him welled up in me.

He stayed around the hotel most of the day, in and out of the show room. He did not demand any attention, but was available if I wanted to say something to him or to introduce him to someone. He read the greeting cards in the display rack, the newsletter, my brochure and the tape covers. At one time he picked up a copy of my *Finding Your Life's Purpose* workbook, and read a few pages here and there. By the end of the day I was happy, but exhausted. Charlie stayed and helped me pack all my things and put them in my car. Then he asked if I was too tired to go to dinner with him.

That night I tried to go slow in telling Charlie about my beliefs and my experiences. I usually waited for him to ask me questions. I had no intention of trying to explain being an extraterrestrial "walk-in" to a fundamentalist!

On about the third date, Charlie looked at me and asked, "You are not from here, are you?"

"No, I'm from Texas. I lived in Oklahoma City for six years before I began traveling," I said.

"No, I mean you are not from here, from Earth, are you?"

Not believing he was seriously asking such a question, I hesitated in my response, but my soul pushed me to continue to divulge my truth.

"No, I'm not, actually. I'm from the Nova system, which is beyond this Omniverse. I came into this galaxy through the system of Venus to get permission to 'walk into' a body on Earth in 1969." I sort of ran it all together, holding my breath as I waited for his reaction.

"Venus. Of all the places I could have guessed you were from, Venus is the one I would have said," he replied.

"What would possibly cause you to ask such a question anyhow?" I inquired.

"I'm not sure. You just don't seem like you are from Earth. You are not like anyone I've ever met before."

I stared at him, wondering if he was being fed these questions unconsciously by his soul. Then he asked, "Could you explain more to me about what it means to be a 'walk-in?' I've never heard that term before."

I talked for about an hour. He watched me and listened intently. When I finished, he explained that he had eaten lunch that day with the minister of music from his church. The man had tried to convince him that I was "of the devil" and that the spirits I converse with are "demonic."

My body tensed as I listened to this ignorant judgment being passed on me by someone who had never even met me! Then after a few moments I took some deep breaths and tried to remember my own ignorance in 1982, when I had begun hearing the voices. That was before I knew the truth about what it is to be psychic or the difference between being a psychic and being a mystic.

I heard Charlie's voice saying, "I listened to what John was saying and then I thought about last night when you did the Cellular Release process for me. I remembered how loving and

'of God' the energy felt. I had to tell him that I thought in your case that he had to be mistaken. I told him I had not felt anything evil in your presence, that I have felt nothing but love coming from you or the people around you. I tried to tell him that you talk about God, Jesus and the Holy Spirit, and that you also talk about a lot more. But his mind is so closed!"

Charlie and I spent a lot of time together during the rest of my stay in Oklahoma City. He confided that after his divorce he had checked himself into a recovery unit to deal with his co-dependency. He had felt a total loss of identity when he ceased to be a husband and an in-house father to his two daughters. Apparently the twenty-eight days of therapy opened him to himself, his feelings, his spirituality and his ability to verbalize his feelings.

When I left for my home in Albuquerque, I left Charlie copies of the workbook and some back issues of the newsletter. I did not really expect him to read any of them.

When I arrived home on December 21, a message was on my telephone answering machine from Charlie. His trip to visit his brother over Christmas in Montana had been canceled because of snow. He knew I would not be returning to my home until after Christmas, but when I did, he wanted to talk with me.

I called him immediately. It felt right to forgo my intention to be alone during the holidays and to invite him to drive out for Christmas Eve and Christmas Day.

He responded with, "Let me pray about it until tomorrow. I'll call you back after I check to see if it feels like the right thing to do."

I was greatly surprised that he did not give an immediate answer, yet glad he was going to check with his soul, in his own way, to see if it was "right" or if it was just what he wanted to do. I was also amazed at how well-developed his intuition was, even without his understanding how to depend on it.

He called early the following morning. We both decided I needed two days to take care of my mail and unpack. He would drive in on Wednesday.

We had a wonderful four days together. One night when we were talking, his soul began speaking through me. It told him that he, too, is a "walk-in" and that it took place in September 1969.

At that, every hair on his body stood on end, and he became very emotional. That was proof to him that the information was true. He also said it did much to explain the many events of his life the past years.

All in all, it was one of the best Christmas holidays I have ever spent. I never felt he was an intrusion into my space or my thoughts. In fact, I was not ready for him to leave when Sunday came. But we both agreed that we had to get back to our work; that God would have to arrange how and when we would see each other again.

Charlie returned to Oklahoma. We had agreed that he would come to New Mexico for New Year's Eve.

The day before he was to drive out, he called and said, "I have just one question . . . Am I Jovan?"

I was appalled that he would ask me this over the phone and could not imagine where he had even heard the name.

"Where did you hear that word?" I demanded.

"I just read the May issue of the newsletter in which Lady Venus explained to you that one of your main missions is to ground the energies of the Goddess Psyche and Eros on the planet and that Jovan is coming to assist you. I need to know if I am Jovan. If not, I need to stop falling in love with you because it will be very difficult for me to give you up when Jovan does arrive." He was very matter of fact in his explanation.

I was amazed to hear such expressions coming out of the mouth of a fundamentalist! No skepticism, no doubt, no fear were present in his voice.

"No, you are not Jovan, but I must tell you that the soul says you have the energy potential to allow his energies to merge with your body. This is because we are all a part of the same Oversoul. You will keep your own personality. You are the only one who can make this decision, and you do not have to make it now. Let's talk about it when you are here in person. I'm not comfortable talking about it on the phone."

"Well, I have to tell you I'm not scared. I want to do this if it means I will get to be with you. What do I have to do?" he inquired.

Tears flooded my eyes and I could no longer speak. When I gained composure, I replied, "You only have to be willing. When the time is right, Spirit will let us know what needs to be done and when." My body trembled as the soul accepted his agreement.

As I hung up the phone I came back into present time with a jolt. Getting my thoughts together I realized that this was December 1992, little more than a month after I had poured out my longings and loneliness in verse! Now, a tall, gray-haired man named Charlie from my same Oversoul was going to join me for the planet's celebration of the New Year!

He arrived in Albuquerque for the holiday as planned. At 2 a. m. on January 2, he awakened abruptly, startling me. "What's the matter?" I questioned, somewhat alarmed.

"I heard these voices. They asked me if I am sure I want the merger to take place. I was thanking them for giving me the opportunity to serve with you and assuring them that I want to do it," he muttered. "I have to go back to sleep now. It is time." He kissed me briefly, turned over and was quickly asleep.

Shortly after his breath had deepened, Charlie's body began to vibrate. Energy tremors went through him for six hours. He perspired as if he were breaking a high fever.

I lay beside him, stiff with fear, frightened that he was dying and that I would again be left alone. (My faith in what the soul was doing was far from strong!)

Charlie woke the following morning feeling wonderful, energized and cleansed! (I was exhausted and felt as if I had just given birth!)

He returned to Oklahoma as planned, but flew back to Albuquerque the following weekend. The two of us decided I would move to Oklahoma City in early April 1993.

40

Space Ships and Moving to Oklahoma City

February 1993

On February 20, 1993, I was driving from my home in Albuquerque to Memphis, Chattanooga, Tennessee and Birmingham, Alabama. I had reached Oklahoma City and was on my way to Memphis when, by 4:30 p.m., it became so foggy that visibility was down to one block.

About twenty-three miles east of Memphis I decided to stop for the night. After a light dinner, I went to bed early and meditated. Matthew, my Eighth Dimensional higher self, told me that I had arrived at the correct location for the work that we were to do.

The "work" was that of strengthening the New Madrid Fault Line that runs along the Mississippi from below New Orleans, north to the Chicago area. Matthew said I was needed to give Human permission for a fleet of ships (from the fifth dimension) to enter the dimensional portal I was under. The ships were to be anchored energetically and stationed along the fault line.

Just as I dozed off, I established telepathic contact, gave permission for entry and allowed my body to be used as a grounding device for each ship. Then a fleet of seven beam ships took formation above the area. After the seven ships were in place, I thought the job was finished and so returned to sleep. However, within an hour I was made aware of another seven ships in formation above the portal.

Sixty-three ships in all were brought in that evening, each in a seven-ship formation. Apparently, I had made it clear that I would not be returning to this area of the country for quite some time and that if they wanted entry, the time was now! They took me at my word and brought in as many ships as they expected to need to keep that area of the country stable.

After all of this, I continued my trip to Chattanooga and Birmingham.

Interestingly enough, a lot of ship activity can set off tremendous weather changes. And so it was that a couple days after I left Birmingham, a severe blizzard hit the area. But then I didn't feel so bad about this weather disturbance when I weighed a harsh snowstorm against that of drastic earthquake activity, which would have potentially included loss of life and property, had the ships not moved in! Indeed, I felt the best choice had been made.

On my way home to Albuquerque, I stopped in Oklahoma City to become better acquainted with Charlie and to decide on a place to live.

We took a six-month lease on a two-bedroom apartment in the complex where Charlie had been living. Out of 600 units, it was the only one with mauve/pink carpeting! (Matthew, my Eighth Dimensional higher self, and Charlie understand how important color is to me.) I would have room for my office/studio. Marian gave me some of the furniture from the condo in Albuquerque so we could furnish the remainder of our new home. (I have always been told that if I would divest myself of my belongings each time I move, they would be replaced comparably.)

Charlie and I agreed to marry sometime in the future, as this seemed at that time to be the desire of our Oversoul. I had (and still have) a great resistance to marrying again after three times. But Soul assured me this marriage would have a cosmic and planetary purpose concerning the creation of a new matrix of balanced partnerships to replace the old paradigm of marriage. To emphasize that I would eventually marry again in 1989 when I left Charlotte, North Carolina, to return to Denver, the Spiritual Hierarchy gave me a wide gold wedding band. They ask me to hold it as a reminder that it was time to give up my resistance to being legally married again.

In 1990, they sent a large emerald ring. The ring was to serve as my cosmic engagement ring and to be used to assist in opening the eighth chakra of Humanity and the Earth.

After each of the rings appeared, I asked, "When will the person be sent?" They replied "soon."

As we are aware, cosmic "soon" and Earth "soon" are two very different definitions! I was, however, grateful that "soon" had finally arrived! (Then, as now at this writing, I encourage those of you who were seeking partners not to give up. Rather, spend time <u>becoming</u> that which you seek. For example, have you become as emotionally balanced, physically attractive, honest, loving, financially stable, trustworthy and spiritually dedicated as that which you seek in another?)

MORE ON THE RAPTURE

I arrived home in Albuquerque February 26. On March 30, my impression of the "Rapture" began. The Hierarchy expected it to take approximately six to eight months for all the unawakened souls to be exchanged into Oversouls and be replaced by aspects of the Oversouls from higher vibrations.

The activities of the Rapture would not be immediately observed in the mass consciousness as a positive change. It would seem chaotic; people would probably feel the intense increase in the amount of energy in this dimension. They might feel jittery. The paranoia in many people might increase also.

I saw the Rapture as essentially a walk-in/walk-out situation, although "soul-braiding" would take place in some situations.

In a walk-in situation, the aspect of the soul originally inhabiting the body would eventually leave it and return to the Oversoul. The walk-in aspect would remain with the body. In a soul-braiding situation the two – and sometimes more aspects – merge or braid the essences together. When several aspects of one soul choose to use and incorporate into one body, it is referred to as a "composite consciousness." Personality changes are usually less dramatic in braiding, than in walk-in situations. Composites happen over longer periods of time. Additional aspects join the host body one at a time, usually every six months to a year, leaving time for integration to take place.

Children under age thirteen would not be affected by the above energy shift because most of them came directly here from the ships. They are members of the new species that will replace the Homo sapiens and will be called Homo universalis. These beings began to be born in 1985. They have a four quadrant etheric brain, where the Homo sapiens have a two hemisphere brain. They take in and store information in a totally different way than the Homo sapiens. They also have an etheric 12-strand helix to their DNA and the Homo sapiens have a two-strand helix to their DNA.

It will take a while for these etheric changes to be physical and visible to scientists, but we are already experiencing how difficult it is for them to be still and to focus on one activity at a time. This is why so many are being diagnosed with ADD (attention deficit disorder) and drugged to slow them down to the vibration of the Homo sapiens teachers and parents.

THE MOVE

On April 18, 1993, I moved from my home in Albuquerque to Oklahoma City. For the first month or two I was quite involved with just "living and being." In fact, I was so involved with "living and being" that I did not have time to report on "living and being" (didn't write Newsletters). I was adjusting to my "relationship."

I had not been in this type of relationship before, one in which I was challenged and willing to be so present, or to work so diligently to be open, honest and available to another person.

I realized that for the past eleven years, I had been entirely "relating" mostly to my soul and to my clients. Even when I was in a male/female relationship, the people I was in relationship with were satisfied with very little of me being present and were not interested in participating in "relating." I would "relate" with my soul and then, on occasion, express or explain to my partner what I was doing or going to do. I did not "relate" about the decisions while they were in process. This form of being causes it to be very difficult to be a "we."

With multidimensional persons (persons who are consciously expressing life in several dimensions and having more or less constant communication with some level of their souls), Third Dimensional communication oftentimes seems meaningless, redundant or unnecessary. I tried explaining this to Charlie during our early stages of friendship. While he did not totally comprehend what I was saying, he did continue to WANT to understand and participate.

When my gaze became fixed and he could tell I was listening to something not obvious to him, he tried not to interrupt. He would wait until he felt my energy return again, and then sometimes ask, "Where were you?"

It is not always easy to explain where we have been when we stretch ourselves to be in so many places at one time!

Charlie and I are projections of the same Oversoul, and I think that helped a great deal. Often, the soul gave him intuitive insight into what was happening with me and, therefore, he didn't have to ask many questions. Or, the soul would give him the right questions to ask!

However, there was one frustration I suffered and that was that I didn't seem to be getting enough "done." Since I had always been project and goal oriented, I had often worked twelve to eighteen hours a day when I was living alone and traveling.

When I moved to Oklahoma, I made a decision to slow down to working "normal" hours and to take weekends off. I committed to painting, writing, relating and playing more.

This felt very strange to me. I seemed to be in a constant state of feeling behind and non-productive, causing unnecessary tension in my body. Several alternative healers and body workers assisted me in remembering how to relax.

Being a metaphysician, I naturally understood that my body followed my mind. So I was constantly releasing tension, resistance, concern and anxiety to the Oversoul for release and transmutation. I also spent a lot of time working with the situation on the Mississippi. Plus, I worked with the energy of the Pope and the throngs of people who attended the gatherings generated by the Pope's appearance in Denver.

The team of cosmic workers I was assigned to had the responsibility of creating a protection system for the Pope, since he was in danger of assassination during the trip to Denver. We were also committed to implanting thoughts (images of the wealth of the Church superimposed with images of starving and homeless people) into the minds of the Pope and Cardinals.

The perfect situation to do that – to reach large numbers of people – was set up for us by the gatherings in Denver. Our intention was to (a) instill the idea of individual thought and freedom of choice, and (b) to connect the chords of the Cosmic Christ Consciousness into people's hearts.

We anchored seven ships over the Denver area during the Pope's visit.

One of our missions is to anchor the energies of the Cosmic Christ Consciousness into this organization and to open it to Truth.

We witnessed the Pope's admitting to the fallibility of the Church and all Popes. Prior to this time the infallibility of the Pope had been one of the main tenets of the Church. As he left Denver, from the steps of his plane he admitted that the things he told people from his pulpit are <u>his</u> suggestions and not dictates. He admonished people to seek Christ personally and to follow their own consciences. He said those who did not choose to strictly follow the tenets of the church would still be welcomed within the church. This is amazing progress! We also felt later that we were seeing results in the exposure and treatment of priests who had abused children, as well as in the children themselves.

Then in June, at Spirit's request, I went to the Portland/Vancouver area of Oregon and Washington for two weeks. Many wonderful people assisted me there. I did six groups and one TV show and had several personal sessions.

The TV show was an interview about being a walk-in.

That reminded me that by this time many people were feeling the effects of the "Rapture," which had begun some three months earlier. Massive numbers of walk-ins were arriving on the planet. Most of the sessions we did in the Pacific Northwest had to do with facilitating and educating walk-ins who were just becoming aware that they *were* walk-ins.

Most people who are walk-ins are not initially aware that they are walk-ins, any more than I was. The confusion can be painful and tremendous. Those who suspect they or someone they know is a walk-in should ask to receive confirmation from their own souls.

It is important to release the first soul aspect at the appropriate time. It is important also not to hold on to that which belongs to the first aspect, after that aspect has ascended back into the Oversoul. Not doing so causes confusion to the life and hampers the second aspects being able to get on with the soul mission.

Walk-ins come from the same Oversoul as the entity whose body they join. They must agree to complete the karmic contract of the original soul aspect before they are free to follow the planetary contract they come with. In my case this included co-creating two bodies for the souls that Betty Jean had originally contracted to create. When her karmic contract was accomplished, I was free to leave the life she had created and to begin to work on the planetary contract I had come to accomplish.

ENERGETICALLY WORKING WITH THE WEATHER

After moving back to Oklahoma weather predictions came to my attention.

I stated then (and it is just as essential now) that we realize we are NOT helpless to change weather patterns. Many of the destructive patterns are caused by the karmic accumulation of negative thought forms. The Earth only has a few ways to transmute these accumulated thought forms: water and fire. They can be better transmuted through Human intention and the use of the Violet Flame and by calling forth the Twenty-first Ray of Climate control when the thought forms have actually already created a weather threat emergency. We can call on the Master of the Twenty-first Ray, Master Eufaschia and the Angel Josiah and ask them to orchestrate the Elemental Kingdoms to dissipate built-up energy. Use the word DISSIPATE three times after the invocation of the Ray. Some intense weather patterns are caused by the intense magnetic buildup resulting from the extraterrestrial ships moving into our atmosphere.

In cases where it appears that the ships were causing massive rain storms, we would do well to remember that things could have been MUCH WORSE if many had not consciously cooperated with the ships to slow up the changes and to energetically hold the land masses together!

I advised people to focus their attention and thoughts on what they desired to happen, rather than on what was being predicted. Those who insisted on watching news broadcasts and predictions were asked to focus on reversing the negative thought forms sent out by the broadcasts, instead of buying into them as inevitable. It was my understanding we were all sent here to <u>assist</u> in the evolution, not to roll over or to run for cover.

If we would listen to our souls, we could know the right things to do to assist and would always be in the "right" place for us.

JAPAN

Sometime during the summer of 1993, I received information that it was time for me to go to Kyoto, Japan, to pick up another aspect of my Oversoul, a Shinto Priest. The occasion was "right" for me to merge with his consciousness so his body could leave the planet.

While I had known since 1989 that the soul desired for me to go to Japan and merge, I felt some confusion about a related matter:

Each of us has, during any given lifetime, "windows" – times when we are allowed by soul to exit the life. Since I have been in body, I had asked the soul several times, "how long do I have to be here?" The reply, prior to June of 1993, had always been "93." I had assumed that meant until I was 93 years old. In June I was feeling so overwhelmed, underfunded and overworked that I again asked my soul the question.

Soul's reply was very matter of fact: November 21, 1993!

I was a little surprised by the answer and a little disappointed too, since

I was enjoying my life with Charlie, having a home space and not needing to continually travel in my car. On the other hand, I must admit I was also a little relieved to hear I would not have to continue the daily struggles.

The thought of working from other dimensions, where it feels as if we accomplish things more quickly, also appealed to me, as I'm sure it does occasionally to many others.

I did a great deal of thinking about the option facing me: Was I living my life the way I wanted to? If I had only five or six months left, how did I want to live them?

My children, who are very psychic, picked up on the possibility I might be leaving the planet and called to determine why they felt that way. I explained the situation to them. We spent time together. I also visited friends, bought life insurance, consolidated my bills, rested, read more for fun than education, painted more, thought, listened and spent more time with Charlie and my daughter Kelley.

In August, Kelley moved to Oklahoma City for her own soul's growth and also to be closer to me.

AS LONG AS WE ARE CONCENTRATING ON SOMETHING TO HEAL, RELEASE OR OVERCOME,
THERE WILL BE SOMETHING TO HEAL, RELEASE OR OVERCOME.
WHEN WE SWITCH OUR FOCUS TO GOD,
THERE IS NOTHING TO HEAL, RELEASE OR OVERCOME.

41

Japan

September 1993

Mid-September 1993, I went to Dalton, Georgia, for a few days. While there I received a message from Soul that it was time to go to Japan.

While I had known for four years that Soul desired me to go to Japan, it was confusing to me that I would go, accomplish the merger, and then leave the body and planet life.

I did not know how I could afford the trip either, other than by using my credit cards. However, since my intention had been to become debt free, I did not consider the cards an option.

Actually, at this time, I felt nearly as confused about affording the trip as I had in 1988 when I was directed to go to Peru. Fortunately, I had a little more experience under the belt now, and things didn't throw me or puzzle me quite as much as they had before.

One of the reasons I wasn't quite so puzzled is that I had learned that when Soul asks us to do something, we are allowed to state reasonable conditions under which we will attempt the action. This is made possible because of the gift of free will and because our lives are to be co-creative experiences between us and our souls. Therefore, I agreed to go to Japan IF the trip could be arranged without incurring more debt, and IF it could be fun and comfortable.

I called Jean, my travel agent in Denver, and asked her about the fare to Kyoto. She said it would be $1,200 each way. Two days later she called to tell me she had lunch with another agent the day after our talk and that woman asked her if she had seen the just-posted offer from United for travel agents to fly to Kyoto for $299 and take a guest at the same fare?

Through her the Universe moved to create a special fare with an airline. Also, several friends, who are very attuned to their souls, sent money immediately. They did not know that the trip was eminent, but they did know they were to make contributions. Another friend who also did not know about the trip, sent $1,000. One more friend, who I had just met in Denver, gave me a check for $1,000 the morning before the flight! The trip to Japan was easy, fun and graceful, thanks to Jean who took care of all the travel arrangements.

Jean had also interpreted a vision I had had back in 1989. The vision had occurred three times in exactly the same way: I was riding on a very fast-moving train. It was silver, very streamlined and futuristic-looking. In the vision, as I gazed out the window, I saw a large snow-covered mountain. Then I was walking up a very well-defined pathway, much like one in an Asian garden. As I passed under a red archway, walking to meet me was a bald monk in robes. In the vision he held out his hands, palms up. I placed my hands in his, palms down. At that moment energy passed between us, from him to me. I had the most amazing sense of peace and an absolute understanding that I did not have to "do" another thing. From that moment on, I would only be required "to be." The day following the vision in 1989, I lunched with Jean. She said she thought the train in the vision was the "bullet train" in Japan; that the mountain was probably Mt. Fuji, and that the gates were called Tori gates marking the entrances to all Buddhist Temples and Shinto Shrines. She also gave me a copy of a travel magazine about Japan. In the magazine were pictures identical to my vision, including the gates and a picture of a bald Shinto priest!

At the time of the vision in 1989, I was in a live-in relationship with a male friend in a suburb of Denver. A few weeks after the vision, he was retired from Honda against his will. A part of the separation agreement included two round-trip tickets to Japan and $1,200 spending money! As unbelievable as it might seem, the man was so angry with the company for retiring him that he refused to accept the trip, even though I had told him about the vision and my need to go to Japan.

I accepted his decision and in so doing I trusted that my soul would find another way to get me to Japan. I kept the trip in the back of my consciousness, knowing that sometime in the future I would make the trip. I felt no "pressure" to go until I received the message while in Georgia. Once I became "willing" to go, as has been my experience, the arrangements were easily accomplished.

Upon arriving in Kyoto, Japan, Jean and I did not know exactly where I should go to actually merge with the energies of the priest. So the first day, we went to several Buddhist Temples, and Jean merged with a member of her Oversoul who had been a Buddhist priest. Neither of us had been told this would occur.

The second day in Kyoto, my soul woke me, telepathically giving me the name of the Temple/Shrine we were to visit. But later, when we showed the name to the taxi driver, he did not know where it was. However, with the help of two additional taxi drivers, we arrived at our destination.

When we reached this Temple/Shrine, we realized it was different from the many others we would visit. For one thing, there were very few other visitors. Nearly all of the other places we visited were teeming with visitors, especially school children who were on holiday the week we were there. At this Temple/Shrine just one group of children was leaving the grounds as we arrived. The youngsters waved and shouted "Herro, Herro" and made the sign of 'peace.' (They have difficulty pronouncing "l's".) Also, all the children we encountered while in Japan made the sign of peace.

As we walked toward the Shrine, Jean stopped suddenly. Half under her breath she uttered, "bj! Look up ahead!"

As we passed under the red Tori gates, we saw a bald, robed monk moving toward us on the path. (It was unusual to see people in Japan in native dress.) He appeared to be about 50 – younger than I had expected him to be from my vision.

Although he never made eye contact with me, as our bodies passed each other, an energy force struck my body between my sternum and my navel. The force was so strong I actually doubled over. I also felt powerful emotions of fear, guilt, anger, sadness, grief, pain and anxiety. As these welled up inside me, I felt as if the energy was purging me of lifetimes of these emotions. It felt like years of pent up PMS hitting all at once.

Just as I was about to burst into sobs, a little hand tugged at my long skirt. I looked down into the face of a small Japanese boy about three years old. I was aware of how unusual it was for a Japanese child to approach a stranger. Small Japanese children are very shy, private people. Even teenagers waited until we approached them before they tried to communicate. The small boy carried a plastic bag filled with a type of acorn he'd collected on his walk through the park. He spoke no English.

I bent down to his level, admiring his find, mostly by smiling and nodding my head. I put my hand on his head and silently gave him a blessing. As suddenly as he had appeared, his mother arrived, smiled and bowed several times and whisked him away. I put my attention on the path leading to the shrine.

The emotions were now choking me. I turned to see where the priest had gone. When I noticed he was no longer in sight, the sobs began. Although I was determined to make it to the steps of the Shrine, the sobbing was so intense I found walking quite difficult. This particular Temple/Shrine was being renovated. Workmen were everywhere, hammering and sawing. After a while a man in a suit and tie began moving toward us. He appeared to be overseeing the work and motioned for Jean to move me from the shrine steps to some folding chairs that had been set up alongside the temple area. After a while the emotions subsided, and I was able to walk again. I felt dazed for several days, almost as if I were in shock.

We strolled through the park, the other temple buildings and the cemetery. At a day school for small children on the grounds, we asked permission to use the restroom. The teacher was very gracious and showed us where to go. The stalls inside were miniature, with only one large one for the teacher. The Japanese have special plastic slip-on shoes they slide into before entering the restrooms.

Merging with more of my Oversoul was just one of several missions I had to accomplish while in Japan. Interacting with the children was another. As cosmic timing would have it, junior/senior high school children were on holiday during our stay and were everywhere we went. Since English is a required course in Japan, they were eager to talk with us once we approached them.

We learned that the best way to approach them was to ask to take their pictures. After that, they would quickly want to have their pictures taken with us. Then they would ask for our address so they could eventually send us a copy of the snapshot. Most children carried the Fiji disposable camera.

We seemed to be a novelty, almost as if we had been dressed in full American Indian costume! Of course, to us, we looked perfectly normal, and since they do not usually wear their traditional dress, their apparel is very western also, but in subdued colors, mostly grays, blacks and browns. It was indeed unusual to see anyone in a kimono.

Although the children were on holiday, they had an assignment. It was to interview someone who spoke English. They were to ask these questions: What is your name? How old are you? Where are you from? What do you think of Japan? What places do you intend to visit?

We printed our answers on pieces of cardboard provided by the children. They needed written answers so they could share them later, and write them in their notebooks. We also spoke our replies. We had brought along some items to share with people as gifts. The items included postcards of Colorado, bookmarks and greeting cards I had painted, key chains Jean had made, a few copies of the *Celestine Prophecy* by James Redfield and boxes of chocolates. The people were very appreciative and always wanted to give us something in return.

Another mission I was to accomplish while in Japan was fulfilling our souls' request that we go to the Kyoto University Campus. There we were to allow the Intergalactic Federation to anchor a ship over the University. We were also told to leave a copy of the *Celestine Prophecy* on a chair in the cafeteria. We were further directed to go to Nara, a town near Kyoto, and allow a ship to be anchored over a huge, 52-foot-high bronze statue of the Buddha.

We achieved all we had set out to do in Japan. I came away with sense of peace and accomplishment.

> "God is infinitely creative and wise.
> We can trust and move through the fear to the adventure . . ."

42

Universal Light Language Symbols and Soul Paintings

After I came home following my trip to Japan, Charlie and I rented a 1,700 sq. ft. house in a quiet, older neighborhood with lots of trees. This provided us with a large office for Namaste, Inc., and a separate studio and guest room.

I looked forward to allowing more and more creative energy to flow through me. I became increasingly aware of the Universal Light Language symbols. Further, I noticed a strong desire to write the characters of the Japanese language in calligraphy, using a brush! I became intensely busy obtaining brushes, rice paper, oriental watercolors, an ink stone and a book about how to make the Japanese and Chinese language characters. All of the materials became immediately available to me in the shops we visited.

I began to remember that one of the things I had agreed to do in my soul contract for this incarnation was to bring the symbols of the Universal Light Language through in physical form.

I recalled some information on symbology I had channeled during a group meditation in Mount Shasta in March of 1991. It was:

"It is now important for you (all of the group members) to understand symbology, the curve, the tachyon energy of the pyramidal structure, so you can henceforth use and remember that which you knew before. In the issuing forth of these symbols into your joint consciousness we (Spirit) can activate memory of your pasts, of your previous experiences, and of some of your simultaneous experiences in other dimensions which are going on concurrently with your life in this dimension.

"We have now instituted these symbols into the etheric structure, as well

as in your cellular structure. You can now access them as keys to unblock the memories that you say you choose to remember.

"As you perceive, stare at, and meditate upon these various symbols, it will be as if golden giant keys have been given to you to unlock the storehouses, the treasure rooms of your mind where you have stored previous knowledge; where you have veiled this knowledge from the conscious self. You hid the knowledge from yourself so as not to be tempted to misuse it; so as not to be lured into giving it out to individuals prior to the time of their (or the masses) readiness to assimilate and use it in an ethical manner."

I also was told that the symbols for Japanese, Chinese, Hebrew, Sanskrit, Russian, Mayan, Incan and Egyptian languages are all derivatives of the Universal Light Language symbols. These symbols were brought to Earth by extraterrestrials.

I was told too, that at one time, we knew that specific symbols combined with certain colors or Rays of energy – and with certain tones or sounds – could reverse gravity, transmute the molecular structure of ourselves or another substance, cause alchemy and dematerialization. I became aware that even before I had gone to Japan, I had begun seeing symbols around people. I also had seen large, very complex symbols when I went out-of-body into space. The symbols resembled what would happen if someone took a laser device, wrote letters in the air in golden white light or fire and just left the images hanging in the air.

Spirit then instructed me to begin creating paintings with the Universal Light Language Symbols in them – Soul Paintings or Soul-Mission Paintings.

The symbols in the paintings represent the lifework of the individual he/she contracted with before this incarnation was begun. The paintings also reflect the energy that could most assist the individual to accomplish his/her mission.

The way I learned to produce such paintings might interest you:

When I would tune into the soul of an individual, certain symbols and energies would come. These energies were vital to that person and were those with which he/she should connect. The symbols represented information the person needed and had agreed to be responsible for bringing to the Earth plane.

I then would draw the symbols I had received, on white watercolor paper and cover them (the symbols) with Resist, which is the consistency of rubber cement.

After the Resist dried, I would take watercolors, acrylic or ink, whichever

I had intuitively and telepathically been given, and allow energy to pour onto the paper through my body and the paint. The colors represented the energy frequencies the individual needed to expose themselves to, or the frequencies that would assist him or her to consciously remember and accomplish his or her mission. The symbols served to return more of the Cosmic Christ vibration into the third dimension.

After the Resist had dried, I would rub it off. The symbols then appeared white on the paper I had watercolored. I then was instructed to paint the white symbols with iridescent white, gold, silver or copper paint. I was told each symbol could represent as much information as is contained in a set of encyclopedias!

I understood that exposure to a person's soul painting increased that person's ability to make conscious connection with his/her mission, and also provided the information and energy _needed_ to _accomplish_ that mission.

Delivery time for individual soul paintings was about six weeks, depending, of course, on how many people ordered.

I offered no "readings" or interpretation with the paintings. It was to be an energy-absorbing experience for the persons receiving the paintings, exposing themselves to the symbols and energy. The information was "grocked" into the recipient's consciousness.

Sometimes while I was actually working on a painting, a few words would be given. Sometimes I taped and sent music to the person receiving the painting and suggested they listen to it while viewing the painting. Once in a while, certain books were recommended or, in some cases, a video.

I did not guarantee anything other than the painting, which was the best impression I could create of what the person's soul gave me. The interpretation had to be between the recipient and the recipient's soul. The reports that came in from recipients were VERY encouraging. Most reported positive changes and awareness.

Some of the higher vibrational colors I needed were not available in tube watercolors or acrylics, but in the spring of 1994, I began seeing (in my mind) liquid paint in bottles. The bottles had eye droppers in them. I had not seen watercolors or acrylic paints in liquid form. My inner guidance sent me to an engineering supply store, even though I did not know this store carried art supplies. However, there on the shelves were the paints I had seen in my mind's eye!

The energy intensity of the liquid colors was amazing. My hands actually began to vibrate as I held the bottles. On paper the colors were even more amazing.

The name of the paints was "Dr. Ph. Martin," and the manufacturer was Salis International, Inc., in Hollywood, Florida. I was asked by Spirit to call Dr. Martin and to ask why he had not marketed the other formulas he had been given by Spirit. At that time, according to Spirit, Dr. Martin had been given the formulas for iridescent, pearlescent, metallic, opalescent, fluorescent and permanent colors in vivid shades. I needed these colors to accomplish the works of art Spirit wanted. I was hesitant to call yet another person I didn't know and to deliver a message from his soul, but if he did indeed have the formulas for the paints, I could hardly wait to use them.

I finally called and a man answered. I asked to speak to Dr. Martin, but the man who answered said the doctor wasn't available and asked if I would like to leave a message. I didn't want to leave such a message to be delivered by someone else who might not deliver the message or who might modify what Spirit wanted to say. I asked when it would be possible to speak with the doctor. The man assured me that he was the doctor's business manager and that he would deliver the message. I finally gave in and told him who I was and why I was calling. I ask him to tell Dr. Martin that Spirit understood that he was disappointed with the market reception the paints he had already put out were getting, to the extent that he didn't want to manufacture the others. I told him that Spirit said that the formulas were necessary for artists to be able to paint the new energies coming in to Earth and that he had a spiritual responsibility to get the paints on the market. The man said he was grateful for the message and would be sure to deliver it verbatim. He told me the doctor couldn't speak with me because he was depressed, due to the public's lack of response to his original formulas.

Within a couple of months I found he had created and begun to market the colors I needed in watercolor, acrylic and calligraphy inks.

MEDITATION TO RECEIVE INSPIRED ART, MUSIC OR WRITING

In an earlier chapter, I mentioned that Georgia O'Keeffe often works with me when I paint. I also stated that O'Keeffe told me that many of the masters – including her – are quite willing to help artists who know how to project energy into their creations. (That way, the masters help bring through energies that facilitate the renaissance we are experiencing now.) This help is also available concerning music and writing. However, the masters cannot come through <u>unless they are asked</u>.

It seems appropriate here to include a meditation one can use to receive inspired writing, music or art.

When people do the meditation the first few times, I suggest they take a shower to symbolically cleanse their auras. I further suggest wearing loose clothing, taking the telephone off the hook and lighting a white candle.

When you are ready to meditate, sit with your spine straight and bare feet flat on the floor. Place a pencil and a pad of paper in your lap. Repeat the following prayer, or the Lord's Prayer:

"I deliberately seal this room on the North, South, East and the West, the ceiling and the floor against any negative influence or entity. I invoke the presence of my master guides, teachers and Angels to be present and receptive to me. I deliberately open myself as a channel for my Oversoul, the Holy Spirit, the Cosmic Christ Consciousness and the 49 Rays of God."

Take a deep breath and, while exhaling, deliberately send beams of energy from the souls of your feet down into the central core energy of Mother Earth.

Take another deep breath and, as you exhale, deliberately open your heart in love and appreciation for Earth, yourself and all levels of your own Oversoul.

Take another deep breath and, as you exhale, deliberately open the crown of your head and send a beam of energy from your heart, through the high heart and through the middle of the brain into the highest level of the Oversoul that your physical body can stand energetically. Deliberately seek communication with the Cosmic Christ Consciousness level of your own Oversoul. At the middle of the brain are two glands, the pituitary and the pineal glands, between the two is a tube called the "Z" tube. It is useful to focus there to activate the soul contact and intuition.

Allow yourself to begin relaxing . . .

Take a deep breath and hold the breath at the center of the brain, while counting (to yourself) three . . . three . . . three . . . Then exhale. Take another deep breath and hold the breath at the mid brain while counting two . . . two . . . two . . . Then exhale. Take another deep breath and hold the breath mid-brain while counting, one . . . one . . . one . . . Exhale. Breathing normally, but still focusing on the mid brain, count s-l-o-w-l-y backward from ten to one.

Sit peacefully and without expectation, but with the intention to communicate only with your own Oversoul.

Write ANYTHING that comes into your mind. The first thing you write may seem to come from your own thoughts, but beginning to write will start the flow of energy. Write, even if it seems to be only your grocery list, or your "to do tomorrow" agenda.

My own experience with such a meditation may encourage you. For example, <u>my own thoughts</u> seem to originate on the left side of my brain, while communication from Spirit feels as if it happens on the <u>right side of my brain</u>. My hand does not write by itself. The words I receive are telepathically imparted into my consciousness, not in a voice, they are just there. Oftentimes, it is more of an idea that comes to me than it is individual words, and I have to create words to explain the idea. The energy of the transmission, the syntax of the sentences (pattern of speech) and the vocabulary used all give clues as to whether I'm writing my thoughts or Spirit's. Spirit seems to use words that are not in my normal everyday speech or thoughts.

Don't let yourself become discouraged. Continue trying. Do so without expectation, but with the INTENTION to communicate.

> **"If we fail to fulfill our creative purpose,
> it is nonsense to expect life to support our better living."**
>
> - Kennedy Schultz

43

Loving Responses and Universal Law

January 1994

In January, 1994 Namaste mailed out 300 letters to our mailing list explaining we needed another, newer computer, and offering to do Soul-Mission Energy Paintings. The response was tremendous.

We were given a fully equipped Macintosh with printer and software. The items had never even been out of the original boxes and were still sealed in cellophane! We also received a 386 Packard Bell with expanded hard drive and lots of software. (We added more RAM memory to it, later, so we could run the software programs we used to publish the newsletter.)

We were also given a Tandy laptop that we traded for a carousel slide projector. We planned to use the projector to show slides of our travel to spiritual spots on the planet locations.

As for the computers, the week before they arrived I had programmed to have someone who is computer literate come to set them up, program them and teach me how to use them.

That person arrived the week after we received the computers and agreed to stay on as part-time office help. Her name was GRACE. She was most appropriately named.

Grace told me she had known since the first time she heard me speak, several years before, that we would eventually be working together.

Another thing: Charlie and I had been getting along for nearly a year with just one car. Then a friend from New Mexico came through and left a car for me to drive for a while. It was a 300Z convertible.

I had never thought of myself as the sports car or convertible type, so it seemed to me that Spirit had a great sense of humor.

It was wonderful to have my own transportation, since I was so active at that time, lecturing, socializing and framing and shipping paintings. Charlie and I were most grateful to Hal and Marian for their generosity.

Charlie, too, was very busy and doing well. His business steadily improved, and he was trying to reach more people with his singing.

Charlie's voice and the energy he channels when he sings are quite healing. He agreed to sing at local events when I was asked to speak, and it made an amazing difference in the audiences.

Interestingly, though Charlie and I are projected aspects of the same Oversoul, an idyllic relationship, with no complications, was not guaranteed.

When Charlie had allowed Jovan to merge with his body in February 1993, his spiritual attitudes changed dramatically. (Jovan was my counterpart from aboard the Venusian mother ship I left to take this body.) He made the quantum shift from religion to spirituality with no hesitation.

Cellular and cultural programming still plagued him with insecurities about the longevity of our relationship, as did his judgments of the "spirituality" of my past relationships. Continued reminders and my communication with these individuals caused him some conflict. His great sense of humor helped, though. Unfortunately his insecurities pushed him to read my private journals while I was traveling, which ultimately caused us to breakup.

UNIVERSAL LAW

In early 1994, I had a real lesson in Universal Law.

In May we held an art show in Tulsa, Oklahoma. I had spent 16 months painting in preparation. I also had greatly extended my credit to print and post the newsletter, print a new brochure, duplicate some tapes, print more workbooks and frame my paintings. Very few people attended the show. By Third Dimensional expectation, it was not a success. Beth, Sandy and Charlie were very depressed as they dismantled the show.

My depression waited until the next morning. I awoke aware of my doubts and fears. I had extended myself financially, feeling strongly that I was following guidance. What had gone wrong? I was so depressed and exhausted from weeks of preparation I could not get out of bed. I napped, prayed and meditated in an effort to try to understand.

Finally, I remembered something my guidance had told me years before. It was, "When things do not make sense Third Dimensionally, seek THE LAW," meaning the Universal Law pertaining to the situation. I prayed again, asking, "What IS the Law?"

Matthew, my Eighth Dimensional self, replied,

"Third Dimensional expectation is to put energy into one place or thing and to expect the energy to return through that place or thing. For example, you go to work for an employer from 9 to 5, five days a week. You expect a paycheck from that employer.

"But the Universal Law says, 'Do the next single thing in front of you to do, and the energy will be returned to you from whence it is <u>karmically</u> correct. This means you painted the paintings, you took them to the place we suggested to you. If you expect money (energy) to return to you from that action alone, you close off millions of other avenues through which the Universe can return your good or energies – money.

"Had you done the paintings with the awareness of THE LAW, you would be open to money and good coming from <u>any</u> avenue that is deemed appropriate, karmically, by your soul."

Once I remembered THE LAW and adjusted my focus, money and goods began coming in from very unexpected directions. The expenses for my trip to Chicago were even completely covered two days before I was scheduled to leave!

In my heart I thanked everyone who had been involved with my lesson in Universal Law.

**"A miracle happens
when we become aware of an illusion previously held as a truth."**

– Unknown

44

Chicago, Lansing and Grand Rapids, Michigan

May 1994

I spent three weeks traveling to Chicago, Lansing and Grand Rapids, Michigan. I had wonderful sponsors in all three cities.

The night before I left Oklahoma, Spirit distinctly told me NOT to call my sponsor in Chicago to confirm she would be picking me up at the airport the next day. Rather, I was to <u>trust</u> that she would.

When I arrived at the airport, no one was there to meet me.

I searched my address book. A slip of paper on which my Chicago sponsor had dashed some information for me two months before dropped out.

I then remembered she and her husband had driven to Oklahoma to visit Charlie and me after her first telephone reading. At that time she had said, "Let me give you ALL our telephone numbers in case you ever need to reach us."

I first dialed the couple's home and got a recorder. I left a message that I was in the airport. Then I called their respective offices, first getting machines and then an answering service.

The operator with the service listened attentively as I described my predicament, then she held me on the line while she paged and also called several numbers attempting to locate somebody. She kept reassuring me she <u>would</u> find someone to rescue me.

Finally she reached my sponsor. She said she thought my plane was coming in at 10 p.m. instead of 10 a.m. I was assured someone was on the way to retrieve me. (They live 1-1/2 hours from the airport.)

I sat down to wait and read.

In the exact length of time I had been promised it would take to reach me at the airport, a delightful woman named Joy arrived to get me. I had read for her on the phone a few months before.

We had a wonderful conversation and drive. She had been cleaning the house where I was to stay and had recognized my voice on the recorder. She had left immediately for the airport.

We all laughed for several days at Spirit's sense of humor . . .

The first night I spoke in Chicago, about 50 people came. They were sitting in chairs, on the floor and even standing, in the home where we met.

The Light coming through these folks brought tears of hope. They were so open, ready and willing to consciously hear and practice their multidimensionality. As I shared the story of my journey and awakening, they laughed, cried, nodded agreement and smiled encouragingly.

I had intended to speak for an hour and then break to free them from their restrictive bodily positions. But they were so responsive and encouraging we went on for an hour and a half. They lasted through an additional hour of questions and answers. (It takes a lot of interest and dedication to sit still and attentively in an uncomfortable position for three-plus hours!)

Later during my stay, my sponsor, who is a gifted psychic and counselor, and I did counseling sessions together for her clients. We both learned a lot and felt mutually supported by these people, each other and our guidance.

My sponsor's husband is also a counselor. He had an ongoing men's group that explored heart and Spirit. I was invited to speak to the group one of the evenings I was there.

Interacting with 12 open and responsive males was a fascinating and enlightening experience. This was especially so since one of my major life lessons, for this incarnation, is to learn to understand maleness in myself and others.

While in Chicago, I became aware that people need written material about Universal Laws, done in an easy, comprehensible format. I recalled that for years my guidance had encouraged me to read and rewrite the material previously offered in *The Secret Doctrine, Isis Unveiled* (four volumes) by Madame Blavatsky. The writing was to be in condensed and written in language people could understand. I was encouraged to do the same with the blue books (at least 25 volumes) by Alice A. Bailey and the *I Am Discourses* of St. Germain.

I committed myself to write a three-volume series of the above material, WHEN MY FINANCIAL DEBT WAS REMOVED AND I HAD A YEAR'S INCOME SECURED.

The six days I was in the Chicago area felt like six weeks because of the intensity of the work those folks accomplished.

When I left I felt as if I were leaving with many wonderful gifts, and I knew I would stay connected to this group. (One of the women who had attended, a writer, even traveled to Lansing to attend my workshop the next weekend.)

I flew from Chicago to Grand Rapids on my way to Lansing. Jonathan, a man I had met briefly at the Spiritual Frontiers Fellowship Retreat in Olivett College in Michigan four years before, picked me up. He drove me the 60 miles to Lansing.

My energies and his were so powerful together that we missed the turn off to Lansing three times. We were an hour late arriving at my next destination.

We finally became aware that the delay was deliberate. Then, energy passed from me to him that he needed to receive before his birthday the following Tuesday.

The lectures in Lansing were not as well attended as in Chicago, but all the "appropriate" people were there. The love of the people moved me deeply.

The Creativity Workshop was attended by four women. They were all at turning points in their lives. They were also all artists and writers, so we really enjoyed the information that was shared by our souls.

It was the first time I had offered a workshop on enhancing creativity. I learned that I knew and practiced more than I realized! (According to the *Course in Miracles*, we are always teaching what we want and need to learn.)

I went to Grand Rapids from Lansing. The lecture there was attended by only six persons, but their reactions were positive.

While I was in the Great Lakes area I worked continually to bring many more ships into the Fifth Dimension and to anchor them in strategic places. One was anchored over the Chicago Museum of Art. On that particular day I was fortunate to get to view ten of Georgia O'Keeffe's original paintings.

During the three weeks, a great deal of work was also done to secure the upper end of the New Madrid Fault Line, which runs from the Great Lakes to New Orleans and beyond into the Gulf. At that time a team of people from the Namaste network were in the New Orleans and Memphis areas to also work on this fault line.

I returned home to Oklahoma City to learn that Mary Jo, my adopted mom, had been diagnosed with inoperable lung cancer. She had been given only a few months to live. I knew I would be using much of my time to serve her.

Many "earthly" happenings took place as the months moved from summer into fall. Charlie and my children changed employment; the offices of Charlie's previous employer were gutted by fire shortly after Charlie terminated his work there; Charlie's daughter got married, necessitating association of estranged family members; close friends went through serious illnesses. At times, I felt as if we were being prepared to write a cosmic "soap opera."

Then an opportunity presented itself for me to meet my Chicago sponsor in San Francisco. Barbara Thomas invited her and me to spend a few days at her Creativity Retreat at Ben Lomand, California (near Santa Cruz). From there we drove down to Carmel to experience the ocean and the Monarch butterflies.

The drive was quite significant because for several months I had been seeing Monarch butterflies in my meditations. (These butterflies migrate to the Carmel, California, area in the fall.) On the drive, a wonderful painting came through to me of the Earth, butterflies, dolphins, whales and a rainbow.

We also did a lot of energy work, which was fun and exciting.

After California I went to Colorado to be with my spiritual family and to work on the Rocky Mountain Fault Line.

I returned to Oklahoma City a little earlier than planned. My adopted mom, Mary Jo, made her transition into Spirit. I took care of arrangements and performed the funeral service. She left me a $25,000 CD, which cleared by debt for the first time.

MALE/FEMALE BALANCE

At that time in 1994, balance between our male/female essences and our sub-personalities was the most important issue for us to work with. My friend Janet Dian had just released the third in her series of books about the Oversoul entitled *In Search of Yourself; Finding the Balance*. She said that in writing the book she had developed a great respect for the process of balance for all the sub-personalities that come together to create the main personality one expresses. (Sub-personalities include love, hate, anger, guilt, jealousy, compassion, fear, control, manipulation, possessiveness, suffocation, etc.)

We were dealing at that time with challenging situations, just as we are today. These situations were due partly to astrological influences and partly to what was going on with Humanity and Earth's evolution. I liked what Janet said of challenges: "Challenging situations push you deep into your inner resources. In order to survive emotionally and/or physically, you reach into places inside yourself you didn't even know existed.

"You may be pushed beyond your ordinary limits. Once you have done this you know that you will never be the same. These experiences accelerate your learning process, quickly moving new and different experiences into your life.

"In addition, this clearing and cleansing process reveals more of whom and what you are, and continues to specifically define your potential. Consciously recycling your energy is another fascinating step on the journey of self awareness."

It is very important that our actions become dependent on, "What do I think?" rather than, "What will others think?

TIME
By Charlie

No one has been given any more time than have I
And it's up to me just how I choose to use it.
A lifetime is just minutes that have somehow turned to years.
I can love the joy of life, or just abuse it.
I can tip the glass of time and drink each day as nature's nectar.
I can give away a smile because it's free.
I can know that smile is understood when it's done in any language
And know the best thing I can do is just to see.

I can see that if a single man achieves the highest love, That love can spread and change the hate of millions.
I can say that if we learn to give and share instead of taking
We can change the frame of mind that keeps us killing.

bj King

I can learn that life and death are both a great adventure.
I'll not shrink from living life nor fear to die. I will tell the World that
might's not right and don't abuse your brother.
And the bigger man is not afraid to cry.

I will hear my soul keep saying success is getting what you want,
But happiness is wanting what you get.
I'll keep my sight within my heart and not just in my eyes.
I'll not fill my present with yesterday's regret.

If I can leave a gift that speaks of what I've done or said
Let it be that I heard much more than I spoke.
Let me think on how to mend things instead of how to spend them.
And let the chains of hate be the only thing I broke.

Let me know I can't spell brothers until first I have spelled others
Let me share the Source of Light through happy thoughts
Let me know that love's best part is in the giving not the getting
Let me share the warmth and love that Spirit brought.
Let me know that my whole life is God's most treasured book
And that each day is just a turning of a page.
Let me write a tender love note on each treasured piece of parchment
And make my life a thing of freedom, not a cage.

45
Colorado, Fairfield, Iowa and Ploarus

January 1995

January 10-20, 1995, I rode with a friend to Colorado to complete the work on the Rocky Mountain Fault Line begun in November. The trip was satisfying and the energy work was easy: We gave permission to the Pleiadians to change out the ships they had hovering over Denver. Also, we anchored a Ray of Cosmic Christ energy into the "Living From the Heart Wellness Center" in Morrison, Colorado. A group from that center joined us in our efforts. Classes were held in the center, and people came from these groups to swim with the dolphins (in the future).

We also attended the IMAX presentation, "Africa: The Serengeti." I became acutely aware that my once worst fear was ultimately going to become a reality! My soul WOULD ask me to go to Africa!

I recalled that this fear was the one thing that had kept me from committing my life to God at a much earlier age – fear I would have to serve as a missionary in Africa.

While I was in Morrison, I became "willing" to go to Africa, provided I could take a group of friends with me. At the moment this took place, I was talking with people from the "Living from the Heart Center."

I recalled how, as a child in fifth grade geography class, I was touched by the magic of Africa. After studying the continent I had been especially drawn to the shape of the trees and to some of the animals.

I had also been fascinated by the tall, slender, ebony-carved statues of the Masai people. When I was 13 I collected six of them. Although I don't know what happened to them in all the moves, the memories remain.

I went back home to Oklahoma City from Colorado. Then February 11-12, Charlie and I had fun traveling to St. Louis, Missouri, to view an exhibit of Georgia O'Keeffe's early water color paintings. As I viewed the paintings I kept exclaiming, "Wow."

Charlie finally said, "I obviously don't see what you see that is so special about these paintings. I think yours look better. What am I missing?"

"These paintings are done on manila folders. If her work was this uncoordinated when she started, there is hope for me to become a better painter than I am."

While in St. Louis, we once again gave permission for, and assisted with, the changing out of the ships anchored over the Mississippi River. The ships monitor and maintain the New Madrid Fault Line.

In March, I journeyed to Fairfield, Iowa, to speak to a group. I also had the most intensive reading schedule I had ever attempted – 40 readings in five days! These were in addition to small group discussions some evenings.

Fairfield is a small town where a University was founded because of the transcendental meditation (TM) movement. Thousands of meditaters live there. Many choose to go twice daily to the domes (one for men and one for woman) to practice the form of meditation taught by Maharishi Mahesh Yogi. The domes look like giant space ships that have landed in a corn field.

Since I am a Westerner, not schooled in the Vedic traditions, I was intellectually illiterate about their beliefs and practices. Instead, I HAD to observe and participate in their lives energetically and from the level of my soul and their souls.

At first, I couldn't imagine why I had been invited to Fairfield. John and Jaya, my hosts, and I had met somewhat peripherally while we were all living in Charlotte, North Carolina, years before. They had not attended the classes I had taught during my time in North Carolina.

Since then, however, as has apparently happened with many of the people within the TM movement, John and Jaya had become what I call "spiritually restless." For example, the people I read for were hungry for practical spiritual advice and knowledge that would help them to understand many of their "seemingly" unusual experiences, some of which included encounters with extraterrestrials.

The first evening I was in Fairfield, I spoke to a standing-room-only crowd of about 70 folks. For the first time, I was personally nervous, although I am always aware that what I am saying is coming "through me" and is designed to answer questions in the minds of the audience.

Before I speak to a group I take a deep breath and anchor my body to the central core energy of Mother Earth. I take a second breath and open my heart to my soul. I take a third breath and send a beam of energy from my mid-brain into the highest level of my Oversoul that I can connect with without having my voice quaver. I take a fourth breath and connect my Oversoul to the Oversouls of the people in the room. The talk is then made up of questions and concerns that the audience may be carrying with them. Their souls tell my soul what the talk should include. Even when I am telling my personal stories and experiences the souls of the audience members indicate that these are the stories they need to hear at that time. I always begin my talk with a disclaimer that everything I say is my opinion, which is based on my personal experiences, and should not be taken as the truth for someone else until they have filtered the information through their own discernment. That night I spoke, as is usual, about my own experiences and personal spiritual opinions, formed from my experiences.

The group was restless and stiff when I began, even after a friend played superb meditation music on the piano. Interestingly, the first time I mentioned the word GURU, which I apparently pronounced differently from many of them, because of my accent, a discernible noise-like "crack" was heard and felt energetically in the room. Then, the first time I evoked a laugh, the energy became considerably more relaxed. But it wasn't until I used a West Texas distinctive title to explain my discernment theory (the need for a spiritual "BS detector") that the group members really opened themselves energetically. After the ice was broken, they were a warm, sincere and loving audience.

The last evening I was there, after most of the people had left, I was sitting on the floor answering a few questions that had arisen. I had been hesitant to mention that one of the reasons I had come to Fairfield was to give permission for two Saturn ships to be anchored in the Fifth Dimension over the meditation domes. (The energy was to affect a radius of 100 miles in all four directions.)

As the conversation proceeded, however, my soul asked me to give out this information.

I explained that the purpose of the ships was to spotlight any deceit and to keep the energy stirred up so that people's minds could not focus on life as it HAD been, and also to force them, energetically, to consider the bigger picture of all events.

I was further explaining that usually the anchoring of the ships sets off huge electrical storms; that one way to determine a normal electrical storm from ship activity was to watch the lightening. If the lightening is normal, it strikes the Earth and is grounded. If it is ship activity, when the bolt strikes the Earth it connects with the magnetic grid and seems to bounce back toward the ships.

Just as I said the above, a bolt of lightening struck! The room shook much like an earthquake, and the thunder was deafening.

It was the most dramatic and emphatic demonstration of energy, while I was in the immediate process of making an explanation, that I had ever experienced!

The people did not appear to be fearful. They got up immediately and went out to the large Victorian porch to watch this demonstration of energy.

A few weeks after we returned home, I was sitting in the bathtub meditating when Matthew, my Eighth Dimensional higher self said, *"About Ploarus . . ."*

I responded with, "What is Ploarus?"

"Ploarus is a planet which is presently being created and which will ultimately be similar to Earth."

"I am curious why have I never seen this planet? Since I travel all over the Omniverse, it is unbelievable that I would not have already been aware of such a place.

"I asked you about such a place back in 1990-91, when I was living at Mount Shasta. Others were channeling about a 'dust planet' where the laggards would go. You neither confirmed nor denied the information. You simply stated that it was not my concern at that time. Now you are telling me that it does, in fact, exist." I was not happy to get this news.

"When we stated that it was not something you were to be concerned about at that time, we were telling the truth. You had many more important matters to learn about at that time.

"The information that was being given to your friends was not being given down by the Spiritual Hierarchy, but by astral entities trying to provoke more fear in Humans.

"Now, the time has come for certain individuals to be aware that this creation is taking place and that a certain part of their consciousness is dedicated to assisting Devas to move certain plant and animal thought forms to Ploarus. This is in preparation for its eventual occupation by Homo sapiens.

"At this time there is no plant life there. An atmosphere has just now been created and contained within a 'ring-pass-not.'

"You have never seen this area, since you do not go into the Fourth Dimension, or astral plane, but GO THROUGH the fourth. The corridor through the Fourth Dimension was created for the purpose of aware individuals not to become embroiled in, or distracted by, the activity of the astral plane as they move through into the Fifth Dimension.

"Now that this area is separated from, but still within the Fourth Dimension, certain individuals will be expected to begin energy work there with us."

I asked Matthew "Is this why the television program <u>EARTH 2</u> was created? To prepare people's consciousness for the idea?"

"Yes, exactly. All of the water on Ploarus is currently inside the planet. The first root race of Ploarus will be Homo sapiens who do not choose to evolve at this time into Homo universalis.

"These Homo sapiens will incarnate there, go through the agricultural evolution, the industrial evolution, the technological evolution and ultimately the cosmological evolution that Earth and Humans are experiencing now."

"The greatest danger to the Human species and Earth is not maliciousness, but apathy."

– **The Saturn Council**

46

The Bombing in Oklahoma City

April 1995

April 19, 1995, I was sleeping on the couch to avoid Charlie's snoring. I heard an enormous boom and fell off the couch. As I lay there, listening to the rattling of the sliding door, I was so shocked I couldn't think clearly at first. The noise was so loud and the vibrations so intense I thought it must be the explosion of an atomic bomb. I immediately turned on the TV. It seemed only seconds later pictures of the Murrah building collapsing from the detonated bomb were on the news. None of my immediate family was involved. I sat back on the couch and began to pray for the people of Oklahoma, the families of the victims and the people of the World. During the ensuing days I noticed the change in the waves of energy coming toward Oklahoma City. The first wave was, of course, shock. The second was fear, the third anger, the fourth was an overwhelming amount of love and compassion coming from all directions around the globe. The fear did not end when it was determined that this act of terrorism was accomplished by white, male Americans. In fact, this information increased the fear, uncertainty and anger. How could an American hate other Americans enough to cause such devastation? The explosion caused so much upheaval in people's lives, physically and emotionally.

There were scads of reported incidents in which people either did not go to work on the day of the bombing, did activities not generally part of their daily routines, shuffled their usual schedules, or made last-minute decisions to live differently that day. Many stories were reported about people not taking their children to the day care center at the Murrah building that morning.

An example of the above is a friend of my daughter's who, on a "whim," decided to take her granddaughter shopping that day instead of attending her usual college classes. She picked up the little girl at the nursery in the Murrah Federal Building early that morning. (The child's mother worked in the building and was missing for some time in the debris after the explosion.)

Karmically, before being born, the child had contracted to be raised by the grandmother and step-grandfather. However, such "divine agreements" do not help the emotional devastation people feel and must come to grips with in this Third Dimension.

On the surface, much positive good was demonstrated. For instance, people in the area seemed softened by the event, displaying emotion that, for many, might have been the first time in years and years. People who normally did not ever even consider touching, touched others. Parents hugged their children. Others looked at each other – particularly family members – as if they finally understood that they can't take their presence for granted. Many persons donated their time to help others, gave money, articles, clothes. Mental health services were offered free of charge for months and months after the bombing to anyone who felt they needed it. Many of the survivors, the firefighters and police were suffering from traumatic stress syndrome.

Cosmically, the event was to karmically balance the incident in Waco, but there seemed to also be some strange Moslem or Arab energy influence involved.

In our Sunday evening meditation group hours before the explosion, we had been asked by Spirit to invite in the Over-lighting Devic Presence of the entire Oklahoma Metroplex area. We were also asked to invite each of the Over-lighting Devic Presences of each of the suburbs, Edmond, Midwest City, Warr Acres, Bethany, etc. In addition, we invited the Archangel Michael and the Band of Mercy to come in to clear out all possessing and all hovering astral plane spirits. We were further asked to give these Angels permission to remain in the area and to work actively with the people of the Oklahoma Metroplex area.

We were not aware of the reason the Hierarchy felt the need to do this additional investment of spiritual power until the bombing. We were not allowed to have precognitive awareness of what was about to happen. Apparently, the events would have been much worse, and people would have been less able to positively deal with it all had not so many Angels been present. The additional explosive devices would not have been located in time to be deactivated and the Court House, employees and records would also have been destroyed.

After the bombing, Gerald G. Jampolsky, author of *Love is Letting Go of Fear* and founder of the Attitudinal Healing Center in Tiburon, California, set up offices at the Unity Church and the Church of Religious Science locations. He and his crew members from various parts of the country did counseling with family members of victims. Some of the Attitudinal Healing Center trainers stayed for a while to train and meet with anyone interested in creating a Center in Oklahoma City. (An Attitudinal Healing Center has since been formed in the City.)

I could not help realizing that hidden in any crisis, whether big or small, personal or planetary, lays the opportunity for growth and expansion. Ancient Chinese philosophers were well aware of this. Their symbol and word for crisis, "wei-chi," is depicted as a combination of two characters: one means "danger," the other, "opportunity."

Following is a poem Charlie wrote about the time of the bombing:

MAKING GOOD FROM BAD
By Charlie

May 2, 1995

It was two after nine when that unthinkable deed struck terror in the heart of our land,

It forever changed lives and it took quite a few and left a pain that's so hard to understand.

In the face of this anguish it may be hard to accept that life has a reason for all,

But lest we forget we all enter this journey with a mission to fill, be it big or small.

And if you stay in your head to make sense of it all that reason will likely never come,

But if this crisis can make you look down in your soul then you can see where the sense can come from.

The positive side of a crime of such horror is it causes us all just to think

To somehow acknowledge all the gifts that we have and how they all can be gone in a blink.

That father that leaves every morning so quickly without a hug or a kiss for his child or his wife,

Can now know the treasure of spending just one more moment for those hugs, kisses and smiles.

And he can take those few steps it will require to embrace that sweet loving partner who cares

And make certain they know in the time that he's gone that the love never leaves, it's still there

And that hard-working mother who drops off her children and then rushes off madly in haste

Can take a few moments to assure that small loved one that time spent in loving is not waste

Or that nice smiling someone who works down the hall that you've chosen 'til now to ignore

You can now feel the need to give back a little sunshine and be amazed when it makes you smile more.

It can make you feel a tug to make a short phone call to talk to that Mom or that Dad

Or to somehow forgive that one thing that you've harbored that now just doesn't seem all that bad.

It can make you rekindle a friendship that has withered from an angrily spoken remark

Or it can bring to your mind the real lasting treasure of a picnic or a walk in the park.

And last but not least it makes brothers of strangers as they work side by side day and night, .

And it shows us the wisdom of loving and caring and how killing and hating can't be right

So, let us learn from this mayhem that though we yearn for revenge and we may want to settle the score,

That the lives that are taken can help us to love and if it does that's what their mission was for . . .

47

Mexico, the Dolphins, and North Carolina

April and May 1995

Despite the devastating events that happened in Oklahoma City, I was able to go to Mexico and be with the dolphins, April 29 - May 6, 1995.

My friends from Chicago, Denver, California and I did not get to actually swim with the dolphins, but we were able to watch other people swimming with them. Somehow, Spirit did not tell us we needed to make reservations in order to actually swim with them.

But the trip to Mexico was successful and fun. We took the ferry early in the morning to Isla Mujeres and a taxi to the dolphin swim reserve.

As I stood off to one side beside the pools where two younger untrained dolphins were swimming, I noticed they were very eager to communicate. They would stop below me on the dock and come up out of the water with their faces and make their sounds. Then they would swim away from me, building up energy by going around both pools. When they had built up momentum they would leap up in front of me.

One of the dolphins swimming around built up such a charge of energy her belly turned pink. Then she turned over in front of me exposing her pink tummy and released a charge of love energy into my heart chakra. (I had had the same experience with the baby whale Orca at Sea World in San Diego a few years before.)

After a while, we went under the pavilion for something to drink. While we were there the dolphins invited us to go out of our bodies and to enter theirs and swim with them from within their bodies!

What a trip that was, to feel the power and grace of their bodies and movements. It was fun to see through their eyes, too. Their eyes, located on the sides of their heads, permit them to see everything on both sides of them, but nothing out in front. Rather, they FEEL what is in front of them. Then I knew why they came up under me when I was on the dock and turned their heads to the side to be able to stare directly into my eyes. They looked as if they were flirting or posing for pictures.

While our itinerary did not include it, we took a couple days to visit the Chichen Itza pyramids. This was because a few days before our departure for Mexico, we received a letter from a woman who lives in Piste, Yucatan, near the pyramids.

The woman received the Namaste newsletter. She understood we were coming to Mexico and invited us to stay at her inn at the entrance to the park near the pyramids.

We rented a car and drove through the jungle, enjoying the day. We stopped at a village just before Piste, and anchored a ray of Cosmic Christ energy in a church. We also had lunch at a delightful garden restaurant.

Upon our arrival, we were greeted by Carole, originally from Pennsylvania, and her charming husband who is a Mexican National. We were also greeted by a man named Enrique who had been visiting the Inn for two weeks. He had a travel agency in Mexico City and Cancun. He was a Mayan astrologer. He had been instructed by Spirit to come to the Inn and stay for a while.

There is a pyramid tomb on the Inn property where several priests and priestesses of the Itza culture are buried. Carole's father is also buried there.

The energy there is so strong, the hair stands up on your arms just upon entering the lobby! Also, the gardens around the spring-fed swimming pool are amazing. Banana trees, orange, lime, mango, papaya, avocado trees and many Mayan medicinal plants grow in the garden. Carole and her husband have started a spiritual Retreat Center on the property.

After this delightful trip and a few days at home, the last of May rolled around and it was time for me to travel to North Carolina.

One evening while there, I was preparing to do a slide show about the spiritually significant places I'd visited when a young man came up to me and asked if I had any slides of Africa.

I explained my long-term fear and resistance to going there. I also told him I had finally agreed to go if God would arrange a safe, easy trip with someone who knew and understood Africa and her people; that I also wanted to have fun with trustworthy traveling companions. Having someone who could get me an introduction to the Masai people was in order, too.

Then he told me that he had "heard" my name from a friend a couple hours before and "knew" that he was supposed to come to the slide show and meet me. He had driven an hour to get there!

He asked me where I needed to go in Africa. I explained that my guidance had been to go to Zimbabwe and to meet with the Masai people. I also explained that I did not know if the two locations indicated were even close together.

He replied, "Fortunately, they are about a 45-minute plane ride apart, and I happen to be an honorary member of the Masai tribe. My name is Ray Johnston and the name of my safari company is Pure Wild Safaris. I take special interest groups into Africa, and I've been sent to be your guide."

This really took me by surprise! Although a few months before I had finally become "willing" to overcome my early fear and go to that continent, I was appalled that Spirit had met my conditions so soon! And the guide they had sent! Ray was a highly developed intuitive, auric healer and, according to my soul, had absolute spiritual integrity.

(Actually, after that evening, plans were put into motion for a trip to Africa October 7 -23, 1996. However, because of a mass hovering of ships to take place about that date here on the North American continent, and my extreme fatigue of body and emotions, the trip was canceled.)

BOOKS I HAD REVIEWED

About this time, several books had been written and were being read by many persons, books I'd been asked to comment on.

Two were *The Kryon Books* by Kryon and *You Are Becoming A Galactic Human* by Virginia Essene and Sheldon Nidle.

I was surprised Virginia had put her name on the *Galactic Human* book because I felt all of her previous books were 100 percent on target energetically with the Cosmic Christ Consciousness.

The *Galactic Human* book did NOT feel that way to me. However, at the end of the book, Virginia stated that the information did NOT come through her; that she was asked by her guidance to put her name on the book.

I felt better knowing that Virginia was aware that these two books were challenges for people to <u>fine tune their discernment factors</u>. (The "Masters Degree" lesson in Discernment is possibly the toughest we have to pass!)

The two Kryon books contained much truth (and much misleading fiction) in my opinion. And also, <u>I in no way believe that any of us should invite or allow any form of implants!</u> Implants are no longer appropriate and should be removed.

If individuals suspected they had implants, I suggested they contact a competent energy practitioner who could feel or seek out such implants and have them removed!

THE POSITIVE MEMBERS OF THE EXTRATERRESTRIAL FORCES AND OUR OVERSOULS ARE NO LONGER USING IMPLANTS!

<u>The time of our need to be controlled or monitored through devices IS OVER.</u>

ACKNOWLEDGE THE SHIFT

Before I close the chapter, I want to say this: As we move from the Piscean Age, which was ruled by the Law of Karma, into the Aquarian Age, which is ruled by the Law of Harmony and Grace and Balance, IT IS IMPORTANT <u>to acknowledge this shift</u>.

To do this we should <u>personally claim and accept moving OFF the wheel of Karma</u> and <u>ask and accept</u> moving INTO a state of harmony, grace and balance. Claim moving yourself, your family, all your possessions and properties OFF the wheel of Karma – out from under the Law of Karma – and into the Aquarian Age. Also, claim this for the Earth. This requires active participation and is not automatic.

We may need to spend more time sleeping and in meditation. Much is being accomplished cosmically, which requires our being out of our bodies.

I recommend people make use of the skills of chiropractors, osteopaths or massage therapists who have the ability to do Cranial Sacral work. This loosens the sutures between the plates in our skulls and allows the brain room to breathe and expand.

The Homo universalis, the species we are mutating into, will have four quadrants to the brain, whereas we now have only two.

Our memories are being stacked, much like the computer programs which stack the files on our hard drives. The long-term memories will begin to be more in black and white and have less emotion connected with them.

The short-term memory will not be as easily accessible, which will require taking more notes and keeping the post-a-note folks in business. This expansion and stacking process makes way for the galactic mind to merge with the Third-Dimensional mind. The galactic mind understands cosmic structure and communicates with symbols from the Universal Language of Light.

INTERESTING ITEMS

A Hughes Aircraft employee, who has great appreciation for the environment, got an idea on his drive home from work one evening: He should look in his refrigerator for the solution to the problem of the Ozone layer being depleted due to Chlorofluorocarbons. (This industrial chemical is blamed for the erosion of Earth's protective Ozone layer).

The man cooked up a citrus-based substitute for the widely-used chemical. The solution worked! He once again proved that sometimes there are low-tech answers to high-tech problems.

Also, we are usually in an Alpha state of consciousness when we are driving our cars. So we should pay attention (listen) to the messages we receive when we are driving!

Electronic Devices: The electronic devices used at check-out counters in grocery stores to scan purchases deplete the energy value of food. Therefore, it is extremely important that persons reinvigorate their food each meal BEFORE beginning to eat.

Food can be reinvigorated through prayer, or by placing the hands on either side of the plate, thereby creating an energy field between the hands. Thank the Devas for creating the plants, animals and minerals for our food and raise the vibration of your food, supplements and medications higher than the vibration of your body before taking them into your body.

Time Capsules: When we came into incarnation (and some of us later) we had in our systems what appear to be "time-release capsules." These capsules contain information.

If we do not know about these capsules, we may have a tendency to misread them energetically in other people (if we can see etherically).

In order to activate these capsules – to break apart the "gel cap" as it were, so the tiny pill can escape into our streams of consciousness – we must s-t-r-e-t-c-h our bodies, physically.

If you're like me, such a suggestion is not too entertaining. Many of us just don't like to exercise. However, Guidance has said that if we choose not to stretch, that the areas in which these capsules are located may begin festering and giving us considerable discomfort.

Well, I still wasn't interested in exercising – until the aching began, that is. Then I tried negotiating: "Can't I just visualize myself exercising?"

"NO," Guidance replied.

Then I had to resort to praying for inspiration and desire to exercise before I could motivate myself out of bed and accomplish the task.

Many persons are being intuitively guided to swim, walk or practice yoga or Tai Chi. Looks as if we need to do this in order for the information we need (and what we brought in for the collective) to be released within us.

TERRA
By bj King

Evolutions of man
Survival of the fittest,
New Age challenges beyond war
To Universal peace.

Seeing Earth as an ally, a ship that we ride
Through time and space,
Giving loving maintenance to our vessel Terra.
It is time.

48
My Travels, Decisions, World Congress, and Charlie

July 1995

I drove myself from Oklahoma City to Amarillo, Texas, on July 11, 1995, to do a session on the reconnection of the 12-Strand Helix of the DNA. As I drove along, I was aware that "conscious relationship" was a continuing path between Charlie and me and that the challenges were many.

While in Amarillo, I was treated by my wonderful healer friend, Dr. Lou Ann Hall. We focused on clearing up relationship issues that might be left in my body or inherited from my family. We centered on my WILLINGNESS to GIVE UP ALL EXPECTATIONS about the relationship with Charlie. Dr. Lou Ann had in previous years helped me to clear and overcome allergies to foods, odors and many environmental pollutants.

I moved on to Lubbock with much curiosity. I was also a little apprehensive. Since moving away from there some years before, I had been back only to visit my family, not to teach or to do any readings. Before going to Lubbock, I did not know where I was to stay. The woman who sponsored me lived with her aging mother and could not host me. I called for motel reservations and found every motel was full because of an FFA convention.

I prayed about this and was guided to call a woman who receives the newsletter but whom I had never met. She had sent me a letter several years before offering her home if I ever needed a place to stay in the area.

The woman had remarried and could not offer her home. However, she suggested I might wish to stay in a house she owed and rented to others, since it was vacant at the time. She moved a bed, chairs, table and a lamp to the residence to accommodate me. My guidance had caused me to get a cellular phone, so the lack of a phone in the house was no problem.

Before I left Lubbock, Spirit suggested I call Charlie and have him meet me in Amarillo. The two of us were then to go to Denver for a few days where I would do some readings and a group session.

Charlie was agreeable and joined me. We left his car in Amarillo and drove to Raton, New Mexico, for the night.

For about a year, Spirit had asked me repeatedly to plan to attend the World Congress on Illumination in Colorado Springs, August 11-16. I resisted because of the expense and because I felt I needed to be home writing the newsletter, painting and spending time with Charlie.

I did not want to tell Charlie I needed to be gone for the entire month of August, if I was to follow Spirit's suggestions. (Spirit wanted me not only to attend the Congress, but following that to get Charlie to Amarillo so he could drive his car back to Oklahoma City. Then I was to go from there to Albuquerque to spend time with a group of women gathering at my friends Hal and Marian's. The women were preparing for a vision quest at Chaco Canyon and Hopi Land. The women were from New Zealand, Canada and various sections of the United States.) I remained silent about the mental activity I was going through until we arrived at the Antler's Doubletree Hotel lobby in Colorado Springs. Spirit had asked us to stop there on our way to Denver to allow the energies to start setting up in the hotel for the World Congress on Illumination, in the Garden of the Gods and in Manitou Springs. We were also to anchor the energy of World peace at the Broadmoor Hotel complex.

Charlie had no resistance to stopping. As we sat in the lobby, the currents of energy that hit our bodies made every hair on both of our heads stand on end. He was amazed and impressed by the power.

"What did you say was going to happen here?" he inquired excitedly.

I explained as much as I knew about the Congress and its plans.

"Well," he stated after a while, "it's clear to me that you are expected to be here. When does this thing start?"

After I'd given him that date, he reasoned, "Then it would not make much sense for you to try to return to Oklahoma between these two trips. Maybe you should just plan to stay at Judi's in Denver, get some rest, and do some painting and then come on to this Congress." I began to cry. It was clear that Spirit was placing this suggestion in his heart and mind to make it easier for both of us. It was good for it to be his idea, since I had not included him in my decision. This has been a repetitive problem for me in relationships, making my decisions internally with Spirit without discussing them with those with whom I'm in relationship.

We left Colorado Springs with much lighter hearts and a reservation for me to attend the conference.

The meetings in Denver went well. Charlie and I had one day to spend together in the mountains, then he flew to Amarillo and home to Oklahoma City. I proceeded to Albuquerque and the blessings of LaMadera Canyon and being with Hal and Marian.

The women at the vision quest were delightful and invited me to visit New Zealand. I stayed four days in the Canyon, and then drove back to Amarillo and Denver.

On the trip to Denver, Spirit suggested it would serve the Divine Plan if I didn't stay in Denver, but proceeded to Grand Junction, Paonia, Durango and Pagosa Spring, Colorado, to offer the DNA connection.

I opened my address book to call my friend Marie Yeager in Grand Junction, Colorado. To my surprise I found a folded letter from Pam Cameron in Pagosa Springs. She had written me last fall and invited me to visit her while I was in Denver. (I had not been able to accept the invitation then because of my adopted Mom's death.) All these months I had been carrying the letter with me in my briefcase! Then I chuckled with delight at the synchronicity that happens in all of our lives when we let Spirit lead instead of our logical minds!

I called Pam, but was unable to reach her. I found this strange and a bit unsettling, since I was sure Spirit intended I should stay with her. I decided to proceed as if the arrangements had already been made.

On the drive to Grand Junction, Spirit asked that I stop in Dillon and call a woman I had met in San Francisco eight years before. I had recently reconnected with the woman, a film maker, over the phone. She was interested in producing the extraterrestrial film script idea that had come to me in Mount Shasta in 1991.

She met me for coffee and gave me the name of a person in Pagosa Springs she felt I should meet. We would get together later in the week. The synchronicity continued . . .

My friend Marie was most generous and accommodating. An overflow crowd from area towns near Grand Junction attended my presentation. I did a few readings the following day and then went on to Paonia where my dear friend Honey Lee lives. You may remember Honey Lee is the Namaste accountant that I met by following Spirit's guidance to go to the KOA campground in Cottonwood, Arizona, outside of Sedona.

All the driving I had done up to then gave me lots of time to think about my life, my path, my intentions, and to listen to Spirit's suggestions.

I came to the decision to separate from Charlie. Most of our relationship had worked well for both of us and we were pretty compatible, except for two areas of our lives. I felt I simply could no longer afford to be in partnership with someone who was out of integrity in these two areas.

Spirit agreed with me so I mentally and emotionally began preparing myself to make the separation upon my return to Oklahoma.

I admit here that I was very angry with Spirit for yet again bringing me a partner who was not willing to embody the Jovan energy or to "walk their talk" and live from their center. He had allowed the Jovan energy to merge with his body for the first year and then had rejected it.

I fussed and fumed. I was quite upset emotionally when I arrived in Paonia.

I had planned not to mention all of this to Charlie, but to remain superficial in my conversations with him until my return home. Spirit, however, had another plan.

When I called home to give the family my number in Paonia, Charlie asked me to tune in to the possibility of our moving to Dallas, Texas. I was a little surprised because he seldom asked me to tune in psychically to anything.

I truthfully answered that I felt a possible move for him to Dallas, but not for me; I did not feel a move in my future until January, and that, at best, was only a possibility.

His immediate response was confusion. He asked me if that meant we would not be moving together.

I had to be honest and tell him that while I did not fully understand what it meant, I did feel there was a very real possibility we would be separating.

He was devastated by this and, of course, demanded to know why.

When I explained the reasons, he became angry and sarcastic.

When I hung up the phone, Spirit asked me NOT to call Charlie again and to be unavailable if he called me.

In the days that followed, I tried to focus on my own feelings and my paintings. I was able to create several soul paintings while sitting beside the Crystal River that flows past Honey Lee's mountain cabin. I also rested some.

I called a friend in Durango, my next stop after Paonia, and learned she was in California with her mother, who was dying of cancer. (Sena was the person to whose home we went to view the video *UFO Contact the Pleiades* in Sedona. That was also the night we saw the fleet of ships come in and made our first telepathic communication with the Intergalactic Federation.)

By the time I arrived in Durango, Sena's mother had made her transition, and Sena was back in town. This enabled me to complete a rather sensitive event: During one of the days I had sat painting by the Crystal River near Honey Lee's cabin, Sena's mother approached me in Spirit on the day of her death. She instructed me to make Sena's soul symbol painting and deliver it to Sena "from her mother." The presentation was a very emotional time for everyone present.

That night, while I was trying to rest in my motel room in Durango, an energy began to return to Earth. The energy was that of Poseidon. (Poseidon was a continent, apparently in the Fifth Dimension energetically, not unlike Avalon.) The energy was apparently being rebirthed onto the planet through the bodies of several women who I spoke with that week. They all suffered birth pain contractions similar to those I felt for four days.

The pain was intense. My colon continued spasming for days afterward. Fortunately, I was among many healers who generously assisted me through the experience of continuing to release the anger I carried toward my soul.

I drove on to Pagosa Springs where I spoke to healers and metaphysical teachers at a noon meeting. The following day I was in pain again, but was treated by a wonderful chiropractor there.

Following that, Spirit asked me to go to a certain restaurant for lunch, to carry the book *Losing Your Mind* with me and to place it on the table there. The book is written by Karen Alexander and Rick Boyes, and I highly recommend it.

I placed the book on the table and then struck up a conversation with two women sitting at the next table. They invited me to join them for lunch (which lasted two hours). The women also came to my car to view my soul paintings.

One of the women was moving that week from Colorado Springs because there was so much anti-New Age sentiment there among its churches. I had to laugh as I confessed that even the New-Age bookstore owner had written me requesting I remove the store's name from my newsletter mailing list. (The woman felt this was the reason why the Congress of Illumination was being held there!) We had a delightful time.

I felt rejuvenated – renewed – as I made the beautiful five-hour drive through the mountains from Pagosa Springs to Colorado Springs. I felt myself beginning to connect with the energies of the Congress as they kept building.

I called home with the number where I could be reached in Colorado Springs. Charlie was distraught and immediately confronted me with the "shoulds" and "should nots" of my telephone conversation with him some days before and the fact that I had hung up on him.

Spirit moved my hands and gently pushed them down on the button and hung up the receiver. I was told I could not afford, at that level of energy, to engage in his anger, nor could the participants in the Congress afford a negative thought (mine OR theirs). Spirit also asked that I not pick up the phone again that week when I knew, energetically, it was Charlie calling.

Of course, Charlie was furious and felt very rejected. His frustration and anger grew. All of this was apparently necessary to <u>push him</u> toward relinquishment to his soul.

That night in Oklahoma City, Charlie explained what had happened to the members of the meditation group who met in our home. He did not ask for sympathy, but for help. And said if anyone received a message for him from Spirit, he would be receptive to learning what it was.

After the meditation, the message was delivered that he had been resisting the Holy Spirit's efforts to speak to him for over six months; that the Holy Spirit was standing there, waiting for him to recognize Its Presence and that It (the Spirit) had something to say to him and something to share with him as well.

Charlie asked if what the Holy Spirit had to say would help our relationship.

The answer came back, "This has nothing whatsoever to do with whether you and bj stay together. This has to do with <u>you</u> and it is time for you to <u>listen</u>." (Charlie had previously not felt the messages given through the channel God chose had much meaning.)

This particular one, though, caused goose bumps to cover his body from the top of his head to the end of his toes. He relinquished his judgment. He got the message.

After the group members left, he went into his studio and played a song Spirit had asked the two of us to buy the week before I left on the trip , "Holy Spirit Touch Through me."

He became engulfed in the power and energy of the Holy Spirit. He wept. He released all resistance. The following morning he began taking steps to correct the conditions and situations I had not been able to tolerate any longer. He wrote the following:

> An answer came into my mind as I worked out in the yard,
> An answer to a question that I've sought.
> That question is why growth must hurt and why must it be so hard,
> And He whispered, "There's a lesson to be taught."
>
> You have to fight this battle on your own, inside your soul,
> And reaching out to others is just a hinder,
> For in this war your "will to fight" is your biggest single foe,
> For all you have to do to win is just surrender.
>
> Give up the notion in your mind that you have held so long,
> The notion that you need someone's approval.
> Rejoice in your new truth that to know you're weak will make you strong,
> And that a must for "Real" new growth is pride's removal.
>
> I don't mean you must be wimpy or hang your head and mope about,
> As a matter of fact, just the opposite is true,
> For when you have your faith in Me, your joy will make you shout,
> For I have told you that through me there's nothing you can't do.
>
> So why the pain and why the tears and why the fuss and stewing?
> Just feel my changes, they cost nothing, there's no bill.
> So clear your heart and hear my voice for I know what I AM doing,
> And the only thing you have to do is "Peace be Still."

While Charlie agonized in Oklahoma City, I had a restless night in Colorado Springs, curled up with hot towel packs to calm the spasms which had returned. All night I used the mantra, "Be still and know that I am GOD." I dreaded the Congress ending and my having to return home to Charlie's disappointment and anger.

It was thus far my most strenuous lesson of staying focused and in the moment. The following day was the first day of the World Congress on Illumination. The Congress, the energy and the meditations are not describable in words. Patti Cota-Robles is an amazing spiritual teacher and facilitator.

Our collective assignment from the Spiritual Hierarchy was such that The Hierarchy was doubtful it could be accomplished during the 4-5 days of the conference. However... it was completed the first day!!!! The rest of the week our accomplishments went far beyond the expectations and goals of the Hierarchy!

It isn't possible to explain the feeling of being in a room of 160 persons, totally dedicated and focused – for hours – in guided meditation to change the outcome of the prophesied horrors, to that of a potential future of heaven on Earth. I was SO GLAD I had given up my resistance to being a part of this awesome group.

Group members took a trip to the Garden of the Gods and one to Pike's Peak. They also went on a river rafting trip. While Spirit did not instruct me to go on these trips – nor was I physically able – I WAS totally present for the meditation work.

All of us had a delightful time with old friends and new. I even found time to see two movies, *Pocahontas* and *Walk in the Clouds*. Much of the music from *Pocahontas* was played at the Congress. The colors of the skies in the *Pocahontas* movie are the colors our bodies remember from the time of Poseidon. During the Poseidon time frame this continent was apparently a Fifth Dimensional place energetically.

Following the Congress I started for home, rather dreading my arrival. But to my amazement, Charlie had changed so much, energetically, he was difficult to recognize as the same person! He had shaved off his beard and moustache. That really added to his strangeness. His commitment was different too. His following poems help to explain what happened:

"I took the longest trip of my whole life these past few days,
And I wasn't on a boat or on a plane,
And along the way there were some times I thought I'd lose my mind
But I wasn't really going crazy, I was going sane.

The first place that I came to was a spot called Point Rejection,
It's a quaint little village right next to Ego Falls.
And that led me to a lively town that's known as Anger City
Where I got stuck until I made some calls.

I got directions to a little known city that's called Complete Surrender,
But to get there I had to pass right though Cape Fear.

bj King

And I knew about that location because I've lived there off and on
For the better part of fifty years.

So I thought I'd go around it and when I talked to my tour guide
A cordial fellow by the name of Holy Spirit,
He suggested that we take the route through Trusting Pass and Quiet Valley,
And we'd avoid Cape Fear completely, not even go near it.

So I dropped off two pieces of luggage,
one called Pride and the other Judgment,
And I noticed right away my load was lighter.
And as I saw the rest stop between Forgiveness and Releasing,
The scenery seemed to get considerably brighter.

And as I looked down at my tour card I was so surprised to see
My final stop was just called Peace be Still,
And when I asked what the cost would be if I just got off there,
This Holy Spirit fella just smiled and said the cost is nil.

You see the guy that built Be Still is a fella known as God,
And if you ask him I bet a home to you he'd give.
And he was right and I loved it there so I moved in next to God
And I'm pleased to say that's where I'm gonna live.

And you know, God wasn't surprised at all at the distance I had traveled.
He said "I always knew you'd get here, it just took a while."
And as he took my hand he said that trip can be a rough one
And as I sat to rest I'm sure I saw Him smile.

49

Dolphin Days, Energy Work and The Ruins

October 1995

The days flew by and soon it was October 1995 and time to swim again with the dolphins and whales.

These creatures are representatives from the star system of Sirius. They have come to Earth to hold the energies of heart healing and expansion for the Human species. They also interface with the inner Earth civilizations, keeping a close reading on the magma of the Earth's core. They report this back to the ships through their soundings. Interacting with these creatures can be a profound healing and spiritual experience, as well as one of pure joy.

At the airport in Dallas, I met friends from Amarillo, Texas, Charlotte, North Carolina, and Niagara Falls, New York. When we arrived at the airport in Mexico, we were greeted by my friends Hal and Marian from New Mexico.

Several years before, I had made a "Manifestation Journal." One of my entries was that eventually I wanted to have the abundance to meet my friends in exotic, fun places to do energy work for the planet and also to play. That desire has been realized, and I am so grateful people agree to join me to do this energy work and celebration.

From the airport all of us took a ferry to the beautiful island of Isla Mujeres, which translates to The Island of Women. The ride took about 20 minutes. When we docked, we took taxis to the Marina Isla Mujeres, a small delightful Mexican resort on the beach within walking distance of the Dolphin Discovery swimming area. Since I had needed to get more exercise, I was amused and pleased when it was announced that I was to stay in a penthouse at the top of a winding three-story staircase!

The room was large and private, with a king-size bed and refrigerated air. It had a magnificent view of the beach, the ocean and the sunsets.

The first evening, the 40 of us, 25 of us from the Namaste network, met for dinner at an open air, screened-in area on the beach. We were divided up into "pods" of six for the dolphin swims.

Three out of the six days there we walked, or took taxis, to the Dolphin Discovery area and swam with the dolphins. Some days we had organized swims in which the dolphins pulled us through the water, pushed us from the soles of our feet through the water, or jumped over poles we held up out of the water.

One day we had what was called an "encounter time" with the dolphins in shallow water. They would swim by us and stop for hugs and talking. For all of us this was our favorite time spent with these creatures.

Many persons reported healing experiences during the week. It was wonderful receiving body work by the healers and body workers who went on the trip both to perform these functions and to swim with the dolphins.

In addition to the swims, the group members met on the beach in a circle each morning and evening to pray. We grounded energy, set our intention for the day and gave thanks for the day's events.

According to the Spiritual Hierarchy, the group was extremely successful in accomplishing the energetic mission it had agreed to do.

Part of the mission had included enlisting the assistance of the Sirian energy to avert war in the Middle East. According to our spiritual sources, at that time atomic weapons had already been moved into the Middle East.

We also worked on the energy in Cuba.

The island we were on was one of the places closest to Cuba. It was also the safest place available to us.

One evening a group of us was asked to go to the ruins where the lighthouse is on Isla Mujeres. We were to anchor energy of the Seventeenth Ray of personal empowerment for the people of Mexico and Cuba. That same night the taxi drivers of Isla Mujeres went on strike to own their own cabs and set their own rates. We were amazed by the quick reaction. Even though they were striking, the cab drivers we had met and communicated with earlier did not let us get stranded in the downtown area after we had eaten dinner there, not knowing about the strike when we left the resort. Energy was also directed for peace in the Middle East and Bosnia. At the time the energy was sent through the communication station inside our moon, we felt the vitality move very strongly through our bodies. As I held my hands up toward the sky flexing my fingers to acknowledge and thank the Hierarchy for its love, communion and assistance, The Hierarchy radiated out concentric circles of energies in various colors to show its appreciation for our assistance! It was one of the most moving displays of energy and phenomena I had witnessed in ten years of working consciously with the Federation and Spiritual Hierarchy. These conclaves within our moon are held during the time of each full moon.

Later, back at the Marina we described the experience to our friends who were on the beach and I suggested we try the connection again. We did so and the response from the moon was the same! We were told that Sanat Kumara, the father of Venus, and other members of the Hierarchy and the Intergalactic Federation were holding a conclave within the communication chamber inside the moon. Their energies were there for the week of the full moon. Many persons with whom I spoke later, mentioned the unusual powerfulness of that particular full moon. Usually the conclave lasts from the day before the full moon, the day of the full moon and one day after. It was unusual for it to last for a full week. The meetings involve discussions of what would be the next influence allowed by the Hierarchy and the Federation to speed up the evolution of Humanity.

One day, a group of 25 of us took the ferry to Cancun, boarded an air-conditioned bus and went to Chichen Itza. On the way to Pyramid Park we stopped at the Pyramid Inn and picked up our friend Carole. At the Temple of Venus we invited the lowering of a chamber from the Fifth Dimension back into the third dimension. As the molecules of the chamber were transmuted, the intensity of the energies hitting our bodies was amazing and undeniable. The chamber, according to the Hierarchy, held the records of the Itzi people's relationship to the extraterrestrials.

It had not been appropriate for these records to be discovered before now, which is why these chambers – and the chambers under the Sphinx – were moved into the Fifth Dimension many years ago. In previous years, archeologists seismographically tested for chambers under the Sphinx and under the Temple of Venus and agreed that none were there; it was solid. Later tests now show there to be space under these structures.

However, since we moved the chambers under the Sphinx from the Fifth Dimension to the third three years ago, the chambers are now being detected. We expect the same thing to happen at Chichen Itza. Archeologists often stay at Carol's Inn, so she planned to speak with them about it.

Another interesting happening at Chichen Itza: On our way there, group members programmed a cloud cover in the sky to lessen the intensity of the sun while we were in Pyramid Park. We were successful! We had cloud cover! However, when about 20 of us were ascending the top of the Temple of Venus to invite the lowering of the chamber, the intensity of the energy set off a terrific rain shower!

Later, many of the folks who agreed to participate in the energy circle, confessed they had not believed anything would happen . . . that they were more or less going along with the idea, but didn't really believe that what I was suggesting was going to take place!

The other three days of the trip I spent painting on the beach, doing readings, shopping and visiting.

Dr. Steve, a psychiatrist, and his wife, Macy, were co-founders of "Living From the Heart." Although he passed through transition in June of 1994 from a very aggressive brain tumor, he continues to play an important role in the dolphin-assisted therapy. Five percent of the cost of our trip went into the Steve Jozsef, MD, Memorial Fund. The fund pays for a patient, unable to finance his/her own trip, to go on a dolphin swim.

Several years before, I was attending a Silva Mind Control class (against my will). After the first class meditation, Steve had walked over to me from across the room and said, "We're from the same place, aren't we?"

I had never met Steve Third Dimensionally. At first I didn't know what he was talking about. I thought possibly he had recognized my accent and that he was from Texas, too. Upon very quickly checking with Spirit, the answer came that we were both Novan/Venusian. So I responded, "Yes, we are." And then, just to see what he would say, I asked, "What does that mean to you?"

He told me that during the meditation he had received information that we were from the same place, but he didn't know where it was.

When I arrived in Dallas on my way home from Mexico, I was shocked to learn that Yitzahk Rabin, Prime Minister of Israel, had been assassinated.

The death "seemed" contradictory to peace. However, reporters the next day mentioned several times that the death seemed to be bringing countries together in a search for peace. Whenever we give permission for energy to be sent to an area of Earth to heal, cause World Peace or change a condition that exists, we always release the energy to be acted out within the Divine Plan of the Creator.

Through the many years I have been working consciously with Spirit I have learned that our form of logic is not always the path of Spirit. We must always <u>trust</u> the bigger plan. Our responsibility is to pray and give permission for Divine intervention – permission to override the Law of Free Will. The Federation and the Hierarchy cannot intervene without Human permission to override Human free will or to intervene in any way on behalf of Earth or Humans.

Each of us on the trip received a complimentary tape of ourselves swimming with the dolphins. Sharing the tape with friends, after returning home, brought back the energy of the trip. It also extended the "high" of the experience. And it was impossible not to smile at it all, because of the energy of the dolphins and the relaxed atmosphere.

> **Expect your every need to be met,**
> **Expect the answer to every problem.**
> **Expect abundance on every level,**
> **Expect to grow spiritually.**
>
> **– Eileen Caddy**

50

Los Angeles, Washington and Oregon

1996

I've often said that Spirit does not understand the principle that the shortest distance between two points is a straight line, as the following seems to illustrate.

In late 1995, I had been invited to go to Los Angeles in January 1996 by a woman attendant with US Air. I wasn't very excited about going. The last time I had driven myself out there, Matthew, my Eighth-Dimensional self, had said, "*You will never have to do this again.*" I had assumed he meant I would never have to return to Los Angeles.

When I asked him about the invitation to go, he <u>and</u> the Spiritual Hierarchy were clear that the trip WAS VERY IMPORTANT. Matthew also explained that when he had said, "*You will never have to do this again,*" he had meant that I would never have to <u>drive myself</u> to Los Angeles again.

When I checked with the flight attendant at US Air about the trip, she assured me she could get me a "pass" from her airline, but I would need to get myself to Kansas City through another airline; US Air does not fly out of Oklahoma City.

I was not disturbed by this, since Southwest Airlines had a $19 round trip fare from Oklahoma City to Kansas City. Also, my consciousness translated the word "pass" as meaning "free." I felt any inconvenience on my part would be worth the financial trade-off.

After several calls to the attendant, the ticket finally arrived. I learned, though, that I was being charged for it. In addition, when I called my travel agent, I was told the $19 fare was not available; it would cost me $80 to get to Kansas City.

My Guidance told me to return the ticket to the US Air attendant and get a ticket with another airline.

Meanwhile, the attendant (I had been counseling her for several years) told me she had changed her mind about sponsoring me to go to Los Angeles and turned my trip plans and seminar over to another person, a former US Air employee. I had not met nor read for this person.

The man called me about my trip plans and said he would be sharing the responsibility with yet another woman and that I would be staying in her home. I had never met this woman either.

By now, as well imagined, I was quite confused and wondered if I wanted to go at all!

However, Spirit kept encouraging me, telling me that they really needed me to go.

Then the first airline attendant, who was originally to handle the trip, called me. She admitted that she had recently had a reading from someone on the east coast and that the reading was totally different from the one she'd had through me. Therefore, she no longer wanted to sponsor me. (She was unable to discern which reading was energetically accurate! She was very confused.)

However, her call did dissolve much of the perplexity of the whole thing for me and certainly made clear why there had been a charge for the US Air ticket I'd first received.

As the particulars fell into place, I recalled that three years before another woman, Carole Wilke from Los Angeles, had written several times offering to sponsor me. Each time she had written, Spirit suggested I not go at that time.

As I continued working out plans for the trip, I kept wondering why I was not being given a more direct – and seemingly eager and more clear route – to Los Angeles.

When I finally arrived there, James Buckley met me at the airport and escorted me to the home of my hostess, Wynnona, and her roommate, Carol. After all the initial confusion, these three dear persons really made my stay convenient and easy.

And lo and behold, I learned that Carole Wilke who had wanted to sponsor me three years before was living in the same suburb as Wynnona! Had I not gone the less direct route to California, these folks, who were ordained by Spirit to meet, would not have done so at my seminar.

Spirit's form of "efficiency" seldom looks that way to Earthlings. However, the results are in Divine timing and the people who need to meet, get met . . . and the saga goes on . . .

While I was in Los Angeles, Carole Wilke worked on my body. Carole is an amazing healer who uses the Zenith method, which was channeled by a man in Las Vegas who received the information from the Pleiadians.

I also met an interesting woman named Judith Block. She had had a kidney transplant. She was a tremendous artist and created a line of cards, the profit from some of which went to help the Transplant Recipient International Organization. Some of her cards were of African drawings.

The trip was successful. I did what Spirit wanted me to do. The ships came in to stabilize the fault line, bringing rain as usual. Even the temperature dropped. Those persons who had done their spiritual work and qualified for spiritual initiations were taken aboard the ships for six nights; while their bodies slept, the initiations took place. The energy was tremendous and we all enjoyed tremendous growth.

My hosts arranged for me to visit the J. Paul Getty museum on my way to the airport. Getty collected many Grecian and Roman artifacts. He built a replication of a beautiful villa overlooking the ocean where he placed the treasures for Humanity to see.

It was a delightful experience and put me in the energy of Greece prior to my trip there the following month.

I went home for about twelve days. Then I flew to the Vancouver, Washington – Portland, Oregon, area. Several months before, I had tried to cancel that trip because I had felt so tired, and also had not wanted to "overdo" before going to Egypt.

When I called my sponsor in Vancouver in November to say I was begging off, she agreed to let me out of the commitment. However . . . Spirit was not so agreeable. In fact, my Guidance was adamant that the trip to Portland/Vancouver needed to take place!

I flew to Portland on February 7 with the understanding that 26 people in that area were qualified for initiation aboard the ships. When I arrived, my Guidance told me there was potential for an 8.9 earthquake in the area the following day! The quake would set off volcanic eruptions in Mount St. Helens and Mount Hood!

The Hierarchy needed permission (from a planet dweller) to bring in 13 additional ships to join the seven-ship fleet that is permanently assigned to the Portland/Vancouver area.

The ships came in and stabilized the fault line. However, the magnetic energy disturbance brought pouring rain for several days. The Earth, already saturated from normal winter rains, simply couldn't hold another gallon. The flood came, the likes of which hadn't happened in that area in years – maybe never. It was very severe with accompanying extensive personal property damage, mud slides and closed highways.

I was a little tense as I sat in my sponsor's home on top of a hill for four days getting reports on TV and watching the Columbia River rise to alarming heights, debris of all sorts sweeping downstream, and boats breaking away from their moorage docks.

Then the rain stopped and the sun came out. The worst was over.

The amount of destruction caused by the rains seemed great, until I compared that with what <u>would</u> have resulted from a gigantic earthquake and volcanic eruptions!

Where we Humans were in evolution at that time in 1996, with the amount of negative energy that had to be transmuted, it was most fortunate indeed that we were able to <u>invite</u> extraterrestrial intervention and aid to minimize the potential damage.

The erratic weather patterns are caused by sun flares and by misqualified energies in the Fourth Dimension. Each time the "ring-pass-not" energy barrier, just beyond the fourth dimension, is tightened; the energies in the Fourth Dimension become more intensely pushed into the Third Dimension. Then the weather gets crazy and time speeds up.

The molecules are condensed, therefore the clocks continue registering the same 24 hours. However, as I've mentioned before, we actually had. at that time, approximately 16 hours in a day to accomplish 24 hours of activity. In 2008, the time is now shortened to 11-hour days. Our only hope is to become more efficient, learn to use the Holy Violet Flame of Transmutation, simplify our lives, and to <u>pray and give permission</u> for extraterrestrial and Hierarchical intervention.

The trip to Portland/Vancouver was considered successful, despite the flood. Few lives were lost and scores of people met one another and joined hands in various projects to help each other. Many learned the lesson of priorities: how important are physical belongings compared with Human life and spiritual growth? Also, all of the initiations on the ships took place. The ships were able to depart the area more slowly, when the time came, without causing any other major weather changes.

In fact, about 8:30 the morning I was leaving to come home, Edith Durfey, with whom I had stayed the closing days of my visit to the two states, had rushed downstairs and said excitedly, "bj, there's a funny-looking cloud out on the horizon."

In the east, on a cloudless blue horizon, she had seen a deep apricot-colored cloud shaped a little like a boot. It really aroused her interest and curiosity.

I explained to her that for some reason, those aboard that ship had felt it important that she see it take off.

I and many others were MOST GRATEFUL to our friends within the Intergalactic Federation for their help in stabilizing and transmuting energies and for bringing the severity of this and the California situation to our attention!

THE PHOTON BELT

THE PHOTON BELT, which in 1996 was making its way toward the Earth, is the energy of the Cosmic Christ Consciousness.

In order to greet this energy gracefully, it is imperative for us to increase the Cosmic Christ Consciousness tri-fold flame in our hearts; to consciously invite the increase in the intensity of this flame in each of us individually and collectively.

If we accomplish this successfully, when the wave hits the Earth, the larger portion of the Earth and her inhabitants will only feel the blessing of the increase.

If we continue to ignore and to fear the coming, the energy will not match the energies of Earth and Humanity and will feel devastating to us.

Photon energy is not energy of duality, but the energy of Oneness.

Letting go of opposites – dark and light, good and evil, male and female; plus exclusive energetic identity, as well as racial, cultural and religious splits – and choosing Oneness instead is the hope of the future.

Pentimento: Diary of a Walk-In

EARTH
By bj King

Mother Earth is crying, her sobbing
comes as earthquakes to the cities of the World.
Her tears flow lava-like from volcanic ducts.
The acid rain of thoughtlessness
kills her vegetation and her streams.

What happened to her dream of Eden? And
Man and Woman sharing life in a garden
of beauty and love?
It's coming, but first, the rain of remembering
must fall into every heart
To wake the "Being" there who understands
Mother Earth is Us and We are She . . .

51

New York, Greece and Egypt

March 1996

When going to Egypt was suggested by my sponsor in Vancouver, Washington, I had been a bit resistant, because I didn't personally know the leader of the trip, and I couldn't imagine keeping 45 people together well enough to accomplish anything energetically. However, Spirit was so adamant that I agreed to become a co-creator for the trip and invited participants from the Namaste network to join with me.

As soon as I agreed to go, I began having trouble with my left arm and shoulder. I went to many healers and chiropractors. Nothing seemed to touch the pain or totally identify the cause, other than the message "it is soul trauma."

There were many "hitches" and problems concerning the trip's organization, including financial details and receipt of tickets.

As departure time drew near, I became even more suspicious and leery of the sincerity, honesty and candor of the woman in Sedona who was organizing the trip. I even informed people who were going that I felt the possibility of problems on the trip.

But my Guidance continued urging me not only to go, but to give the woman an opportunity to come into financial and spiritual integrity. I felt a little better when several people, who I trusted energetically, signed up to join us for the trip.

I must mention here that Hal and Marion, my friends from New Mexico, signed up early for the trip. However, before the venture to Greece and Egypt, the two of them also had the opportunity to go to New Zealand.

They had asked Spirit, through me, what they were to focus on while in New Zealand. The answer was that they were to enlist the assistance of the Maori people, in a group, to activate the large ruby crystal in the ocean between New Zealand and Australia.

According to Spirit, approximately 21,000 years ago a curse had been placed on the land where the countries of the Middle East, Yugoslavia, Turkey and Greece are now located. The beings made the possible reversal of this curse very complicated. They did not believe that any souls with the correct Universal Language of Light symbols would ever incarnate. Neither did they believe such souls would ever meet each other, nor become conscious enough to determine the necessary process for reversal of the curse.

Unraveling the curse had to start with enlisting the assistance of the Maori people of New Zealand (the reason Hal and Marian were so drawn to New Zealand just before going to Greece. At the time, we did not realize all of this was part of a much larger mission that would be revealed to us later . . . once we were in Greece.)

To disentangle the curse, Hal and Marian did ceremonies with the Maori people to reactivate and increase the volume of energy flowing through the giant ruby crystal. Because of this, the Maori people continued praying with and for our group throughout our trip to Greece and Egypt.

Getting back to the planned trip to Greece and Egypt, I became aware (through energetic investigation) that the trip involved the very important mission of lowering a crystalline etheric capstone from the Fifth Dimension to be placed atop the Great Pyramid in Giza in the Third Dimension. This capstone was created aboard the New Jerusalem, which is the city of Light anchored above the Yucatan. The New Jerusalem at the equator keeps the Earth from being able to shift the poles from one to the other.

The leader of the Egypt trip claimed to channel the Pleiadians and that the mission to place the obsidian capstone on the Giza Pyramid was for the highest good of Earth and Humanity. I perceived her to be a young spiritual recruit and channel with very little discernment or integrity.

I was further made aware that this "obsidian" capstone contained the negative thought forms from Atlantis – in fact, it had held the negative energies of Atlantis, which have been held contained, off the coast of Bimini. If the obsidian capstone were to be placed atop the pyramid, once again these negative thought forms from Atlantis would be unleashed into the grid system of the Earth!

Therefore, this trip to Greece and Egypt – the presence of those of us making the journey – was imperative, according to the Spiritual Hierarchy.

If we did not intervene, there was a possibility this other group would accomplish the placement of the "obsidian" capstone.

The changes that had been made in the Earth's grid system (December 23 - 28, 1995) had doubled the system. Placing the crystalline capstone (which vibrates at the frequency of the Cosmic Christ Consciousness) atop the pyramid would cause the energy to flow out into the new grid system!

The Hierarchy expected a reaction from Human consciousness, which they predicted would be 2,700 times stronger than the effects of the Harmonic Convergence (1987). These changes might possibly be discernible after the Spring Equinox (1996).

With gratitude and appreciation to a friend who secured a round trip ticket for me to and from New York, I left Oklahoma City March 1996. I arrived at the airport in New York during a snowstorm!

I was to meet a friend from Buffalo, New York, upon my arrival, but she was not there. After much checking, searching, asking and phone calls, I learned that my friend was snowbound at the airport, as well. She advised me to go on to the Waldorf-Astoria without her; that she would find her way there.

Another friend from Denver was to meet us in the lobby at the Waldorf. I could not check in without my friend from Denver, since the room was in her name. (She gets a discount because she is a travel agent, and that's why we were staying in such a posh place.)

The taxi ride from the airport to the hotel was $48 with tip. I wondered to myself how people afford to live in New York City – or, moreover, why they would want to! So many people, so little space . . .

When I arrived at the hotel I explained my circumstances to the bellman. He checked my bags at the door and invited me to wait for my friend inside the lobby.

The lobby is VERY elegant, old and busy. The ceiling is gold and very ornate. A beautiful, big clock stands in the middle of the lobby and chimes at every opportunity.

There were so many people from every walk of life, it seemed, waiting and milling about in the lobby. So many languages were being spoken around me; they seemed to add to my feeling of disorientation. FINALLY, after walking through several VERY expensive shops in the hallway, I noticed a chair had become vacant in the lobby. I sat down and began reading the mystery paperback that had successfully put me to sleep on the plane. I "people-watched" for more than an hour before my friend from Denver arrived.

It is fun – and a relief – to see a familiar face after traveling so many miles to such unfamiliar surroundings! The order and organization of the Universe, plus today's communication abilities, <u>do</u> make meeting like this possible. Yet it still thrills and amazes me when we all show up in strange places.

We laughed together, hugged, babbled and were joyous. Then the bellhop showed us to our room. It was small, but elegant with two twin beds.

As she tipped the bellman, I noticed my friend's eyes get big and wide. Later, I learned she had assumed that the two beds in the room would be double. (It had not dawned on me that there were three of us to sleep in two twin beds!) We laughed and said we'd just make do. On our way to dinner, a little later, we practically ran over our friend from Buffalo who had just come into the lobby. She had arrived by bus from the airport moments before, following her snowy trip from upstate.

After good food and baths, we fell into bed and managed to sleep very well, in spite of the narrow beds and noise.

The following morning we awakened early, had breakfast and called a taxi to take us to the United Nations, our first stop on our energy work schedule. Before leaving Oklahoma City, Spirit had indicated that because it was such a critical time, energetically, for the planet and because of the potential of war, doing energy work at the United Nations, as well as the World Trade Center, the Empire State Building and the Statue of Liberty would be helpful.

As the three of us entered the United Nations area, the energy was truly amazing. One of the first things we noticed was a sign that read, "WE ALL HAVE COMMON NEEDS. WE SHARE ONE WORLD."

The emotion began. By the time the three of us had finished reading the astronaut's quote, "Only One Earth," we were in tears. It read, "Before I flew I was already aware of how small and vulnerable our planet is; but only when I saw it from space, in all its ineffable beauty and fragility, did I realize that Humankind's most urgent task is to cherish and preserve it for future generations."

The purpose of the United Nations is stated to be, "Enhancing people's sense of their own wellbeing – to generate home – to help people discover their paths to a peaceful future."

We learned that the United Nations has 185 member nations and that its bell rings on March 20 – Earth Day, the day we would be placing the new capstone on the pyramid in Giza!

After anchoring the energies of World Peace at the United Nations location, we went to the World Trade Center and the Empire State Building where we did the same anchoring. After all of this, we "treated" ourselves to the movie *Up Close and Personal.*

One would assume that a movie theatre in downtown New York City would be nice. Not so. The tickets were $8 each, and we were herded into a very small area (where people were smoking) to wait for the end of the feature so we could take our seats. (It was much too cold and windy to wait outdoors.) Our friend from Buffalo bought popcorn, which tasted terrible.

But the movie was great . . . until the end. We walked out in a state of shock and disbelief at the ending. But we were grounded by the experience.

The next day we enjoyed a leisurely breakfast, did a little shopping and took a cab to the ferry on our way to the Statue of Liberty.

Because of timing, weather, etc., we did the energy work from the dock in view of the statue rather than from the land itself.

When it was time to take a shuttle to the airport and Greece, our friend from Buffalo and I said goodbye to our friend from Denver, who was leaving for Florida to help her sister settle her affairs after the death of her husband.

We had our last American meal for a while, joined friends who were going to Greece with us, and boarded the plane for the seven-hour flight to Athens. I was able to sleep a little on the flight.

It wasn't too long before we learned that the travel agent had NOT provided vegetarian meals on the flight as promised. But we were entertained by the movie *An American President* and our excitement carried us through the inconveniences.

Customs and baggage retrieval went easily in Athens and a bus took us to our hotel, the Philippos. The front of the hotel looks out on the Acropolis, an amazing spectacle, especially at night.

As we took in many of the sights on the trip we felt as if we were viewing movie backdrops. We had to constantly remind our minds and our bodies that "this was the real thing;" we were really there; it was not a video on PBS!

I might mention here that several years before, I had met a woman, Vittoria Marangoni from Greece, at the Interdimensional Interspecies Communication Symposium in Ashland, Oregon. She and I had corresponded in the ensuing years and in a letter to me she had said she would be joining us on the Greece portion of the trip.

True to that message, she came to the hotel each night and had dinner with us.

All of my American friends fell in love with Vittoria, who is a psychiatrist at a mental hospital housing 2,000 mental patients. She lives in a room in Athens to be close to her work, but also has a home in the mountains outside the city. She invited us to return to Greece in the summer, sometime in the future, so she could escort us in her car to many other sights. She also asked us to stay in her mountain home when we come. Her mountain home was later destroyed by Albanian refugees so we never got to see it.

The first two days in Greece were lovely, with very little stress or hassle.

The third night the rest of the group arrived. The tension between the tour agent and me was a bit evident. Also, it became obvious that she had spoken to several other members of the group (who did not know me personally) in an attempt to influence their feelings toward me.

I was able to maintain composure and did not allow myself to engage with her energetically. This had been Spirit's advice to me, continually: "Do not engage with her at her level of energy."

During the first meeting between her and me in Athens, she admitted she had overcharged me $200, but said she would give me a check to cover it, although it would not be good until her return to Sedona (some weeks hence).

I accepted the check without comment, knowing she was attempting to manipulate good feelings between us, and that the check (at that time) was not covered. (She later covered the check after her return to the States.)

This woman had written a successful metaphysical book and had taken a group of people to Egypt the year before for what she called the 12:12. She believed she channeled the Pleiadians.

My experience with channeling was that her body was being used to manipulate not only her, but the group, by the "clones" trying to put the obsidian capstone into place on the pyramid.

Listening to this type of channeling can be very seductive and convincing if the energies are not traced to their source.

Also, there is more than one faction of Pleiadians. One group belongs to the Federation. One group does _not_ and does not have the highest good of Humans and Earth in mind. There are also groups of astral entities <u>claiming</u> to be Pleiadians, who channel through individuals. They use much of the same terminology, but their aim is to control and manipulate energies and to steal the energies of their audiences.

Each night the group from the Namaste network and I meditated in one of the motel rooms. The meditations were strong. We claimed the energy of the entire group and sent love and forgiveness to the agent. We also sent energy before us each night to prepare the way for the following day's activities. In addition, we built an energy bridge between the Yucatan (the location of the New Jerusalem where the capstone was created), and Giza where it would be installed.

We were given a chant to use to continuously increase the energy of the bridge. The chant was RA MA NA HA SA HO. One person pointed out that the RA MA NA sounded Egyptian, and the HA SA HO sounded American Indian.

We were awakened early each morning. Breakfast consisted of white bread, cream cheese (like feta cheese, creamed), jam, coffee or tea. Eggs were available, but at that point my body was allergic to eggs and to milk.

Because of parasites, we were admonished not to drink the water nor to eat any fruits or vegetables that weren't cooked or peeled. This limited the diet of those of us who normally live on vegetables and fruits. No baked potatoes were available. Actually, the diet of persons who live in Greece and Egypt appears to consist of lots of meat.

We did an enormous amount of walking, which our bodies adjusted to after a few days of aching legs.

It was much colder than normal in Greece and rainy during the nights. The sun came out during the day, though. The arrival of so many ships to accomplish the energy work always changes the weather patterns. So we could only smile and wear coats and several layers of clothing. Fortunately, I had packed turtle necks and sweaters, even though we had been promised spring weather, so we shared clothes.

All in all we maintained reasonable comfort – and usually, our sense of humor.

Buses took us to many temples and museums. Delphi was one of them and was very powerful for many group members. Some picked up aspects of their Oversouls there.

We also went to Corinth and the Acropolis. Paul had given speeches in both places. While we were there I experienced his energies asking for our forgiveness for things he had preached, and how they had been used by the Church to manipulate people and his attitude toward women.

We took a ferry to the Islands of Poros, Hydra and Aegina.

Everything we did in Greece seemed to be rushed. We felt herded about and saturated with lectures about ancient history, all most of us wanted to do was just _feel_ the energy of the various places, quietly do our prayers and enjoy the beauty.

I felt that the ceremonies that were scheduled by the tour leader and held were ostentatious and attracted unnecessary attention to what we were trying to accomplish. For example, the tour agent demanded that everyone be smudged with sage and incense before entering the circles – even after we explained our allergies to these substances. She played music and chants on a cassette player to "invoke" the energy of Shiva (a God of destruction) although I feel she probably thought she was playing OM Niva Shivaya [sic] and invoking the Creator God.

We were sorry to leave Greece, but were relieved that Vittoria was going with us to Egypt. We also knew that many of the members of the Namaste network would someday return when the weather was warmer and we were less rushed. We did return by cruise ship in October 2011.

We flew to Cairo, claimed our luggage and were taken by bus through the very, very crowded city, over the Nile to our hotel in Giza, a separate city from Cairo and located across the street from the three large pyramids.

As we had been promised, our first glimpse of the pyramids took our breath away.

Our hotel was old and large, but beautiful. We were grateful to unwind for a few hours, since nothing had been scheduled until the next morning. A few people bribed the night guard and went to the largest pyramid the first evening and had their own adventure.

We held our usual evening meditation. A few additional people joined us. Some came once out of curiosity; some continued to join us. The following morning we once again boarded buses to cross the street to view the pyramids – from outside only – and the Sphinx. The tour agent had arranged for two buses to take us everywhere, even though the 44 of us could easily have been accommodated on one bus. She had hired a guide for each bus. One guide was a Moslem woman who spoke fair English, but with a heavy accent. The woman had a very limited knowledge of Egyptian history. She constantly repeated what she knew to fill up time.

The other guide was a very attractive Egyptian man who spoke excellent English and had a tremendous background in Egyptian history and the sites. Half of the women on our tour were in love with him by the second week.

As for passengers on the buses, the woman agent who arranged our tour was overheard telling the bus guides that she wanted my friend from Buffalo and me on separate buses to break up our energies. The agent put herself on the same bus I was on. The Moslem woman was the guide.

A few people were dropped off the bus so they could ride camels to the pyramids. The sand was blowing across the dunes. I remained on the bus and took photos of the others. Later, one woman was seriously bitten on the leg by a camel. She required stitches and rabies shots. This woman had come on the trip from Florida. She did not realize it was a spiritual pilgrimage, but she learned a lot and had lots of guts. She had been terrified of shots before the trip. She felt she had created the camel bite to heal herself of the fear. She said she didn't feel the shots when they were given.

The Sphinx is near the pyramid and smaller than I had imagined. Reconstruction was going on there and people were not legally allowed to go between its paws. That is where we go in meditation to get into the chambers beneath the Sphinx to do the intergalactic work. I felt the chambers beneath, energetically.

Again, we were not given much time to be alone or to feel anything energetically before being whisked off to a papyrus museum to purchase paintings done on Egyptian papyrus paper. The paper is made by slicing the stalks of the papyrus reed plant, soaking them in water for several days, and then weaving and flattening them until dry.

I bought one of the paintings of the Egyptian alphabet with an unusual drawing of the Eye of Horus with numeric dimensions.

The next morning we were awakened early. We usually had only about 6-1/2 hours of sleep a night after our evening meditation. The tour agent did not hold regular meetings, other than the circle ceremonies, nor any evening meditations.

We were taken by bus to a train with sleeping cars. The cars were small with bunk beds. The toilet was down the hall. My friend from Buffalo, who had the upper berth, couldn't sleep and stood out in the hall most of the night talking with a friend of mine from Iowa. Shelagh had given me some earplugs, which made it possible for me to sleep.

We rode the train all night to get to the ship, Ramses II, for our cruise on the Nile. The next morning we felt drugged from the chemical fumes on the train. We were pleased and relieved to finally get aboard the ship and finally have the <u>same</u> bed for six nights.

The Nile valley is fertile and we viewed a continuous show of passing life in villages as we sailed by.

One participant sponsored me to fly to Abu Simbel to see the huge statues of Ramses in front of the great temple. It was an awesome experience. The plane flew over both the old and new Aswan dams. Spirit warned of potential terrorist activity to explode the dam during the meeting of World leaders, which began that day. Temples downstream would have been destroyed by water had there been an explosion. We invoked the assistance of the gods and goddesses of Egypt to help prevent such from happening. Since the people of Egypt had saved their temples, which would have been destroyed by the water as it rose behind the new Aswan dam, the ancient gods were willing to assist our efforts.

We also continually worked to influence the meeting of the World leaders with positive energy to end terrorism and war. In addition, we connected energetically with people we knew were meditating with us in other countries – the United States, Mexico, China, Canada and New Zealand. Simultaneously, two women I know were in China during our trip and had agreed to join with us energetically. When their energies arrived in China physically, they were to set off a series of events that potentially lead to a bloodless revolution for the freedom of the people of China and Tibet.

We visited the Valley of the Kings and the Valley of the Queens. At one of the Temples of the Goddess, the agent had arranged a ceremony. During the ritual a very tall, thin, Amazon - looking woman (an actress friend of the agent from Sedona) moved into the circle and began dancing, like a whirling dervish. Toward the conclusion of her dance, she stood directly in front of me doing mudras (hand motions) and seemed to be daring me to make eye contact.

I had the impression she had energetically opened herself and invited the presence of the energy of the Cat Goddess. This Goddess is one of the energies of Isis, the personification of destruction. (On one other occasion during the trip the woman had collapsed after allowing an entity to channel through her.)

I refused to make eye contact with her. Instead, I stared at her combat boots. She later explained to some of the others that she had been sent on this trip to overcome evil forces, which she perceived to be personified in me!

We visited Luxor and Karnak, and in each place we invited the energies of these planetary gods and goddesses back to the Earth. We assigned their energies to the task of assisting with World peace, the protection of women and children from abuse, and the end of terrorism and violence. (We were told by Spirit that many of these huge beings were Titans from the planet Titanus and the planet Karnak.)

These words were engraved in English on a wall in one of the temples: "Let us discover the significance of birth and the joy of living."

I was very moved by the energy at Karnak, as were many of the group. I would have loved to have been able to stay several hours there among the columns.

At each site we visited, we were required to have one-pound notes to pay the people who took care of the rest rooms. Sometimes the attendants handed us toilet tissue and sometimes we had to use our own. But we were always expected to pay.

We visited the ancient site of Memphis and lowered the etheric blueprint of the original city back into the third dimension. Many temple names became a blur to me as I continued stretching my energy and focusing on the big picture of our mission.

One night while we were on the cruise, we were invited to have a party. Since everyone was encouraged to wear Egyptian dress, most people either bought or rented costumes from the gift shop aboard the ship. I had brought an Egyptian dress and jewelry from home. The items had been given to me several years before.

Half of the ship housed Belgians who were sharing the cruise with us. Although many of us retired about 10:30 p.m., we could hear the party go late into the night.

After the cruise was over, we returned to Cairo and yet another bus ride across the busy city to our hotel in Giza. We were grateful to be able to unpack for a few days.

A few nights before the Equinox, the group that met each night to meditate, met etherically in the chambers under the Sphinx during meditation. They met to do the necessary ritual to open Star Gates 42 through 47. (These Star Gates had been closed since the curse was established 21,000 years ago.) The rainbow bridge of energy – the pathway for the capstone – had to move through these Star Gates to arrive over Giza.

We left a portion of our energies in this chamber for three days. The second day we placed a portion of our consciousness aboard the capstone itself. To me, it felt like an actual Starship made of a crystalline substance. For most of this group, it was the first time they had had to challenge themselves, while conscious, to hold their focus in three places simultaneously.

In meditation I had been told that we were to have people both inside and outside the pyramid during the landing of the capstone. I was told the Federation needed columns of energy from each corner of the pyramid to balance and ground the capstone.

The night before, I approached the tour agent with this information to give her one last opportunity to cooperate.

She refused. She declared she knew what she was doing and that we were all to be in the King's Chamber and would <u>later</u> go to the various corners.

I also requested that the tour agent not burn sage or incense in the King's Chamber during the ceremony because of my allergies to these substances and the allergies of others.

Her reply was, "It's a big room."

The group met for a meditation. I explained the need for each individual to receive their own information about where they were to be. I advised each person to ask if they should be inside or outside, and if their answer was "outside," question in which direction they were to stand.

We retired early that night to prepare for an early rising the next morning.

We were to be at the bus at 4:30 a.m. to go to the pyramids. (The tour agent had paid the guards extra for permission for the group to go inside the Great Pyramid for three hours.)

I knew the capstone landing was to begin at 5:47 a.m.

The agent and most of the group went inside. Seven persons were standing with me after the others had left to enter the Pyramid. Each person knew exactly where he/she was to go without my even having to tell them. I was very proud of the way they had paid attention to their own guidance.

I explained to George, the tour coordinator, that some of us needed to stand outside at the various corners of the Pyramid. He was distressed, but spoke with the guards.

One guard accompanied each group of two people to their respective sites. The guards wore and carried guns. They did not speak English. They did not understand what we were doing. (Apparently, others who had come to the Pyramid requiring special attention had wanted to climb to the top, or wanted to go into the inner chambers.) We took our places in the dark.

I seated myself in the lotus position on one of the corner stones. The stone was very cold, but I was determined to tune in. My friend from Buffalo chose to stand.

The two of us became totally silent and still. Not a muscle moved. The guard became very frightened. He could not determine if we were asleep, dead or what.

He paced up and down, his walkie-talkie squawking in Egyptian, with much static. He shifted his gun and chain smoked. Occasionally, he inquired, "Lady?" loudly.

We never moved, in spite of the mosquitoes landing on our faces. The energy was intense. The situation was tense . . .

Then, we connected and claimed the energy of the group for the

Hierarchy, the Cosmic Christ Consciousness, the Federation and all members present in Egypt and everywhere on the planet.

As we drew back to our bodies, the parts of our consciousness from beneath the Sphinx and the parts aboard the capstone, a roaring took place in our heads and up and down our spines. We connected to the central core energy of the Earth and the landing began.

There was a physical reaction in our bodies when the capstone lowered, and a distinctive sound when it locked into the grid. The sound was almost like tumblers fitting into place and locking.

The landing was complete at 6:02 a.m.

My friend from Buffalo and I left our post and walked to the other corners of the Pyramid to join physically with our friends and their guards. Our guard went with us, of course, grinning from ear to ear with relief. The other six had experienced similar reactions and were just as elated and high as we were. We all laughed and were happy as we went from corner to corner rejoining each other. Then we all gathered at the entrance to the Pyramid. There, we decided to make the climb into the King's Chamber.

We could hear the group inside still singing the agent's chants. She had refused to accept the one that Spirit had given to me.

When we reached the King's Chamber, we noticed many of our group standing in each of the four corners of the room, rather than in the circle. They were quietly chanting to themselves RA MA NA HA SA HO. We waited until the group had dispersed and moved to the Queen's Chamber before we entered the King's Chamber. We lay on the floor for a while, just to experience the intensity of the energy and to give permission for the gradual increase in frequency in the grid system. We were told the frequency would be progressively increased for the six weeks that followed the capping.

When the Agent's group moved to the Well, we moved to the Queen's Chamber and on out of the pyramid. We walked back across the street and went to breakfast. When we had awakened that morning so early, we considered we might return to the motel and sleep. However, we were so high, we did not need to sleep!

We laughed our way through breakfast and then a group of us from the Namaste network spent several hours by the pool chatting, painting and reading. We shared a lunch of pizza, and I went inside to take a nap.

Some of the others went on yet another shopping expedition. The vendors were so demanding and aggressive I was not in the least bit interested. Also, I was aware that we might need our funds later for other more basic necessities.

Later that day George, the tour coordinator, told us that some of the checks that the woman agent in charge of our money had given the tour company in San Francisco had bounced; that we were in jeopardy of losing our services as of noon the following day unless she or the group came up with $4,400 in CASH. And George's company, where he'd worked for seventeen years, threatened to fire him if he didn't "fix" the situation.

The tour agent barricaded herself in her room and refused to answer the phone or the door.

One of the members of the Namaste group pushed a note under her door requesting she speak with him. The note stated he would help her in whatever way he could.

He was already aware that there were financial problems. When he and his partner had arrived in New York on their way to join us in Egypt, the tour agent was having heated words with the people of Olympia Air. They demanded she come up with additional funds of about $1,200. She kept negotiating with them until they lowered the amount to around $750. She claimed to have no cash and convinced them to take her personal check.

The tour agent later admitted that three times her Guidance had directed her not to go on the trip, but to return to Sedona to take care of the financial matters. She made the decision to come to make sure "everything got done," <u>even though her Guidance advised her to return to Sedona</u>. She did not bring the financial records of her transactions with the tour company with her to Egypt. She later admitted that she had spent some of our money, which was to go to the hotels, airlines and guides.

We were all disturbed by the news, but boarded the bus for the day's sightseeing.

Even though there were two buses, this time we all got on one. A couple of people were late. Everyone was nervous. Rumors had been passing back and forth, but no one had spoken to the collective group about what was happening.

Some of the people had been pre-warned, through correspondence with my sponsor in Portland, that the agent had been less than honest with her and me. They were a little less shocked than the others.

People began chanting my name and insisting that I get up and say something about the situation. I had deliberately NOT spoken in any of the group meetings the agent had arranged because she clearly made no space for this to happen after the first meeting, when she did invite my comments.

My Guidance had been that I should not energetically engage with her. I did my best not to get into a public state of conflict with her.

As I got up to take the tour-guide mike to speak, the agent's friend from Sedona stood up, pointed her finger at me and screamed, "I'm not listening to anything this bitch has to say. She doesn't know anything. I'm the one who knows what's going on here. I'm the one who should be talking. I should be leading this trip now!"

I was shocked, but calm. I assured her that I would be glad to turn the mike over to her so she could give her version of what was happening as soon as I finished saying what Spirit was asking me to say.

She continued to scream, "Let me off this bus! I'm not listening to anything you have to say!"

At this point the bus driver, who didn't understand much English, opened the doors and the woman got off. Two of her friends followed her.

The doors closed and I began explaining – not about finances – but that the agent had tapped into a very real fear; that she was irrationally reacting to the present events because she had connected to another set of circumstances that had happened 2,700 years before. At this point an actor, 6'5" tall, about sixty years old, with a booming voice and shaved head covered with an Egyptian skull cap pointed his finger menacingly at me and began yelling, "Liar, liar, you don't know what you are talking about. I'm not going to listen to anymore of your lies. Let me off this bus!"

The door opened, and he got off.

Some of Spirit's assignments are more difficult than others. I swore I would never again be involved in a tour with so many people, especially people I did not know.

The bus was shaking with the energies of its startled passengers. I still felt calm – violated, but calm.

I shrugged my shoulders and began speaking again, giving my version of the event 2,700 years before when members of this particular group had actually killed the agent for being out of spiritual integrity. I also explained that I understood that as spirits, we had agreed to come back at this time with her to give her repeated opportunities to come into spiritual and financial integrity; that we had a responsibility to remain conscious of this, regardless of her behavior, and to pray for the situation. I then offered the mike to the agitated woman as she climbed back into the bus.

The group stopped the woman and demanded she calm herself before she spoke, which she did.

The woman explained that she and another member of the group had been acting as the agent's financial advisors during the trip's preparation. She went on to explain that the day before, they had taken the agent to the tour offices in Cairo and tried to get her to straighten out the financial mess. She had refused, denying that she had done anything wrong. She declared that all of the problems lay with the tour company, which tried to overcharge her.

Speaking further, the woman explained that she and the friend took the agent to lunch and tried again to calm her and get her to agree to do something about the finances. The woman claimed the agent had personally taken advantage of her financially, as well.

The bus got us to the Cairo museum. We were to be there for two hours. (It would take a week to see everything.) I prayed that while we were there, Spirit would make it possible for our friend, who had stayed behind, to be able to reason with the agent.

A few of us left the guides and went to see the Tut exhibit and the statues of Akhenaton. There we had amazing energetic experiences. During our viewing at the museum, the tall male actor who had called me a liar aboard the bus, came up to me and apologized. He said he felt he was being affected by energies from 2,700 years ago and that he was currently working through the feelings he had experienced. The women never did apologize.

We were then taken on another shopping trip. I felt as if I were walking around in a daze. The entire scene was unbelievable and unreal.

When we finally returned to the hotel, I went to the room of our friends who had stayed behind to give them their return airline tickets. George, the tour coordinator, had given us our return tickets earlier in the day. We felt better, just having our return tickets in our hands.

We then learned from George that unless we came up with the $4,400, our nightly room rate would increase from $55 to $143. Several of us got together to discuss our options.

Our friend who had stayed behind had encountered the tour agent having breakfast in the coffee shop and assured us after meeting with her that she was emotionally and mentally incapable – and unwilling – to be of any assistance; the group was on its own to find a solution to the difficulty.

We agreed to have a group meeting before what was supposed to be our "celebration dinner," and to ask each person to contribute $100 toward solving the problem.

Some of the people were leaving the next day and did not want to contribute. Some were leaving the next day, but were willing to contribute for the group benefit. Some were unwilling to contribute because they had been through a similar scenario before and didn't feel the agent should "get away with this." In fact, they wanted to turn her over to the tourism police who would confiscate her ticket and her passport until she came up with the money. Someone mentioned that she had left Athens owing money there too!

The atmosphere was mixed hostility, acceptance, resignation, compassion and forgiveness.

Our friends from New Mexico assumed the role of "group parents." They accepted money and made a list of contributors and those who agreed to contribute after they returned to the States. Some people had to go to the bank and draw money on their credit cards because they had over shopped or simply were not prepared for any financial emergency. Three of the group agreed to get money on their own credit cards to finish out the amount they were not able to collect immediately.

Our friends from New Mexico volunteered to remain in Cairo the next day and to go with George, the tour coordinator, to the tour company with the money. This would assure us of hotel accommodations. Several members of the group were to leave that next day for the Sinai. I, as well as another group, was taking a bus to Alexandria.

Before dinner that night, my friend from New Mexico notified me that the tour agent was in the driveway getting a taxi to leave the hotel. Some of the group members were trying to detain her. My friend felt I should come with him to make sure nobody harmed her.

Going with him was the <u>last</u> thing I wanted to do! I wanted to be home. I wanted this whole nightmare to end. I was reaching the end of my patience, but, of course, I went with him.

Several members of the group were gathered around the agent who sat on a ledge at the edge of the driveway. As we approached her, we heard her say tearfully, "I just don't understand why everyone is being so mean to me. I tried so hard to make this trip perfect for everyone and everything has been so hard."

The agent claimed she was on her way to the Embassy to speak with a man she had apparently been talking with on the telephone.

Group members were trying to console her, to get her to go back to her room. They wanted her to talk with George, to come up with a solution to the problem instead of once again running away from the responsibilities she had accepted.

She finally agreed to go back inside and to talk with George, but only if she could speak with him alone. It was obvious her nerves were breaking down and that she was not capable of tracking mentally or of focusing on any kind of solution to anything she had created. Then my friend learned she had managed to get her ticket changed so she could get herself out of Egypt the next day and back to the States.

At that, he recommended we assist her to leave Egypt, rather than get her involved with the Embassy, or any other authorities. We agreed to do that, and she left the next day.

She did make it back to Sedona, because when I got back home, my check cleared. Also, she had a friend send us all a note saying her father had died the day the capstone was lowered on the pyramid, and that she would be in Florida dealing with her grief and unavailable. The day she left, several members of the group did go to the Sinai. Our friends from New Mexico stayed in Cairo to deal with the tour company and 13 of us went to Alexandria to lower the blueprint and previous contents of the Library of Alexandria into the Third Dimension from where it had been stored in the Fifth Dimension.

The trip was much less tense, even though many of the members of the group were not aware – nor willing – to participate in the lowering of the energies. They were nevertheless respectful of our need to do so.

Our guide was a sweet, young, well-spoken tourism graduate student from the University.

The Library of Alexandria, as it was being reconstructed, is a beautiful, modern version of various pyramidal forms, with lots of glass overlooking the sea. It is located very near, or next to, a military base.

Because of the construction, we were not permitted to be on the premises nor to even be across the street, since this is a military installation. Fortunately, however, there was a small green strip of park between the Library and the military base.

The bus driver dropped us off next to the green strip and a few of us gathered inconspicuously next to a tall military monument.

We prayed and called forth the original architect of the Library, whose name one of our group had researched. We also called forth Ramses, Akhenaton, and the energies of many well-known spiritual scholars, such as Socrates, Plato, Aristotle and others. We asked them to lower the blueprint of the building and its contents. We also called forth the energies of all nations of the World to release copies of documents containing the true history of the World.

(In October 2011 a group of us returned to Alexandria and the library.

Most of the contents of the library have been digitalized and are now available free through any computer.)

We then hopped back into the bus, elated and ready to eat.

We were taken to a wonderful restaurant overlooking the sea. We were fed more rice and meat. Then we were rushed to a jewelry museum for a 12 minute run-through to see the jewelry of the family of Mohammed Ali (not the boxer). It was one of the most amazing mansions I had ever seen. This could have been an all-day visit, with all there was to see just in the decorations of the mansion itself.

We were then driven to the Citadel By the Sea and took pictures of the Mediterranean.

By then I was exhausted and remained inside the bus. I did, however, negotiate with a young man outside the window to buy a shell for my sea shell collection.

That night we had our last meditation and completed our energy work. We were informed that the volume of the Cosmic Christ Consciousness energies coming into the grid through the pyramid was continuing to increase and would for the next six weeks, as we had already been informed. We were very much aware of the energies in our bodies.

The following morning we awakened early again, but with such a sense of excitement! We were going home!

We were at the airport early and passed easily through customs. We spent our remaining "pounds" in the gift shops there, then waited.

The trip back was longer than the one going over – 10 1/2 hours. We were aching, and many of the members were sick with stomach problems and sinus infections.

We were all VERY ready for American food. However, the food on the plane was once again disappointing, even though vegetarian meals had been arranged to accommodate us, before we left Egypt.

My ticket home to Oklahoma City from New York was not valid for two days, so my friend from Buffalo and I checked into a Holiday Inn. She graciously postponed her trip home to Buffalo to stay with me.

We stayed in bed most of the two days sleeping, reading, watching an occasional movie and eating, mostly from room service. We tried to get our bodies to agree with the time change before going home to families who would expect us to eat and sleep when they did! My trip home from New York was peaceful. I did not have to sit next to anyone, so was able to stretch out, read and nap. Charlie met me at the airport with a big smile, a hug and yellow roses.

I was so tired that I found speaking difficult. I tried to give a mini-version of what had happened on the trip, but did it very inadequately. For several days he felt that I was just "not back." I felt as if I were in shock. I was grateful to be home, yet I was not able to do anything except sleep and lay in the chaise lounge. I did read the mail, but felt unable to answer it adequately.

The phone rang incessantly. So many persons called wanting to know how the trip went. All I could say was that it went well, energetically, but that I had never been so glad to be through with an assignment! I had personally picked up two large aspects of my Oversoul and was in the process of integrating these. I had also released an aspect of myself to the Oversoul. I was both grieving and integrating. I had no idea how to be the "new me."

Since the Egypt trip, people have asked why did I suppose I had to do such an important mission under such adverse and strenuous circumstances.

All I can say is that apparently, these particular persons, as a group in Spirit, agreed to do this mission to give the tour agent the opportunity to serve and to come into integrity. All of us set ourselves up for a massive lesson in discernment. We did just that, and under the circumstances, we did it very well.

I am sure that each person who was there had his/her own version of what took place and why. As with an accident, for example, each person witnesses it from their own prospective. We do not see things AS THEY ARE. We see things as WE ARE.

I take responsibility for my part in the creation of the events of this trip.

I will always appreciate, from the bottom of my heart, everyone who went physically on the trip, and their sacrifices. I am also so grateful for the financial support of so many and for the prayers for our safety and the success of the mission. For those who stayed at home, but accompanied us energetically, every day, thank you, thank you, thank you. Without each of you, it would not have been possible to have accomplished the mission. Don't discount your importance. I, personally, felt good about the outcome of the trip and am hopeful for Humanity and the planet.

For the first few weeks after coming home, I did not feel "driven," as I had since 1985 when I agreed to begin traveling for the Spiritual Hierarchy and the Federation to do such missions. Finally being free of feeling driven felt strange to me.

According to Spirit, with this mission I had now completed the singularly most important part of what I agreed to come to Earth to do. That in itself brought relief, but also the next question: What do I do next? I'm being facetious here, but there is an old Zen saying that the gracious women who made up the address list of those who went on the trip and sent it out, attached these words to that list, "After ecstasy, the laundry..."

52

Activation of Seed Crystals

1996

At the first Sunday night meditation of our group in Oklahoma City after I returned home from Egypt, the Hierarchy asked us to focus energies on beginning to activate and release large seed crystals from their holding patterns. These seed crystals were planted within the Earth at the time of her preparation for Human life.

According to the Hierarchy, Earth and the Human species have now reached a point in evolution in which the crystals are ready to be released and activated. The anchoring of the capstone and the doubling of the grid system made this possible.

When the etheric tip of the crystal touches the atmosphere and is activated, a huge laser beam of energy shoots out into space to the galaxy and to the group that originally planted the crystals within the Earth. The group is thereby notified that we are ready to receive contact once again.

The meditation group was asked to focus on a symbol in the foyer of the Chartres Cathedral in France. This symbol is known as the labyrinth. It is inlaid in the stone floor and is approximately 42 feet in diameter. Legend has it that the design was part of King Solomon's Temple and was carried to France by the Knights Templar.

This is a Spiritual Tool Whose Time has Come

With one part of our consciousness, group members traced the pattern, or walked the labyrinth. With another part of our consciousness, we focused on the location of the crystals to be activated.

The first crystals to be activated were located as follows: in the Mediterranean; Stonehenge; Mount Shasta; Jenny Lake (at the base of the Grand Teton); Canyon Lake (near Wimberley, Texas); Banff, Canada; Milwaukee, Wisconsin; Detroit, Michigan; and Tuscaloosa, Alabama.

After we had assisted in the activation of the first few crystals, I began receiving calls from people who wanted readings. Spirit gave an assignment through me to everyone who called to activate a crystal. A woman called from Albuquerque. She and her family were on their way to Nova Scotia. Spirit told her where to go to activate a crystal off the coast of Nova Scotia. Also, a man called from Michigan and was asked to activate one off Point Barrow in Alaska.

Group members were made aware of the labyrinth symbol before the request to activate the crystals came in our meditation.

One of the members of our meditation group attended a seminar presented by Dr. Artress and lent us a copy of her book *Walking a Sacred Path: Rediscovering the Labyrinth as a Spiritual Tool*. (It is published by Riverhead Books, a division of Putnam Sons Publishers.) Jean Houston has been using the labyrinth as a tool in her Mystery School for several years. This tool can help us prepare ourselves for the "transformation of Human personality in process" and aid us in accomplishing a "shift in consciousness" as we seek spiritual maturity as a species.

According to Dr. Artress, this ancient mystical tool dropped out of Human awareness more than 350 years ago.

Dr. Artress takes this symbol around the country, offering workshops where people walk the labyrinth. This process seems to offer people gifts of insight, wisdom and peace. Some report feeling as if they have touched the Holy Spirit.

Dr. Artress and her group have created a large portable canvas reproduction of the labyrinth. Another reproduction has been made in carpet at Grace Cathedral in San Francisco, and one in tile on the terrace there.

Dr. Artress believes the labyrinth is an incredible gift: "It is grace busting into our experience to help us be the co-creators we are, instead of the creation destroyers we have become."

She goes on, "A division has emerged in Western culture. We have confused religion with spirituality, the container with the process. Religion is the outward form, the 'container,' specifically the liturgy and all the acts of worship that teach, praise, and give thanks to God.

"Spirituality is the inward activity of growth and maturation that happens in each of us."

Dr. Artress quotes Ruth Burroughs in her book, *Guidelines to Mystical Prayer*: "Lights-on mysticism is explicit, conscious experience of Divine presence. These experiences awaken us, encourage us, and sustain us when our daily lives seem dry and uneventful. They help us discover that we are loved.

"Lights-off mysticism is devoid of direct, conscious contact with the Divine. Instead, we are sustained through faith, the teachings of the church and Scripture.

"Those who attempt to teach spirituality without some personal experience of the Sacred are like the painter who has never painted a picture. They have an image somewhere inside them, but neither they nor the World will ever benefit from it.

"Those who have had the experience of the Sacred, teach from their very Presence."

I love her saying: "Religion is for those who are scared to death of hell. Spirituality is for those who have been there."

"Spiritual Law is never defeated.
It operates regardless of our approval or disapproval."

53

Texas

After my return home from Egypt, I had a few weeks to recuperate and catch up.

However, I noticed I was very uncomfortable being at home. I kept feeling I wanted – needed – to go "home." But I didn't know where to go to satisfy the feeling. I felt very much like a different person than the one who had gone to Egypt. I could not as yet figure out at the personality level how to express all the consciousness I had picked up there.

My friend Mark called from North Carolina and invited me to come to Dallas for a day and a night to visit, since he would be working there for a week.

It seemed the perfect answer: I would drive myself, spend time <u>by myself</u> listening to what I should do next, and hopefully see the bluebonnets of my home state. I felt I needed to see something familiar, because my home surroundings and Charlie felt very strange. The same day Mark called, I received another call from a friend in San Marcos. That was enough synchronicity for me. I told Charlie I was going.

He was very disappointed at my leaving again so soon after getting home. He felt rejected that I seemed to prefer to be alone, or with someone else, rather than at home with him.

On my way to Texas, at the first sight of the bluebonnets, I burst into tears and had to stop driving. Something in my solar plexus was being healed, released and changed. Once I was with Mark and, later, my other friends in Texas, everything seemed to make me emotional and I'd burst into tears. I had no logical explanation for this. I later realized it was cellular memory that was still in the body from Betty Jean's life. Although she had returned to the Oversoul, I still had her cellular memories to deal with. This is one of the challenges of being a walk-in. Sometimes we get blind-sided emotionally by things the previous entity has experienced or identifies with that mean little to us or to our planetary mission. This is the reason I chose the word "Pentimento" for the title of this book. The previous entity's experiences occasionally "bleed through" into my daily experience unexpectedly, just like a painting that has been painted over a previous painting sometimes begins to bleed through the new painting.

I drove around in the Texas hill country, alone, listening and watching for signs. For many years I had felt that ultimately, I would have a home, a Namaste Center, in the hill country of Texas. It would be a place where people could come to rest and to open up to their forms of creativity. The area location felt right, but I did not see the exact place. This, and the location, was a dream Ed and I had shared and intended to actualize after our marriage. I thought the dream had died with his death.

I met several interesting metaphysical people in Wimberley, Texas. A man at the metaphysical bookstore there told me that Wimberley was on the same ley line as the Great Pyramid in Giza. At his statement I had goose bumps and told him I had been there only a few days before.

I asked him if he knew of a lake nearby. He, and several other people, mentioned Canyon Lake, so I drove out there. As I headed my car in the direction of the lake, energy intensified in my body, and I knew I was going in the right direction.

When I arrived at the lake, in my inner vision I saw the crystal beneath the water. I split my consciousness, traced the labyrinth and awakened the crystal. It began to surface etherically.

As soon as this was accomplished, I felt complete again and drove back to San Marcos and had dinner with a friend. Later, while I was driving back to Oklahoma, I felt no less emotional, because I became aware the guidance was suggesting it was time to tell Charlie that I needed him to move out.

At the logical level, this made no sense to me. However, on the emotional level I realized I could not continue living in an environment requiring censorship of all my thoughts, while monitoring his reactions before I expressed them. The environment with him in it no longer felt emotionally safe. In order to do my work, I needed an emotionally safe space in which to recuperate between assignments.

He was shocked and hurt when I told him of my decision.

During the days that followed, he had direct communication from Spirit on two different occasions. Both times he was in the bathtub and he said before each message he felt as if he had been hit in the head. One message concerned judgment; that he was in judgment of me (which he had denied previously) and that the judgment had to stop if we were to stay together. (He realized he had inherited from his family the "right," or tendency, to judge.)

The other message concerned his attempts to control relationships "passively." He had heard that before in counseling sessions, but had never understood.

After that, our relationship changed and we were able to communicate more fully and honestly. We were both more able to let it be "one day at a time" and to enjoy it for what it was. We discovered that our relationship did not have to die, but the way we were living it had to change.

There comes a time in life when it is as if your casing is too tight, like a snake needing to shed its skin; when you can no longer continue the way you're going. Sometimes one finds this to be in a relationship, a job, your residence, or the <u>way</u> you are living. You have two choices: you can die or you can change.

I became aware – and it seems proper to mention it here – that the energy increase was/is bringing inherited and genetic beliefs to the forefront for people. Beliefs come from our culture, family heritage, or from our parents at the time we were conceived.

Events in people's lives will now clearly reveal these beliefs to them, as well as the effects that living out the beliefs will/is having on their lives.

It is indeed time to make personal choices about what we <u>choose</u> to believe, instead of <u>continuing</u> to live unconsciously out of these beliefs.

The last of June on my trip to Mexico to swim with the dolphins, a seed crystal was raised off the lighthouse coast point of Isla Mujeres.

I went to Minneapolis in mid-July to present "Insights for the Spiritually Restless," and "Oversoul Communication - Co-creation as a Way of Life." I also did some private sessions and attended the Walk-In Conference.

Several readings were particularly interesting. For one woman, from Japan, a message surfaced that she had come to Earth to assist the healing of the energies between Americans and Japanese with regard to Pearl Harbor, Nagasaki and Hiroshima.

I felt a little uncomfortable suggesting this. Since she was very young and a student, there could not possibly have been any physical connection between her life and these events. However, her body reacted immediately to the information.

Apparently the woman had not been in body at the time of these happenings, but other members of her Oversoul were. She had agreed to come back to heal these events through her physical body, which at the time of our meeting was in pain because of automobile accidents.

I worked with her body using sound and energies, and loosened up the trauma. She rested for a bit in my room while I sought the help of two other healers who were on the trip.

Later, the four of us worked for about two hours. The process was more intense than anything I had ever done. Her body went through tremendous energy releases, which left us all exhausted. It was an expanding experience we will not forget!

Another reading involved a couple who, at the end of their session, asked about their Arabian horses. These two horses had been born in different parts of the country. Yet when we tuned in to them, we were told that the consciousness that now inhabited the two bodies had last inhabited the body of one elephant in India. But now it had chosen to come back in the form of two agile and beautiful horses, and to come back together in one location.

The owners had a good laugh because the horses exhibit behaviors not common to horses. For example, they'd raise one foot and hold it up, like an elephant, while throwing their heads back like an elephant tossing its trunk. When anyone was around who had been eating peanuts or even peanut butter sandwiches, the horses would get in the face of the person who smelled of peanuts.

Prior to the reading, I had no belief in the transmigration of animal consciousness from one species to another. I still do not believe in transmigration from animal consciousness to Human consciousness, but my beliefs are constantly changing based on my experiences . . .

To continue about readings, one person received one about his father who was old (in his 90s) and seemed to have no reason for hanging on to life in his body. He slept much of the time. The person was told that many people who do not finish their missions before their bodies wear out begin new lives before their present lives are finished, in the form of babies. In other words, in the case of this old man, a baby had already been born – and was living – which he (the elderly man) would become once he died. He was stretching his consciousness between the two life streams – between the baby and his life as an elderly man – each body sleeping much of the time.

In such cases, persons in old bodies become more and more childish, as the greater part of the consciousness moves to the baby. The process is complete when the aged persons finally relinquish their adult bodies in death.

This may be one explanation of senility and comas . . .

On this same trip, I met an interesting woman, Connie Shaw, from Loveland, Colorado. She had been a visionary of the Mother Mary and had written a book called *Mary's Miracles and Prophecies*. It was about her visions and other Mary visionaries. She had also made 20 trips to India and many visits to Sai Baba's ashram, besides having traveled in 50 countries.

Although I had never personally felt close to Mary or Sai Baba, during our conversation Connie and I found we had many similar beliefs:

a. We must be willing to move in spiritual awareness beyond phenomenon, no matter how pleasant (the phenomenon) might be.

b. When one needs to cross the river, the boat will be there. c. Go where you are invited.

d. Those of us who have access to Spirit are not spiritual vending machines. We have a right to privacy and a right not to be available to others every waking hour.

e. Each person must ultimately attune within and receive his/her own guidance in order to grow and attain. We cannot ride on another's spiritual coattails.

f. The reward for service (well done) is more service.

Time spent at the walk-in conference in Minnesota was good. Several scheduled presenters did not show, so I did more than one session.

The last evening in Minneapolis, after completing all of the presentations and readings, I stretched out on the carpet to rest my back and eyes before dinner.

Almost immediately, balls of energy, about the size of golf balls, began making their way up my spine, exploding in my throat and third eye.

The process was uncomfortable, but not painful. It continued for about two hours.

When it slowed, I arose and got into the bathtub to discharge some of the energy, which was beginning to make me nauseous. The energies quieted and I decided to forego dinner and go to bed.

I slept soundly until about 1:30 a.m. when I awakened thinking I had to go to the bathroom.

When I had fully come into my body, I realized that my throat was extremely sore. Upon looking in the mirror I discovered blisters on my tongue and throat. I felt as if they continued down my throat all the way to my sternum.

I gargled, prayed and went back to bed. Since I could not sleep, I continued reading *Mary's Miracles and Prophecies*. The chapter was entitled, "Symptoms of Spiritual Awakening - Samadhi Activation." It was about the possibility of Kundalini activation and explained many symptoms people are undergoing.

Although relieved to have the information, I still had to go home and deal with a very sore throat . . .

"Anticipate the future with hope and gratitude for the present."

54

The Spiritual Gift of Discernment and Discernment About Predictions

When I was still an Episcopalian and a member of a Bible study group, we read about the various spiritual gifts that are available to us from the Holy Spirit.

Since I did not want a gift that others would know I had, I prayed for the gift of discernment.

Today, of all the spiritual gifts I have received from my soul, I consider the gift of discernment my greatest asset.

I recommend that you ask your soul to establish an inner Discernment factor within you.

IT IS GROWING MORE AND MORE IMPORTANT TO USE YOUR OWN DISCERNMENT: BELIEVE ONLY WHAT FEELS RIGHT TO YOU, REGARDLESS OF SEEMING ENDORSEMENTS BY PEOPLE YOU WOULD NORMALLY TRUST. EXPOSE YOURSELF ONLY TO WORKSHOPS AND CONFERENCES THAT FEEL CORRECT TO YOU AS INDIVIDUALS. ALWAYS TRUST YOUR OWN GUT-LEVEL FEELINGS ABOUT THE ENERGY OF EVERYTHING YOU READ AND HEAR! MANY TESTS FROM OUR SOULS ARE CREATED TO EXAMINE OUR OWN ENERGETIC JUDGMENT.

In this Chapter I want to discuss <u>discernment</u> and its importance to you.

Many psychic nets are being put into place over some of the major energy vortexes of the Earth, places where spiritual seekers normally gather. The reasons for these psychic nets is (a) to make soul communication difficult and (b) so the impostors of the "dark force" cannot connect themselves as your guides and find channels for their energies. (The nets over Mount Shasta, Santa Fe and Sedona have recently been removed.)

Many of you do not believe in a "dark force," convinced that everything is of God.

I believe everything originated with God, was created by God. However, there are aspects of energy and parts of souls that have forgotten they are God and are standing in the shadows. These I refer to as "the dark force."

These entities are astral or lower Fourth Dimensional beings. They are beings who have died in a state of confusion and without spiritual awareness. They actively work to stop the spread of spiritual awareness on the Earth. They are very clever and very observant.

These astral entities masquerade or clone themselves in the image of high spiritual teachers and enter the meditations and dream states of spiritual seekers; they interfere energetically with the spread of truth and soul communication.

These impostors create Master Degree Lessons in DISCERNMENT for us! For example, if you do not feel divine love and compassion coming from an entity who approaches you, or from one you hear being channeled by another – whether in person or in written form – be very wary of the information being presented.

Much is being said by these beings about the destruction of Earth, erroneous timing and dates of energy openings. Such information is to produce fear in spiritual seekers and to limit the conscious use of these energies by spiritual seekers.

Keep in mind that true spiritual masters <u>do not preach fear or intimidation</u>. They teach connection to God, peace, love, joy and harmony!

Because of the high-energy vibrations being sent to Earth, people are rapidly opening up to them (the energies) or they are leaving this dimension. Those actively working to hear spiritually, or to become aware psychically, must act with discernment. Put another way, if we open ourselves to the world of Spirit without proper knowledge of how to do this safely and effectively, we CAN communicate, but with disastrous results.

Many entities in the astral realms observe this phenomenon – of masses of Earth entities choosing to open to channel or communicate with spiritual entities.

Many astral entities are very enterprising and energetically strong. They can impersonate such entities as Babaji, Hilarion, St. Germain, Michael, Matthew, Andrew, Mark, John, Luke, Gabriel, Kuthumi, Ashtar, Sananda and others to deliver their messages. Thus they can use this means to control individuals and groups. They seek to promote what I call "guruISM" – making you believe you need someone outside yourself to teach you and from whom you are to get your answers. They preach, "Follow me. I have the answers."

I personally receive many tapes, books and written channeled manuscripts to review every month. Much of what is coming through – AND PUBLISHED – is coming from these entities. Their desire is to confuse, increase fear and control.

We will continue to be subjected to such information, which is fear-based, oppressive and disheartening.

I am not trying to discourage people from meditating or from exposing themselves to material being brought in by others. I <u>am saying this</u> to admonish people to pray to their souls for the gift of discernment of truth and energies!

Seek communion with only your own soul at all times. To seek communication directly with God, the Source, the Creator, keep the name of God on your lips, and in your minds and hearts at all times through the use of the mantra of GOD. Breathe the word GOD!

At all times, request the protection of the ARCHANGEL MICHAEL and your own Guardian Angel, especially before meditation and before sleep.

It is good practice to challenge any entity or energy that approaches you in meditation or otherwise by asking, "Are you of the Light?" Confront the entity three times. By spiritual law, entities can lie to you twice, but not three times! I later realized that they could lie about being of the Light, because everything is made of light. I changed my question to, "Are you of the vibration of the Cosmic Christ Consciousness?"

Usually if you challenge an entity, it will disintegrate or disappear and seek someone who is less aware.

It is also very important to deal with energies by approaching them as a master yourself, not as a student. If you stand in the truth of that identity, you are very unlikely to fall for an untruth.

Everyone has the authority to call upon the Archangel Michael for assistance. He has accepted this commission to protect us and the Earth from any evil or interfering influences.

I also recommend sealing the room in which you are meditating before beginning your reflection. Say something like, "As I enter the realm of Spirit (or seek to communicate with my higher self or Oversoul), I call forth the energies of the ARCHANGEL MICHAEL and the Band of Mercy to clear this room of any negative energies or entities." (Pause for a time so such can be accomplished.)

Then proceed with an intention to seal: "I deliberately seal this room on the north, south, east and west. I seal the ceiling and the floor against any negative entities or energies. I invite my master guides, teachers and Angels to be present and receptive to me. I open myself as a channel for the power of the Holy Spirit, the Cosmic Christ Consciousness and the 49 Rays of God, and I ask that only the highest form of truth be allowed to come through me."

I highly recommend that you only open yourself energetically to your own Oversoul. Ask to communicate with the highest level of your own Oversoul that your physical body can tolerate. Become familiar with this energy and make an agreement, an intention, that this level of your Oversoul will be your "gatekeeper" or your "receptionist" and that if any other spirit or soul desires to speak with you it will first speak to this level of your Oversoul, and the message will be given to you, if it is your business to communicate with this Spirit and to your highest good.

Following is an experience that will help explain why discernment is so important.

For several years I had been uncomfortable with an energy I had heard several persons channel and had read much about. This energy came through in the name of "Sananda."

When I first began hearing this name, I asked people, "Who is that? Why do I not know this energy in the world of Spirit?"

I was told by these people that it was a new name for the energies that were on the Earth plane as the Master Jesus. Some of the people said they were told by their Spirits to refer to this energy as Jesus Sananda to identify Jesus' energy now on the space ships (Sananda being his "space name").

I became even more uncomfortable, as I was personally subjected to people channeling energies that called themselves by this name. I would feel excruciating pain in my body and psychic discomfort. Therefore, in my normal "no nonsense" approach, I confronted my soul for MY truth concerning this matter.

The response: "Sananda is an anachronism."

When I sought the dictionary for an exact definition of the word, I learned it referred to, "A crediting of a person or thing to a time other than the actual period; anything out of its proper historical time."

I further confronted my spiritual guidance. "Is this the Christ energy of the one who walked the Earth as the Master Jesus?"

The response from soul was, "No. Sananda is an energy 'thought form' created by the Silver Ray (an aspect of God) as a challenge or lesson modality for the learning of DISCERNMENT during this time in the spiritual evolution of Humanity. It is also an 'acronym,' a created word to represent an energy which would explode star seed memory in the DNA of individuals at this time."

There is another energy being channeled that is an extraterrestrial, personality-centered individual calling himself "Lord Michael," and hoping people will accept him as the ARCHANGEL MICHAEL, which he certainly is NOT. Be aware of this!

We all must make our own discernments about this and any other energy to which we are subjected. Use your own discernment when listening to channeling and when having personal psychic readings done through others.

We must become our own authorities.

For example, I am not your authority, nor is anyone else. I write about my experiences and what I hear from my Spirit. You must discern your own truth always, otherwise you may be drawn off your path into meaningless activities that have nothing to do with your soul's mission.

Seek to communicate with your soul. Your guides will then be members of your Oversoul who have a vested interest in communicating with you personally and in assisting you in accomplishing that which you agreed to do before you came to the Earth.

Practicing discernment energetically in the physical is also important.

When we develop our level of discernment and soul communication, we know where to be when, and with whom to associate. We are able to determine when individuals do not have our highest good in mind, as well as knowing that every individual may not be honest.

When I first became involved with metaphysics and spiritual studies, I was extremely naive. I believed all people seeking spiritual enlightenment or studying spiritual principles were honest. We, as Humans, are struggling with separation, with overcoming the belief that we are separate from God, of not accepting our omniscience: our old beliefs that we are to be humble, or to practice humility, all beliefs that get in the way of our accepting ourselves as co-creators.

It is not separation to determine energetically that you choose not to associate with individuals whose vibrations are uncomfortable to you. It is not separation to determine energetically that certain persons are not practicing honesty or do not have your highest good in mind. It is not separation if you choose not to associate with such people, even if they are members of your biological family.

It IS SEPARATION, however, to judge them as not a part of God, and therefore not a part of you, and to send them anything less than positive thoughts and Christ Light.

Maintaining that we are separate from God and others is the ultimate act of pride, not humility. But, choosing to "hang out," or associate personally with people whose vibrations are offensive to us is foolish.

(See the Chapter in this book entitled, "Intention, Exorcism, Healing" for related information.)

DISCERNMENT ABOUT PREDICTIONS

Predictions about all kinds of events (mostly negative) are really flying around. <u>Thoughts collect</u> in certain areas, depending upon the events that took place there over the centuries.

It is important to remember that we Humans were given the ability to see the future IN ORDER TO CHANGE IT. We were <u>not</u> given the ability for the purpose of concentrating on the predictions, becoming panic-stricken, or giving up.

Predictions are to set in motion our <u>co-creative abilities to solve them or transmute them. Also it is important to remember a problem cannot be solved at the energetic level it was created. We must seek a higher vibrational answer to the challenges we are facing</u>.

Many people are unaware of their own power. When they read predictions, hear about them or watch such programs on TV, they concentrate <u>unknowingly</u> on the calamities. Such concentration assists in the <u>creation</u> of disasters. We get confronted with this a lot, since we live in what some people refer to as "tornado alley." While the weather forecasters and storm chasers are revving up the audience's emotions about the storm and projecting fear, and in some cases actually hoping it will happen to up their viewing ratings, we have a responsibility to be calling forth the Twenty-first Ray of Climate Control, the Master Eufauchia and the Angel Josiah to orchestrate the Elemental Kingdom to dissipate the energy of the storm.

Earth has three means of dissipating these pockets of negative energy: water, fire and wind. We have the responsibility to use thought and to call on the Violet Flame of Transmutation, the Seventh Ray, the Master Saint Germain and the Angel Zadkiel to dissipate and transmute these pockets of negative energy or potential storms.

This truth helps us to realize the importance of concentrating on what we DESIRE TO HAPPEN, what we DESIRE TO EXPERIENCE, not what we don't desire.

Thoughts are things. They do not dissipate unless they are deliberately dispelled energetically, or canceled or replaced by positive thoughts.

Collectively, Humans <u>have</u> the mental power to change what has been predicted. But it takes concentration, intention, cooperation and the energy of group focus to change what has been put into motion.

Many people in power on Earth consider war <u>economically essential</u>. We have a responsibility to project the thought, "Peace is economically feasible, possible and preferable."

It is the responsibility of all Earth Humans to <u>think</u> and <u>act</u> peacefully.

From my soul I have channeled a CD designed to clear our energy bodies and negative soul record experiences from our cellular bodies.

The CD is called "Release of Fear, Trauma, and Negative Beliefs at the Cellular Level." This tape will also accomplish an exorcism if you have additional energies sharing your body. However, the reaction may require additional energy work through a competent practitioner. It is also best facilitated for you the first time by someone who knows how to channel Seventh Ray energy.

As we learn to listen to our own Souls, our God Selves, we will always be in the right place. It is time for us to become Masters, to learn to materialize our needs and desires instantaneously without the need of fear or lack, to learn and practice the UNIVERSAL LAWS OF CO-CREATION.

55

The Oversoul, Travel and Soul Merger

Presently, as well as in the last few years, people have often felt the urge to travel, to go to another country, a little-known part of the World, or even just to a remote place or location. Frequently, they have no logical reason for wanting to go.

Indeed, if the desire is not to return to their place of origin or childhood, to attend a reunion, a funeral, a family gathering, a conference or school, or some similar function, people can find such urgings hard to accept.

Spiritual growth happens in a spiral. When it is time for us to move up to the next rung of the spiral, it is often encouraged by our soul to return to the place of our birth or to reconnect with the vehicle through which we came to Earth, the body of our mother. This makes sense to me if I look at the energy as operating in a spiral. If I complete one cycle, by returning to the beginning, I slip easily into the next octave of energy operation. That doesn't mean I like to return to my place of birth, and my physical mother is not still in this dimension. Sometimes while we are shifting from one energy octave to the next it feels like we have lost communication with our souls, our guides, our higher selves. This can feel like the dark night of the soul. If we understand what is happening we can understand that the wires are down, because we are being rewired to reach a higher vibration and we can endure or wait out the change more gracefully.

In fact, if such persons do not truly understand their multi-dimensionality, it is easy to disregard such promptings because no "logical explanation" accompanies them. It is simple to brush away the desires with such justifications as, "I don't have the money to go . . . no time. . . too far away . .

. don't want to go alone," and a hundred others. And people actually believe these excuses are the real reasons for "squelching" the urgings!

When I first began opening to my Oversoul and hearing and seeing multi-dimensionally, I noticed a phenomenon which I did not understand: When I stared into someone's eyes, my perception would shift – as if I went through that person's eyes and up through the crown of the head, while following an energy cord. The cord seemed to connect that individual to a series of energy fields and, ultimately, to a much larger energy mass. Eventually, the cord connected to what appeared to be the Source of all energy.

The energy fields resembled continually exploding roman candles, with descending spirals of energy forms coming from the Source energy toward Earth. These spirals of energy moved out in all directions, connecting all the stars and planets. Let me describe this another way: When I look into a person's eyes and go energetically back up to the Source, I see something that looks like a giant fireworks display – as if the Source sparked off energetic parts of itself and those parts are large enough to spark off parts of themselves and to bring down those "aspects" of themselves into lower vibrational frequencies for the purpose of experiencing life in these various dimensions. These "aspects" are all energetically connected.

I have drawn a simplified sketch of my version of an Oversoul. It is helpful to remember that I am attempting to describe, two-dimensionally, something that has a multitude of dimensions. As far as I'm aware there is no set number of members in one Oversoul.

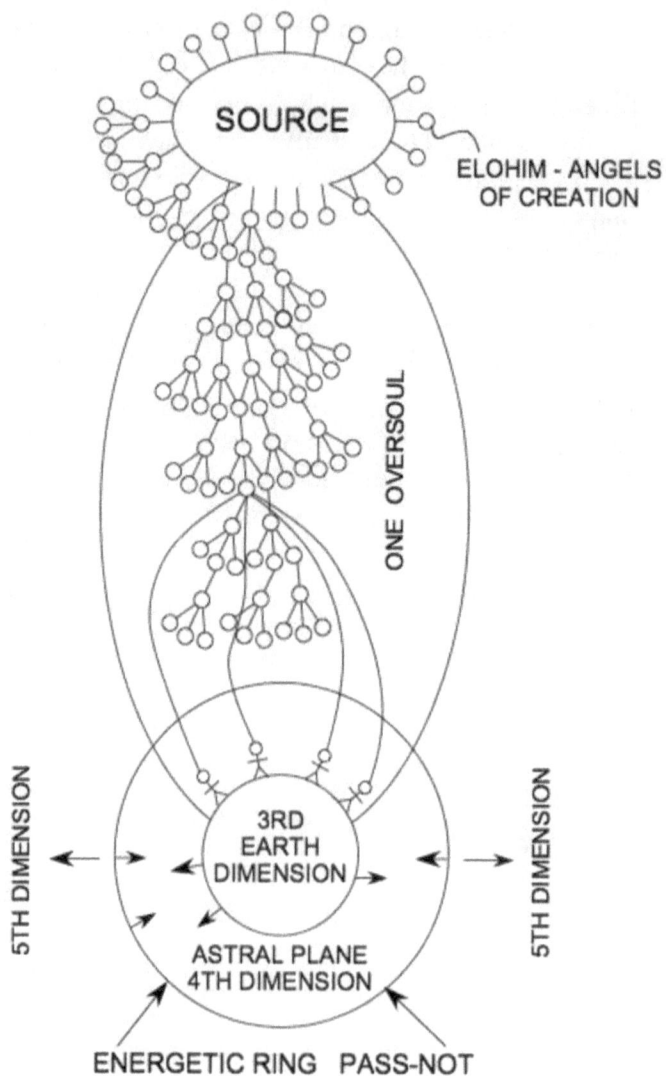

Then I began leaving my own body etherically, through the crown of my head, to explore my own soul's structure. Understanding began coming more fully, and eventually, I connected with an "aspect" of my soul in the sixth dimension of consciousness. This soul aspect referred to itself as my "Source Self" and welcomed me to call it Matthew. I questioned Matthew about the descriptive terms he used.

He explained that ASPECTS or CO-BEINGS are terms used to describe one unit of soul consciousness operating as a separate personality in a vehicle created of Light particles and infused with soul essence, sometimes physical.

SOURCE SELF is the Aspect of the soul choosing to send a portion of its consciousness into another Light body, or physical body, for an additional set of experiences.

Matthew further explained that the OVERSOUL refers to a group or family of souls (similar to a family tree) descended directly from the Source.

I understood that if anyone could trace his/her true family tree far enough back, the person would encounter the Source of everything.

All souls are connected. However, there are levels of vibrations and planes of experience operating simultaneously, with seemingly separate existences. The separateness appears to be more realistic, or pronounced, between the physical and non-physical dimensions. This is because of the "veils" between the levels of consciousness and the dimensions of vibration.

Matthew's explanations were always precise and as simple as he could make them, while clarifying such complex subjects! He also continued to explain that translating spiritual principles into English is very difficult because English is a language designed for commerce, not spiritual expression!

However, he continued his explanation, saying, "'Co-beings' or 'Aspects' enjoy a shared memory and a shared sense of self at the level of the RNA/DNA memory. The soul memory, or dianetic memory, includes the pattern of experiences of the entire Oversoul, not just experiences of a single personality."

This explained to me that if I allowed myself to regress many, many times to past life experiences, I would begin to see a chronological overlap in what I experienced as linear time.

I understood that in order to create space in our cells, or DNA, it is wise to erase negative and traumatic memory patterns from our DNA.

Various methods of DNA clearing are available to us. Radionics is one. "Circles of Life processing" is another. Still another method, which Matthew channeled to me, is given on the CD I previously mentioned called the "Cellular Release of Trauma, Fear and Negative Beliefs."

My understanding of all of this about the Oversoul was that when our system was created originally, the Source sparked off parts of itself and created the 24 Elohim, or Creator Spirits, usually referred to as The Builders of Form. These entities sparked off parts of themselves and created what are known as souls. They worked with certain extraterrestrial groups to create the original Human prototype; then on through the various stages of Human evolution from cave man to Cro-Magnon, to Neanderthal, to Homo erectus, to Homo sapiens and now to Homo universalis. These powerful and creative beings sparked off energies which became souls, or the higher aspects of Oversouls. The matrix for the Human containers – bodies – have been upgraded through evolution and through extraterrestrial and spiritual influence through the centuries.

An Oversoul is a family whose members vibrate at a higher vibrational frequency (a non-physical frequency) than that of the third dimension. I refer to the Oversoul's family members as "kindred spirits, aspects or units" of the Oversoul. I do not use the term "soul mates" since it has been misused in a romantic context.

Each of us is a part of a more complex energy field – a member of an Oversoul. Aspects of our Oversouls experience life in other dimensions and in this dimension simultaneously. Some aspects are on other planets; some are a part of other star systems, or in inner Earth civilizations; and some are aboard light ships or in other bodies here on the planet.

Oversouls project aspects (of themselves) into this Third Dimension at different ages. Put another way, many of our Oversoul family members may be of a different age or sex than we are.

Often we will meet someone who is embodied who is from our same Oversoul If they are near our age often the energy is so strong between us that we assume the meeting is to be a romantic, sexual relationship, and we jump in bed with them, because we have no other Human category of relationship for this kind of energy intensity. This is seldom the reason two members of the same Oversoul are brought together. Usually it is because one or both members are going through intense periods of growth or healing, and the soul can pour down more energy into the situation if they have two bodies present and even more so if the bodies are of different sexes.

Other members (or aspects) of our same Oversoul family have vested interests in communicating with us and in assisting us to accomplish the missions we came to Earth to do. When an aspect (or member) of an Oversoul decides to incarnate on Earth to experience physicality, a contractual agreement is made, to wit, the aspect will work toward certain types of growth for the benefit of the entire Oversoul. Everything the incarnate accomplishes spiritually assists the growth of every other aspect of the entire Oversoul.

The agreement is in the incarnating aspect's super conscious and can be accessed or remembered by the personality – self – through meditation and soul communication.

The part of the Oversoul agreeing to lower a portion of itself (an aspect) to become physical consults various expressions of the Oversoul and the Karmic Board (as part of the agreement). Considered, for example, are features and characteristics of the Oversoul family that could stand strengthening or increasing. (Because of the Universal Law of Karma – the Law of Cause and Effect – energies must stay balanced to enable the Universe to function as intended.)

When a member of an Oversoul is aspected into Earth's third dimension, its contract or agreement spells out the race, sex, economic conditions, country, parents and certain "classes" it will take while on Earth – even the potential of how many bodies it will create for other soul members to inhabit. Classes may include such things as: physical handicap, incest, alcoholic parents, divorce of parents, being raised by a single parent, being adopted and the like.

Further, an incarnating aspect sets up what I call certain destiny points or tests, as part of the agreement. These tests are to happen at certain ages and are for the purpose of determining spiritual growth. Tests may include events like graduation, marriage, accidents, severe health challenges, divorce, bankruptcy, or death of a parent, a child or a close friend.

When the aspect, or person, reaches the destiny point, or age, the event happens. How a person responds to or reacts to the event – and how severe it needs to be – is a gauge by which spiritual understanding and growth can be measured. To illustrate, it is obvious that at certain times in our life experience, a divorce would feel totally devastating – we could feel as if we had lost our entire identity, our entire reason for living. At another time, if we have spiritually progressed to understand who we truly are, we might be able to view it as both a release from karmic agreements, and freedom to move on up the path toward a new and more exciting future.

EVERYTHING BETWEEN DESTINY POINTS IS CREATED BY

OUR DAY-TO-DAY THOUGHTS, BE THEY POSITIVE OR NEGATIVE ATTITUDES.

This contract does not determine predestination it only sets up possibilities. We always maintain our free will.

I want to say here again, that the Oversoul who aspects a part of itself into the Third Dimension has an energetic investment in that aspect accomplishing its goals. The Oversoul UNDERSTANDS THE DIFFICULTY OF THE ASSIGNMENTS. (Remember, though, since evolution happens in accordance with Divine Plan, the Plan has been in effect for a very long time.)

Multi-dimensionally, various aspects of our Oversouls (and, therefore, of ourselves) are having many different types of experiences simultaneous to ours. Some of these aspects may be of the same sex as we, or opposite; some will be androgynous (containing equal masculine and feminine energies). Some will be extraterrestrials. Some will be very much like ourselves, except operating in alternate realities, or what we think of in linear time as alternate pasts and futures. (This is because all time is simultaneous in the time-space continuum.)

If we were to accomplish regression, or progression through hypnosis, we could possibly experience some of these simultaneous alternatives. Occasionally, we may glimpse them from the altered states of sleep or meditation.

These aspects of our souls may serve in the roles of guides, teachers, mentors or protectors.

Human beings have the ability to communicate with these other aspects, i.e., to ask them for assistance and advice. However, because of the Universal Law of Free Will and Non-Intervention, these soul aspects may ignore us, to a certain extent, <u>unless we seek out and specifically ask for their help</u>.

Matthew jokingly stated, "*When a Human begins meditating and asking for assistance, it is as if a 'blue light special' begins pulsating above your heads. Oversouls watch and wait and hope for these lights to begin pulsating.*"

Once we become acquainted with these other aspects of our Oversoul (of ourselves) we can consciously merge with their energies. Thereby, we can gain greater volumes of information, resources, spiritual knowledge and energies.

Some of our soul aspects will also be incarnate on the Earth plane when we are. Oftentimes, we are brought together with them for group interactions, projects, and just to have emotional, physical, psychological and spiritual companions in our journey back to the Source.

We can usually recognize a soul aspect through a resonance of energy that feels totally comfortable and reassuring to us. And this familiar energetic reaction will happen whether the aspect of the Oversoul is in physical body or spirit.

However, there is nothing to say that this will be a positive energetic reaction. These beings can be very clear mirrors to us of our unresolved issues. Feeling agitated by someone from your own Oversoul is possible too, because of past life experiences. While such beings can assist us with much soul growth, all may not be fun or without confrontation. This is why I do not advocate that people seek their soul mates, or another member of their Oversoul as a mate, this is, however, up to each person's personal choice. It is usually easier to be in a mated relationship with someone not of our same Oversoul.

Also, there are those Oversoul aspects who were sent to Earth <u>before</u> us, who became awake and aware during their Third Dimensional stay. They understood that those of us who would come after them would need energetic assistance with our mission, especially during this critical period in the evolution of Earth and Humanity.

For us to accomplish spiritual growth, it is helpful to work toward communication with the various levels of our Oversouls, through intuition and sometimes through telepathy.

In some cases, when certain vibrations are reached within the body (and in accordance with some prior-to-reincarnation agreements) other aspects of the Oversoul will join, braiding themselves into the consciousness of an aspect using one vehicle (or body). This is called "soul braiding."

Usually, there is a subtle, but not dramatic, personality shift when this braiding occurs. The aspect that comes does not bring personality, only consciousness, but the expanding of consciousness will often cause changes in a person's personality.

Several aspects can braid themselves into one life stream and work through one body, during the course of a lifetime. When more than one aspect braids into one body from the same Oversoul, this being is then referred to as a composite. Many walk-ins later agree to become composites, in order to have as much of the Oversoul energy as possible available in this dimension.

Soul braiding is not to be confused with a walk-in situation. In a walk-in situation, the original aspect returns to the Oversoul and leaves the body to another aspect. Neither of the instances of "soul braiding" nor "walking in" is possession.

Possession is the unlawful overshadowing of one consciousness (or more) in physical body, by a consciousness from the astral. This is contrary to spiritual law. Soul-braiding and walking-in are in alignment with spiritual law and the aspect walking-in is always from the same Oversoul.

Some individuals now on the Earth plane made prior-to-reincarnation agreements to allow their vehicles (bodies) to be used by what is known as "group mind." This constitutes several Oversoul aspects "braiding" into one life stream, or "group energy" moving through the vehicle periodically, without braiding their consciousness permanently into the vehicle (personality).

"Group energy braiding" is identified by some people as a form of channeling. Some persons are experiencing this without understanding what is taking place. An explanation here is that it is a vibrational activity and can happen without conscious understanding at the personality level.

When an aspect of the Oversoul dies or leaves the physical body, it may or may not rejoin the Oversoul immediately. There are options: (a) It can retain the personality and energies and reside near the Earth plane to assist others. (b) It can surrender its personality identity and rejoin the energy pool of the Oversoul. (c) It can retain its energy on the Earth without a body and wait to give its energy and consciousness to another of its Oversoul aspects. (d) In the case of an Oversoul aspect(s) who came to Earth before us, it can leave its assigned energy and wisdom hermetically sealed in the Third Dimension in the location of their physical death.

Regarding the hermetically sealed energy/wisdom, those of us who have come to Earth at this time, come with Universal Language of Light symbols in our energy fields, which make it possible for us to merge with Oversoul hermetically-sealed essences when we come in contact with a location where previous conscious Oversoul members have hermetically-sealed portions of their consciousness to be retrieved at a later time by someone who can use the consciousness to serve the Earth and Humanity. Likewise, in the case of energy and consciousness waiting to be given to another, aspects (Humans on the Earth) will be drawn energetically to locations where previous entities resided so the merger can take place.

Oftentimes, the TRUE purpose of people's urgings to travel is to "soul merge," or "pick up" an extra energy or energy aspect of the Oversoul. This energy aspect may either be ready to leave Earth life and willing to donate a portion of the consciousness it has carried, or it may have already left its earthly life, in the physical sense, and left a portion of its consciousness hermetically sealed in this dimension.

If the aspect has already left physical life, as explained, it may be waiting energetically to give its energies and consciousness to one who will be committed to using this portion of soul energy for the benefit of the entire Oversoul.

Soul mergings are not something to fear. They are great gifts offered us by our Oversouls. I recommend you follow your <u>intuitive</u> urges to travel.

People may or may not be totally aware physically or consciously at the time they merge with other aspects of their Oversoul. But their consciousness and energy will expand. They don't even have to do a ritual – or do anything – to cause it to happen. All that is required is that they (people) travel with INTENTION TO MERGE WITH HIGHER LEVELS OF THEMSELVES. EVERYTHING IN THIS DIMENSION IS BASED ON INTENTION.

Occasionally, an aspect of the Oversoul may die without having developed any spiritual awareness. The aspect may, therefore, have difficulty getting out of the astral plane and into the Light.

When this happens, persons who have Oversoul communication may be asked to call forth the Archangel Michael and the Band of Mercy to retrieve this aspect energy and escort it to the Light.

In either case, I recommend that people understand fully how to accomplish this successfully before agreeing to do it.

Oftentimes when such mergers take place, people (Human beings) are not conscious of what has happened. They may feel expanded, briefly disoriented, or maybe sad or elated for a short time before continuing normal expanded awareness and energy. Some time may be needed for the physical body to adjust to the additional energies. If people are aware of such possibilities, they are advised to consciously request the merger take place with "no negative side effects and without resistance." They should also ask the Oversoul to transmute the energies <u>before</u> they (the energies) are merged with those of the people doing the merging. This is so the transmutation AFTER THE MERGER will not have to be done through the physical and emotional bodies of the ones doing the merging.

It is VERY IMPORTANT now for people to work through <u>and only accept guidance</u> from their own Oversouls. Seeking guides and teachers from one's Oversoul family insures receiving the greatest amount of assistance and personal Truth.

It is important NOT TO CALL IN extraterrestrial forces or other spiritual teachers other than those of one's own Oversoul.

For readers and healers, it is especially IMPORTANT that if you wish to call in guides, (yours or those of the person you are reading for or healing), that you try doing it through CONTACTING YOUR OWN Oversoul first. Ask your Oversoul to contact the other person's guides from THEIR Oversoul. (I do this by mentally intentioning a beam of energy sent into my Oversoul, just as you would if you were plugging a cord into a switchboard). This is much less confusing and is easier for your body. It will also get you clearer, more complete information you can trust.

Here is an effective method that can be used to contact your Oversouls: When you meditate, ground yourself by sending beams of energy from the soles of your feet into the core of the Earth. Seal the room in which you are meditating from astral interference.

Begin pulsating energy at the point of the mid-brain (the pituitary and pineal glands are located at the mid-brain), and open the crown chakra (top of your head). Through thought and intention, send a beam of energy from the mid-brain up through the corridor in the astral plane (or fourth dimension) to the Fifth Dimension of your Oversoul.

You may want to ask your Oversoul for a name or identifying sound, symbol or vibration as recognition that you have successfully made contact. Usually, the flood of love and concern that overwhelms you is sufficient for you to "know" you have been successful.

While contact with the Oversoul may not always occur, I feel strongly it should be sought during every meditation.

As our energy vibrations expand and increase, we are able to reach more and more aspects of the Oversoul in all dimensions, eventually reaching our Guardian Angel and the Source.

After your soul vibration and your body vibration synchronize, you will be able to consciously merge with each aspect and level of vibration, incorporating increased consciousness and access to the Oversoul's combined knowledge. When I first started working with Matthew in 1982, his energy was of the fifth dimension. Through the years as we have both progressed, his energy and mine are of the eighth dimension.

Many people deliberately avoid meditation and soul communication for fear of what they will hear, what will be expected of them, fear of change, or of having to give up familiar or known lifestyles. Avoidance behavior is futile and makes life more difficult. The entire purpose of life and the incarnating process is to remember, to communicate and to accomplish the life's goal.

If we spend our lives in avoidance, the soul continually co-creates circumstances with us to promote growth and complications to encourage us to seek communication with God and to reach out to the soul for help.

If we procrastinate too long in avoidance, the soul, after many attempts to get our attention, withdraws its energies from the physical and personality (self), and the body dies. The soul energy then returns to the Oversoul to evaluate its progress and to be reassigned by the Oversoul to another life and body to work out the same issues and learn the same lessons, similar to having to attend summer school.

Immediately upon leaving the body, a hologram of our life's events flows before us. As our own judges, we compare the events with the agenda, or agreement for the life we made before incarnating. We can then see where "we missed the mark." In archery, this term is defined as "to sin."

One of the reasons people fear death is that during the current lifetime they shun or shy away from doing what they were scheduled to do for the Oversoul's benefit on the inner planes. Since we Humans are "dipped in the bath of forgetfulness" at the personality level before each incarnation, we do not remember our purpose, agreement or previous lifetimes <u>until we consciously seek to remember</u>. In each successive lifetime, we increase our awareness and knowledge.

The more conscious each aspect of the soul becomes during each incarnation, the quicker the memory of the soul is restored, and the stronger the Oversoul becomes, proportionally.

Many children are being born now (sometimes called Star Children) with thin veils – or no veils at all – between their personality selves and their Oversoul selves. These children will be more difficult to control and confine and will have trouble conforming to our standard educational programs. This is because they remember Universal truths and will not accept dogma, convention or lies as a way of life.

GROUP MINDS

Within the various levels of our Oversouls are what we could think of as terminal mainframes (using computer terminology). These mainframes house vast quantities of information.

In spiritual terms these "mainframes" would be referred to as "group minds." The various "Brotherhoods," i.e., the Great White Brotherhood, the Brotherhood of the Rosy Cross, the Sisterhood of the Shield, The Order of Emerald Fire, The Order of the Golden Feather, The Order of Amber, The Order of the Golden Dawn are names given to just such spiritual orders.

After Humans have done a certain level, or volume, of spiritual work, clearing of negativity from consciousness, and have begun to communicate and follow the soul's guidance, they may receive an invitation to become an active conscious member of one, or several "group minds."

These groups have various spiritual functions and focuses. Some are healing orders, some with teaching, some with politics, some with economics, some work primarily with Human evolution, some with Earth evolution, and all with spiritual evolution. Being inducted into an Order is called initiation.

Receiving this type of invitation denotes that the spiritual student has reached a certain level of integrity, discipline and dedication. It is similar to a job promotion in a corporation, or receiving a "password" into a level of information to which we have not previously had access – or a "key" to the executive washroom . . . This type of access is <u>not lightly</u> offered a spiritual student. Nor should the student accept it lightly. The more knowledge we receive, the more we are expected to share with others. The more we know, the more spiritual laws or principles we are required to practice.

As further explanation, say Person No. 1 was given access to the Akashic records (soul records) of Person No. 2. A great deal of discernment and integrity is required of Person No. 1 concerning what to reveal or repeat of what is viewed to Person No. 2 – such as during a psychic reading. When a person is first given access to the Akashic records, it is as if they are given a library card that only allows them access to the first floor. Once the person's integrity has been proven in the use of the information access, additional access is allowed. It is my experience that to enter the Akashic records, a person must request permission each time, just as you would be required to give your library card each time you use the library. It is my experience that I don't go anywhere to get the information. It is not like a library in that way. The information comes to me from the other person's soul to my soul and then to me as knowingness.

"To accept the truth is a first great step. But only when we begin to live it and demonstrate it in order to prove it for ourselves is it truly ours. Jesus proved everything He taught us by demonstration and through living – even death and resurrection – to prove the illusion of death."

– Matthew

56

Intention, Exorcism, Healing

In this Chapter, I want to discuss Intention, Exorcism and Healing. Actually, Exorcism and Healing are a part of Intention.

Many metaphysical teachers teach that visualization is extremely important in the process of manifestation. Many of us thought we were "flunking" spiritually because we could not visualize or hear. Actually, for a thought form to be visual it has to vibrate at the third or fourth dimensional level. Therefore, to try to visualize not only lowers the vibration of the thought, but lowers OUR vibration as well. For a thought form to be auditory, it must vibrate at the Third, Fourth or lower Fifth Dimensions. Therefore to <u>see</u> or <u>hear</u> Spirit messages indicates fourth and lower Fifth Dimensional activity.

Most of us came into this World spiritually vibrating at Fifth Dimension and higher. Our souls are not supporting the idea of our trying to "see" (clairvoyant) or to "hear" (clairaudient). We came in "knowing," which is higher Fifth Dimensionally and higher vibrationally.

For those who can't see or hear spiritually, I suggest beginning to operate from <u>knowingness</u> – using one's intuition. "Knowing" is the highest form of spiritual awareness before "beingness." Therefore, I recommended if we desire to manifest, that we create a physical and word picture of that which we desire to manifest.

Everything energetic happens as a RESULT OF INTENTION. The INTENTIONS or THOUGHTS we hold in mind ultimately CREATE OUR REALITY, because ENERGY FOLLOWS INTENTION.

Energy does not have a mind of its own. It is directed through thought. Therefore, when we set up deliberate intentions through writing and physical pictures, we are setting up a framework to be filled in energetically by Spirit. For example, if we hold the INTENTION of living a soul-infused life, guided by Holy Spirit (our soul, or God) it will be so.

It is our responsibility to claim the authority assigned to us by God (to be in dominion). By the authority of the Cosmic Christ Consciousness we can affect healing, weather control, exorcism and all that Jesus said we were capable of doing as He did, and more.

If we do not claim this authority, the energy is just "there," not being assigned a task or service – not being used. Worry is misuse of creative energy. Instead, redirect the energy, through thought, to what you REALLY DESIRE to happen. Train yourself not to use the words "want" and "need" because the soul and the subconscious take us literally and believe we desire to stay in a state of wanting or needing rather than having.

Following is a prayer of <u>Exorcism</u> and <u>Clearing</u> you can use:

"Holy Mother/Father God of Light, Divine Creator of All That Is, through the authority invested in me by the Cosmic Christ Consciousness, I deliberately call forth the energy of the

Archangel Michael and the Band of Mercy to enter this building, the body of _____ (the automobile, place of business, cemetery, hospital, nursing home, bar, etc.). I ask that all negative influences, energies or discarnate entities be removed and escorted into the Light that they might continue to grow and prosper.

"I ask that this be accomplished with no negative side effects and totally without pain or trauma. I ask that _____'s body be triple sealed against any further invasion, use or abuse by discarnate entities. So It Is. AMEN, AMEN, AMEN."

At this point, I tone. (Toning is best done audibly, but can be silent if necessary due to the circumstances. It is an intuitive tone you choose. It creates a beam of light that the discarnate entity can follow, like a path into the Light.) You do not need to have the person's permission to do this Prayer of Exorcism, because possession is against spiritual law. However, it is easier if you do have permission and the person or persons is/are <u>willing</u> to be cleared and, therefore, feeling cooperative and invested in not being open to astral plane entities.

ASTRAL, CEMETERY, OR DISEMBODIED SPIRITS RELEASE PRAYER

"I call upon the energies of the ARCHANGEL MICHAEL and the Band of Mercy to enter this dimension and area to escort all souls represented by these graves (or all disembodied entities in this area, or a specified area by address) into the Light, that they might continue to grow and prosper. I (we) ask that this be done in love and totally without pain." TONE

The reason we say "graves" instead of "headstones" is because often burial grounds are layered and other graves from previous civilizations may be buried beneath what are obvious graves with headstones and the discarnate entities may have hung around for centuries.

HEALING

Following is a powerful prayer for Healing:

You do <u>need</u> permission of the individual, or that person's Oversoul, to do this ritual.

"Holy Mother/Father God of Light, Divine Creator of All That Is, through the authority invested in me by the Cosmic Christ Consciousness, I deliberately call forth to the BODY INTELLIGENCE of _____ I ask this Intelligence to override any beliefs in _____ 's emotional or mental bodies and subconscious mind that believes it needs or wants this disease. I ask _____ 's Oversoul to replace these beliefs with belief in perfect health and the total balance of all of the body's, magnetic and mental systems.

"Because it has been promised that where two or three are gathered together in the name of Christ, the energy of miracles is present, we now claim this healing through the power of the Holy Spirit and the Cosmic Christ Consciousness. And so it is. AMEN, AMEN, AMEN.

ACTIVE INTERCESSORY PRAYER

Another powerful healing tool is called, "Active Intercessory Prayer."

A PROBLEM CANNOT BE SOLVED AT THE ENERGETIC LEVEL IT WAS CREATED. Therefore, Universal Law allows us to use this ritual to reach an individual for whom we have concern or deep love, a person with whom we have no luck communicating Third Dimensionally, a situation that needs healing, or a condition we cannot solve.

We <u>do not need the person's permission</u> to do this ritual.

The most effective means I have been given to accomplish this kind of healing is to write a letter to the individual's Oversoul and Angelic Presence, stating our concerns for the individual and seeking intervention on behalf of that person from their Higher Self. For example, we can ask the person's Oversoul for divine intervention on behalf of that individual to come into a state of awareness, balance, harmony, perfect health, etc.

A letter should be written every day for fourteen days. Letters may be repetitious, but need to be retyped or rewritten daily.

Your letter should read similar, but not exactly as the following:

"I ask for divine intervention for my relationship with _____ (or healing for). I ask for healing of body, mind, spirit and emotion. Recognizing that I do not fully understand the karmic implications in this situation, I ask the Oversoul to intervene. I ask for healing from addiction (or anger, disease, etc). I ask that_____ become aware of their true divine nature, their mission and their Oversoul.

"Because it has been promised that if we ask we shall receive, I recognize that by writing these letters for fourteen days in a row and on the fourteenth day burning the letters, I am acting in accordance with spiritual Law.

"I now release this person and his/her condition to Higher Power for resolution."

When you have done your first letter, read it carefully and ask yourself if you are doing this out of love for the person, or because of your need to control. What might be the attitudes <u>you</u> hold toward that person that make communication difficult? Also examine personal judgments you might be holding that are similar to what aggravates you about the individual. You may need to reword the letter, depending upon how you answer the above questions. BE HONEST ABOUT YOUR MOTIVES. When you burn the letters, do so ceremoniously and RELEASE the person to God and ask for the highest good for all concerned. This is equivalent to a prolonged intercessory prayer, without accruing negative karmic consequences, because you release the person and circumstances. Fire energy assists in transmuting the situation.

The spiritual purpose of the letters gives the Oversoul the authority to override the person's free will for six weeks. You should wait four weeks before again writing another set of fourteen letters (if you feel the situation needs further attention). This gives the Oversoul time to intervene. Waiting only four weeks instead of six, you are creating a situation that keeps the

Oversoul in a permissive state of overriding the free will of the individual without creating karma for you, the person or the Oversoul.

Many times the Oversoul will arrange a series of events that causes the person we are concerned about to seek help. The Universal Law of Free Will is superseded by the Law of Love through a special dispensation by the soul, because of the act of faith and love on our part to invest the time and energy in writing the letters and burning them.

If you should miss a day of writing during the 14-day period, just keep writing until you have written 14 letters. You may write letters for addicted individuals, but I would do the Exorcism also, as most addicted people are periodically possessed and not fighting their addiction for just one person!

You can also write letters for the Earth, a country or a condition that is present on the Earth.

This letter-writing ritual is the only way I am aware of that allows the Oversoul and Guardian Angel to have spiritual permission to override the person's <u>free will</u> for six weeks to positively influence the person's life.

This Intercessory Prayer also works well if the person is in a coma or is experiencing Alzheimer's or senility.

Many miracles have been reported through the use of this prayer technique.

At one time, I had a person living with me that did not take care of the room were living in and drank and smoked pot daily (not in my home, but before they came home). I didn't want to throw this person out of my home, but I wanted them to leave. I wrote the letters and asked that the person would "find a place they would rather be." I was only on the fourth day of the letter writing when the person came home and said, "I know you don't want to live by yourself and you may feel I am abandoning you, but I have found a place I think I would rather be." It was very difficult for me not to laugh. The person used the exact words I had used in the letters. More recently I used this method to assist a neighbor who had many large, noisy dogs to find a place they would rather be in the country, rather than living next door to me and upsetting my quiet and solitude. You can even use this method in legal situations, writing to the Oversouls of participants, judges, lawyers in a legal situation or any situation where one-on-one communication isn't working.

bj King

WHAT CAN ONE PERSON DO?
By bj King

What can one person do To save the World From Hatred
Guilt, Deceit
Destruction
From Mankind's madness?
We can talk
About our plans
For Peace
Love
Co-operation
Interdependence
Co-creation.
We can love ourselves
The Planet, each other.
We can see a World,
a species
Whose aim is PEACE.
We can feel gratitude
Instead of greed,
Compassion
Instead of hatred –

Even toward ourselves.
We can live lives
Of co-created beauty and abundance
With God
Instead of fear, struggle
And existence.
We can take time
In groups and alone
To see the good
And magnify it,
See the disturbing
And replace it
With a vision of alignment and grace.
We can use the tools we've been given
By our Source

To change the World
And ourselves
By multiplying through focus
Beauty
Harmony
Love
Peace
Kindness
Sharing.
Where poverty now exists
We can SEE plenty
Illness replaced by health
Greed replaced with sharing
Competition eliminated through cooperation.
Pollution exists
Because we are unwilling to see clearly
And perform with clarity
That which we know is true.
We know the difference
Between order and chaos
Truth and deceit
Cleanliness and filth
Beauty and ugliness.
We can't change anyone except ourselves
And only then if we open our eyes
To see how we are a part of the problem.
Are we criticizing instead of complimenting?
Hating where WE could love,
Griping when we could fix it ourselves,
Challenging when we could support
Laying blame instead of pardon
Judgment instead of insight?
Could we do better than we are?
I believe we can.
I believe groups of people
Deliberately sitting together
To focus love
Order
Abundance

bj King

Beauty
Sanity and Peace
Can change and save the World.
We can see bombs and weapons
Defused and dismantled,
Bodies fed, housed, clothed, and whole
Love's made productive through cooperation
Housing and gardens
Clean water and air
New forms of energy generated
To replace the pollution of petroleum
And atomic fuel.
We can see
The energy of the tides the Planets
And the Sun warming and cooling
Fueling and driving our factories
And our homes.
We can see light instead of darkness
In the hearts and minds of everyone.
Expect the best instead of the worst From everyone
Knowing full well we've all come together
From the same Source
And shall return.
As long as one of us suffers,
We all do.
We can see pain replaced by joy,
A planet surviving,
A people thriving,
A God who cares.
We can change it all
If we think it to be so
And know . . . . . SO IT IS

57

The Earth, Humans and Addiction

For several years I had experienced what energetically appeared to me to be a large funnel above my head. The Spiritual Hierarchy deposited information into this funnel. The information was in the form of symbols, Universal Light Language symbols. The symbols looked like large oriental hieroglyphics drawn in light. When the funnel became too full of the Universal Light Language symbols, I tried to stop and allow the symbols to take the form of English words, so I and others could understand the messages.

The following was my impression of what I was given: The Earth is a Third Dimensional entity inhabited by the Homo sapiens species, by plants, animals, minerals and water. All of these operate at a vibration of Third Dimensionality. The Earth and the substances and creatures upon it are experimental and are in various stages of evolution. The Earth has undergone many radical changes during its evolution, as have the other species that ride upon her.

This particular stage of the evolutionary experience timed for now, the Aquarian Age, involves the Earth and the Human species EVOLVING into the Fifth Dimension. This evolution includes a molecular vibrational change, which would not be observed as physical by Third Dimensional vision. It also means a change in the helix of the DNA. The Homo sapiens' DNA is being changed from a two-strand helix, to a twelve-strand helix; the Earth is moving vibrationally from being Third Dimensional to Fifth Dimensional.

When the Human species was seeded upon the Earth, it was given FREE WILL and certain UNIVERSAL LAWS were set into motion. This caused the Earth to act and react in specific ways within this particular galaxy of the Milky Way.

Humans were given DOMINION over the planet and its plants, animals and minerals. DOMINION is a term referring to a level of the Angelic kingdom, meaning "to steward" and "to co-create with that which is present."

Humans misconstrued this noun to be a verb and have placed themselves over the Earth, plants, animals, minerals and resources. They also have ruled and destroyed, rather than stewarded, nurtured and co-created with that which is present.

Out beyond the Third Dimension, at the edge of the Fourth Dimension (a vibration, not a place) an energetic barrier exists called the "ring-pass-not." This "ring" was designed by the Hierarchy to encapsulate the negative thought forms created by Humans. It was installed at the time that Humans decided to split the atom. Splitting the atom without the boundary of the "ring pass not" would have allowed a chair reaction of destruction to move out through out the Universe. The "ring" is to hold these thought forms and energy close to the Earth, rather than permit them – and therefore the Human species – to contaminate the Galaxy and the Universe with negativity. The ring-pass-not is tightened periodically to bring the Fifth Dimension closer to Earth. Each time this happens, time speeds up. Every molecule in this dimension speeds up at exactly the same frequency, including watches and clocks, so nothing looks different. We feel that things are happening faster, but it is deceiving because the clocks and watches still make us think we have 24 hours in which to accomplish what we want to do in one day. In actuality at the time of this writing we have a ten-hour day as compared to life in the 1940s.

Each time the ring is tightened, it also forces the Fourth Dimension, filled with these negative thought forms and lower vibrational discarnate spirits who have not transcended into the Light, in on the Earth. Before the Earth can make the vibrational shift to the Fifth Dimension, it must release, transmute, absorb, translate and transcend these thought forms and release these entities.

This Fourth Dimensional space is filled not only with negative thought forms, but also with soul aspects of beings who have died in a state of confusion, addiction or disbelief in a spiritual reality. Many refer to this dimension as purgatory, limbo or the astral plane. This is the dimension Christians would refer to as hell. (Many people refer to everything not Third Dimensional as the astral plane.)

I prefer to call the Fourth Dimension the astral plane, and to refer to the other dimensions by numbers, i.e., Fifth Dimension. (These dimensions, as I've mentioned, are <u>frequencies of vibration</u>, not actual places of matter, such as the Earth plane.) Without definitions of terms, it is difficult to understand the subject of metaphysics.

Metaphysics can possibly be more easily misunderstood than any other subject, since the subject concerns non-physical reality and non-linear time. Also, the English language, which we are using, was not created for describing spiritual ideas and thoughts, but rather to facilitate commerce and intellectual principles and impressions.

It is my belief and experience that when an addicted person dies, h/she still has that addiction even though h/she is no longer in a physical body.

If the person is spiritually aware before leaving the body, and knows enough to call forth Angels to help with the crossing, h/she is taken to a "way station," similar to a hospital. The person is placed in a state, similar to suspended animation, until the addiction is transmuted energetically.

Addicted persons who have no faith or knowledge of spiritual reality – nor anyone near who is aware enough to call forth Angels or assisting spirits to help them into the Light – are contained in the astral plane of consciousness without bodies. They remain addicted. Such beings are able, through thought, to create a copy of the Third Dimensional substance to which they are addicted, but the use of it does not relieve their addiction, because they have no physical bodies. Addictions may include nicotine, power, money, sex, food, drugs, co-dependency, anger, alcohol or control.

The only relief such beings can obtain is to merge with the body of a person practicing their drug or behavior of choice, and to vicariously feed off that person's use, practice or reaction.

The magnetic bodies of unhealthy or addicted persons often appear as gauze or even fish net and may have several tears, rips or exploded holes. Astral entities join and use these physical bodies through such ruptures. The magnetic bodies of healthy individuals are closely woven and bright, with no holes. Most persons who are suffering addictions of any sort are not feeding the addiction of just one individual, but may be feeding or acting it out for many additional beings.

I have experienced one body being used by as many as 90 entities! This is why it is important for a person entering a treatment or recovery center to be exorcised of any additional entities and energies. Such persons need their auras thoroughly repaired and sealed if they are to have an effective recovery from addiction. If these methods were taught to counselors and facilitators in recovery units, chances of recovery would be appreciably improved. It is the responsibility of those of us who know, to assist in the release of these beings from the astral plane.

Never get into a direct confrontation with a spirit being or anyone whom you suspect to be possessed. (The scenes you might have seen in *The Exorcist* are not exaggerated.)

Fear is not helpful. Wisdom is. Do not fear these entities. They are lost and confused; therefore, do not confront them. Help is best given through prayer to call forth the Archangel Michael and the Band of Mercy to do the clearing.

Anyone can accomplish this by declaring, "Through the authority vested in me by the Christ Consciousness, I deliberately call forth to the energies of the Archangel Michael and the Band of Mercy to enter the body, residence, school, work, automobile and all places frequented by_____(name the individual) and remove all negative influences, energies and invading discarnate entities.

"I ask that these beings and energies be taken into the Light that they might continue to grow spiritually. I ask that this individual's aura be triple sealed against any further invasion by negative forces. AMEN"

Also, a letter of "Active Intercessory Prayer" may be written on behalf of addicted persons, IN ADDITION to doing the Exorcism.

An example of the "Active Intercessory Prayer" letter is given in the chapter in this book entitled, *Intention, Exorcism and Healing*. Other tools for healing are also given in that chapter.

CO-DEPENDENCY, INDEPENDENCE & INTERDEPENDENCE

A few years ago I began hearing the term "co-dependency," through friends who were therapists and worked with addictions. As with any new buzz word, when I first started hearing it I thought, "what does that mean?" (I ask that question a lot about many words in use today.)

Finally, I asked one of my friends. She explained that co-dependency describes the condition of being dependent on another person for identity; when one simply cannot exist independently, but only co-dependently. They believe they are the "roles" they play and have no self identity beyond their roles. I was one of these people in 1979 when I left my family in Texas and moved to Oklahoma City. In order for me to learn who I was beyond the roles I played for others, all the roles I had been playing were taken away over a nine-month period. I found myself in Oklahoma City, with no lover, no husband, my children were living in Lubbock with their dad, so I was not a daily "mom," my mother had just died and my Dad married a new person almost immediately and focused entirely on that person's family, so my role as a daughter was being unused. My friends had turned against me because in their minds I had run away with the priest, and I was excommunicated from the Episcopal Church because we were not yet married when he died in my bed. I was unemployed. I was completely alone. I spent hours sitting with a legal pad on my lap, rocking in a rocking chair attempting to figure out who I was if I didn't have any roles to play. I would write "I AM" and try to figure out what to put after that. I didn't remember ever hearing the term "The I AM." It was years later when I realized I was giving myself the answer. Before, during and after all the roles we play we are the I AM Presence, the aspect of us that is connected to the divine.

There are people who are afraid of having identities of their own out of fear it will be the "wrong" identity. Some people become so obsessed with another's life that they ignore their own feelings and goals. Their very personalities and thoughts are based on what someone else thinks or says or does, not on what they believe or feel. If they decide that someone else no longer loves them (and they obviously don't love themselves), they feel there is literally no reason to continue living.

Co-dependents have difficulty experiencing appropriate levels of self-esteem, setting functional boundaries, owning and expressing their own reality and taking care of their adult needs and wants. Co-dependency is a dysfunction that is caused by lack of self-love, self-worth, self-trust and self-esteem. Such people try to solve their personal deficiencies by "pretending to be normal," or by finding a mate for life who will give them what they cannot give themselves.

Co-dependents live in fear, fear for their identity, fear of being discovered, fear of doing something wrong and losing the source of their happiness, their mate or their child.

Living in fear requires a life of controlling others.

A major symptom of co-dependents is that they spend their lives compulsively worrying, defending, controlling, and otherwise fussing over others. The result is they never have time to examine themselves or their own motives. This is a true addiction, because it does a good job of mimicking love . . .

Our task is not to seek for love, but to seek and find all of the barriers within ourselves that we have built against love! It is not necessary to seek for what is true, but it _is_ necessary to seek for what is false.

SPIRITUAL ABUSE

Spirit says that "spiritual abuse" is the only true sin, meaning it has severe karmic consequences carried from one life to the next. When one person deliberately entangles, enmeshes, or interweaves his/her life so thoroughly with another's to keep them from their spiritual path, that person commits spiritual abuse.

Parents often do this with children by trying to live their own lives through the lives of their children. That way, they (parents) do not have to take direct responsibility for the results, but can take direct credit . . . Also, when a particularly strong child is born to weak parents, the child is often beaten, either physically, verbally or emotionally, into submission and, therefore, is deterred from following his/her own growth or soul path.

Often, through co-dependent needs, one partner will try to hold another (or themselves) back from spiritual growth so as to maintain a status quo in the relationship, or threaten to leave in order to control the other's growth.

58

The Rays

As already mentioned in an earlier chapter, while Jan, Kathy and I were in Hawaii in February 1992, we connected with a group of spiritual beings referring to themselves as THE FOUNDERS. The Founders is another name for THE ELOHIM, a spiritual group who originally participated in the creation of Earth and its species. They are sometimes referred to as THE BUILDERS OF FORM.

THE FOUNDERS requested that the three of us ground seven new Rays into the Earth at Kee Beach on Kauai. These Rays constitute the adjustment or amendment to the Universal Laws affecting the Third Dimension and governing the density and structure of matter. These Rays were a gift to Earth, dedicated to the evolution of the plant, animal and Human species. They were in addition to the original seven Rays first given Earth at the time of the great flood and the rainbow covenant. Five additional Rays seem to have been added at, or near, the time of the Harmonic Convergence in 1987. There are now a total of 49 continuous Rays of energy aimed at the Earth and available for use by us to assist the planet and Humanity. The Founders told us (in 1992) that our scientists would eventually begin to notice the Rays.

I had not been aware of the Rays until 1988 when I was asked to make the meditation tape, *The Gift of the 12 Rays*. In later years, we were sent back to Kauai to assist the Hierarchy to anchor additional Rays of energies into the Earth. After all 49 were anchored, a group of us go to Kauai to Kee Beach during the Summer Solstice, June 21, and the Hierarchy adjusts the percentage of frequency of each of the Rays and anchors them through our bodies for the benefit of Earth and Humanity. The amount of each Ray coming to Earth affects the evolution of everything on Earth. The Rays and their use are available to anyone who chooses to know about them and to call them forth. I later wrote the *Meanings And Uses Of The Forty-Nine Rays* as a book, which the Hierarchy channeled. The book is available from Namaste.

Each Ray is controlled and monitored by a Master or Chohan and his female complement and an Angel. Each Ray has a fragrance, flower, minerals, music, and color that coordinate with the Ray.

59

Universal Law – Synchronicity – Serendipity

Our Universe is perfectly balanced by natural and spiritual Laws, which maintain order. We can learn to depend on these Laws and live in alignment with this order. We live on a dualistic and physical planet. Because of this, we often find ourselves facing a seeming paradox – caught in an endless loop of contradictions. However, it is important to remember that if we turn on a tape recorder and record our voice, when we play it back, we hear our voice saying exactly what we recorded. If we plant a spinach seed, spinach will grow and not cauliflower.

WHAT WE SOW IN CONSCIOUSNESS, WE REAP.

If we think of ourselves as Humans trying to become spiritual, the lives we live will look like this: If we feel we have to have more time and more money before we can attempt or accomplish certain things, our lives will always feel a little out of balance; we may need to be propped up by addictions, possessions, relationships and roles.

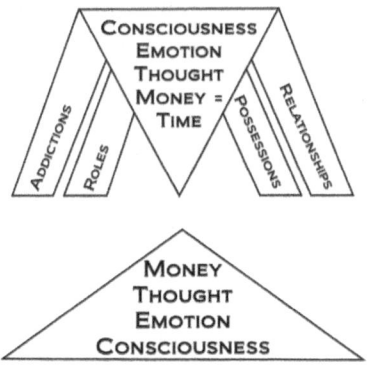

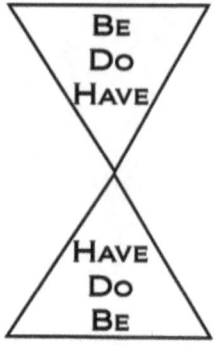

However, let's invert that assumption and ACCEPT that we are spirits inhabiting Human form, for the purpose of having certain experiences AND to co-create a Third Dimensional reality. Our lives will then be very different. The pyramid will sit on the firm foundation of KNOWING WHO WE ARE – beyond the roles we choose to play. We are SURE of who and what we are: Spirits inhabiting matter. We have less need for props. We have less need to be co-dependent. We have NO NEED at all for addictions or fears.

We can look at ourselves and life in a more simplified way. Say that we Humans <u>think</u> we have to HAVE more money, or MORE time in order to DO certain things so we can BE stable, or creative or successful. Then our pyramids are inverted to reflect HAVE MONEY, DO OUR PASSION, BE SUCCESSFUL, but if we consciously BE a spirit and DO that which we <u>enjoy</u>, then we HAVE money, success and reward or fame.

Until recently, we have lived in a World that was under ACCUMULATIVE KARMIC LAW, THE LAW OF CAUSE AND EFFECT. However, since the recent cosmic dispensation was passed, we now have the opportunity to balance, by choice, <u>all the karma</u> from past lifetimes for our <u>entire Oversouls</u> and to move into what is called, "instant karma." (*The Cellular Release CD*, available from Namaste, Inc., is an excellent tool to use for this. To order, see order form on the web site: Namasteconsciousness.org) Clearing past negative memory, trauma, judgment and fear from our cellular bodies readies us to move consciously out from under the Law of the Piscean Age, the Law of Karma, and to deliberately move ourselves into the Aquarian Age, which is ruled by the Laws of Harmony, Grace, Beauty, Balance and Love.

Once you are reasonably clear you can decree: "I now deliberately move myself, all my possession, property, pets and family out from under the

Law of the Piscean Age, the Law of Karma. I deliberately move myself, all my possessions, property, pets and family into the Aquarian Age and we are now ruled by the Laws of Harmony, Grace, Beauty, Balance and Love.

Other methods to accomplish this are now available through spirit.

Once we clear our karma, that which we do and think reaps its return virtually immediately because it is not filtered through all of our past karma. We are in a state of instant karma. Scientists have worked to prove the laws of physics, the laws affecting our physical universe. But they have not considered spiritual law or the fact that we are a self-evolving species and that our thoughts control our evolution!

Scientists try to convince us (a) that we live in a World in which everything takes place in relationship to deterministic laws that unfold in linear time, and (b) such are, therefore, unresponsive to Human thoughts or affairs.

In the past, such experts have said that "chance events" only produce patterns that are random; that to see meanings in such patterns is as pointless as searching for messages in the "snow" that appears, at times, on our TV screens. To believe that certain chance events are a manifestation of "some underlying patterns in nature," or the result of an "acausal connecting principle," would be utter nonsense to them.

These experts are, however, beginning to suspect that even chaos has a pattern. Despite the appeal that "scientific" views of nature give us, "chance" or synchronistic events do occur. They can be dismissed as "coincidence," true. Such an explanation makes little sense to those of us who have experienced synchronicity.

Synchronistic events ARE meaningful and DO play a significant role in our lives, especially if we pay attention while they are happening. It is usually easier to identify them when we look back upon life events, than when they are happening. It is spiritual maturity to recognize them WHILE THEY ARE HAPPENING and to invite them into our lives and learn to build on them.

It is my personal theory that such events are synchronized, or "set up," by our Oversouls, or by "the hand of God." That their purpose is the arranging of certain encounters, or events, to surprise us into a lesson or in order to assist us with our goals. (It is my experience that sometimes they are simply for the purpose of cosmic humor.)

"Seriality" is an interesting word describing a kind of synchronistic happening, to put it simply. Serialist events seem to take place under the influence of acausal connections, rather than by means of the familiar causal pushes and pulls of physics. Therefore, they produce an argument for the existence of an underlying harmony, or mosaic to nature, which includes Human thoughts and feelings affecting science or Universal Law.

What truly differentiates a synchronicity from a mere coincidence is the inherent meaning given to the event by individuals or Humans. We are each a result of a balance between intuition, thinking, feeling and sensation. The more of our past karma and fears we release from our bodies and our subconscious, the more space we have within us for these functions to take place. Without the clutter of the past, we can become systems that function in synchronicity with nature and Universal Law.

If we add to this, a conscious awareness that we are active members of much larger soul families (we have an Oversoul), with whom we can communicate and receive intuitive impulses, or messages of how to live "in the flow," we increase the occurrences of synchronicity and serendipity in our lives.

SERENDIPITY is defined as the faculty of making happy and unexpected discoveries by accident or events that happen when we begin to "dip" into life with "serenity." Webster defines it as "the gift of finding valuable or agreeable things not sought for." Actually, serendipity is the discovery of goals that one stumbles into (or which stumble into us) while we're searching for an altogether different goal. Another way of putting it is the UNEXPECTED discovery of something worthwhile during a search for an EXPECTED something worthwhile. The challenge is to <u>accept</u> the unexpected, or at least to pause to analyze what these "unlooked for" happenings may mean in relation to the total business of living.

Like many of the finest things of life – happiness, tranquility, fame – the gain that is most precious is not the thing sought, but that which comes of itself in the search for something else. Such are many scientific breakthroughs, e.g., penicillin and the nicotine patch, etc.

Many people live their lives as if they believe things simply happen and that they have no choices or control over events. When a person begins asking his/herself, "Do things simply happen, or are they brought about?" that person is entering spiritual maturity. This is especially so if the person begins taking responsibility for that which he/she is creating. If we live our lives INSIGHTFULLY, PHILOSOPHICALLY, and if we TRUST OUR GUIDANCE, our lives will be filled with serendipitous events, and we will experience synchronicity.

Let me explain these words. To me, being INSIGHTFUL means observing my life <u>AS I AM LIVING IT</u>, not living from an unconscious perspective. To be PHILOSOPHICAL means to understand that everything has meaning, even if that meaning may not be immediately known to me. For example, if we accept all of our duties as a part of our divine mission, we can do those must-be-done daily things in a state of joyfulness and with the best of intentions. We can also maintain the attitude that something good and enjoyable can happen while we're doing those chores. Such an attitude creates a space in which serendipity can happen.

TRUST YOUR GUIDANCE. Even if you have not reached a point where you believe you have reached knowingness from your soul, you can learn to trust your intuition. If your inner prompting is wholesome, clear and in the rhythm of your life, obey it. If it has a heavy feeling, question it. If it has a light touch, follow it.

We must always ask for guidance and assistance, since the Oversoul is not allowed to <u>force</u> guidance on us. This is because of the Universal Law of FREE WILL.

The serendipitous test of guidance is threefold: it always motivates us (we do not motivate it); it always fills one with a sense of rightness; and it always leaves a person – and our World – in better spirits than before.

Everything moves in cycles: the planets, the tides, seasons, day and night. There are industrial cycles, political cycles, and fashion cycles. At present, we are in what is known as the Information Age, or cycle; the Age of receiving and disbursing, or networking, information. Each one of us also has his/her cycles. It is very important that each of us become aware of our own cycles and get in tune with them. We can only accomplish this by observing ourselves and attuning with our souls.

Life is a wheel. Fate does not turn the wheel, we do. The thoughts and attitudes we assume and the way we look at things, determine the spin and velocity of that wheel and where life is taking us. When we stay relaxed, receptive and inwardly confident, knowing that we are spiritual beings experiencing life as Humans, we can remember the bigger picture and accept our role in that bigger picture. We can get synchronized with life's rhythm. When we are in a "down" cycle it is important to understand that it is a time for learning and to demonstrate patience and gratitude. During the "up" cycle it is important to express gratitude. When life does not seem to be moving-when we feel stuck- it is important to be <u>both</u> grateful and patient. Gratitude and patience are two of the keys to living synchronized and serendipity-filled lives.

60

The Eye of Hours, The Ankh, The Star of Ddavid

In about 1991, a friend insisted that I have a reading with a channel in Portland, Oregon, by phone. I never seek out having readings with or through other people, because I feel that my soul will tell me everything that I need to know. The friend gave me the session as a birthday present, so I called the gentleman. Our phone connection was bad, and I struggled to hear what he was saying.

The gist of the conversation was about the Universal Language of Light and my connection to it. At the time, I didn't know what he was talking about. He said that I was part of a galactic team of people who came to Earth to assist in the setting up and evolution of the Egyptian civilization. According to him we brought the symbols of the Language of Light and taught the Egyptians the formulas for using them to build the pyramids and other structures and to do amazing art work. He said that after the destruction of Lemuria and Atlantis, many of us came from the stars to upgrade the civilization of Egypt, bringing with us symbols from the Universal Language of Light and that I was one of this team of beings. (I thought he was nuts, because at that time I had heard nothing about the symbols or Language of Light from my soul. It all sounded pretty far-fetched to me. I discounted everything he said at the time. Later when I visited Japan and merged with the aspect of my Oversoul that carried that knowledge, I felt I owed him an apology, but had no memory of his name or how to contact him.)

We taught the Egyptians that when the symbols were combined with certain sounds (tones) and Light Rays or frequencies, the gravity of Earth could be overcome; that objects could be lifted to build the pyramids and that molecular structure could be rearranged alchemically in the same way.

Consider that the Rosetta Stone, discovered by French soldiers in 1799, was planted by extraterrestrials to cause Humans to believe that they had a code-breaking device with which they could decipher the Egyptian hieroglyphics. This was allowed so that Humans would not discover or remember the formulas and the true meaning of and use of the symbols when combined with sounds, colors and vibrations.

During the time of the Pharaohs, many of us came from the stars to assist in the upgrade of the Human species. We brought the device known as the Ark of the Covenant. We tuned into the power of the Ark by using the devices in the shape of the Ankh.

We assisted in the creation of the pyramids and the Sphinx by using symbols, sounds, and the energy of the Rays through color. Beneath the Sphinx were third-dimensional chambers, in which we worked adjusting the energies of the Earth and contacting our Space Brothers and Sisters. We did this by using symbols and sounds. To enter the chambers, we walked up to the Sphinx. We wore robes and carried staffs. We tapped the left paw of the Sphinx three times with the staffs. We intoned certain sounds and when a door opened, we descended the stairs into the chambers.

When we left Earth and returned to the stars, we took the formulas and the true meaning of the symbols with us, because Humanity had not evolved sufficiently to be trusted with the formulas. We also moved these chambers – in their entirety – into the fifth dimension. We did this by raising the vibration of their molecular structure.

Archeologists have believed that logically there would be chambers under the Sphinx, since there are chambers beneath the pyramids. However, when they have checked seismographically, they have been unable to locate such chambers. (This is because the chambers did not truly exist Third Dimensionally.)

In January 1994, it came time to place these chambers back in the third dimension. Many records are stored in these chambers relevant to destroying the myths Humans have lived with for thousands of years. Later, when the archeologists tested seismographically again, they discovered that there are indeed chambers below the Sphinx, but excavation is not allowed.

Many members of the Namaste team were involved in this restoration.

To explain more about toning and using symbols, I'll go back a few years.

Some members of the Namaste team moved to Spain and Portugal in 1993-94 to work on the energies of Cuba from that location. The Hierarchy noted there was a buildup of arms in Barcelona Spain. It was about the last place on Earth such a buildup would be expected. The arms buildup was not for Spain's benefit, except monetarily. The weapons were for use by other countries. Anchoring the energies of the Cosmic Christ Consciousness THROUGH INTENTION was the only way known to us to change that buildup of negative vibrations.

Another way to change such negativity is to learn (or remember) how to invoke the Rays, and to use symbols and intonations to transmute such vibrations.

I've related my story and the events of my travels and the energy work I've participated in with other Humans, the Spiritual Hierarchy, Angels and the members of the Intergalactic Federation to let you know there are many of us walk-ins here on Earth at this time and many more of us coming to help with this state of evolution of Earth and all life on the Earth.

Epilogue

In 2001, I wondered if there would ever be an actual Namaste Creativity Retreat Center for me to live in when a friend called from Denver. She had received a message from her soul to refinance her home, take out her equity and buy a place in Oklahoma City for me to live in and use as the Namaste Creativity Retreat Center. I was amazed, and of course I asked, "Are you sure you want to do that?"

She replied confidently, "Yes, I'm tired of people promising you they will help you and then backing out at the last minute. Go find the place and I'll buy it and rent it to Namaste."

In my description of the location for the Center that I had written I had indicated that I wanted it to have a view of a large body of water. The first place I looked at was across the street from the city water tower. I had to laugh at Spirit's sense of humor and attempt to make me more explicit in my description of my desires. I rewrote the description to be a view of a lake or river.

I went to the post office the next morning and must have been smiling more than usual because the agent asked me what I was so happy about. I told him I was finally going to have my own home, and he reached in his shirt pocket and took out a business card. He had just passed his real estate exam. "If you haven't found a realtor I think I can help you find what you are looking for."

He came to my home that afternoon and looked at the pictures in my manifestation book and said, "I think I know the exact house you are looking for, but it is a disaster right now because the bank is redoing it. It has been repossessed by Wells Fargo."

"Take me to see it anyway. I'll be able to tell right away if it is the right place," I said.

He called the agent, and we picked up my daughter and went to see the house. Just as we approached the front porch, I looked down and there was a blue jay feather on the grass. I had to laugh.

As we walked up the inside stairway my daughter said, "The spirit of the house is saying, 'Rescue me. Rescue me.'"

Judi, who is the secretary of Namaste, came from Denver and signed the contract and we moved in January 10, 2002.

A couple of years later the upper story of the house needed to be repainted. Neither Judi nor I had the money to pay to have it painted, and I really desired to have the upper story covered in vinyl siding in a light color. I had never liked the color Wells Fargo had painted the wooden part of the house. Judi could not find a way to refinance the house to get out the money for the siding. I put a picture of a similar house with light siding by my phone and energized the picture every time I answered the phone. At that time one of my energy assignments was to go to the local Indian casinos to create vortexes of energy to bless the Indians and the people who came to play there. Every time I went to this one casino the same man would be there gambling, no matter what day or time of day I was there. He always seemed to play a large amount and to win large amounts. I always watched him, but never spoke to him.

A few days later a crew began to put what I considered to be my siding on the house next door to mine. I was furious and kept asking God, "What part of my address did you not get?"

I got over being mad at God and went next door and asked one of the men to ask his boss to come over and give me a bid on what it would cost for them to put siding on the center. When his boss showed up at my front door it was the man from the casino, so I was sure I had the right person to do the job, but I still did not know where the money was coming from.

I kept remembering and affirming what Maharishi had said to Deepak Chopra when Deepak had asked Maharishi where the money was going to come from to build all the meditation temples he had planned. The answer: "The money will come from where ever it is now."

Another friend called at that time and mentioned that she was getting in meditation that something was going on with me that she was supposed to be part. I explained about the siding and the man from the casino. She said she and her husband had a line of credit and that maybe they could loan me the money. I waited for a couple of weeks and heard nothing from her. I kept energizing the picture and doing the affirmation: "The money is on its way to me from where ever it is now."

I had been unable to convince the man who owned the siding company that if he started the job the money would come. He said, "I believe in God, but not when it relates to money and business."

Little did he know God was sending him business whether he believed or not.

A group of us were meeting in Sedona, Arizona, at that time to do some energy work of moving Shamballa from the Gobi Desert over Sedona. When my friend and her husband showed up in Sedona, she was embarrassed that she had not called me back. I assumed that her husband could not go along with the idea of loaning me $10,000, which was going to be the price of the siding. When she apologized, I assured her that the money was on its way. She said, "My husband doesn't know Judi and technically we would be loaning the money to Judi, since she owns the house, even though you would be the one paying the money back. What he would be willing to do is to buy the house from Judi, redo the mortgage and take out enough money to buy and install the siding and pay off the note you are now paying on for the sunroom you had built. We will give you life estate to the property and keep the rent the same as you are paying now and be one hundred percent responsible for the maintenance."

I was astonished. When I write out my desires I always end the request with the affirmation, "I now accept this or something better, through the grace of God and to the highest good of all concerned." Once again God had a bigger and better plan than any I had imagined.

The couple bought the property from Judi and I've been living here for ten years now and using it as a bed and breakfast retreat center. I still travel with groups to do planetary and galactic energy work when it is called for by the Spiritual Hierarchy and the Federation. I still paint and do spiritual consulting and speak at conferences.

If you would like to contact us, our web site is: Namasteconsciousness.org. Namaste,

bj King
February 14, 2012

www.ingramcontent.com/pod-product-compliance
Lightning Source LLC
Chambersburg PA
CBHW030238170426
43202CB00007B/36